CINEMATIC UNIVERSE

A CELEBRATION OF DC AT THE MOVIES

DK | Penguin Random House

Senior Editor Cefn Ridout
Project Art Editor Jon Hall
Production Editor Marc Staples
Senior Production Controller Laura Andrews
Managing Editor Rachel Lawrence
Managing Art Editor Vicky Short
Managing Director Mark Searle

Packaged for DK by Bullpen Productions
Editor Alan Cowsill
Editorial Assistant Melanie Scott
Designer Gary Gilbert

Cover Steve Anderson

First published in Great Britain in 2024 by Dorling Kindersley Limited
DK, One Embassy Gardens, 8 Viaduct Gardens, London, SW11 7BW

The authorised representative in the EEA
is Dorling Kindersley Verlag GmbH. Arnulfstr. 124, 80636 Munich, Germany

Page design copyright © 2024 Dorling Kindersley Limited
A Penguin Random House Company
10 9 8 7 6 5 4 3 2 1
001-338583-Sep/2024

A CIP catalogue record for this book is available from the British Library.
ISBN 978-0-2416-5003-5

Printed and bound in China

ACKNOWLEDGMENTS
DK would like to thank Nick Jones and Win Wiacek for their text and expertise; Benjamin Harper, Josh Anderson,
and Shane Thompson at Warner Bros., and Michael McCalister, Doug Prinzivalli, Benjamin Le Clear, Jay Kogan,
Hector Lobos, and Clay Eichelberger at DC for vital help and advice; Michael E. Uslan for his gracious foreword;
Steve Lansdale at Heritage Auctions (HA.com), Jim Bowers at Caped Wonder (capedwonder.com), and Alan Davis
at BFI (bfi.org.uk) for image permissions, Alex Evangeli for picture reasearch; Bullpen Productions for packaging;
and Kayla Dugger for proofreading.

www.dk.com

MIX
Paper | Supporting
responsible forestry
FSC™ C018179

This book was made with Forest
Stewardship Council™ certified
paper – one small step in DK's
commitment to a sustainable future.
Learn more at **www.dk.com/uk/
information/sustainability**

DC
CINEMATIC UNIVERSE
A CELEBRATION OF DC AT THE MOVIES

WRITTEN BY NICK JONES AND
STEPHEN "WIN" WIACEK

DK

CONTENTS

MODERNIZING THE MYTHOLOGY

EXPANDING THE UNIVERSE

FOREWORD

From the 1940s to '50s, movie theaters showed escapist live-action movie serials featuring popular comic book characters such as Batman, Superman, Captain Marvel (now known as Shazam!), Vigilante, and Blackhawk. In 1967, a feature-film version of Adam West's TV series, *Batman*, made its way to the silver screen. But it was the blockbusters starring DC's A-listers—Superman, Batman, Wonder Woman, and Aquaman—that truly garnered worldwide attention. The films based on DC characters have spanned decades, explored different genres, and revolutionized Hollywood in the process.

Yet some enduring achievements also occurred on movies with the tiniest budgets. In 1982, I produced the independent feature film *Swamp Thing* on a below-the-line budget of $1.9 million. Directed by my dear friend and legendary director, Wes Craven—who went on to create the *Nightmare on Elm Street* and *Scream* franchises—it was a fun throwback to the 1950s rubber-suited monsters that used to prowl "popcorn movies," and became a cult classic.

In an era before CGI and VFX, Wes directed a fire stunt sequence that is considered one of the greatest in film history. Our stuntman extraordinaire, Tony Cesar, with a partner, created a new gel that coated Tony's entire body, which slowed the fire burning through to his skin for up to a minute. This was the first time fire stunts could be done without cumbersome asbestos suits. The drawback was that Tony had to close his eyes and gel his eyelids, which meant he had to climb, jump, run, and dive totally blind, while we were blowing up our main set in the middle of a very real swamp infested with rattlesnakes, copperheads, cottonmouth, coral snakes, and alligators!

And who could forget the out-of-the-box creativity and talent of Francis Lawrence in his directorial debut as a feature film director—prior to his phenomenal work on *The Hunger Games*—on our Keanu Reeves version of *Constantine* in 2005? Francis's cinematic interpretation of both the devil, played by Peter Stormare, and archangel Gabriel, stunningly portrayed by Tilda Swinton, were a revelation as to how old tropes and stereotypes could be successfully reinvented on screen.

But the most important turning point came from the genius of Tim Burton. In what I call his "Big Idea," Tim declared that if we were to make the first dark and serious superhero film work for adult audiences who have never read a comic book, the movie could not be about Batman. Instead, it must be about a driven, obsessive Bruce Wayne. And that was the game changer! Tim also believed that Gotham City had to be the third most important character in the movie. From the opening frames, audiences had to believe in Gotham City and (without laughing) that a guy dressed up like a bat could be running around the city fighting a guy who looks like The Joker. The rest, as they say, is history!

My favorite recollection of the first Tim Burton *Batman* movie was having my family on set one day. Though my children were only eight and four, I got the okay to bring them into the soundstage and up onto the roof set, where perhaps the most iconic scene of the film was about to be shot. My little daughter sported a head full of Shirley Temple-esque blond curls. As she stood just beneath Michael Keaton's right elbow, he grabbed the bad guy and, in a moment frozen in time for me, uttered the words, "I'm Batman!" Every time I see this scene on a big screen, I stare at Michael's right elbow looking for that blonde curl! The DC cinematic universe may be just that, a universe, but for me, I will never forget these small, personal moments.

In fact, DC contains myriad universes representing some 5,000 comic book inhabitants, each with their own unique story, colorful cast, and powerful themes, all waiting to be discovered, uncovered, or rediscovered by each new generation of filmmakers and writers who have the spirit of adventure and sense of wonder to captivate seasoned and new audiences alike. As proclaimed in Warner Brothers's trademark tagline, "It's the stuff dreams are made of!"

This book richly and thoroughly covers the inside story, from the creation of the DC comic book universe through its successful transformation into the DC cinematic universe. It acknowledges and celebrates how it all began with larger-than-life characters representing our modern-day mythology, as told through entertaining, compelling, and inspiring stories steeped in messages of hope, goodwill, and redemption. But, just as importantly, the book turns the spotlight on the filmmakers who brought those beloved heroes and villains to life on the big and small screens. Filmmakers guided by a creative, contemporary vision, as well as a passion for and understanding of characters first realized in the four-color pages of DC comic books, which have, for generations, sparked the imagination of fans throughout the world.

Michael E. Uslan
2024

Michael E. Uslan is the originator and executive producer of the *Batman* movie franchise. His first job was with DC in 1972. He has written Batman, The Shadow, and Stan Lee's Batman for DC, as well as the graphic novel *Batman: Detective #27*. Michael's memoir, *The Boy Who Loved Batman*, which was first published in 2011, is being produced as a Broadway play by The Nederlander Organization, with the working title of *Darknights and Daydreams* and a planned 2025 opening.

"I'm Batman!" Michael Keaton enters DC cinematic history with his definitive portrayal of a new and deadly Dark Knight in Tim Burton's game-changing feature film, *Batman*.

LIGHTS ... CAMERA ... ACTION COMICS!

Since its birth in the 19th century, when the Lumière brothers screened 10 short films to an astonished, paying gathering on December 28, 1895, motion pictures have been the paramount entertainment form for mass audiences. Arguably an equally old, if more personal, art form and, for much of the 20th century, the primary province of kids, comics also dominated the free time and interest of millions.

"Creativity requires courage."

Paul Levitz (writer/former DC publisher)—
Superpowered: The DC Story (2023)

In 1935, National Allied Publications—what we know today as DC—started publishing comics. Within three years, the company's efforts changed the world with a revolutionary character who reshaped popular culture. Superman inspired a wave of imitations, founded a new genre of storytelling, and quickly migrated to newspaper strips, radio—and movies.

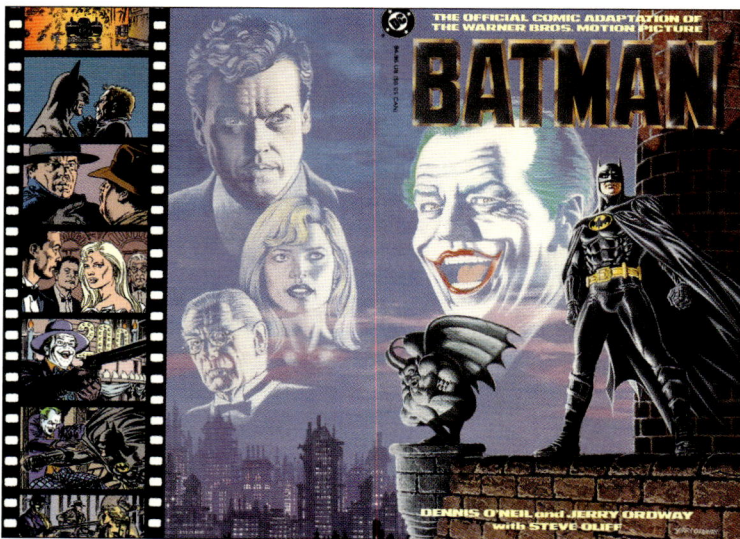

Legendary DC writer Dennis O'Neil teamed up with artist Jerry Ordway and colorist Steve Oliff for the official adaptation of Tim Burton's *Batman*.

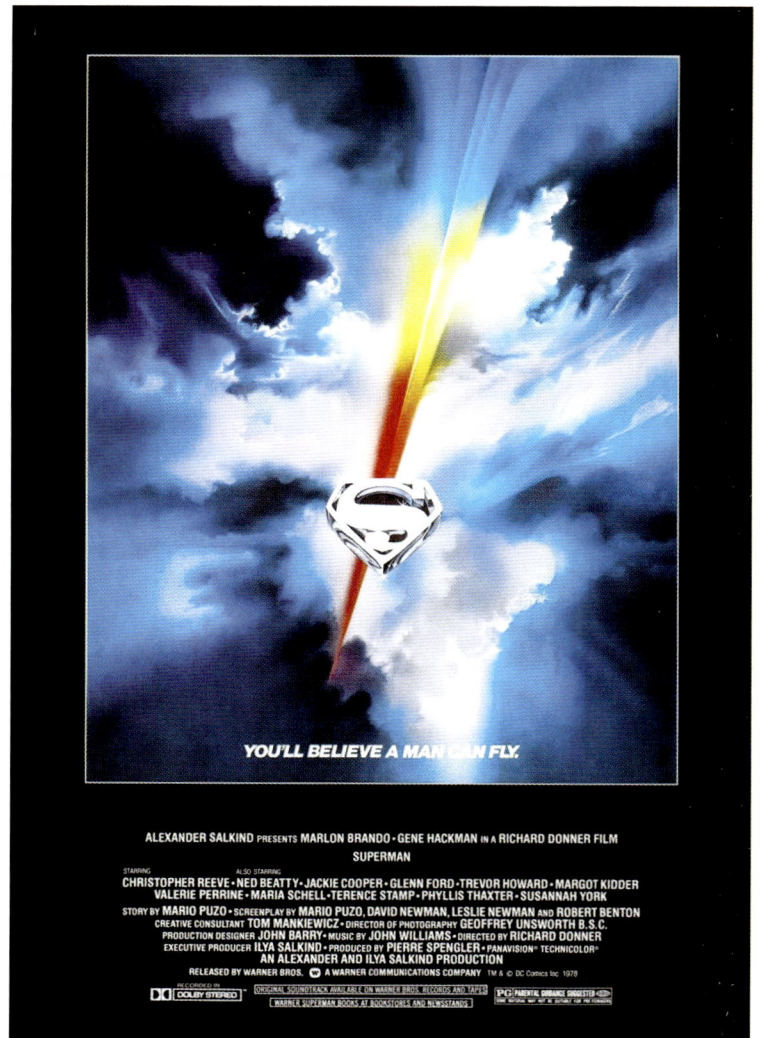

Above and right: Posters for the theatrical exploits of DC's tentpole characters reflect the changing times and sensibilities.

As this compendious coffee-table celebration demonstrates, DC has long proffered paper heroes for the silver screen, and since popular entertainments thrive by capturing their times, the company has changed and evolved to suit those times. This has been a two-way street, with film successes repeatedly enhancing comic books, and since the 1940s, DC has published many titles based on or adapting cinema releases.

When DC's comic book stars first crossed over to movies, the commercial priority was to make them as widely accessible to as many moviegoers as possible. However, just as printed comics sought to attract and retain older readers, so too did their cinematic interpretations. All-ages megastars like Superman and Batman grew darker, grittier, and even morally ambivalent as the 20th century closed and, inevitably, film producers shifted their attention to the likes of Swamp Thing, Constantine, Jonah Hex, and Watchmen. Reconfigured for modern sensibilities, tastes, and storytelling, these characters already appealed to mature audiences while also fitting established genre niches. Even villains such as The Joker, Catwoman, Harley Quinn, and the Suicide Squad have become box-office sensations.

This book reveals how DC's early movie offerings developed and coalesced into today's shared cinematic universe. From the

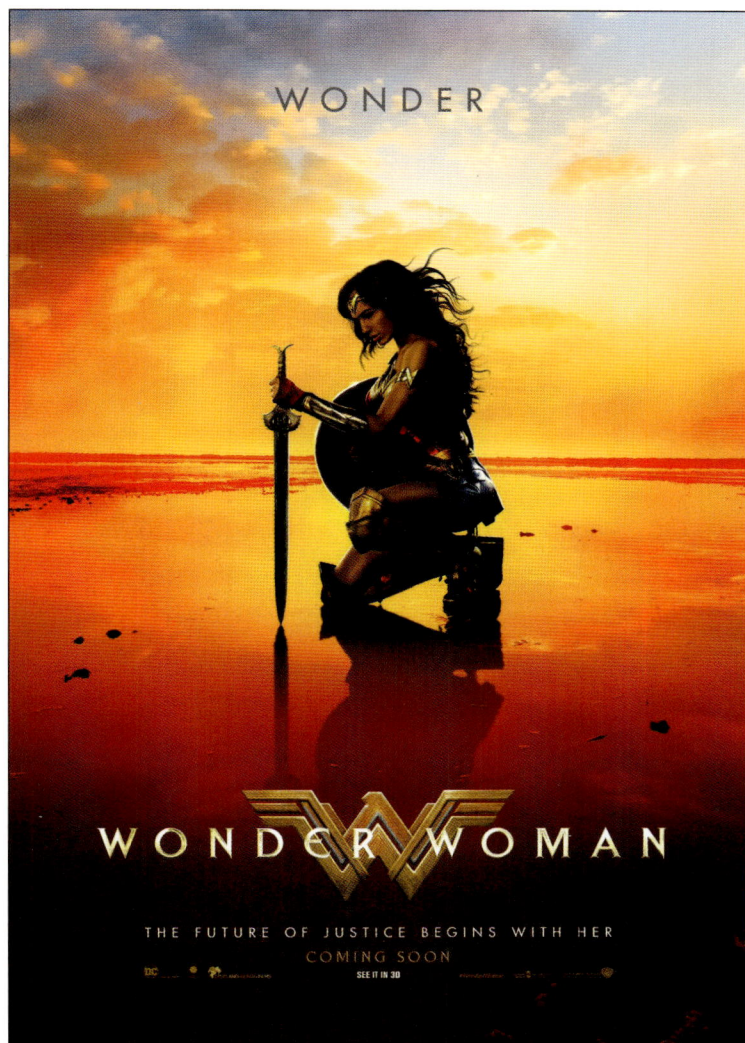

trailblazing 1940s cliffhanger serials to the superhero's celluloid coming of age in Richard Donner's *Superman* (1978), to the myth-remaking of Tim Burton's *Batman* (1989), to Christopher Nolan's revitalization of the Dark Knight in 2005, to the formation of a DC extended universe in the 2010s, the movies have leaned into and built on their comic book roots. It provides a solid grounding from which to enjoy the impending dawn of a new, meticulously planned and interlinked "DC universe," courtesy of director James Gunn and producer Peter Safran, DCEU alumni and co-chairs of the newly formed DC Studios.

Their ambitious slate of movies includes *Superman*, *The Authority*, *Supergirl: Woman of Tomorrow*, and *Swamp Thing*, while projects set outside the DC universe, such as Matt Reeves's *The Batman Part II* and Todd Phillips's *Joker: Folie à Deux*, would fall under the banner of DC Elseworlds—a term coined in the early 1990s for comics set in alternate realities and outside of established DCU canon. Also in the works are television series *The Penguin*, *Waller*, and *Lanterns* (featuring the Green Lantern Corps) all within the ambit of Gunn and Safran's "Chapter One: Gods and Monsters" masterplan.

How to use this book

For those unaware of the scope and range of DC's eight decades of movie credentials, *DC Cinematic Universe* offers an entrée into when and how comic book dramas became live-action epics. It doesn't cover films based on licensed/creator-owned properties published by DC or its specialist imprints such as Vertigo or Paradox Press.

Divided into coherent eras of achievement rather than decade by decade, the book explores DC's forays onto big and small screens through extensive research and candid behind-the-scenes revelations. Presented in chronological order of production and release, the entries delve into many aspects of filmmaking, including scripts, concept design, storyboards, cast,

makeup and costuming, and special effects. Supporting sidebars highlight comic book source material and how it was adapted for the screen; celebrate significant actors and achievements; and examine tie-ins and spinoffs, including live-action and animated TV series.

From low-budget game changers, to state-of-the-art blockbusters and must-see theatrical serials, to view-on-demand streaming series, this is the first time DC's screen adventures have been surveyed in one lavishly illustrated volume. *The DC Cinematic Universe* is an insightful resource and celebration of DC's movie milestones for newcomers to get up to speed and fans to rediscover past screen gems, all in preparation for the new era that beckons.

SCREEN ADVENTURES

Created to repackage newspaper strips aimed at general audiences, comic books became a sensation in the late 1930s, in the wake of the spectacular success of writer Jerry Siegel and artist Joe Shuster's ground-breaking Superman, which debuted in *Action Comics* #1 (June 1938). The invention of the superhero and the subsequent proliferation of comic books also affected cinema in the 1940s.

At the time, traditional and hugely popular serials used extended storylines with tantalizing cliffhanger endings to attract and retain predominantly younger audiences. Serials offered excitement, wonder, adventure, and romance, with cinemagoers being enticed to return each week to see their favorite characters save the farm, find true love, or escape certain death.

So how could Hollywood, already mining prominent pulp fictions, newspaper strips, and radio serials, ignore the rising stars of best-selling comic books, whose exploits so closely mirrored the thrills and spills of Saturday-morning cinema?

ADVENTURES OF CAPTAIN MARVEL

Release date: March 28, 1941
Rerelease date: April 15, 1953 as *Return of Captain Marvel* serial and in 1966 as a four-hour movie
Starring roles: Tom Tyler, Frank Coghlan Jr., William Benedict
Director: William Witney, John English

Screenplay: Ronald Davidson, Norman S. Hall, Arch B. Heath, Joseph Poland, Sol Shor
Cinematography: William Nobles
Music: Cy Feuer
Running time: 216 minutes/ 12 chapters

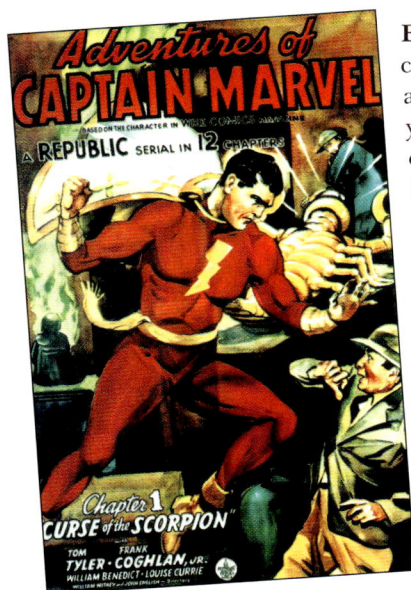

Tom Tyler's superb physique took him from prop man to action hero. His athleticism made Captain Marvel an imposingly authentic on-screen presence.

By 1935, movie serials were crucial to filmmaking, but only as action-packed teasers to attract youngsters. In this, they mirrored comic books, and studios soon began adapting top-sellers to the screen. Three years later, Superman debuted. Hugely popular in all media markets, he inspired a new story form and much opportunist imitation. Foremost was Fawcett Publications' *Captain Marvel*— a magical Super Hero who soon outsold Superman.

Republic Pictures was prospering. Once considered a second-rate studio, they had steadily climbed in prestige and profit and sought something special for their first comic book foray. Bargaining hard for industry leader Superman, when protracted negotiations failed, Fawcett approached Republic and history was made.

HERO OF THE GODS

Historically one of most beloved Super Heroes in American comics, Shazam's champion was created by Bill Parker and Charles Clarence Beck. *Whiz Comics* #2 (February 1940) saw homeless orphan Billy Batson chosen to battle injustice by channeling six mythical gods and heroes. Speaking an ancient wizard's name— an acronym for Solomon, Hercules, Atlas, Zeus, Achilles, and Mercury—Billy transformed from puny boy to brawny adult Captain Marvel. Before evolving an affable personality, the Captain was brusque and characterless, with his juvenile alter ego the true star. Billy was an archetype of self-reliant, resourceful youth overcoming all odds through determination, gumption, and grit. These characteristics informed the serial.

In *Adventures of Captain Marvel*, the origin is changed and Billy works for American scientists in Siam. When the Malcolm Expedition uncovers a fantastic scorpion-shaped mechanism that transforms matter and emits death rays, Batson refuses to be a tomb raider and the wizard appears, empowering him to prevent the ancient weapon from causing harm. Escaping violent uprisings, the scientists disassemble it, each hiding a key component, but hooded villain The Scorpion kills them all to reconstruct it, with Billy and his friends Betty and Whitey unable to stop him over 12 fantastically exciting, high-quality episodes—until the fiend is finally foiled and Billy relinquishes his powers.

On screen, Captain Marvel lets Billy take the limelight as the film's true protagonist. Seeing action through valiant but naive eyes was a gift for Frank "Junior" Coghlan (1916–2009), whose 129 screen roles began in 1920—in silent film dramas, *Our Gang* comedies, Andy Hardy films, *Gone With the Wind*, and as young Jimmy Cagney in *The Public Enemy* (1931).

Captain Marvel shrugged off bombs, bullets, blades, blistering electric shocks, and even boiling lava as he thrashed gangsters and bandits on two continents.

Insidious fiend The Scorpion eradicated every member of the Malcolm Expedition with such efficiency that viewers were only able to deduce his identity in the final chapter.

Offering exotic fantasy, gangster thrills, murder mystery, and frontier adventure, the serial rated high production values and top creative support. Dubbed "the father of action films," director William Witney was brilliantly innovative, pioneering editing as a story clock for film shooting. He handled all action scenes, leaving acting sequences, setting the mood, and advancing the complex plot, crafted by a team of writers, to dramatic specialist John English.

"Shazam!"
Billy Batson/Captain Marvel

This commitment to quality set a formidable benchmark for successive celluloid comic superheroes and sparked a mountain of merchandising. Betty and Whitey joined the comics' cast and Beck and Otto Binder created a print sequel for *Captain Marvel Dime Action Book*. In 1994, the serial informed the graphic novel *The Power of Shazam!* (Jerry Ordway), leading to a triumphant return for the hero and enemy Black Adam and presaging today's movie franchise.

Although played a little older than his preteen comic book counterpart, the cinema Billy Batson was a loyal, honest, and clever kid with the added benefits of gun, driver's, and pilot's licenses.

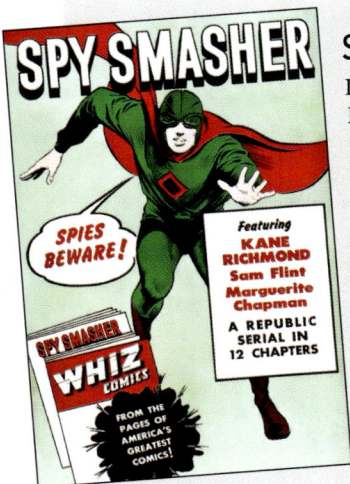

Spies beware!

If Captain Marvel was Fawcett's answer to Superman, their Batman was Spy Smasher. Alan Armstrong was a millionaire inventor whose amazing inventions helped him fight America's foes as the eponymous hero. Another Parker/Beck co-creation, Spy Smasher also debuted in *Whiz Comics* #2, winning a solo title (#1-11 Summer 1941 to February 26, 1943) long before America officially joined WWII. Posthostilities, Armstrong became Crime Smasher: a film noir-inspired private eye in *Whiz Comics* (#76-83, July 1946–March #1947) plus a 1948 *Crime Smasher* one-shot.

With Captain Marvel unavailable, Republic made *Spy Smasher* their follow-up comic chapter-play. Directed by Witney and starring serial veteran Kane Richmond (*The Shadow, Brick Bradford*) and Marguerite Chapman, it was

Chapman's big break into movies and television. Over 12 explosive episodes—filmed from December 22, 1941, to January 29, 1942—the "Defender of Democracy" was pitted against Nazi nemesis The Mask, who was attempting to destabilize still-neutral America with counterfeit currency and sabotage.

Scripted by Ronald Davidson, Norman S. Hall, William Lively, Joseph Poland, and Joseph O'Donnell with amazing stunt-work from Yakima Canutt, Carey Loftin, and David Sharpe and special effects by the Lydecker brothers, it was Republic's most expensive and acclaimed release of 1942. Comic sales exploded—*Spy Smasher* #1 had sold 338,935 copies, but by the serial's end in 1942, circulation topped 1,114,526. In 1966, with the *Batman* TV show sparking a superhero boom, the 214-minute saga was trimmed to 100 minutes and rereleased as *Spy Smasher Returns*.

THE BATMAN

Release date: July 16 to October 22, 1943
Rerelease date: Columbia rereleased to theaters in 1954 and 1962
Starring roles: Lewis Wilson, Douglas Croft, J. Carrol Naish, Shirley Patterson, William Austin

Director: Lambert Hillyer
Screenplay: Victor McLeod, Leslie Swabacker, Harry L. Fraser
Cinematography: James S. Brown Jr.
Music: Lee Zahler
Running time: 260 minutes/ 15 chapters

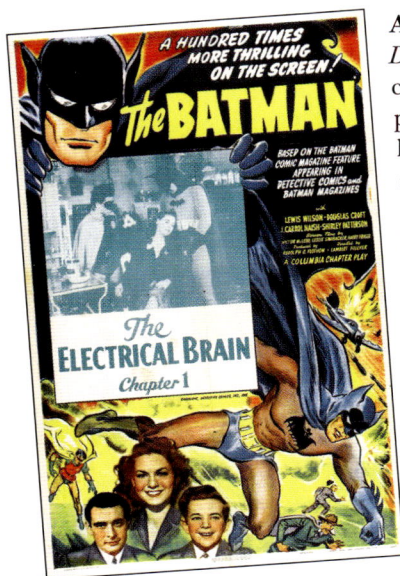

After Batman premiered in *Detective Comics* #27 (May 1939), creator Bob Kane with silent partner Bill Finger detailed the hero's influences—radio and pulp stars like *The Shadow*, Leonardo da Vinci's drawings and films like 1930's *The Bat Whispers* and Douglas Fairbanks's *The Mark of Zorro* (1920).

Kane and Finger frequently used films as reference and inspiration and their new hero resonated with every kid at newsstands or in the cheap seats. Finger was a true devotee, infusing his stories with the imagery of German Expressionist classics like *The Cabinet of Dr. Caligari* and *Nosferatu*. It made the Dark Knight a huge comic book hit and Hollywood soon wanted in on the action.

Scored by Columbia Pictures' chief composer Lee Zahler, produced by Rudolph C. Flothlow (*Crime Doctor, Ellery Queen*), and directed by Lambert Hillyer (*The Invisible Ray*), *The Batman* begins with the release of convict Martin Warren (Gus Glassmire). Before reuniting with his niece Linda Page (Shirley Patterson), he is abducted by gangsters working for Japanese spy Dr. Tito Daka (J. Carrol Naish). Asking boyfriend Bruce Wayne (Lewis Wilson) for help, she's unaware he and his ward Dick (Douglas Croft) are federal agents working undercover as vigilante heroes Batman and Robin.

This serial uses all Batman's skills—fighter, detective, forensic scientist, escapologist, even disguise artist when he infiltrates the gang as "Chuck White." Replete with action—especially extended fistfights—the plot sees the heroes repeatedly foil Daka, confiscating his radium-powered disintegrator pistol and frustrating attempts to obtain more weapons or sabotage infrastructure with electronically enslaved living zombies.

SERIOUS BUSINESS

The Batman was announced in trade journals on April 17, 1942, with writers Victor McLeod, Leslie Swabacker, and Harry L. Fraser beginning at year's end. Opening three-reel episode

The Batman was 23-year-old Lewis Wilson's third role and screen debut. He worked as an actor until 1973 and is best remembered as the first Dark Knight.

"The Electrical Brain" (26.9 minutes), is followed by two-reel chapters between 14 to 20 minutes duration. The conclusion was 20.4 minutes, with a suitably grisly end for Daka.

Enjoying a publicity campaign equal to that of feature films, ads in *Box Office* (July 17, 1943) and *Motion Picture Herald* were supplemented by comic book plugs. Press releases described *The Batman* as a "Super Serial" and Columbia's biggest series to date. The timing indicates movie serial and comic scriptwriters all collaborated, as the series saw the debut of Alfred (William

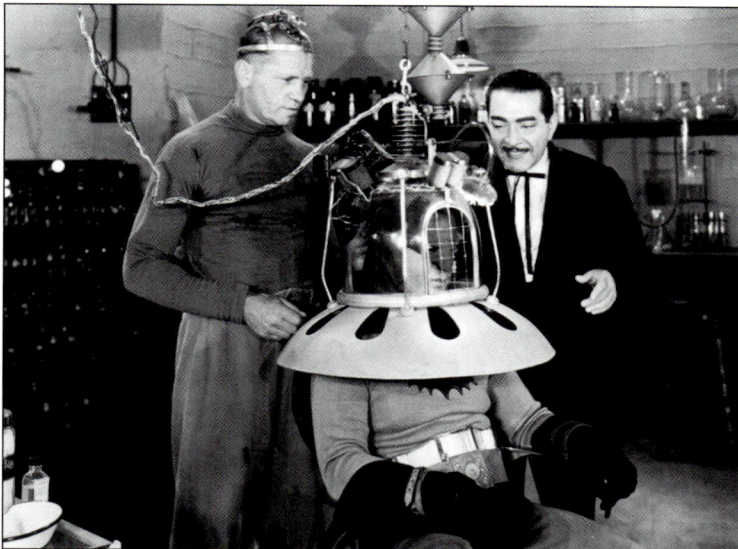

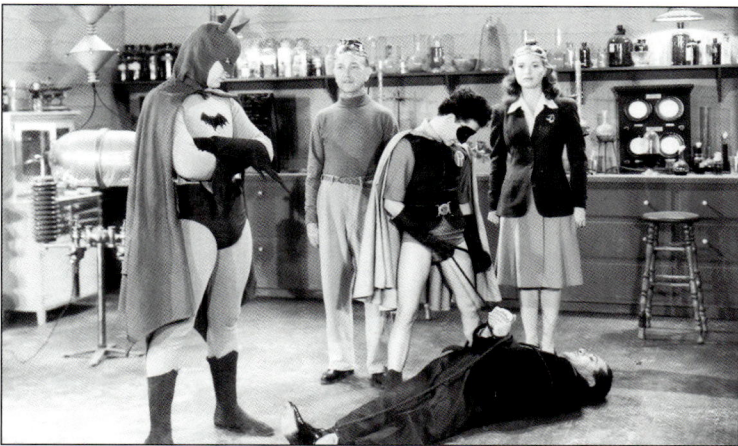

Ultimately, creeping imperialism and sinister super-science proved no match for patriotic valor and the Boy Wonder's flying fists.

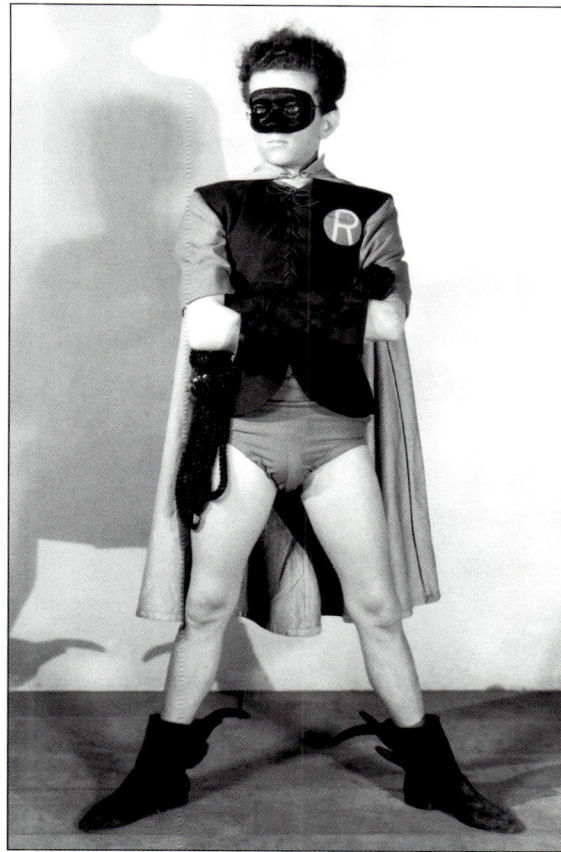

Far left: Dr. Daka's process for creating mindless zombies was lifted straight from pulp tales of the era, and the serial's scriptwriters were nominated for a 1944 Hugo Award.

Left: Noteworthy for his manic, exuberant fight scenes in the serial, child star Douglas Croft (*Yankee Doodle Dandy*) was 16 years old during filming.

Austin), playing comic relief. The Alfred described in the scripts—finished before his comic book debut—was tall and slim. While his comic book incarnation first appeared in *Batman* #16 (May 1943) as short and stout, he abruptly changed and by *Detective Comics* #83 (January 1944) was more like his movie counterpart.

"Destroy The Batman!"
Dr. Daka

Other innovations copied in comics included a grandfather-clock entrance to the "Bat's Cave." On screen, the subterranean chamber was used to terrify and interrogate captives from Daka's "League of Dishonored Men."

The Batman was a great success, even if it took three years to begin a sequel, and was rereleased in 1954 and 1962 before Columbia bundled the entire chapter-play as *An Evening with Batman and Robin* (1965). Hugely popular with college students, it led to Hollywood reconsidering the celluloid star potential of the Dynamic Duo.

Year of the Bat

In the 20th century, the newspaper comic strip was the Holy Grail American cartoonists aspired to. Syndicated globally, they were seen by millions and accepted as more mature and sophisticated literature than comic books. It also paid better and rightly so. Some of the most enduring characters of all time were devised to lure readers from one paper to another, becoming part of global culture ... and beloved stars of the silver screen.

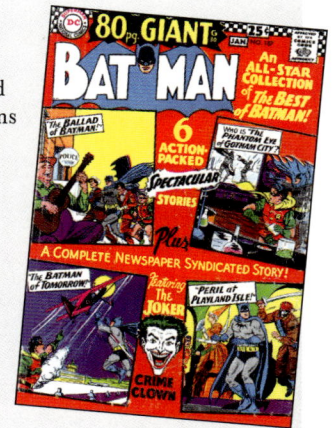

That was why Bob Kane, with silent partner Bill Finger, engaged others (Don Cameron, Alvin Schwartz, Jack Schiff, Jerry Robinson) to work anonymously under his byline in the comic, drew the majority of Batman's newspaper feature himself. Due to wartime restrictions, *Batman and Robin* was slow getting its shot. Confirmation of a film serial probably sealed the deal with the McClure Syndicate, which already handled the *Superman* feature.

When it finally hit the "funny pages" on October 25, 1943, the feature proved one of the best-regarded and highest quality, in both daily and Sunday formats. Sadly, never achieving the circulation it warranted, the strip folded on November 2, 1946. The stories had primarily concentrated on crime capers and human-interest dramas, but had featured The Joker, Catwoman, The Penguin, and Two-Face.

The feature briefly revived in September 1953, for Sunday newspaper supplement *Arrow, the Family Weekly Comic*, edited by the Shadow's creator Walter B. Gibson, but was discontinued after mere weeks. It would take a societal revolution to affirm the Dynamic Duo's star status in comic strips in the next decade.

SUPERMAN

Release date: January 5, 1948
Starring roles: Kirk Alyn, Noel Neill, Carol Forman, Tommy Bond, Forrest Taylor
Director: Spencer Gordon Bennett, Thomas Carr

Screenplay: Lewis Clay, Royal K. Cole, Arthur Hoerl, George H. Plympton, Joseph F. Poland
Cinematography: Ira H. Morgan
Music: Mischa Bakaleinikoff
Running time: 242 minutes/ 15 chapters

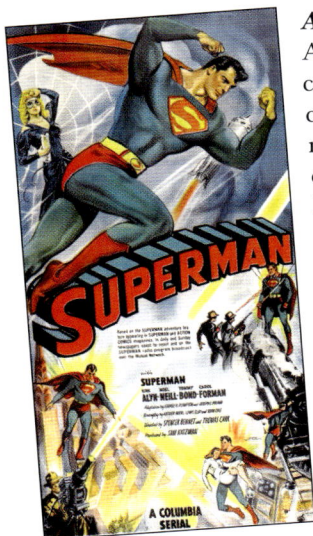

Action Comics #1 hit newsstands on April 18, 1938. Since then, Superman has colonized every aspect of art, culture, and commerce. However, his triumph was never a foregone conclusion. After WWII, concepts of heroism shifted—pristine, pure-hearted champions seemed less believable to audiences. Hard-edged cynicism permeated movies, with the most discernible changes in crime dramas, where soiled, jaded antiheroes abounded. Eventually, they clustered into a movement dubbed "film noir."

Except for DC's top guns Wonder Woman, Batman, and Superman (and the lucky stalwarts sharing their titles), comics book superheroes disappeared. At this time, the company comprised Detective Comics, Inc., National Comics Publications, and Superman Inc., each overseeing specific characters, with the last also supervising a successful newspaper strip, radio show, and ever-growing merchandising empire. For the guys in charge, there was still more Superman could do.

TRIUMPH OF IMAGINATION

One area where nobility still flourished was chapter-plays. As most studios closed serial divisions, Columbia Pictures expanded provision. Under producer Sam Katzman, they boosted output for movie houses still wanting weekly, kid-friendly matinee menus. They were delighted and always sold out when Superman finally made his live screen debut.

Still receptive to clear-cut character directives, kids were also considered less discerning and accepting of heroes and villains at face value. Moreover, plots and special effects were less important to them than action and spectacle. Young eyes didn't see strings and shaky scenery—they saw wonders.

Katzman had produced action, musicals, and serials for Columbia since 1944. Three years later, with nobody else interested, he bought Superman's film rights. He tried reselling them to Universal—just as they quit serials. At that time, feature films for costumed characters were inconceivable.

Also rejecting Katzman, Republic Pictures—makers of *Adventures of Captain Marvel* and once avid pursuers of Superman—declared "a super-powerful flying hero would be impossible to adapt," so he

Although beginning his film career in 1930, Kirk Alyn only achieved star status after the *Superman* serial became his breakthrough role. He was 37.

pitched his idea to Columbia. His recent successes for them included radio/comics properties *Jack Armstrong*, *The Vigilante*, *The Seahound* (all 1947), and *Brick Bradford and Congo Bill* (1948). All paled beside the immense popularity of Katzman's trailblazing *Superman*.

"Up, up, and away!"
Superman

The story begins with Jor-El (Nelson Leigh) sending his son to Earth as his distant planet Krypton explodes. The infant is raised by farmers Eben (Ed Cassidy) and Martha (Virginia Carroll) Kent, who train him to use his incredible powers to help humanity. Now an adult and having adopted the secret identity of Clark Kent, a reporter at Metropolis's *Daily Planet* newspaper, Superman clashes with the technologically adept "Queen of the Underworld" The Spider Lady (Carol Forman).

Far left: The on-screen Clark Kent was a far more forceful character than his comic book counterpart.

Left: Former Disney animator Howard Swift handled special effects, working with a stunt team to recreate Superman's powers.

Another *Daily Planet* staff meeting and once again Perry White (Pierre Watkin), Lois Lane (Noel Neill), and Jimmy Olsen (Tommy Bond) don't notice that Clark is missing.

With actor Kirk Alyn credited as Clark while Superman "played himself," the 15-chapter saga borrowed heavily from a radio show sequence (September–October 1945), with "The Scarlet Widow" transformed for the screen into a criminal mastermind whose gang employ guns, bombs, fast cars, and fists to terrorize Metropolis, and a reducer ray and Kryptonite to keep Superman at bay.

In 1940, Jerry Siegel proposed meteoric element "The K-metal from Krypton" as a means of making Superman more vulnerable, but editors rejected his notion. In June 1943, it was first adopted by radio show writers who frequently employed it to enhance tension and drama. The film serial was the first time fans saw the radioactive menace, which finally appeared in comics with *Superman* #61 (November 1949, "Superman Returns to Krypton," by Bill Finger and Al Plastino).

The Adventures of Superman radio serial (February 1940 to March 1951) starred Bud Collyer as the Man of Steel and Joan Alexander as Lois Lane, pictured here with National Comics (DC) publisher Harry Donenfeld (left). Alexander also gave voice to Lois Lane in the Fleischer Bros Superman cartoons.

Moving pictures

In 1940, Republic Pictures' attempts to secure the first superhero failed because Superman Inc. had signed a deal with Paramount Pictures to produce full-color animated films. That contract forbade all other screen incarnations but resulted in 17 beautiful and breathtaking tales—the first nine from Dave and Max Fleischer (*Gulliver's Travels*, *Popeye*), and the remainder from Paramount-owned successor Famous Studios, with Seymour Kneitel (*Casper the Friendly Ghost*) directing.

Scenarios depicted Superman facing mad scientists, rampaging robots, "bulleteer" bandits, defrosted dinosaurs, escaped animals, asteroids, and natural disasters until—as World War II progressed—tyrannical saboteurs and Asian dictators took over as foes to fight. The first episode, complete with origin, premiered on September 26, 1941, with the last debuting on August 30, 1943.

The entire series cost $530,000 to create, and utterly mesmerized rapt cinemagoers. Among them were Clark Kent and Lois Lane in "Superman, Matinee Idol" (*Superman* #19, November-December 1942 [pictured left]). Crafted by Siegel and Shuster with inks by John Sikela, the story broke the fourth wall for readers, detailing the reporters watching a Fleischer *Superman* cartoon—an exceedingly inventive early "infomercial" for the animated tales.

NEW ADVENTURES OF BATMAN AND ROBIN

Release date: December 1949
Starring roles: Robert Lowery, Johnny Duncan, Jane Adams, Lyle Talbot, Ralph Graves, Don C. Harvey
Director: Spencer Gordon Bennett

Screenplay: George H. Plympton, Joseph F. Poland, Royal K. Cole
Cinematography: Ira H. Morgan
Music: Mischa Bakaleinikoff
Running time: 264 minutes/ 15 chapters

Originally, chapter-plays were an essential component of an extended weekly menu including animated cartoons, newsreels, and a major feature—sometimes two. Rowdy, fast-paced, all-action kids' fodder, they employed traditional themes in established genres, often adapting properties familiar to young viewers: radio and pulp stars, costumed heroes, and the like just for them.

The war changed everything. Tastes altered and television threatened the established preserves of movie houses, strips, and comic books. Cinemas needed proven sellers, and four years after a hit debut, they got the *New Adventures of Batman and Robin, the Boy Wonder.*

Demand for serials was waning. Television even edged out ostensibly "cost-free" radio shows, and most studios ended serial-making divisions to concentrate on feature films, especially B-movies targeting the new phenomenon of teenagers with disposable income. Arguably unsuitable for domestic consumption or sponsored ad breaks (yet), these flicks called consumers out of homes and into theaters and drive-ins—just as car ownership also spiked.

TEENAGE RAMPAGE

The phenomenon might explain why Columbia's new Bat-saga saw Robin with top billing in six of 15 chapters (like "Robin's Wild Ride," "Robin Rescues Batman," and "Robin's Ruse"), while Batman was only namechecked in five. Incidentally, their Batmobile was a standard car doing double duty—a roomy 1949 Mercury convertible.

Complex, convoluted, and employing every cunning artifice of serial storytelling, the plot finds Batman (Robert Lowery), Robin

A former baseball player and boxer, second Batman Robert Lowry also starred in *Drums Along the Mohawk* (1939) and the 1940 epic *The Mark of Zorro.*

(Johnny Duncan), and Vicki Vale (Jane Adams) hunting The Wizard—a hooded mastermind whose stolen "remote-control machine" usurps any mechanism. When not stealing diamonds to fuel it, his gang alternately snatch new technologies like super-bombs and invisibility rays and attempt to kill the heroes.

"Gee, what a character!"
Vicki Vale

An array of suspicious red herrings who could be the villain include inventor Professor Hammill (William Fawcett), muckraking radio reporter Barry Brown (Rick Vallin), creepy butler Carter (Leonard Penn), and even Vicki's convict brother Jimmy (George Offerman Jr.).

Originated by Finger, Kane, and Lew Sayre Schwartz, photojournalist Vicki debuted in *Batman* #49 (October 1948). She was devised as Batman's Lois Lane, a recurring love interest

Anonymous evil mastermind The Wizard was created specifically for the serial—an amalgam of many cloaked and wicked super-geniuses.

Motorcycle rider and dancer Johnny Duncan started his Hollywood rise in the East Side Kids/Bowery Boys films. Aged 26, he was a cool and capable Boy Wonder.

The heroes storm The Wizard's secret submarine in a scene foreshadowing Batman's first feature film 17 years in the future.

Veteran actor Lyle Talbot played the first cinematic Commissioner Gordon. He had begun his career in silent movies, and prior to that was a circus performer like Dick Grayson.

whose nose for news always found trouble for the heroes to save her from. She too spent most of her time trying to prove Bruce's double identity, but Kane always claimed he created her after meeting rising starlet Marilyn Monroe at a Hollywood party.

This film incarnation is far more appealing than her comics iteration, a capable, dogged reporter who doesn't even let her own brother's complicity in The Wizard's schemes and eventual death stop her from revealing the truth. Her comic book career lasted until *Detective Comics* #320 (October 1963), before modernization and reintroduction to the canon in 1977.

She returned to the screen in 1989 as did this serial, rereleased as a VHS set from GoodTimes Entertainment to capitalize on Tim Burton's movie.

Sam Katzman's human touch

Producer Sam Katzman (1901–1973) was a Hollywood veteran who started in the industry in 1914. An independent force who understood trends and people, Katzman never took his eye off the profit and loss columns. Among many pop culture projects—from the East Side Kids film series to 1957's landmark *Rock Around the Clock*—he was responsible for Columbia's serial output from 1945 onward, including all the DC adaptations.

Often producing more than ten features a year, Katzman developed a core team of writers (including Lewis Clay, George H. Plympton, Royal K. Cole, Arthur Hoerl, and Joseph F.

Poland) to work with reliable directors like Spencer Gordon Bennett and Thomas Carr. These were supported by an inventive production team who worked with Katzman on a variety of projects, from musicals to teen comedies to drive-in sci-fi B-movies and horror films.

Katzman's hugely successful Superman serials, the Batman sequel chapter-plays, and other comic book adaptations make him a crucial yet still largely unsung transitional factor in transforming DC's printed universe into today's multimedia mega-monolith.

ATOM MAN VS. SUPERMAN

Release date: July 20, 1950
Starring roles: Kirk Alyn, Noel Neill, Lyle Talbot, Tommy Bond
Director: Spencer Gordon Bennett

Screenplay: George H. Plympton, Joseph F. Poland, David Mathews
Cinematography: Ira H. Morgan
Music: Mischa Bakaleinikoff
Running time: 252 minutes/ 15 chapters

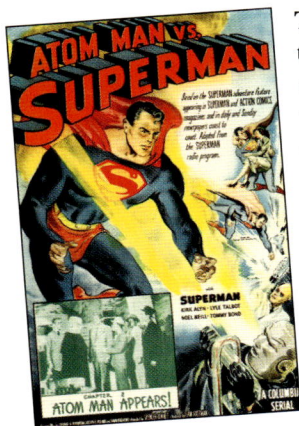

The 1950s signaled vast changes that saw publisher DC fully commit to other media. After its 1940s animations, the previous chapter-play had repositioned Superman as a vibrant, living star. Now a second big screen outing heralded the Man of Steel's first motion picture, while embracing a commonplace comic book plot in a story addressing the burgeoning impetus of the television era.

Batman waited years for a sequel, but Superman's second serial was fast-tracked when its predecessor became Columbia's most profitable chapter-play—grossing over $1,000,000. *Atom Man vs. Superman* did even better but was Kirk Alyn's last time to don the brown and gray suit (the colors that "popped" best depicting Superman's blue/red outfit in monochrome).

VANISHING ACT

Aspiring to the sheer spectacle of Superman's animated features and inspired by radio saga "The Atom Man" (October–November 1945, concerning Nazi science and ingested liquid Kryptonite), the screen version borrowed the name as a mask for the evil genius.

Opening credits included atomic blasts and cited not only print antecedents *Superman* and *Action Comics* but also stated "adapted from the Superman radio program." Reportedly the highest-grossing movie serial ever, it began with technological bandit Luthor (no first name, he wouldn't be called Lex until the 1960s) being sent to prison. After blackmailing Metropolis with terror weapons, Luthor languished inside while enigmatic Atom Man launched a fresh campaign of destruction. Thanks to a teleport machine, Luthor was secretly leaving jail at will, continuing his depredations in a new guise.

Lyle Talbot, top gangster in *The Vigilante* serial and Commissioner Gordon in *Batman and Robin*, played Luthor and Atom Man. His depiction became the character's definitive look in both newspaper strip and comic books for 20 years, despite the serial being Luthor's only live-action appearance until 1978's *Superman*. As Gene Hackman would later do, Talbot donned rubber skin-wigs to simulate the signature bald pate, and producer Katzman—

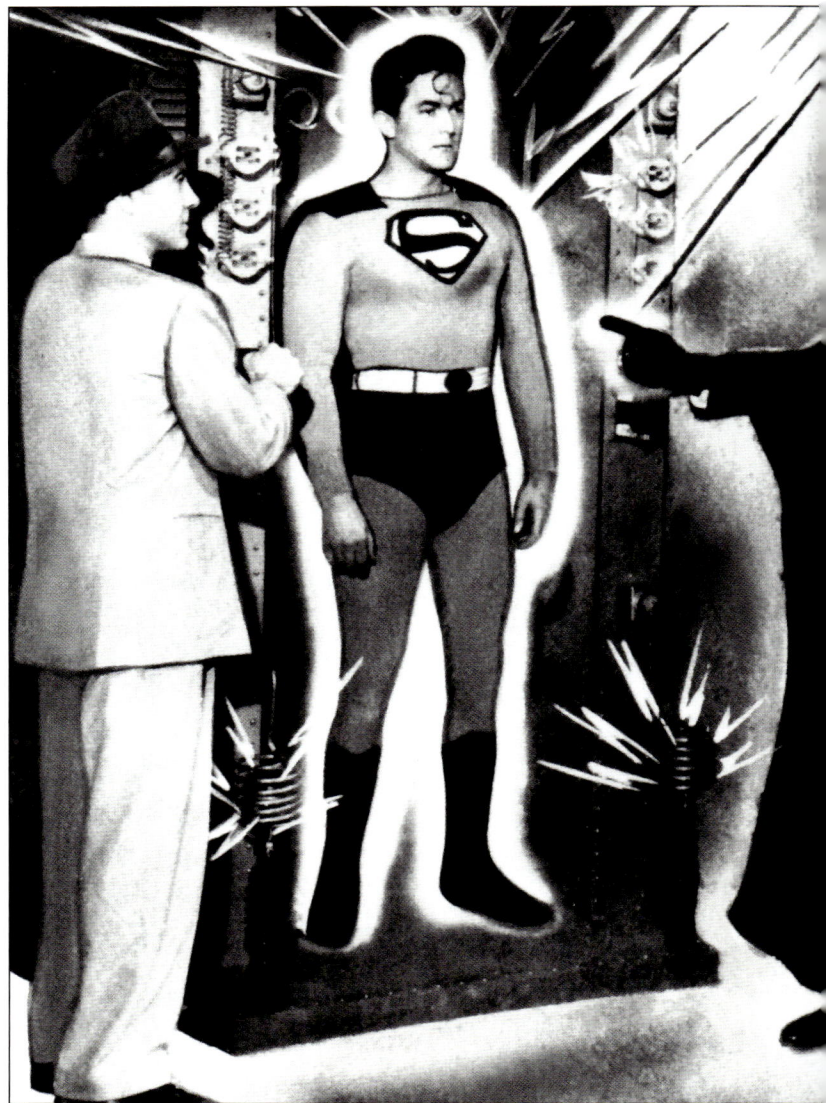

As science-fiction tropes gripped America, enigmatic Atom Man was the first film foe to give Superman a tough time and convincingly endanger his existence.

master of economical fantasy and cinematic expediency—and director Spencer Gordon Bennett draped him in a black shroud and recycled the "Metalogen Man" helmet from 1945 thriller *The Monster and the Ape* when playing the mystery villain. He also spoke with a German accent.

"The world does not know me yet, but it will!"
Atom Man/Luthor

Released as America entered an age of paranoia, the series of extremely engaging episodic clashes sees Clark, Lois (Noel Neill), Jimmy Olsen (Tommy Bond), and Perry White (Pierre Watkin) seeking to expose Atom Man, with Superman countering his devilish devices. These included artificial Kryptonite, bridge-melting death rays, dimensional portals, outer space exile, flying

CITY AT BAY!

ATOM MAN'S FLYING SAUCER

Chapter 13

ATOM MAN VS. SUPERMAN

Based on the SUPERMAN adventure feature appearing in SUPERMAN and ACTION COMICS magazines and in daily and Sunday newspapers coast to coast. Adapted from the SUPERMAN radio program.

Kirk Alyn · Lyle Talbot · Noel Neill · Jimmy Bond

Directed by SPENCER BENNET · Produced by SAM KATZMAN

A COLUMBIA SERIAL

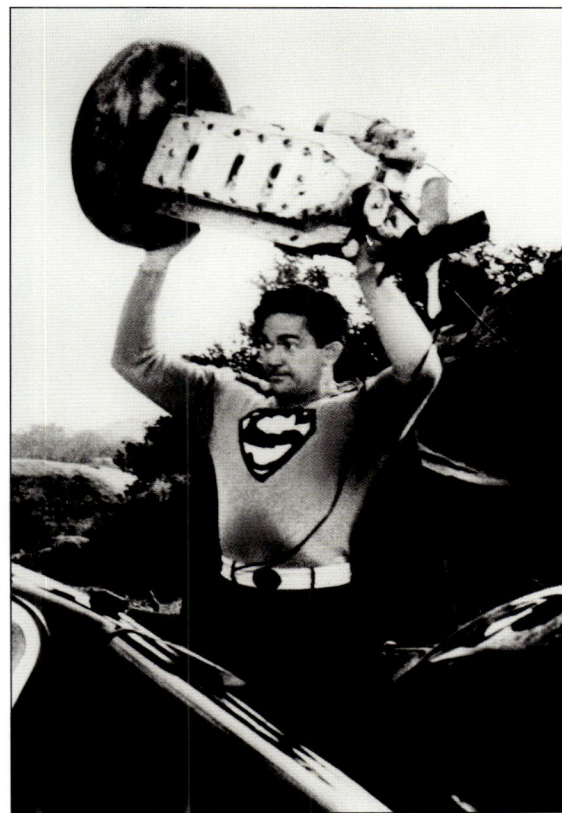

Far left: Convincingly despicable in both roles on screen, off camera Lyle Talbot passed dull moments trading recipes with fellow cooking aficionado Kirk Alyn.

Left: The series' big finish involved an attack by flying saucers, albeit built by Luthor, not space invaders.

Whitney Ellsworth had to be convinced Alyn was right to play clean-cut Superman after the actor's rushed audition—in long hair and goatee beard having just finished a role in a western.

saucers, and aerial torpedoes. In one crucial, momentous segment, the villain's "Empty Doom" (Chapter 8) turned Superman into an intangible ghost—a precursor of the punishment dimension later comic book writers dubbed the Phantom Zone.

Radio days

On February 12, 1940, the Mutual Network first broadcast *The Adventures of Superman* radio show into homes across America. Sponsored by Kellogg's Pep, 15-minute episodes three times a week (in some regions, five days a week) starred Bud Collyer in twin lead roles. Evolving into half-hour installments by August 1942, it spawned a landmark spin-off—a serious novel by George Lowther.

Running until February 4, 1949, the show shifted to an ABC evening slot (and thrice-weekly afternoons) until March 1, 1951, totaling 2,088 episodes and 128 storylines. There was a franchised all-Australian version generating 1040 episodes from 1949 to 1954.

American scriptwriters/directors Lowther, B. P. Freeman, Jack Johnstone, Robert and Jessica Maxwell, Allen Ducovny, and Mitchell Grayson introduced innovations later canonical in comic books—Batman team-ups,

turning an anonymous office copy-boy into Jimmy Olsen, and devising Kryptonite to make Superman vulnerable.

Radio fueled the imaginations of millions and the show embraced the refugee hero's socially crusading roots. In 1946, responding to a resurgence of the Ku Klux Klan, writers attacked intolerance and bigotry in "The Clan of the Fiery Cross." From June 10, 16 episodes detailed a Chinese-American family moving to Metropolis and targeted by hooded racists until Superman stepped in, rallying resistance from every decent citizen.

In 2019, that landmark tale—with elements of radio's Atom Man storyline—was adapted by Gene Luen Yang and Japanese illustration collective Gurihiru for modern comic book audiences.

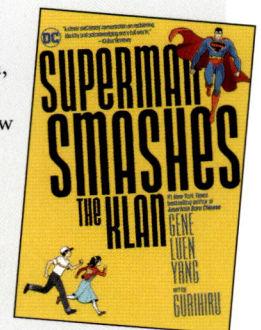

21

SUPERMAN AND THE MOLE MEN

Release date: November 23, 1951
Rerelease date: April 15, 1953
Starring roles: George Reeves, Phyllis Coates, Jeff Corey, Walter Reed, J. Farrell MacDonald, Stanley Andrews, Beverly Washburn

Director: Lee Sholem
Screenplay: Richard Fielding (co-pen name of Robert Maxwell and Whitney Ellsworth)
Cinematography: Clark Ramsey
Music: Darrell Calker, Walter Greene
Running time: 58 minutes

The 1950s belonged to Superman. Headlining in *Action Comics*, *World's Finest Comics* and his own eponymous comic book, the Last Son of Krypton was an icon of the airwaves, with a globally syndicated comic strip and two hugely successful movie serials. But the only way forward was still up.

MAN OF THE MOMENT

Over the decade, Superman's comic book sales regularly topped a million copies, only starting to fall in the mid-1960s when comic books on the whole began to steadily decline on newsstands. Well into the 1970s, DC could honestly declare on Superman covers "Number 1 best-selling comics magazine." Much of this was thanks to a huge boost afforded by the *Adventures of Superman* television show, which replaced the venerable radio institution after its cancellation in March 1951.

However, although the radio series was a blueprint for the small-screen phenomenon that followed and the world was primed by Columbia's serial successes, the path to household dominance was torturous and initially risky.

Tapping into a contemporary zeitgeist of socially critical science-fiction parables prevalent in the era of "Red Scares," *Superman and the Mole Men* was the first ever Super Hero feature film. It was written by Richard Fielding—a pen name for collaborators DC editorial liaison Whitney Ellsworth and screenwriter Robert Maxwell. He had been a producer and writer for Superman's radio show and scripted many episodes of the hit *Lassie* and *National Velvet* television series.

Produced by Barney A. Sarecky (*Kid Dynamite*, *Law of the West*) for independent theater owner/B-movie producer Robert L. Lippert, the entire project was a brazen attempt to move into the wild frontier of television. The film was directed by legendary Lee "Roll 'em" Sholem who for 40 years directed more than

"Since you can't be trusted with guns, I'll have to take them away."
Superman

Superman's first feature film was barely an hour long and released as a "trial balloon" to gauge audience interest in a prospective syndicated television series.

Helping the mole folk return to their underworld, Superman learns there are some things—like misunderstanding and intolerance—that even his mighty powers cannot fix.

At age 37, George Reeves was the joint-oldest actor to debut as Superman. He shares the honor with predecessor Kirk Alyn.

Clark Kent investigates mounting paranoia as mine foreman Bill Corrigan (Walter Reed) shows him glowing samples pulled from their ultra-deep oil well.

Phyllis Coates carried her portrayal of Lois Lane over to the television show but left after season one, with original actor Noel Neill replacing her.

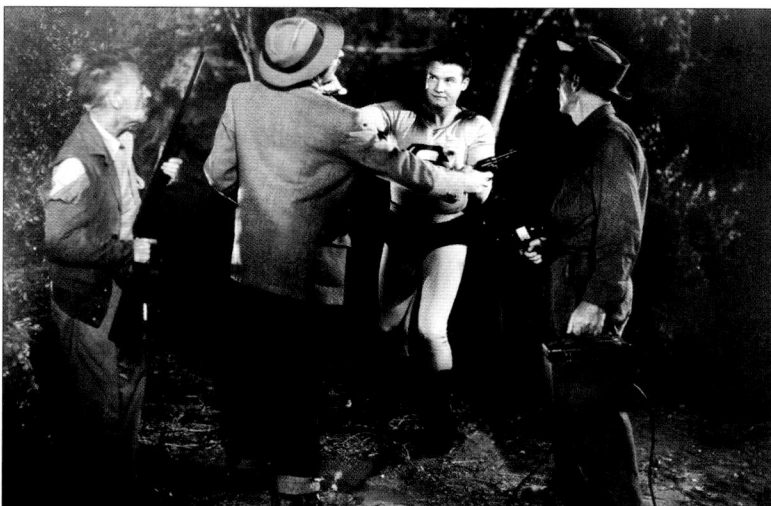

Changing times found the Man of Steel acting as a moral compass, confronting ordinary citizens behaving rashly rather than stopping wicked villains.

1,300 film and TV features (including *Tarzan's Magic Fountain*, *Maverick*). He never went over schedule—a feat unmatched in Hollywood history.

Beginning July 10, 1951, *Superman and the Mole Men* was shot in 12 days on the RKO-Pathé lot—designed as a soft pilot for a TV series. Further work took place in August and September, but then stalled for a year, until Kellogg's agreed to sponsor the series, as they had the radio iteration. Sholem directed many of these *Adventures of Superman*, and when broadcasts began and the show was safely established, the film was edited into two-part story "The Unknown People" and screened in 1954.

In-demand actor and dancer Kirk Alyn had become the go-to guy for serial superheroes. Had it not been for scheduling clashes, he would have played Republic's Captain America in 1944 and become the second actor to play Batman. Now, with two Superman movies under his belt and the entire world knowing him as the Man of Steel, he was the obvious choice for Sholem's movie. However, by 1950, Alyn was done with such hazardous, painfully typecast children's fodder. When the producers made a less-than-adequate offer for him to play Superman again, Alyn rejected it and similarly nixed the role in the planned television follow-up. The part went to dramatic actor George Reeves (*Gone With the Wind*, *From Here to Eternity*), who had been in Sam Katzman's Arthurian serial *The Adventures of Sir Galahad* (1949). A case of right man, right time and place, he came into the frame for Superman after Alyn's refusal sparked a rapid casting call.

Reeves became utterly inseparable from the Man of Tomorrow in public consciousness. When interviewed about his own portrayal of Superman in 1978 , Christopher Reeve admitted that although he couldn't recall ever reading Superman comic books, he was a fan of the George Reeves show.

LIGHT IN THE DARK

The film itself was a timely treatise on intolerance and understanding that began when Clark and Lois (Phyllis Coates) arrived to write about rural, insular Silsby, site of the world's deepest oil well. When their process pierces an unsuspected subsurface enclave six miles down, two strange, highly advanced little beings emerge that night. Roaming the town and investigating everything, the weird duo also innocently and joyously play with a little girl, which absolutely terrifies her mother. Due to natural phosphorescence, these furry creatures shine in the dark and anything they touch glows. When an elderly mine guard (J. Farrell MacDonald) dies of a heart attack, it triggers unreasoning panic and mob violence, led by rabid bigot Luke Benson (Jeff Corey), happily exploiting fears that the little beasts are radioactive.

When one of the strange visitors is shot, Superman intervenes, saving the "mole man." As a mob gathers at the doors of the

hospital where the creature is taken for life-saving surgery, Superman joins Lois to guard the hospital. Meanwhile, the other explorer has headed home, but soon returns with a rescue party and lethal laser weapon. Now, the Man of Steel must save Benson and the rioters, before handing over the recuperating subterranean and allowing the under-earthers to go home and seal the pit.

The budget was small but the crew were highly innovative. The Mole Men's laser gun was built by adding metal shoulder braces to an Electrolux vacuum cleaner frame with a metal funnel affixed to one end. Sadly, there was little they could do to fix the perennial problem and once again, many viewers could not believe that a man could fly. That said, the film paved the way for groundbreaking television series *Adventures of Superman*, which was a monster success in the 1950s. The series was comparatively cheap to make (roughly $15,000 per episode) and ran 104 original episodes across six seasons, from September 19, 1952, to April 28, 1958, and for decades after in syndicated reruns.

At the height of its popularity, the passing of John Hamilton (Perry White) and George Reeves's sudden and controversial death ended the series. Despite many desperate attempts to retool the show and carry on without him, the live-action Superman experience was sidelined for decades. One of the most intriguing "might-have-beens" was Superboy. The Boy of Steel was a postwar sensation offering a fresh take on the legend, and in 1961, Ellsworth produced a pilot starring Johnny Rockwell. Thirteen scripts were completed before Hollywood decided the time wasn't right, and Superboy was left to cartoon capers until a later era brought some rebellious teen appeal to the concept.

Cartoon capers

Superman was the first comic book star with a newspaper strip. His daily feature launched on January 16, 1939, and lasted 27 years, supplemented by a full-color Sunday page beginning November 5 of that year and initially crafted by Siegel and Shuster—who switched their primary focus from comic books to the more prestigious iteration—increasingly aided by their small studio team.

Siegel's episodes established an Alien Wonder dwelling among us, working as a human at a "great metropolitan newspaper" when not crushing evil in a flamboyant alter-ego. Stories emphasized action and the incredible powers of a heroic man of the people. When Siegel was drafted, Whitney Ellsworth provided scripts (1943–1945), as did Jack Schiff and Alvin Schwartz, who was sole scriptwriter between 1947 and 1951. He was part of a Superman writing group thereafter until leaving in 1958.

After the war, the strip comfortably idled. Nothing hurt the hero, nothing changed, and suspense was in short supply. This evolved after the *Superman* cinema serial (and sequel *Atom Man vs. Superman*) boosted circulation, as did television series *The Adventures of Superman*, which benefitted 1950s readership. In all iterations, crime and social crusading gave way to cozy mystery, science fiction, and domestic comedy situations.

They were also frequently augmented by a new category—showbiz and celebrity stories, springing from editorial director Ellsworth in his role as DC's Hollywood liaison and consultant on all their properties for large and small screens.

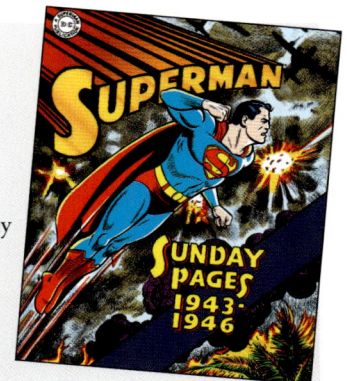

THRILLS AND SPILLS

By 1946, most studios were closing their serial units, but Columbia Pictures carried on crafting chapter-plays until 1956, when US domestic television ownership reached 75 percent. Kids could now stay home and enjoy free fantastic thrills, but between 1946 and 1955, the studio's demand for source material never wavered. National Comics/DC carried many options outside the declining Super Hero trend. Flagship anthology and home of *Superman*, *Action Comics* alone provided two other Columbia serials: Congo Bill and *The Vigilante*. Both supporting strips offered human-scaled fantasy adventure and carried on well into the 1950s.

Hop and Tank's partners in crimebusting were original characters Gail Nolan and her brother Jackie, played by Jennifer Holt and Robert "Buzz" Henry.

HOP HARRIGAN, AMERICA'S ACE OF THE AIRWAYS

In the early 20th century, aviators were folk heroes—stars of books, films, radio shows, and newspaper strips like *Tailspin Tommy* (star of the first strip aviator movie serial in 1934). Jon L. Blummer's Hop Harrigan launched in *All-American Comics* #1 (April 1939), a dashing flier also appearing in eight other titles published by DC's sister company All-American Publications.

In 1941, Hop briefly became costumed hero Guardian Angel, before reverting to a simple pilot, who—with sidekick Tank Tinker—served valiantly in WWII, and as a soldier of fortune afterward. His last appearance was in *All-American Comics* #99 (July 1948).

His newspaper strip was short-lived, but Hop's Monday-to-Friday radio show aired from August 31, 1942, to February 6, 1948. At this time, he had become Columbia Pictures' second DC serial star. *Hop Harrigan, America's Ace of the Airways* was produced by Sam Katzman; directed by Derwin Abrahams; and written by Blummer, Ande Lamb, and George H. Plympton.

On screen and with Earth's existence at risk, in 15 episodes charter pilot Hop (William Bakewell) and mechanic Tank (Sumner Gretchen) were hired by businessman J. Westly Arnold (Emmett Vogan) and scientist Dr. Tobor (John Merton), battling to keep a deadly ray machine from masked mastermind The Chief Pilot (Wheeler Oakman).

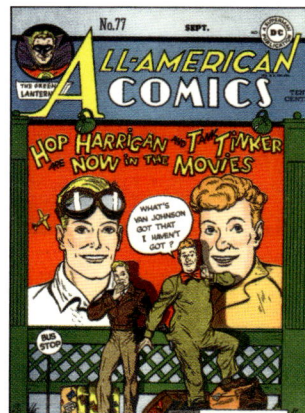

Release date: March 28, 1946
Starring roles: William Bakewell, Sumner Gretchen, Emmett Vogan, John Merton, Robert "Buzz" Henry
Director: Derwin Abrahams
Screenplay: Jon L. Blummer, Ande Lamb, George H. Plympton
Running time: 15 two-reel chapters

THE VIGILANTE—FIGHTING HERO OF THE WEST

Inspired by radio and film trends, The Vigilante was a western-themed masked hero battling modern-day bandits and badmen. Created by Mort Weisinger and Mort Meskin, celebrity singing cowboy Greg Sanders debuted in *Action Comics* #42 (November 1941), running until #198 (November 1954). The hero was one of the Seven Soldiers of Victory in *Leading Comics* #1–14 (December 1941–March 1945).

The cozy cowboy cachet of "The Prairie Troubadour" made The Vigilante a prime contender for serial stardom as westerns proliferated after WWII. Produced by Katzman; written by Lewis Clay, Arthur Hoerl, and Plympton; and directed by sagebrush veteran Wallace Fox, *The Vigilante–Fighting Hero of the West* saw government agent Sanders played by *Dick Tracy* serial star Ralph Byrd. With

THE TEARS OF BLOOD!
CLOSING IN!
Chapter 14
THE VIGILANTE
Fighting Hero of the West

By merging western themes and modern gangsterism with showbiz musicality, *The Vigilante* offered great cross-marketing potential.

sidekick Stuff (George Offerman Jr., a white teen replacing the comic book's Asian hero Stuff the Chinatown Kid), he brought justice to gem smugglers and their boss George Pierce (Lyle Talbot).

The film serial enjoyed a big sales push from National/DC, who produced an *Action Comics* special edition premium free to moviegoers and added a feature on how the film was made to *Real Fact Comics* #10 (October 1947).

Release date: May 22, 1947
Starring roles: Ralph Byrd, Ramsey Ames, Lyle Talbot, George Offerman Jr.
Director: Wallace Fox

Screenplay: Lewis Clay, Arthur Hoerl, George H. Plympton
Running time: 285 minutes, 15 two-reel chapters

Columbia Pictures hired model Cleouna "Cleo" Moore as their answer to Marilyn Monroe, but in 20 films over nine years, playing jungle queen Lureen/Ruth Culver was her only leading lady role.

CONGO BILL—KING OF THE JUNGLE

Very much of its time and closely based on Alex Raymond's newspaper star Jungle Jim (made into a serial in 1937), Congo Bill debuted in *More Fun Comics* #56 (June 1940 and running until #67, May 1941). He moved to flagship title *Action Comics* with #37 (June 1941). It was a solid, reliable B-feature, with enticingly formulaic plots involving uprisings, criminals, rich wastrels, war, plague, witch-doctors, and—as times changed—mad scientists, monsters, and aliens.

Gaining sidekick Janu the Jungle Boy in *Action Comics* #191 (April 1954) and a solo comic book (#1–7, September 1954– September 1955), Bill ended as an animal Super Hero using a magic ring to trade bodies with giant golden gorilla Congorilla (*Action Comics* #224–261, January 1957–February 1960) and later *Adventure Comics* #270–#283 (March 1960–April 1961).

Illustrated by George Papp, Bill had been devised by Whitney Ellsworth, DC's media man and Hollywood consultant for all serials. In 1947, his creation qualified for movie treatment in the venerable jungle picture genre. Thrifty producer Katzman (while preparing a Jungle Jim film series with Johnny Weissmuller) brought the DC character to life in a 15-chapter saga scripted by Plympton, Hoerl, and Clay, and directed by Spencer Gordon Bennett and Thomas Carr.

The series saw Bill (Don McGuire) track down a lost heiress (Cleo Moore) raised as a jungle goddess, opposed by villains and all the perils of nature. Former soldier and journalist McGuire became a screenwriter in 1950, beginning with Dean Martin and Jerry Lewis material before going on to major high points including *Meet Danny Wilson* (1952), 1955's award-winning *Bad Day at Black Rock,* and Dustin Hoffman vehicle *Tootsie* (1982).

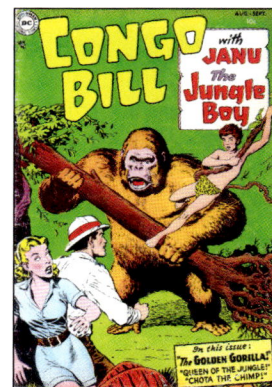

Release date: October 28, 1948
Starring roles: Don McGuire, Cleo Moore, Jack Ingram, I. Stanford Jolley, Leonard Penn, Nelson Leigh
Director: Spencer Gordon
Bennett, Thomas Carr
Screenplay: George H. Plympton, Arthur Hoerl, Lewis Clay
Running time: 15 two-reel chapters

Seemingly born to play larger-than-life characters in snappy costumes, Kirk Alyn began his prodigious film career as a chorus boy.

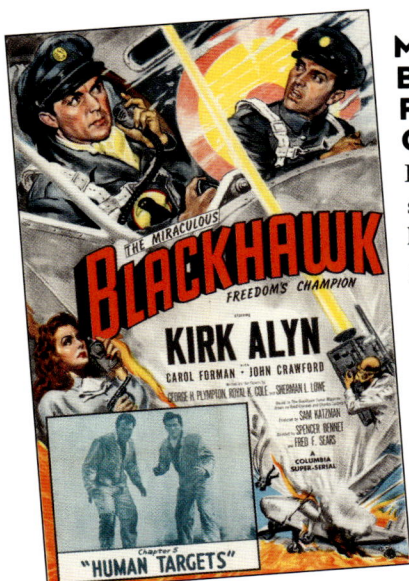

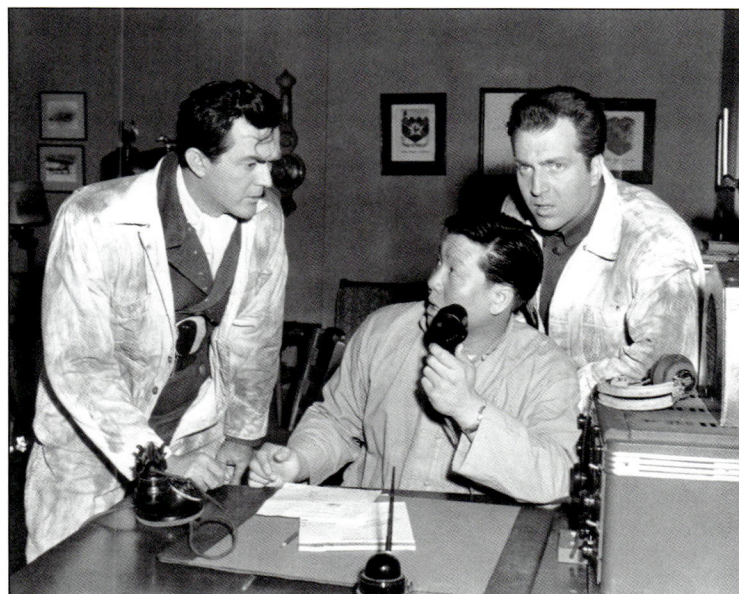

Blackhawk (Kirk Alyn) was a dedicated, hands-on commander of the so-called "foreign legion of the air," even if his on-screen international allies (John Crawford and Warner Levy) were very much American born and bred.

MIRACULOUS BLACKHAWK— FEARLESS CHAMPION OF FREEDOM

Blackhawk was a certified sensation when his flying foreign legion debuted on May 30, 1941, published by DC competitor Quality Comics, and jointly created by Bob Powell, Will Eisner, and Chuck Cuidera.

Military Comics #1 (August 1941) focused on global war while America was still officially neutral. Blackhawk was one series among ten, but outstripped all others with compelling, beautifully drawn tales of intrigue, combat, and vengeance. Ace pilot Blackhawk's squadron of refugee warriors fought against fascism, and stuck together to crush postwar tyranny, pirates, mad scientists, monsters, and even aliens and Super-Villains.

From September 13 to December 27, 1950, a radio adaptation failed to find an audience but did aid Katzman; directors Spencer Gordon Bennett and Fred F. Sears; and scriptwriters Plympton, Royal K. Cole, and Sherman L. Lowe when adapting the "Magnificent Seven" to the dying medium of cinema serials.

With the prospect of a TV series to follow, former Superman actor Kirk Alyn became Blackhawk, whose international brotherhood of air aces defended democracy from a secret US airbase. When enemy agents led by femme fatale Laska (Carol Forman) and The Leader (Michael Fox) attempt to destroy the Blackhawks from within and secure experimental super-fuel Element-X, they begin by replacing stalwart comrade Stanislaus (Rick Vallin) with his evil twin brother Boris.

Despite embracing contemporary science-fiction tropes, the serial failed to reignite Blackhawk and Quality's fortunes. In 1956, publisher Everett "Busy" Arnold licensed his comics properties to National/DC, where the Blackhawks soared on for another decade and have since returned, rebooted and reimagined many times.

Release date: July 24, 1952
Starring roles: Kirk Alyn, Carol Forman, John Crawford
Director: Spencer Gordon Bennett, Fred F. Sears

Screenplay: George H. Plympton, Royal K. Cole, Sherman L. Lowe
Running time: 242 minutes, 15 two-reel chapters

29

BATMAN

Release date: July 30, 1966 (Hollywood), June 19, 1992 (US)
Starring roles: Adam West, Burt Ward, Lee Meriwether, Frank Gorshin, Burgess Meredith, Cesar Romero, Alan Napier, Neil Hamilton, Stafford Repp, Reginald Denny, Madge Blake

Director: Leslie H. Martinson
Screenplay: Lorenzo Semple Jr.
Cinematography: Howard Schwartz
Music: Nelson Riddle, Neal Hefti
Running time: 104 minutes
Box office: $3.9 million (inc. rentals)

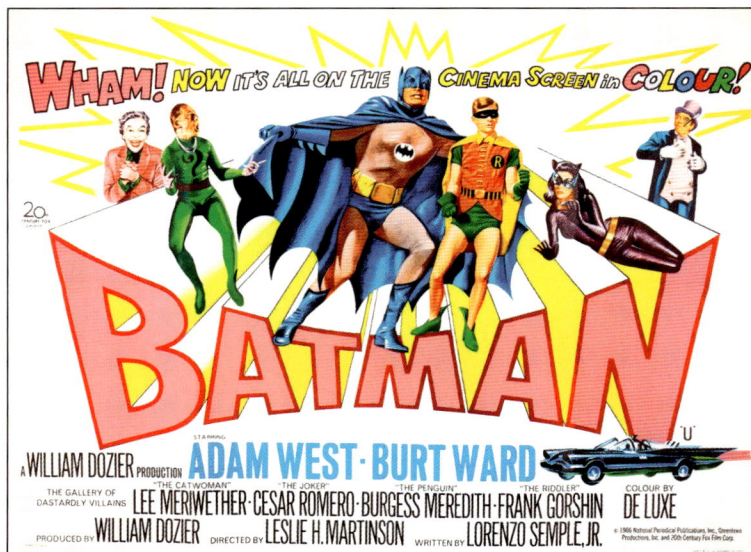

Slick production, bright lights, and lurid colors mimicking comic book hues became the lasting hallmark of *Batman*—not to mention a mountain of eye-catching merchandise.

Batman: The Movie **was released** on July 30, 1966—after the final episode (May 5) of season 1 of a television phenomenon. A frenetic, fast-paced action comedy, the film begins—after the moody credit sequence set a faux film-noir tone—with Batman (Adam West) and Robin (Burt Ward) dashing out to sea in the batcopter to rescue inventor Commodore Schmidlapp (Reginald Denny), who they've been informed is in grave danger aboard his yacht. As Batman is lowered down to help, a trap is sprung. The vessel vanishes, leaving Batman hanging from a rope-ladder and attacked by an exploding shark ...

Batman's first feature film was written in 10 days by Lorenzo Semple Jr. (*Papillon*, *Flash Gordon*). Principal photography took eight more, beginning on April 28. Director Leslie H. Martinson (*Maverick*, *Batman* episodes "The Penguin Goes Straight" and "Not Yet, He Ain't") added three more days of second unit photography. By July, the film was enthralling audiences. Executive producer William Dozier described the show and popular response as the only situation comedy airing without a laugh track.

SAME BAT-TIME, SAME BAT-CHANNEL
On Wednesday January 12, 1966, the *Batman* series premiered on televisions across America. The episode ended on a classic chapter-play cliffhanger as narrator Dozier urged viewers to tune in tomorrow—"same Bat-Time, same Bat-Channel." A huge hit, the show epitomized a new zeitgeist of ironic commentary and satirical mockery of established traditions.

"Some days you just can't get rid of a bomb!"
Batman

Batman ran for three seasons (120 episodes), airing twice weekly for the first two. The third season introduced Batgirl—a fresh iteration of a former character who was soon also a component of comic books and newspaper strips. Internationally, *Batman* sparked waves of trendy imitation and a torrent of merchandise—officially sanctioned and otherwise.

The media dubbed the fan-frenzy "Batmania"—a term originally coined in 1964 by "Bat-fan" Biljo White for his fanzine dedicated to Batman comic books, and itself acknowledging a recent social

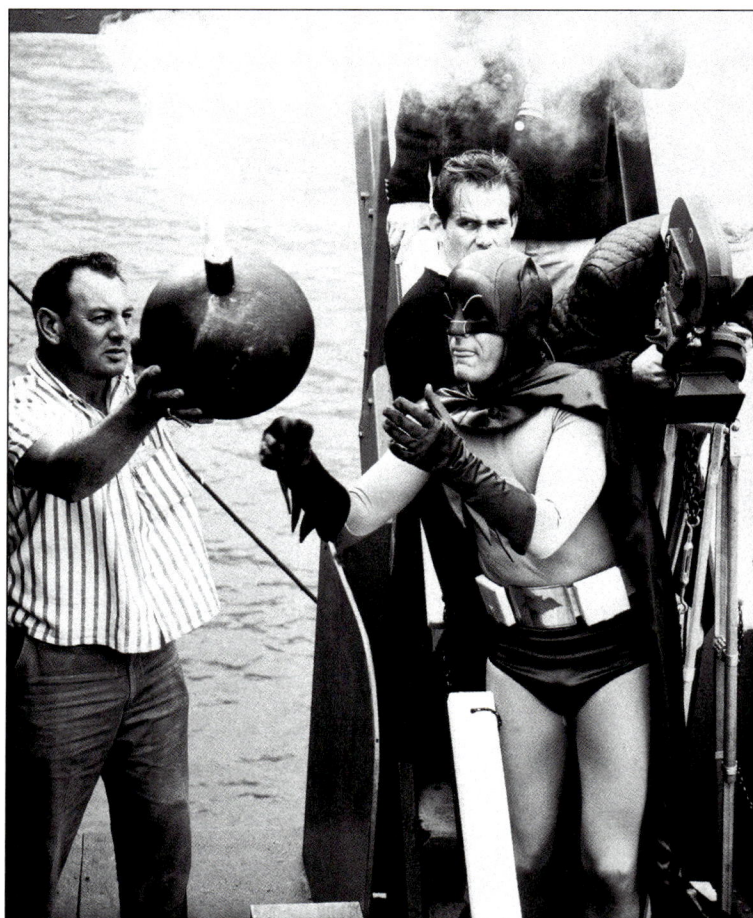

The classically clichéd, silent-film-era comedy bomb that featured in an overtly slapstick scene is now one of the most popular prop replicas collected by "Bat-Fans."

Robin's respectful responses to Batman's stiffly pompous style of deduction was a reversal of the "rebellious youth" image of teenagers then troubling America's establishment.

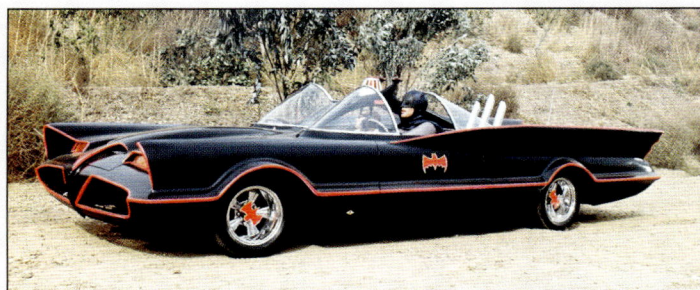

The Batmobile

Although Batman drove a sporty red car in *Detective Comics* #27, the comic book Batmobile officially debuted in issue #48 (February 1941). It has been a constant aid and companion ever since, continually upgraded with the changing times and supplemented by all manner of subsidiary vehicles.

The iconic vehicle built for the television series by George Barris in 1965 is actually five separate cars, with the primary vehicle a modified and converted 1955 Lincoln Futura. This was a prototype concept car from Ford Motor Company lead stylists Bill Schmidt, Doug Poole Jr., and John Najjar of the Lincoln Styling Department. Barris restyled the frame and duplicated on other chassis for different shots and purposes. It was completed in three weeks, at a reported cost of $30,000. So iconic is this model that it perpetually resurfaces in comic books.

The Batmobile has been held to be a copyrighted character under US copyright law—a status generally reserved for sentient fictional characters. This occurred in 2011 after a mechanic making replicas based on Barris's design argued that as an "element of the show" it was ineligible for copyright. The court ruled, however, that the Batmobile was an "automotive character" with its own consistent style, backstory, and theme.

Fight scenes were frequent, lengthy, and highly choreographed, emulating the wildly addictive free-for-alls of the vintage serials the *Batman* show was based on.

Stuntmen Hubie Kerns and Victor Paul doubled for Adam West and Burt Ward, but tight camerawork and revealing masks meant the stars still got their feet wet far too often.

revolution sparked by four lads from Liverpool—Beatlemania. The show ended with the March 14, 1968, episode, but the characters— including Batgirl—lived on in Filmation Studios' animated follow-up *The Adventures of Batman.*

COSTLY CONSIDERATIONS

Dozier wanted a movie release as a pilot preceding his show (as had happened 15 years earlier with *Superman and the Mole Men*) but 20th Century Fox refused, realizing it would have meant their covering the entire cost, rather than sharing it with network ABC. Even so, haggling resulted in a Batcycle (and sidecar), Batcopter, and Batboat, providing stock footage shots for later television episodes. Provided by Texas boatbuilders Glastron, the Batboat cost nothing—made and donated in return for a prominent opening credit and holding the film premiere in Austin's Paramount Theatre.

Expense was always critical. Shooting mainly occurred at Culver City Studios and Warner Brothers Studios in Burbank. The Batcave set alone cost $800,000 and the first episode came in at $400,000. After test screenings revealed audiences disliked it, the studio considered cancelling *Batman*, but went ahead because they had already invested so much money in it. As Dozier said "It was the lowest rating they had ever had on anything!," concluding, "If they [ABC] hadn't already bought the show, it would never have gone on the air!"

Batman captivated viewers and merchandisers (of books, toys, gum cards, apparel, mugs, lunchboxes, puzzles, and more) but actually undid many of DC's plans. After reinventing Super Heroes with a new Flash (in *Showcase* #4, October 1956) and triggering the Silver Age, in 1963, editor Julius Schwartz was tasked with reinventing Batman and Robin. Although appearing in four titles, *Batman*, *Detective Comics*, *World's Finest Comics*, and *Justice League of America*, the franchise was dying.

Far left: Catwoman Lee Meriwether only played the role on the big screen. She did, however, appear in two *Batman* TV episodes ("King Tut's Coup" and "Batman's Waterloo") as Bruce Wayne's girlfriend Lisa Carson.

Left: Frank Gorshin's screen career spanned 1956 to 2005. The actor played The Riddler in 10 TV episodes and the movie, with his performances earning him an Emmy Award nomination.

Burgess Meredith's Penguin was so popular, writers always had a script ready for the next time his schedule permitted a return. Appearing in 21 episodes, he also guested in character on equally outrageous comedy series *The Monkees*.

Schwartz pared back aliens, outlandish villains, and weird transformation tales, and returned Batman to his core concept.

Streamlining rationalization and modernization brought a subtle aura of genuine menace, but simultaneously Hollywood was preparing their series, basing it upon the material Schwartz was emphatically rejecting in the "New Look Batman" and which was currently winning back readers.

THIRD TIME LUCKY

ABC Network had been seeking a fantasy property to develop and—thanks to groundswell interest in revivals of Batman series like *An Evening with Batman and Robin*—they opted for a comic star. Their first attempt was for Superman (the only comics character the general public really recognized), but his rights were tied up in stage musical *It's a Bird ... It's a Plane ... It's Superman!*

Then ABC optioned *Dick Tracy* before losing him to a rival network. Ultimately, ABC's executive producer of choice, William Dozier (*Rod Brown of the Rocket Rangers*, *The Loner*), was assigned the company's successful third choice—*Batman*. Unfamiliar with the material, Dozier proudly stated at the time that he had never read a comic book in his life. "I bought a dozen comics and felt like a fool as I read them, and asked myself what do I do with this?" The answer came by assessing the changing times.

The tenor of the decade had already shifted, with cop, war, and western dramas regularly replaced by spoofs and parodies—fun fantasy fare like *The Addams Family* and *The Munsters* (both 1964), *Lost in Space*, *Hogan's Heroes*, *Get Smart*, *F-Troop*, and *Wild Wild West* (all 1965). Producer Howie Horwitz (*Shane*, *77 Sunset Strip*) and lead writer Semple Jr. and Dozier agreed their project needed to be deadpan funny—overflowing with mock heroism, heavy-handed simplistic satire, intentionally clichéd dialogue, and spoofing the worst excesses of movie serials!

It required really gifted actors to work. Associate producer Charles Fitzsimmons recalled, "It was a tough search because you had to find an actor who was prepared to play Alice in Wonderland as though it were Hamlet."

The series enjoyed a host of celebrity Super-Villains who were naturally granted many concessions. Cesar Romero refused to shave off his moustache, playing The Joker in 22 episodes with it painted white to match his makeup.

Shipwrights Mel Whitley and Robert Hammond built the Batboat from a Glastron V-174 hull in 31 days, making a number of Bat-modifications.

20th Century Fox only leased the Batcopter, modifying a model G3B-1 Bell 47. It was previously used in *Lassie*.

The movie Batbike was a Yamaha Catalina 250 modified by Tom Daniel and Dan and Richard "Korky" Korkes. It was ridden almost exclusively by stuntmen.

The search began in 1965 and soon narrowed to two would-be star pairings—newcomers Lyle Waggoner (later Steve Trevor in *Wonder Woman*) and Peter Deyell, and established actor West (*Robinson Crusoe on Mars*, *The Detectives*) paired with another fresh face—Burt Ward. West and Ward enjoyed crucial chemistry and a boyish humorous spark, signing contracts on September 21, 1965. The comedy element was vital. When Dozier and Martinson tried repeating the process in a more serious adaptation of radio legend *The Green Hornet*, it ended after one season.

Like so many superhero films, *Batman* depends upon villains to carry the action, provide laughs, and provoke empathy. As the Dynamic Duo confers with Commissioner Gordon (Neil Hamilton) and Police Chief O'Hara (Stafford Repp), Gotham City's greatest villains conspire as the United Underworld. The Penguin (Burgess Meredith), The Riddler (Frank Gorshin), The Joker (Cesar Romero), and Catwoman (Lee Meriwether—standing in for overcommitted Julie Newmar) dupe Schmidlapp and purloin his super-dehydrator invention, intent on eliminating Batman and Robin before snatching the United World Security Council.

Repeated attacks against the heroes fail. From their wharfside lair and The Penguin's modified war-surplus submarine, foiled murderous assaults provoke disunity until Catwoman—disguised as a naive Soviet journalist "Kitanya Ireyna Tatiana Kerenska Alisoff, KITKA"—seduces Bruce Wayne and pretends to be captured with him to lure the heroes into an ambush. Escaping that deathtrap, Batman and Robin are gulled into bringing the Bird Bandit and five dehydrated henchmen into the Batcave, where a flaw in the process ends their avian ambush and reduces the thugs to antimatter!

Ultimately, the villains succeed in desiccating and kidnapping the United World delegates, as Batman and Robin make a heroic effort to catch and foil them. In a climactic clash, the powdered politicians are jumbled up together, compelling the heroes to devise a means of separating and restoring the council to ensure global peace.

The show's look and style was unique—celebrity guests playing the Rogues Gallery of villains, a color palate mimicking comic books, items unnecessarily labeled, zany angle shots, and plenty of fights (scrupulously mimicking their serial antecedents) with pop-art graphic effects overlaid. At the phenomenon's height, for a relatively brief moment, mankind went bananas for superheroes in general and most especially went "Bat-Mad." The monster worldwide hit sparked strange reinterpretations. Many countries opted to recolor the drab gray Batsuit to a stylish crimson.

FROM SCREEN TO PAGE

The show's dominance ultimately affected Schwartz's carefully curated renaissance of Batman, success forcing printed stories to emulate the screen tone as sales soared. *Batman* #179—with The Riddler on the cover—went on sale January 20, 1966, and sold out, nearly a million copies and an unprecedented spike

Far left: In comic books, the fearsome foursome have never formed a formal alliance, and smaller partnerships always resulted in betrayal and attempted murder.

Left: The movie's subplot of abducting quarreling world leaders and imminent global conflict was a rare incidence of realism and realpolitik in what was generally considered a frivolous genre.

for the title that eventually overtook even DC's previously unmatchable circulation monolith, *Superman*.

Luckily for devout fans of the darker Batman tales, the show's finish led to a gradual rehabilitation, redefinition, and reclamation of the Dark Knight Detective and his mantle of mystery and fear. As the TV series foundered, so did global fascination with superheroes. The 1960s screen Batman left an indelible mark on global consciousness and became a yardstick all other films, comics, and other iterations were measured against.

Adam West's take on Batman remains a favorite for millions—spawning foreign editions like Jiro Kuwata's *Bat-Manga*, DC's comic book *Batman '66*, and collected editions of contemporary comics tales. West and Ward were wildly popular guests on comics and screen convention circuits for decades and in 2016 and 2017 reunited to voice their iconic characters in two animated sequels—*Batman: Return of the Caped Crusaders* and *Batman versus Two-Face* (with William Shatner playing Harvey Dent).

The animated film was made to celebrate the series' 50th anniversary, with surviving cast joining younger actors in a second clash between the Dynamic Duo and The Riddler, The Joker, The Penguin, and Catwoman.

In the news today

"Batman with Robin the Boy Wonder" began as a full-color Sunday page on May 29, 1966, with the dailies starting the next day. Signed "Bob Kane," stories were written by Whitney Ellsworth and illustrated by Sheldon Moldoff, with Joe Giella providing a sleek, modern finish to visuals. He frequently penciled too, but always inked the strips.

It was a seven-day-a-week job, and Giella regularly called on comic book luminaries like Carmine Infantino, Bob Powell, Werner Roth, and Curt Swan. Dailies and Sundays were generally separate packages featuring their own self-contained storylines. *Batman* started this way, before switching to

single unified storylines in December 1966. Super-Villains and cameos abounded and comedy was king, but gags diminished once the TV show closed. E. Nelson Bridwell, Al Plastino, and Nick Cardy assumed creative duties before E. M. Stout took over on January 3, 1972. Sunday pages ended on July 13, 1969, but invention and guest stars (Batgirl, Superman, Aquaman, Green Arrow, Man-Bat) carried the dying strip until DC's litigious split with the Ledger Syndicate finished it in 1973.

The newspaper Batman then appeared in *The World's Greatest Super Heroes*, created to capitalize on 1978's *Superman* film (running until 1985). The Dark Knight enjoyed a full revival when Tim Burton released *Batman*. Produced for Creators Syndicate, Max Allan Collins, Marshall Rogers, William Messner-Loebs, and Carmine revived classic villains like Catwoman and Two-Face in a newspaper comic strip feature spanning November 6, 1989, to August 1, 1991.

SUPERHERO CINEMA COMES OF AGE

By the 1970s, television was the world's primary entertainment mode—a medium even more trend-driven than cinema. As comic book sales diminished, publishers like DC began migrating characters to the small screen via animated kids shows and mainstream live-action series. These included *Shazam!* (1974–1976) and mega-hit *Wonder Woman* (1975–1979).

TV viewers had already been similarly beguiled by DC stars, with both *Adventures of Superman* (1952–1958) and *Batman* (1966–1968) winning global audiences in their day. Now, thanks to a few visionary comics fans, the film industry responded and adapted, and once again Superman was key to establishing an entirely new genre—superhero blockbusters for sophisticated cinemagoers.

Moreover, on the back of Superman's monumental global success in a five-film franchise and the spin-off TV series *Superboy,* a.k.a. *The Adventures of Superboy* (1988–1992), the door opened to movies for other, darker DC characters such as *Swamp Thing* (1982 and 1989).

SUPERMAN

Release date: December 10, 1978 (Kennedy Ctr premiere), December 14 (UK), December 15 (US)
Starring roles: Marlon Brando, Gene Hackman, Christopher Reeve, Margot Kidder, Jackie Cooper, Ned Beatty, Glenn Ford, Trevor Howard, Terence Stamp, Valerie Perrine, Phyllis Thaxter, Maria Schell, Susannah York

Director: Richard Donner
Screenplay: Mario Puzo, David Newman, Leslie Newman
Cinematography: Geoffrey Unsworth
Music: John Williams
Running time: 143 minutes/ variable
Box office: $300.5 million

The 1970s were tough. War, economic hardship, inflation, rampant crime, and widespread disillusionment even affected the entertainment media. The comics industry had collapsed and almost died while Hollywood forsook escapist fantasy blockbusters in favor of social realism, with smaller, darker movies reflecting troubled times and personal crises. There was never more need for a bright, shining hero. In 1978, Superman saved the day again.

"You'll believe a man can fly."
Promotional tagline

His comic book origins largely forgotten, the Last Son of Krypton was rediscovered by director Richard Donner, who consolidated diverse storylines into a resonant fable for the times. In the mid-1970s, despite animated shows like *The Super Friends* (1973) firmly establishing DC's characters on free-to-view television, the company's comic books were experiencing serious loss of sales, spiraling production costs, and ever-rising prices. With all comic publishers suffering declining circulation, the future was looking less than rosy.

MAN OF METAFICTION
DC's owners, National Periodicals, had taken more than $75 million in combined merchandising sales on the popular 1960s *Batman* TV series and movie, and the company was considered a goldmine of licensing potential for companies such as Warner Bros. Like Betty Boop and Popeye, Superman was deemed priceless in merchandising rather than publishing terms because of his established fame and generational familiarity. No other comic book characters, even the overexposed Batman, were deemed to have the Man of Steel's licensing prospects and simply became part of the package when DC and Warner Bros. became corporate affiliates in 1969. However, in 1976, children's publishing expert Jenette Kahn was appointed publisher at DC and the entire comic book industry began to radically change.

Two years earlier, producer Ilya Salkind had convinced his father Alexander, also a film producer, of Superman's box-office

Stage and small-screen actor Christopher Reeve easily adapted to the wide vistas and epic scope of a fantasy movie.

Far left: Being Lex Luthor gave Gene Hackman opportunity to display his comedy chops, especially as the foil for impossibly dim henchman Otis, as played by Ned Beatty.

Left: As envisioned by director Donner, Lois and Clark were the personification of Jerry Siegel and Joe Shuster's dream couple.

Jor-El (Marlon Brando) and Lara (Susannah York) prepare baby Kal-El (Lee Quigley) for his interstellar voyage to primitive Earth.

John Barry's production design replaced vintage rocket ships with a star-shaped spacecraft to deposit the infant Kal-El (Aaron Smolinski) in Kansas.

Acting icons Phyllis Thaxter and Glenn Ford bestowed simple, decent farming folk Jonathan and Martha Kent with traditional, ethical values.

potential. Their (and partner Pierre Spengler's) protracted negotiations with DC finally concluded with the sale of Superman's rights in August 1974, with the stipulation that—just as with *The Three Musketeers* and *The Four Musketeers*—*Superman* and its sequel must be made simultaneously. The publisher also insisted on an "integrity of character" clause, giving them final say on every aspect of production, including dialogue and casting.

At the senior Salkind's insistence and despite no director being assigned, a search began for a star name to play Superman. Names initially connected to the role included Muhammad Ali, Dustin Hoffman, James Caan, Robert Redford, Burt Reynolds, Steve McQueen, and Clint Eastwood, and DC management approved each one. Eventually, the relatively unknown Christopher Reeve would win the role and make it forever his own. Prospective directors included Francis Ford Coppola, Steven Spielberg, Peter Yates, William Friedkin, George Lucas, and Sam Peckinpah, before the producers hired Guy Hamilton (*Goldfinger*, *Battle of Britain*).

THE WRITE STUFF

A script was the next hurdle. In an era of gritty cinematic verity, a gleaming parable of hope about an extraterrestrial immigrant was a tough sell. When high-profile screenwriters including Academy Award-winner William Goldman (*Butch Cassidy and the Sundance Kid*) and Leigh Brackett (*The Big Sleep*) passed on the job, Ilya approached veteran comics and science-fiction author Alfred Bester (*Green Lantern*, *The Stars My Destination*), who began a treatment highlighting Clark Kent over Superman. Alexander overruled the decision, commissioning Mario Puzo (*The Godfather*) to write a serious science-fiction epic.

Puzo's screenplay was long and suffered from what the producers described as "Shakespearean and Greek Tragedy," yet also contained too many misjudged gags. Puzo left the project after delivering a second draft in July 1975, so David Newman and Robert Benton were commissioned to moderate the comedic elements. When Benton left to direct *The Late Show*, Newman's wife Leslie stepped in, and the two pared down the text for film and sequel.

When it was decided an unknown would play the Man of Tomorrow, casting turned to finding major names and a stellar international cast for supporting roles. Marlon Brando agreed to be Jor-El, which led to Gene Hackman becoming Lex Luthor, a triumph that so impressed Warner Bros. that the studio opted to distribute Superman internationally, rather than just in America.

Far left: By sentencing the Kryptonian terrorists to the Phantom Zone, Jor-El sets up the sequel and primes the audience for the spectacle to come.

Left: Superman in his Fortress of Solitude, created by advanced Kryptonian technology that enables the hero to learn about his true origins.

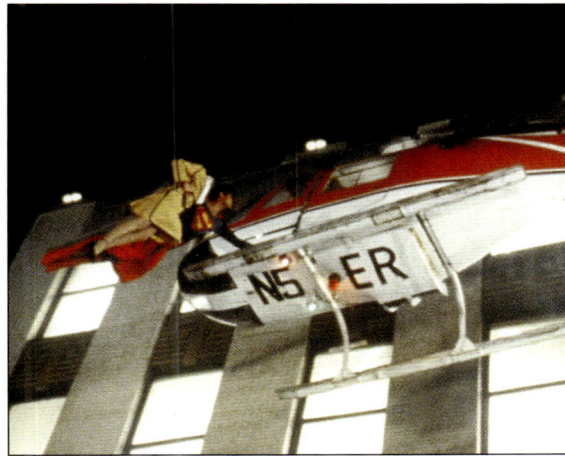

"Who's got you?" Superman makes a lasting impression on Lois Lane, saving her life and protecting the innocents below from a falling helicopter.

Already a big-budget, multinational co-production that included the US, UK, Switzerland, and Panama, preproduction began with sets constructed at Rome's Cinecittà Studios before the Salkinds discovered that Brando could not work in Italy, due to outstanding warrants against his film *Last Tango in Paris*. So they transferred production to England, where Hamilton had directed four James Bond movies.

At Pinewood and Shepperton studios, 350 construction workers and technicians led by production designer John Barry (*A Clockwork Orange*) realized an ancient dying world, an icy futuristic fortress, a criminal genius's subterranean lair, and a modern city that never sleeps, but the move came at a cost. Hamilton was a British tax exile who could only spend 30 days a year in his home country. After briefly considering Mark Robson (*Earthquake*) as his replacement, the producers hired Richard Donner—on the strength of his hit horror film *The Omen*—to direct.

Pinewood was Krypton while Shepperton housed the crystalline Fortress of Solitude. Barry's Arctic scenarios took 100 craftsmen 10 weeks to build on Pinewood's 007 set—the largest in the world—and required inventing many new techniques. Essentially composed of Styrofoam and a water tank, with salt doubling for ice, the Fortress of Solitude wreaked havoc on cameras, lights, and sound equipment, even eating through the crew's footwear and necessitating everybody wearing rubber boots.

The producers also struck gold with their cinematography, securing the services of multi-award-winning cinematographer Geoffrey Unsworth (*2001: A Space Odyssey*, *A Bridge Too Far*) on what

Everlasting romance

The greatest romance in comic books is undoubtedly the first one. Whether as meek Clark Kent or Superman, the relationship between an indomitable woman reporter, Lois Lane, and The Man of Steel is the earliest and most enduring couples dynamic of all superhero stories.

From the moment he launched, Superman was instantly the focus of attention, but even then, the need for a solid supporting cast was understood. Glamorous, sophisticated, and fearless journalist Lois Lane premiered right beside Kent—companion, colleague, rival, and foil from the outset. One thing the ace newshound never realized was that Clark's bumbling timidity was just a mask. Confirming her value, Lois was awarded her own solo feature in *Superman* #28 (May/June 1944), which ran until #42 (September/October 1946).

The comic book Lois was based on movie headline-hunter Torchy Blane (played by Glenda Farrell and Lola Lane in nine Warner Bros. films from 1937–1939) and visually modeled on Jerry Siegel's future wife Joanne Carter. Lois quickly became a mainstay of the cast in all media and once the *Adventures of Superman* television show aired eventually won her own comic title. Following two try-outs in *Showcase* #9 and 10 (August and October 1957), *Superman's Girl Friend Lois Lane* #1 (March/April #1958) launched, running for 137 issues until October 1974.

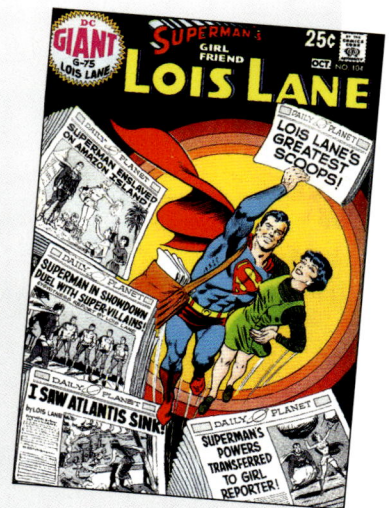

Margot Kidder won the role of Lois Lane thanks to her warm, on-screen chemistry with Reeve, beating 100 other actors to the part.

Marc McClure as Jimmy Olsen is the only actor to appear in all four *Superman* movies and 1984's *Supergirl.*

Veteran actor Jackie Cooper took on the role of Perry White when Keenan Wynn was forced to drop out due to illness.

Director Richard Donner (left) ensured that his actors made every on-screen scene a convincing part of a modern American folk story.

would turn out to be his last completed film. *Superman* principal photography began on March 28, 1977. Due to shooting its sequel at the same time, filming continued until October 1978. Constantly running over budget, the producers received a further $20 million from Warner Bros., by surrendering their television rights.

MYTHMAKING

It was one thing to satirize superheroes on the big and small screen, as had been done a decade earlier with Batman, but to ask an audience to take the subject matter seriously you had to convince them that what they were seeing was plausible, if not real. The key to that, as director Richard Donner stressed time and again, was "verisimilitude." It became a watchword on set and Donner even had a sign in his office with Superman soaring over the word. And it underpinned the movie's famous ad tagline: "You'll believe a man can fly."

As Mike Cecchini, Editor-in-Chief of *Den of Geek* in *Superpowered: The DC Story* explained: "The way to make this movie was to treat it like it was important. Like it was an important piece of American mythology." And the Salkinds pushed the budget out to realize their vision. At the time the most expensive movie ever made, *Superman* was the first American superhero film aimed at adult audiences. While offering fun and excitement, it addressed deeply philosophical, even allegorical themes, depicting the ultimate superhero in almost biblical terms, embracing myth, lost paradises, a selfless savior, an overweening villain, and modern chaos. Rather than assuming no prior knowledge from its audience, the movie instead reaffirmed and embellished a beloved tale everyone was familiar with thanks to comic books, newspaper strips, and four decades of radio and television.

Central to Donner's quest of believability was the man who would be Superman. Christopher Reeve had been an early contender for the role, recommended by casting guru Lynn Stalmaster even before seeking big-name leads. A graduate of Cornell University and Juilliard, he was quiet, well-educated, and utterly devoted to stage acting. Recovering from malnutrition caused by simultaneously acting in *Matter of Gravity* on Broadway and TV soap opera *Love of Life,* with only coffee and chocolate as sustenance, Reeve was recalled for a screen test in February 1977 and wowed Hamilton and the producers.

Accepting the role, Reeve was asked to wear a padded muscle suit, but instead went on an intensive fitness course. At 6 feet 4 inches tall but weighing only 178 lbs, Reeve consumed four high-protein meat-based meals a day while British bodybuilder and actor David Prowse (the body of *Star Wars*'s Darth Vader) drilled him in exercises to maximize muscle mass and definition. Prowse was one of hundreds who had sought the Superman role but was refused an audition as he was not American.

Despite rewrites, Mario Puzo's script remained monumental. Even split between two films, it needed more work and Donner hired screenplay writer/script doctor Tom Mankiewicz (*Ladyhawke,* five Bond movies) to fix it. Due to Screen Writers Guild objections, Mankiewicz could only be credited as a creative consultant, but one lasting innovation later adopted by comic books was his notion that Kryptonians wore symbolic crests.

The story neatly divides into a three-act arc, following the classical Hero's Journey. The timeless tale begins with all-wise Kryptonian technocrat Jor-El dispatching three terrorist outlaws to the Phantom Zone, before failing to convince his fellow ruling councilors that their planet is doomed. Swearing not to be disruptive or leave his world, Jor-El instead prepares an escape vehicle and teaching devices to carry his newborn son to a planet he has been studying—Earth. Baby Kal-El travels from the destroyed Krypton to Earth and, after being nurtured by foster parents Jonathan and Martha Kent (Glenn Ford and Phyllis Thaxter) in rural 1950s Smallville, Kansas (replicated in Alberta, Canada), is called to the North Pole, after his human father dies. Clark Kent spends the next 12 years (and the story's second act) learning from the technological spirit of his biological father before the third act sees his last journey from the security of his Fortress of Solitude to the city of Metropolis ... and his destiny. During his period of study, Jor-El's most strident lesson is that he must not use his extraordinary powers to alter human history.

WORLDS APART

Visually, Krypton was cold, ancient, and forbidding—a barren rock of crystal and light, depicted in muted colors—except for a green memory crystal and baby Kal-El's red, yellow, and blue swaddling blankets. By contrast, Smallville was lush, warm, and hopeful—

With crystal clarity and inspired ingenuity, the production team made the ancient, doomed Krypton a solid and forbidding aspect of Superman's creation myth.

World-Builder

The task of making all the varied worlds of *Superman* "real," fell to British Academy Award-winning production designer John Barry. Born in London in 1935, Barry studied architecture at Kingston College and spent time as a stage set designer. He began his stellar film career as a draftsman on 1963 epic *Cleopatra*, and after a period as assistant art director on the television series *Danger Man*, graduated to an in-demand cinema art director in 1968 with *Decline and Fall ... of a Birdwatcher*.

As well as visualizing action dramas like *Kelly's Heroes* (1970) and even musical fantasies like *The Little Prince* (1974), fantastic worlds and dangerous futures were a large part of Barry's repertoire. After fashioning Stanley Kubrick's *A Clockwork Orange* (1971), Barry worked on Saul Bass's *Phase IV* (1974); Stanley Donen's *Lucky Lady* (1975), which also starred Gene Hackman and boasted the cinematography of Geoffrey Unsworth; and George Lucas's *Star Wars* (1977). At the time, Barry felt that *Superman* was his most demanding assignment. As he outlined in *Superman the Movie All New Collectors Edition* (1979): "In (the movie) there are more that 45 big scenes that involve special effects on a large scale and that doesn't take into account scores of scenes in which characters fly. There's hardly a set in the whole film that someone doesn't demolish, crash into, or smash out of."

That said, the scenes Barry felt would be best remembered by audiences are those on the planet Krypton—before and during its destruction—and the Fortress of Solitude, Superman's secret sanctuary in the frozen Arctic as depicted in his evocative preproductions sketches.

After creating the diverse locations for *Superman* and (most of) *Superman II*, Barry moved into full filmmaking as the initial director for *Saturn 3*. He was working as second unit director on *Star Wars: The Empire Strikes Back* when he died suddenly from meningitis on June 1, 1979.

Barry explained his job and technique by saying "Movie-goers are skillfully manipulated by filmmakers. It's our job to execute effortlessly the 'sleight of hand,' if you will. Images flash across the silver screen pretty quickly and audiences shouldn't have time to dwell on what they see" (IMDb).

The original conception for the ice world of Krypton.

JOR-EL'S LABORATORY.

The escape space pod for the infant Kal-El in Jor-El's laboratory.

The holographic AI Jor-El appearing in the Fortress of Solitude.

Valerie Perrine earned a 1979 Best Supporting Actress nomination (a "Saturn Award") from the Academy of Science Fiction, Fantasy and Horror Films, for her role as Lex Luthor's glamorous aide-de-camp Miss Teschmacher.

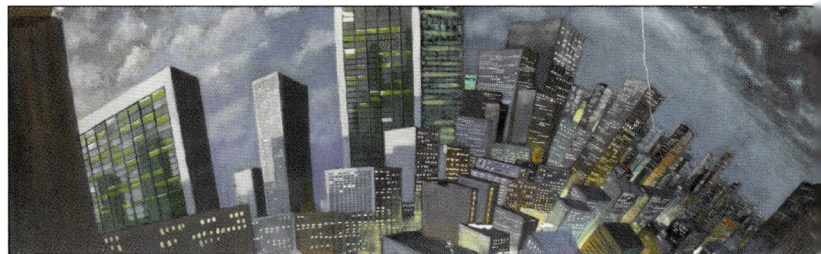

Wielding a sharp mind and a shard of Kryptonite, Gene Hackman's master criminal Lex Luthor ended the era of mad scientist Luthors and heralded the start of the villain as a killer capitalist.

painted in autumnal tones. Nostalgic and elegiac, the rustic idyll of small-town America saw infant Clark grow into a solitary, insular boy with a secret. This was thanks to a loving human father who assured him that he must have been "sent to Earth for a reason."

When Pa Kent died, the teenaged Clark (Jeff East) found a green crystal in the barn and felt compelled to leave the farm. Traveling north, he reached the Arctic Circle where the shard constructed a crystal citadel of Kryptonian design. Here, a highly-advanced interactive hologram of Jor-El spends the next decade training his son in the ways of Krypton and knowledge of the universe.

His time in the wilderness over, the adult Clark ventures into the world, arriving as a junior reporter at Metropolis's *Daily Planet*. The bustling, raucous city is a rude awakening for the shy, awkward Clark, where he is ignored if not actively walked over. New York City doubled as the City of Tomorrow with *The New York Daily News* building providing exteriors for the *Planet*. Interiors were filmed on a custom-built set at Pinewood. Location shooting

Visualizing the impossible

Storyboarding was established in the early 1930s when animators at Walt Disney Productions used sequential drawings to break down and previsualize key plot points, running times, optimal camera angles, and significant moments of proposed features. The practice rapidly became standardized across the entire cost-conscious movie industry, and in 1938, production designer William Cameron Menzies was the first to use the technique for a live-action film with *Gone With the Wind* (1939).

Storyboard artist and visual effects wizard Walter "Wally" Veevers learned his craft on films such as Menzies's *Things to Come* (1936). He went on to make a name for himself on hit films like *The Guns of Navarone* (1961), *Dr. Strangelove or: How I Learned to Stop Worrying and Love the Bomb* (1964), *2001: A Space Odyssey* (1968), and *Diamonds are Forever* (1971), before joining Richard Donner's team on *Superman*.

Having mapped out full storyboards for the movie and most of the simultaneously shot sequel, Veevers turned his attention to realizing his carefully choreographed sequences and preliminary sketches, determined to make the impossible seem real.

To convince an audience that a man could fly, Veevers supervised groundbreaking new flying effects systems (called "gags" on set) and process projection, devising an innovative if painstaking way to mask the wires of harnesses and flying rigs. He also helped develop a front projection unit that was lightweight, mobile, and easily transportable. Working with the rest of the visual effects crew, he was instrumental in making the magical first flight sequences with Superman and Lois Lane so believable, thus fulfilling Donner's chief requirement for the movie: verisimilitude.

Veevers worked closely with director Donner, artist Ivor Beddoes, and the production team to make Superman fly.

Above and left: British artist Ivor Beddoes, best known for his work on *Black Narcissus*, *The Red Shoes* and *Star Wars*, choreographed Superman and Lois' first flight together (left), a sequence that made cinema history. His 13 impressionistic paintings, dubbed "Flying Ballet" (city segment above), were assembled as one 65ft 6in long scroll that showed vignettes from across the globe. Ultimately, however, Donner chose to shoot just against the nighttime skyline of Metropolis.

delays were caused by overly intrusive crowds of spectators, a debilitating heatwave averaging 106 degrees Fahrenheit, and the infamous London-wide power blackout of July 13, 1977.

TURN BACK TIME

Soon, the gentle unassuming newcomer is actively pursuing career woman Lois Lane, but she only has eyes for the astonishing flying man who saved her from a helicopter crash, among many other superpowered feats on the night the world changed forever. That signature scene took six weeks to complete—occurring across two continents and employing five film units.

As romance gradually blooms, the film embraces a contemporary sense of urban decay, tapping into the era's taste for disaster movies with the introduction of the scheming, wig-wearing Lex Luthor and his assistants Eve Teschmacher and Otis. Taking an instant dislike to Superman and his heroic endeavors, Luthor usurps control of two nuclear missiles—one to trigger the collapse of the San Andreas fault, dropping California into the Pacific Ocean, and the other to distract Superman by eradicating Hackensack, New Jersey.

Trying to boost the value of desert land he owns in the most ruthless real-estate scam in history, Luthor also deduces the power of Kryptonite—stealing a meteorite of the alien mineral and using it to make Superman an agonized, helpless witness to his atrocities. The hero is rescued by Miss Teschmacher in return for his saving her mother from death, but the delay causes California to collapse. Employing all his incredible abilities, Superman repairs the fault, saving lives from Gallup, New Mexico, to the

As California crumbles, Superman's desperate but futile efforts to save everyone only emphasize the truth demonstrated by Jonathan Kent's death: sometimes even near-infinite power is not enough.

Golden Gate Bridge, but cannot prevent the Hoover Dam collapsing or Lois from dying in the aftershocks. Bereaved and distraught, he finally chooses to follow Jonathan Kent's advice and abandon Jor-El's commandment, using his powers to turn back time and resurrect Lois in one of cinema's more memorable scenes—as Superman flies around the world to bring her back.

Superman was the second-highest-grossing film of the year, winning acclaim and awards, becoming a firm family favorite, and in 2017 being selected for preservation in the Library of Congress's National Film Archive. For a once-dismissed, if not derided, form of cinematic entertainment, the movie was a game changer, establishing a template and tone for superhero movies to come.

SUPERMAN II

Release date: December 4, 1980 (Australia premiere), April 9, 1981 (UK), June 19, 1981 (US)
Starring roles: Christopher Reeve, Margot Kidder, Terence Stamp, Gene Hackman, Jackie Cooper, Sarah Douglas, Jack O'Halloran, Susannah York, Marc McClure, Ned Beatty, Clifton James, Valerie Perrine, E. G. Marshall

Director: Richard Lester
Screenplay: David Newman, Leslie Newman, Mario Puzo
Cinematography: Robert Paynter
Music: Ken Thorne
Running time: 127 minutes (variable)
Box office: $190.4 million

Superman broke box-office records, hitting all-time highs for the US pre-Christmas week. It also recorded Warner Bros.' best ever opening day and three-day weekend results. A second Superman film had already been started alongside the first and *Superman*'s success made it inevitable.

In 1977, *Superman* and the proposed sequel (originally written by Mario Puzo as one complete three-hour film) began filming simultaneously, before overruns and delays brought things to a halt on *Superman II*. Despite having shot over 75 percent of the sequel, mounting expenses were taking their toll on the overall budget for both movies. So the producers and backer, Warner Bros., decided to concentrate their resources on completing the first film. *Superman* had originally been scheduled for release in June 1978—the 40th anniversary of *Action Comics* #1's debut—but was shifted to Christmas week to allow time for critical postproduction work.

ALL CHANGE

Following the first movie's commercial success and critical acclaim, *Superman II* was green-lit again. However, serious, high-level disagreements over budgets and schedules, as well as story and character direction, resulted in Richard Donner leaving the film.

In his stead, producers Pierre Spengler and Alexander and Ilya Salkind hired Richard Lester (*A Hard Day's Night*, *A Funny Thing Happened on the Way to the Forum*) as the sequel's new director. After working with the Salkinds on *The Three Musketeers* and its sequel—also filmed simultaneously—Lester initially came in as a consultant on *Superman*. So he was primed to take over in 1979 ... and costs went up again.

"Kneel before Zod."
General Zod

Having shadowed, advised, and assisted Donner, Lester was tasked with finishing the blockbuster, but his approach differed markedly from his predecessor's. Tongue-in-cheek humor was inserted into a revised screenplay from David and Leslie Newman. Moreover, key elements of the sequel's big finish were gone, appropriated for the first film. Although not as well-received

In Puzo's biblically themed screenplay, Ursa (Sarah Douglas), Non (Jack O'Halloran), and General Zod (Terence Stamp) were allegories of Satan and his minions, cast out of Heaven to bedevil humanity.

The relationship between Lois and Clark/Superman encapsulated years of comic book subplots, ranging from reluctant colleagues to passionate lovers.

as *Superman* at the time, it was another financial success and work began immediately on a third film, which Lester would direct and could call his own.

The original script for *Superman II* had Lex Luthor's atomic missile shattering the Phantom Zone and freeing Zod (Terence Stamp), Ursa (Sarah Douglas), and Non (Jack O'Halloran). They

Thanks to a diligent exercise regime, Christopher Reeve's body altered visibly during filming both movies and required Richard Lester to reshoot some early scenes for his sequel.

The storm in Metropolis created by Zod, Ursa, and Non, and the subsequent super-breath duel with Superman, was filmed over three freezing November nights at Pinewood Studios.

Terence Stamp's memorable portrayal of General Zod created one of cinema's greatest villains. As Stamp admitted in *DC Special Series* #25, "Zod is a power junkie ... brutal, vicious, and corrupt ... without any redeeming qualities. It's a joy to play a two-dimensional character!"

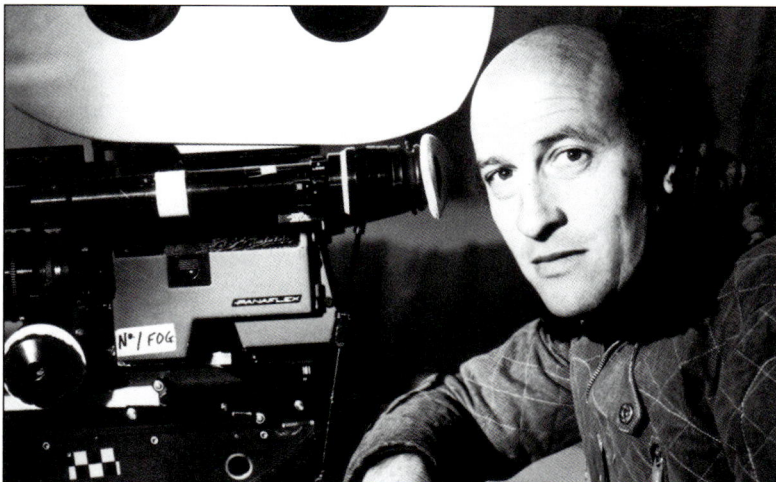

By preference a maker of quirky comedies, Richard Lester was initially brought in to consult, and when placed in charge moved away from mythic blockbuster to a tale of alienated humanity.

destroy Earth before Superman turns back time and defeats the villains. Now, with Donner's epic leanings absent and his conclusion already used in the first film, Lester retrenched, bringing his own vision to the sequel. He, too, faced pressures from the producers to accentuate romance for adults and emphasize good, clean action they felt younger filmgoers and prospective television audiences craved. As Ilya Salkind recalled in *The Making of Superman II* documentary, "The big problem was to respect the audience of children."

As envisaged by Puzo and realized by Donner, the lovers' arc of Clark and Lois—a romantic triangle if counting the unwitting rival Superman—was to be subverted. "It was important that the eternal love story between Superman and Lois comes to a conclusion," explained Pierre Spengler in *The Making of Superman II*, and Margot Kidder's role in the third film was a mere cameo, with a new romantic interest for Clark being created.

BUILDING TENSION

Principal photography for *Superman* and *Superman II* ran from March 1977 to October 1978, and resumed in September 1979 to March 1980. Complex building projects began at Pinewood Studios, including a new Fortress of Solitude, *Daily Planet* offices, Niagara Falls, the Eiffel Tower, and an iconic Metropolis thoroughfare, allowing Lester to reshoot or adjust finished footage and add his own ideas.

Constructed by 162 builders over 16 weeks, Pinewood's 42nd Street cost $4 million and was ground zero for the mighty duel between Superman and Zod's forces. The street battle was supplemented by two identical scale models of the set. When the key Niagara Falls location proved hazardously unmanageable, it was reconstructed in England.

In addition to Richard Lester taking over the directorial reins, *Superman II* also had a number of other changes to principal crew members. Cinematographer Robert Paynter (*An American Werewolf in London*, *Little Shop of Horrors*) replaced Geoffrey Unsworth, who had passed away before the release of *Superman*, while Ken Thorne, who had worked with Lester on *Help!* and *A Funny Thing Happened on the Way to the Forum,* provided the score after John Williams left to work on John Badham's *Dracula*. Tragically, acclaimed set designer John Barry died suddenly on June 1, 1979, while acting as second unit director of *Star Wars: The Empire Strikes Back*, and Peter Murton (*Goldfinger*, *Death on the Nile*) took over, working with Paynter to create more vibrant color schemes that were more in keeping with four-color comic books.

Superman II began by recapping key moments from its predecessor—the exile of the Phantom Zone villains, Krypton's destruction, the boyhood of Clark Kent in Smallville, and the debut of Superman in Metropolis. Luthor's attack on California and subsequent defeat were also revisited, but Jor-El was not seen in the movie. This was because of a dispute between Marlon Brando and the producers that effectively excised scenes that had already been shot in which Brando appeared.

Design pioneer

The design of Superman's suit and fashioning unique Kryptonian chic fell to costume designer Yvonne Blake, aided by Susan Yelland (*The Wicker Man*). Born in Manchester, England, in 1940, Blake worked on *Fahrenheit 451* (1966) and *Jesus Christ Superstar* (1973), and won an Oscar for her designs on *Nicholas and Alexandra* (1971). Despite her accomplishments, *Superman* was uncharted territory. As Blake explained in a presentation to Spain's Fashion Institute of Technology in 2013, "I started prepping long before there was a director or an actor, and worked solely with the production designer, director of photography, and special-effects director. These were innovators on special effects on a grand scale. Now it seems very familiar, but in those predigital days we were like Christopher Columbus discovering the New World."

Superman's costume was one of the first Lycra designs used in a movie and 25 different costumes and dozens of different capes were made, each cut for a specific purpose and shot: flying, landing, close-ups, and action sequences. Blake's focus was making working, wearable outfits that overcame their comic book origins and looked authentic. "It was important that the tights and shorts did not look like a ballet dancer's, so the problem of 'lumps and bumps' was solved by wearing a plastic protection shield normally used by boxers."

However, cutting-edge camera technologies brought fresh problems. Early chroma key compositing "knocked out" the blue of the first bodysuits, making them transparent and impossible to film. Working with front projection screens, testing out different shades for flying scenes, Blake commented "if the Lycra was either too green or too blue, Superman would disappear and all we would see are his shorts, his boots, and his cape."

Another challenge was the Kryptonians' outfits. Blake wanted the clothing to emit light, suggesting energy, but a practical fabric was hard to find. "I consulted the director of photography (Geoffrey Unsworth) who suggested a material called 3M." This reflective fabric, embedded with microscopic beads of glass, was used to create front projection screens. However, its use in costumes was the result of a happy accident when, during a flying test, when it was noticed that 3M lit up on its own. The only downside was that it turned black if touched by bare skin, so crew members had to wear cotton gloves around the Kryptonians.

Right: Blake's first attempt at Superman's suit featured dark-gold colors and an "S" on his buckle. After feedback from fans at the 1976 San Diego Comic Book Convention, she modified the design to reflect his iconic comic book costume.

Right and above: Blake's flamboyant Kryptonian garments were created using reflective 3M fabric.

Gene Hackman had no new scenes filmed for *Superman II*. All his scenes had been shot by Richard Donner for the first film, although Lester employed a lookalike and voice impersonator for minor additions.

The Fortress's crystal chamber allowed Superman to remove his own super-abilities via red sun rays and, when the time came, to render his enemies powerless.

A subplot focused on Lois "friend-zoning" Clark, who was deeply in love with her, while the main plot required a second nuclear detonation to shatter the Phantom Zone. Lester's solution was having Superman save Lois from nuclear terrorists at the Eiffel Tower before detonating their H-bomb in space and inadvertently liberating the superpowered criminal Kryptonians.

After wiping out astronauts on a moon mission, General Zod, Ursa, and Non attack Earth. Meanwhile, on an undercover assignment at Niagara Falls, Lois tests her theory that Clark is Superman by "falling" into the roaring waters, but he manages to save her without revealing his identity. Later, however, a casual slip-up forces Clark to confess his secret—and that he loves her. He takes Lois to the Fortress of Solitude and, after seeking advice from an AI avatar of his mother Lara (Susannah York), he surrenders his powers so that he can spend his life with Lois as a normal man. Clark and Lois return to civilization by conventional means, unaware that while they were away, the Phantom Zone villains had ravaged America, forcing the world to "kneel before Zod!" On learning this, Clark struggles back to the Fortress to undo his mistake.

In the White House, the ever-conniving Lex Luthor, who had escaped prison and discovered the links between Jor-El and Zod, offers the Super-Villains Jor-El's son in return for their giving him rule over Australia. While wrecking the *Daily Planet* in search of Clark, a repowered Superman appears, sparking a cataclysmic battle on 42nd Street that ends with Superman capitulating to stop the aliens from slaughtering helpless civilians. The finale unfolds in the Fortress, where Luthor and Lois witness Superman outwitting and depowering the rogue Kryptonians. Returning Luthor to jail, Clark realizes he cannot cause Lois more pain, and alters her memories with a super-kiss before returning to his lonely life of service and duty.

SUPERMAN II REVISITED

To qualify as co-director, Richard Lester had to be responsible for at least 40 percent of the final film. This was stipulated by the Directors' Guild of America after Warner Bros. asked them to arbitrate in their dispute with Richard Donner. Ultimately, Donner rejected the offer, refusing to share credit, which resulted in Lester jettisoning much of what his predecessor had filmed.

He added new scenes that shifted the tone from a hard-edged, superpowered battle with a tragic, doomed romance at its center to a more family-friendly action comedy. As Lester told interviewers at the time, "I think that Donner was emphasizing a kind of grandiose myth ... There was a type of epic quality which isn't in my nature ... I'm more quirky and I play around with slightly more unexpected silliness." It was a style that he could give full rein to on *Superman III*.

Although the producers had ceded television rights for further funding to finish the movies, they capitalized on the success of *Superman II* by reintroducing deleted scenes to various TV versions they owned and charging the networks for them. When both *Superman* films aired, they were available in different extended lengths and edited versions.

In 2005, however, Donner, editor Martin Thau, and *Superman* screenwriter Tom Mankiewicz began collaborating on what might have been—albeit with necessary compromises. Some footage had deteriorated beyond repair after sitting in

Within the austere Fortress of Solitude, built from repurposed and painted corrugated plastic roofing, Lois Lane is used as leverage in the villainous Kryptonians' vendetta against Superman.

Above: With his powers removed by Superman's devious strategy, it was time for Zod to kneel.

Left: Having averted catastrophe, Superman allows himself one last moment of joy before using a new power to edit his beloved's memory and give her a safer future.

Technicolor's London vault for 25 years, some scenes were never filmed, and new special effects were added, as was a 35mm screen test, which was used for a pivotal scene between Superman and Lois. With permission from the estate of Marlon Brando, who died in 2004, to restore the embargoed Jor-El scenes, *Superman II: The Richard Donner Cut* was finally completed and released in November 2006. Trimming 10 minutes off the original's running time and dedicated to Christopher Reeve, who had also passed away in 2004, this version deeply informed Brian Singer's *Superman Returns*.

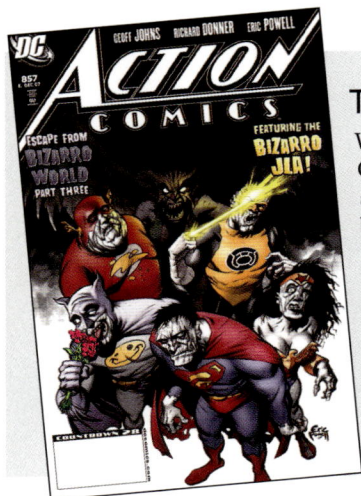

The Legacy of Donner

With the 2006 DVD release of the "Richard Donner Cut," new vistas opened up for fans of the films, not just as a chance to see the director's dream finally realized, but also in brand-new comic book adventures. When then DC Chief Creative Officer Geoff Johns first started working, it was as Richard Donner's intern. That connection came full circle in December 2006, when they collaborated on Superman tales thematically based on the cinematic universe.

Published in *Action Comics* #844–846, 851, and 855–857, and *Action Comics Annuals* #10 and 11, plus a commemorative yarn in *Action Comics* #1000 (June 2018), their stories revisited themes that Donner considered when planning his third and fourth *Superman* films.

In *Superman '78* (2021), Robert Venditti, Wilfredo Torres, and Jordie Bellaire continued to extend the Donner legacy in the comic book universe—detailing the further adventures of Clark, Lois, Luthor, and the rest in stories set after *Superman II,* but not including the events that occurred in *Superman III* and *IV*. Moreover, the six-issue limited series included the true fate of Jor-El, Lara, and the survivors of Krypton, and the director's ultimate dream villain as Brainiac attacked Earth.

51

SWAMP THING

Release date: February 19, 1982
Starring roles: Louis Jourdan, Adrienne Barbeau, Dick Durock, Ray Wise, David Hess, Reggie Batts
Director: Wes Craven
Screenplay: Wes Craven

Cinematography: Robbie Greenberg
Music: Harry Manfredini
Running time: 91 minutes (US), 93 minutes
Box office: Unknown

The 1970s spawned a wave of horror movies, elevating that genre to the upper echelon of critical credibility and box-office profitability. That translated into a number of scary movies whose directors established vibrant subgenres—quasi-religious, satanic, classic revivals, mutant/alien romps, zombie epics, psychological thrillers, and even martial arts and blackly comedic capers. Like comic books, which rapidly adopted all those themes, movies had adapted and evolved.

The decade saw many successful television superhero shows such as *Wonder Woman*, while *Superman* proved comic book heroes could be hits at the cinema, too. Comics were growing more sophisticated and, by 1982, reached a point where they were outgrowing the Comics Code and finding a new, more mature audience—with heroes like Swamp Thing leading the way.

HORROR REVIVAL
Cinema had used age-appropriate subdivisions for years across the world, with horror often confined to an older audience. Michael Uslan and Benjamin Melniker saw the possibilities of comic book horror on the big screen, with Swamp Thing becoming DC's first horror-film hero.

They hired Wes Craven (*Nightmare on Elm Street*, *The Hills Have Eyes*) to write and direct. A former college lecturer who had graduated to horror films, Craven's strict religious background meant he had never read comic books until required to bone up on Swamp Thing.

A SWAMP THING IS BORN
Horror's return to comics had been bolstered by revisions to the Comics Code that had previously restricted content. In the horror anthology *House of Secrets* #92 (June–July 1971), writer Len Wein and artist Bernie Wrightson crafted a gothic thriller that saw 19th-century gentleman scientist Alex Olsen murdered by his best friend and his corpse dumped in a swamp. Years later, Olsen's bride—now the killer's unsuspecting wife—was stalked by a disgusting beast made from mud and muck ...

The tale struck an immediate chord. That issue—DC's best-selling comic of that month—generated fervent and persistent reader response. Initially reluctant to produce a sequel, the creative team eventually bowed to the inevitable, transplanting the concept to contemporary America in a new title featuring DC's first monster star. Wein had been stuck for a title until someone pointed out that what he kept referring to as "the swamp thing I'm working on ..." was the solution. *Swamp Thing* #1 went on sale in August 1972, and was a mammoth hit.

> ## "There is much beauty in the swamp, if you only look."
> **Alec Holland**

Adrienne Barbeau played hero Alice Cable, part scientist, part action hero—hunted by Arcane's paramilitary goons.

Embodying the film's themes, in the final battle between Good and Evil, the unleashed bestiality of Arcane cannot stand against the natural power of Swamp Thing.

Originally a stuntman, Dick Durock was only the second actor
to play a live-action DC character twice, after Christopher Reeve
first reprised the Man of Steel in *Superman II* (1980).

After losing his son Louis Henry to a drug overdose on May 12, 1981, veteran actor Louis Jourdan buried himself in his role, continually reviewing his lines until shooting concluded.

Urbane Arcane was originally meant to mutate into a savage lycanthrope. The idea changed when recent releases *The Howling* and *An American Werewolf in London* made such a transformation commonplace.

Wein and Wrightson's 10 issues formed a multichaptered saga of justice and vengeance: a quest at once philosophically in tune with the times and a prototype for the story-arc/miniseries format that came to dominate modern comics. Each issue also channeled a specific cinematic horror story while advancing a major plot.

Although inspired by and respectful of the source material, Wes Craven heavily referenced Werner Herzog's *The Enigma Of Kaspar Hauser* in the screenplay, underscoring his dislike of "rubber-suit monster movies." He wanted his fourth feature film to be an action movie about "Man against Nature."

When Warner Bros. passed on the project, Embassy Pictures/United Artists took it on. Craven proudly brought *Swamp Thing* in on time and on budget. Shooting began April 27, 1981, but was completed in half the time Craven had wanted. Key scenes were axed and makeup man Bill Munns (*Beastmaster, Return of the Living Dead*) was told his 12-week schedule to create a convincing look for the monsters was halved.

Merging comic characters Matthew Cable and Abby Arcane, researcher Alice Cable (Adrienne Barbeau) joins a secret project in Louisiana's swamp, meeting brilliant siblings Linda (Nannette Brown) and Alec Holland (Ray Wise). Their revolutionary bioengineering work with plant and animal DNA is coveted by a ruthless hidden enemy, and Cable soon falls for Alec's charm, brilliance, and passion.

Meanwhile, decadent Anton Arcane (Louis Jourdan) has already infiltrated the project. When the breakthrough comes—a hyper-volatile formula promoting plant growth on any surface—his forces raid the lab, killing everyone. Arcane personally shoots Linda and when Alec retaliates, he's covered in his formula and ignites like a torch, plunging into the swamp waters never to be seen again in human form.

Stuntman Anthony Cecere—who would work with Craven on *A Nightmare on Elm Street*— devised the effect of Holland on fire. Deciding standard flame effects (igniting rubber cement) wasn't good enough, Cecere tested different gel accelerant formulations—repeatedly setting himself alight and jumping into the family swimming pool to achieve the desired effect.

A rented warehouse became the Holland laboratory and most scenes were shot in the 170-acre Moncks Corner nature reserve of South Carolina's Cypress Gardens. Local schoolboy Reggie Batts played Jude and, sans makeup, stunt doubles Karen Price and Dick Durock, who played Swamp Thing, filled out the cast's smaller roles. During postproduction, additional airboat action scenes were shot on a Los Angeles lake.

Stuntman and actor Ben Bates (*Gunsmoke*) was to play Arcane's monster self, but he collapsed during filming, and Munns replaced him until shooting ended. Durock's job expanded when it was found his flatter, broken-nosed face better suited Swamp Thing's makeup. Wise had expected to play both Holland and Swamp Thing, and four full suits—two each for Wise and Durock—were built, before the double assumed the monster's role. He would return to it throughout his career.

ARCANE TIMES

In the confusion of Arcane's raid on the lab, Cable escapes with a crucial notebook, surviving repeated attempts to capture her, thanks to an incredible humanoid creature who attacks Arcane's thugs Ferret (David Hess) and Bruno (Nicholas Worth). Her efforts

Far left: Vicious killer and prime example of the worst of humanity (a.k.a. "Man"), Hess at last meets something he can't intimidate or destroy as Swamp Thing ("Nature") erupts from the mire.

Left: Imaginative realist illustrator Richard Hescox (*House, E.T., The Dark Crystal, The Howling*) created the evocative poster art, which was faithfully duplicated as the cover of *Swamp Thing Annual #1*.

to evade her pursuers involve the help of a local teenager, Jude, but are ultimately futile. Soon, she is taken prisoner and Jude is dead—until the "Swamp Thing" resurrects him with a bio-restorative healing touch.

When Arcane also captures the monster—revealed to be Alec— he forces it to give up the formula and tests it on his fawning acolytes. Learning that it unleashes and amplifies a subject's true self, Anton takes it himself—devolving into a hideous beast-thing who stabs Cable and battles Holland to the death—his death.

GOOD AND BAD DAYS

Shooting overlapped production of Craven's third film *Deadly Blessing* and was hindered by nature itself. Costumes suffered as much as actors and crew. Tannins in the water and trees ate at them, requiring constant patching as they rotted away. As well as hellish heat, locations were infested by stinging bugs—what locals dubbed "the black caterpillar plague." Already wary of alligators, snakes, parasites, and deadly bacteria, cast and crew risked heat problems by sealing shirts and pants cuffs with rubber bands to avoid debilitating bites. It wasn't all bad—Craven met and married actor Mimi Meyer (Arcane's secretary) on the fraught production.

Swamp Thing was an early cable TV hit and popular in the home rental markets, a fact Uslan and Melniker parlayed into a sequel, two TV series, and a short-lived children's animated show.

Coming off three big hits in a row (*The Fog, Escape from New York,* and *Cannonball Run*), Adrienne Barbeau was urged by her then husband, director John Carpenter, to take the B-movie role. Carpenter was a huge admirer of Craven's early work.

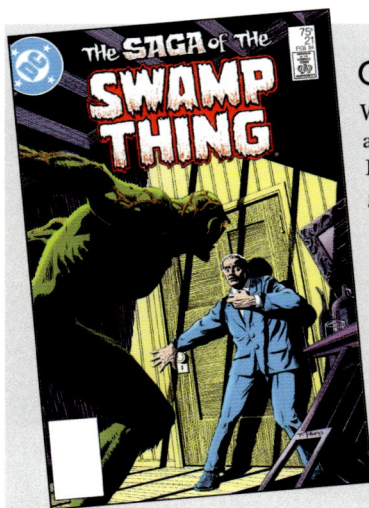

Comic book origins

While newlyweds Alec and Linda Holland (rewritten as siblings for the film) toiled secretly in the Louisiana Bayou on a bio-restorative formula to revolutionize global farming, they had no idea "The Conclave" and its leader Nathan Ellery wanted their research. Despite the best efforts of secret-service agent Matt Cable, their lab was bombed and Linda died. Alec—drenched in his formula and blazing like a torch—hurled himself to a watery grave in the swamp, but did not die.

Holland mutated into a huge man-shaped creature—immensely strong, barely able to speak, and seemingly composed of plant matter. His brain still functioned, however, and over months he vacillated between finding Linda's killers and curing his condition. Cable, misinterpreting the

evidence, became obsessed with destroying the swamp beast, believing it had killed the Hollands.

Swamp Thing traveled the world, facing classic (movie-inspired) horrors and wicked human nature, until British writer Alan Moore revolutionized the concept in "The Anatomy Lesson" (*Swamp Thing* #21, February 1984, pictured left), revealing that Holland was never a man-monster, but that his dying consciousness had imprinted on vegetable matter and detritus from the bio-formula-contaminated bayou.

Although there had been previous rare crossovers with Super Heroes (Deadman/Justice League, Batman, and *The House of Mystery*), Swamp Thing was the bridge between DC's adventure continuity and horror titles, repeatedly teaming up with Batman, Superman, and more, leading to a unified DC universe in print, a young-adult graphic novel, *Swamp Thing: Twin Branches,* and even in assorted cartoon shows.

SUPERMAN III

Release date: June 17, 1983 (US),
July 19, 1983 (UK)
Starring roles: Christopher
Reeve, Margot Kidder, Richard
Pryor, Robert Vaughn, Jackie
Cooper, Marc McClure, Annette
O'Toole, Annie Ross, Pamela
Stephenson

Director: Richard Lester
Screenplay: David Newman,
Leslie Newman
Cinematography: Robert
Paynter
Music: Ken Thorne
Running time: 125 minutes
Box office: $80.2 million

The announcement of a third Superman film was made
at the 33rd Cannes Film Festival in May 1980—months before
Superman II premiered. With a looming deadline of Superman's
45th anniversary approaching, director Richard Lester faced the
recurrent problem of this new genre—whether to embrace comic
book canon, or broaden the appeal to attract wider audiences.

Superman and its sequel proved the public would avidly support
superhero dramas, but many producers and studio execs felt
paying to see outlandish bad guys battle good guys in tights
was still a step too far, and too wild for the general public.
That conviction had already restricted antagonists on live-action
TV shows like *Wonder Woman* and *Shazam!* (1974-1976) to ruthless
billionaires, mad scientists, and common criminals.

FRIENDS OR FOES?

In print, Superman's greatest problem was finding opposition
strong enough to prove a threat. Donner had planned for his
third outing to embrace the Man of Steel's most powerful foes—
Fifth Dimensional imp and trickster Mr. Mxyzptlk and alien
super- android Brainiac. Ilya Salkind had written a movie
treatment (later released online in 2007) to expand the franchise
into the then-booming science-fiction market and extend the
Superman Family by introducing Supergirl.

"Danger goes with the territory, Mister Kent."
Jimmy Olsen

Subsequently, a scaled-back version saw the magical trickster
reduced to an amoral entity, with the marauding alien AI retooled
for the third act as the "ultimate computer." The main villain
became a greedy billionaire trying to get even richer, while
Supergirl was cut out and granted her own film and potential
franchise. The Fortress of Solitude and arch-foe Lex Luthor were
also both absent from the proceedings—although they returned
in 1987's *Superman IV: The Quest for Peace.*

Lester and his scriptwriters—David and Leslie Newman—
reexamined the proposal, repurposing the story to their needs,
and soon had a star of stand-up comedy added to the cast.

Pryor's outrageous spoofing of the US military here may have been fueled by his own service. He was in the US Army from 1958 to 1960, but spent almost all of that time in an army prison.

Far left: Superman's dissolution into a "mean drunk" was filmed at the St. Louis Hotel in Downtown East Village, Calgary, several blocks west of the plaza that featured in the opening comedy title sequence.

Left: Clark Kent's Smallville High sweater was all the visual cue smart cookie Lois needed to trigger her old suspicions. Thankfully, for Clark and his alter ego, she would be vacationing for most of the movie.

Writers David and Leslie Newman had seen Annette O'Toole in a play before casting began, and wrote Lana Lang with her in mind.

Ross and Vera Webster were at the forefront of a change in how villains acted—billionaire bandits who robbed and terrorized countries.

New Zealand-born psychologist, comedian, and actor Pamela Stephenson played Lorelei Ambrosia, seducing the corrupted Superman.

JOKING APART

Richard Pryor's film career was taking off. Following hits *Silver Streak* (1976), *Stir Crazy* (1980), and *The Toy* (1982)—plus an appearance on *The Tonight Show with Johnny Carson* in which he praised the film *Superman II* and admitted to being a fan of the comics—the producers sought him out. In later years, Pryor revealed that he signed on, not simply because he was a fan, but also because he hoped to transition into dramatic roles. He was paid $5 million—the highest salary ever paid a Black actor in Hollywood. On the film's completion, he signed a five-year, $40 million contract with Columbia Pictures.

In *Superman III,* Pryor played recently released convict Gus Gorman, who struggles to survive in the outside world and enrolls in a computer course. Discovering an unexpected talent for programming—he is in fact a true savant—Gus is hired for data-entry at international conglomerate Webscoe. The pay is pitiful, but within a week he has found a way to boost his income.

Utterly naive, Gus gives himself a huge off-the-books bonus, but his flashy spending alerts CEO Ross Webster (Robert Vaughn), his bullying sister Vera (Annie Ross), and Ross's trophy girlfriend Lorelei Ambrosia (Pamela Stephenson). They quickly see the former felon's full potential in the increasingly pervasive digital world. Instead of prosecuting a thief, Ross has Gorman work directly for him, with their first project being to corner the world coffee market. Very much against his conscience, Gus plays along, heading to a nondescript Webscoe subsidiary in Smallville, Kansas, where he can unobtrusively upload new commands to orbiting weather satellite, Vulcan.

Ross Webster is far more like a James Bond villain than a traditional super-foe, although, in truth, Vaughn merely predated the modern trend for evil, overprivileged billionaire one-percenters. In fact, Webster acts very much the way comics creators John

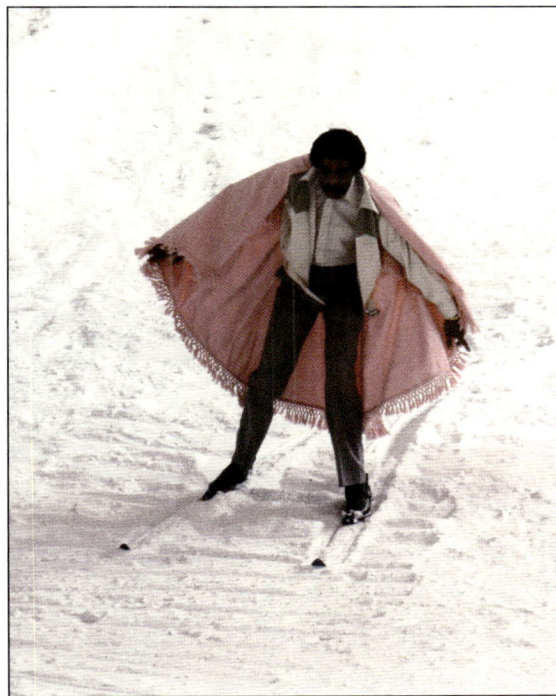

Far left: Spectacular on screen and in comics, Superman battling Clark was a recurring motif and in *Superman III* saw the evil Superman try and crush Clark in an industrial trash compactor.

Left: Webster's acts of conspicuous consumerism included a penthouse ski slope. The set took three months to build at Pinewood Studios and needed 17 tons of salt to mimic the snow.

Byrne and Marv Wolfman reimagined Lex Luthor in the post-*Crisis on Infinite Earths* reboot and Byrne's *Man of Steel* (1987) series.

HOME IS WHERE THE HEART IS

As Lois Lane (Margot Kidder) heads for a vacation in Bermuda, Kent convinces *Daily Planet* editor Perry White (Jackie Cooper) to run a feature on America's heartland. It's prompted by an invitation to his 20th high school reunion. With Jimmy Olsen (Marc McClure) in tow to snap pictures, Clark anticipates quietly reviewing his golden past, but the big-city boys arrive during an unfolding catastrophe. A chemical-plant fire threatens to unleash a deadly acid cloud until Superman saves the day but, in the course of stopping the disaster, Jimmy is injured and benched for the rest of the trip.

Canadian township High River doubled as Smallville, with actual Calgary Fire and Police Department personnel playing cops and firefighters attending the disasters that Superman stops. The only exception was actor Al Matthews, who played a first responder and later narrated 1984's *The Making of Superman III* documentary. With preproduction beginning in April and casting settled, principal photography began June 21, 1982, running until September and divided between England's Pinewood Studios and Calgary in Alberta, Canada. Unique locations included Battersea Power Station, where Lester had shot Beatles movie *Help!* in 1965, doubling as a coalmine, and Glen Canyon, Utah, providing spectacular exteriors for a third-act computer citadel. The junkyard arena where Superman fights himself was Pinewood's backlot, and the ubiquitous 007 Stage became home to the technological trap of the finale.

NO TIME LIKE THE PAST

To achieve his aims, Ross needs Colombia's coffee crop destroyed and has Gorman hack the Vulcan weather satellite to trigger devastating tornados. When Superman ends the weather assault

Boy of tomorrow

In 1938, Superman redefined the concept of a hero and became a global icon. Six years later, Jerry Siegel and Joe Shuster struck gold again, revealing a mighty hero-in-waiting not that different from the kids reading about him. Setting the scene for decades of exuberant adventure, "The Origin of Superboy!" (*More Fun Comics* #101, January 1945) explored lost Krypton, baby Kal-El's flight to Earth, and a childhood full of fun and incident. When television's *Adventures of Superman* ended, *Superboy* was considered for its replacement, but despite a full season of 13 episodes being prepared by DC liaison Whitney Ellsworth in 1961, the result was one unaired episode: "Rajah's Ransom." Viewers had to be content with animated tales of the Boy of Steel until 1988, when Alexander and Ilya Salkind brought Superboy to the small screen.

Superboy (*The Adventures of Superboy* from season 3) ran for four seasons (100 episodes from October 8, 1988, to May 17, 1992), detailing Clark Kent (John Haymes Newton and later Gerard Christopher) and Lana Lang's (Stacy Haiduk) move to Shuster College and their encounters with the strange, the evil, and the unknown. Superboy battled criminals, spies, aliens, Lex Luthor (Scott James Wells and Sherman Howard), and true Super-Villains like Metallo (Michael Callan), Mr. Mxyzptlk (Michael J. Pollard), Bizarro (Barry Myers), Yellow Peri (Elizabeth Keifer), and Toyman reboot Nick Knack (Gilbert Gottfried). Guest stars included Noel Neill and Jack Larson, Ron Ely as an alternate-Earth Superman, and Bond stars George Lazenby and Britt Ekland as (imposters of) Jor-El and Lara.

Many episodes were scripted by comic book writers Denny O'Neill, Mark Evanier, J. M. DeMatteis, Mike Carlin, Andy Helfer, and Cary Bates, who was also co-Executive Story Consultant alongside screenwriter Mark Jones. The show was supported by spin-off *Superboy: The Comic Book* (#1 February 1990). As season 3 opened, the series changed to *The Adventures of Superboy* from #11, ceasing publication with #22 (February 1992), plus a one-shot special edition.

Optical advisor Roy Field said, "Christopher Reeve could hold his body aerodynamically, so when he got into the harness, the whole shot began to come alive."

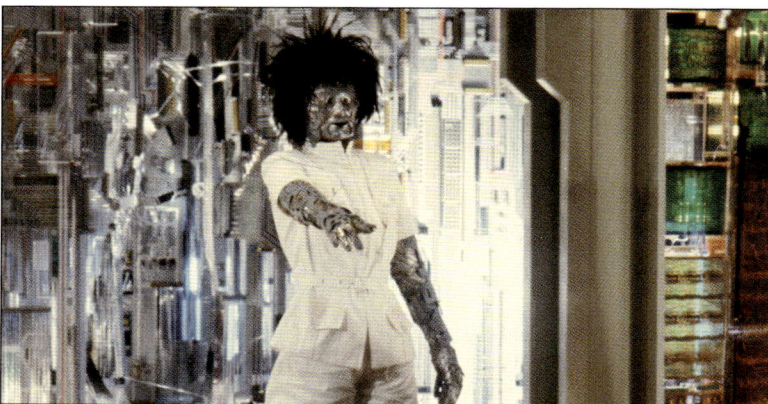

When not transformed into a killer cyborg or playing the villainous Vera, Scottish actor Annie Ross was a renowned jazz performer hired to overdub performers like Sarah Douglas in *Superman II*.

Superman's third-act battle against Gus's ultimate computer was enacted on a sturdily constructed multilevel set on Pinewood's ultra-versatile 007 Stage.

and saves their economy, Ross tasks Gus with seizing control of the world's oil resources. To prevent any more interference, Ross and Vera order Grissom to make Kryptonite and destroy their obstacle. When Vulcan analyzes and catalogs the exo-mineral, it returns a result of "Five percent unknown element," and Gus lazily substitutes tar for the missing ingredients.

Meanwhile, Clark grows closer to his unobtainable school crush, Lana Lang (Annette O'Toole), as well as her son Ricky (Paul Kaethler), despite renewed attacks by his old—and unreformed—class bully Brad Wilson (Gavan O'Herlihy). As Clark and Lana reconnect, Superman saves Ricky from a combine harvester and the town throws him a parade. At the end, Gus and Vera expose the hero to their artificial Kryptonite ... but it does not kill him.

Soon, however, Superman starts behaving erratically: committing acts of petty vandalism, getting drunk, and—after being seduced by Lorelei—blocking world trade and creating deadly oil spills to give Webscoe total dominance. Smug in victory and seeking to keep increasingly rebellious Gus happy, Ross and Vera allow him funds to build the world's most advanced computer in a hidden desert cave, where the contraption quickly takes on a life of its own.

SUPERMAN SPLITS

Eventually the corrupted Superman splits into good and evil halves, struggling for dominance. Reeve filmed each contributing scene twice—good and bad—methodically choreographed as each character, either alone or playing opposite a stand-in. By also using split-screen techniques when both faces were in shot, careful editing sold the illusion in the movie's most memorable moment.

With Clark's personality subsuming his darker side, a reborn Superman sets out to clean up the ecological disaster Webster has triggered, before going after the billionaire. Overcoming all the weapons wealth can command and battling a now sentient and hostile supercomputer that turns Vera into its terrifying cyborg avatar, the hero is aided by guilt-ridden Gus, who cannot bear

The trickiest part of the technological traps in the finale was inventing threats that would enthrall fans without baffling casual filmgoers.

Above: Costume designer Evangeline Harrison crafted outfits to endure harsh treatment, backed up by veteran wardrobe supervisor Betty Adamson.

the thought of being "the man who killed Superman." When the battle is done, Superman is triumphant and both Gus and Lana embark on second starts.

Superman III was the 12th-highest-grossing film in North America in 1983 despite stiff competition from other action adventures like *Octopussy* and *Star Wars Episode VI: Return of the Jedi*. The movie led to a widening of the franchise when Superman's cousin was introduced to planet Earth as *Supergirl* hit cinemas the following year.

Left: As the supercomputer runs amok, the human villains are unaware that they are no longer part of the big plan.

Left: Coalmine scenes were shot at iconic London landmark Battersea Power Station. Decommissioned since 1975, it was redeveloped in 2022.

SUPERGIRL

Release date: July 19, 1984 (UK),
November 21, 1984 (US)
Starring roles: Faye Dunaway,
Helen Slater, Peter O'Toole,
Hart Bochner, Peter Cook, Marc
McClure, Maureen Teefy, Brenda
Vaccaro, Simon Ward, Mia Farrow

Director: Jeannot Szwarc
Screenplay: David Odell
Cinematography: Alan Hume
Music: Jerry Goldsmith
Running time: 105 minutes (US),
124 minutes (International)
Box office: $14.3 million

After 25 years as a subordinate member of comic books'
Superman family, in 1984, the time came for Supergirl to step into
the spotlight. In Hollywood terms, it was a bold move. No female
action hero had headlined a motion picture since Modesty Blaise
in 1966. She, too, was adapted from comics, but even legendary
icon Wonder Woman had, at the time, not hit the big screen.

GIRLS ON FILM

When Pierre Spengler and Alexander and Ilya Salkind bought
Superman's film rights, the deal included ancillary properties
like Superboy and his cousin Kara Zor-El. Having established a
franchise with the Man of Steel, they planned to introduce Supergirl
in *Superman III,* but Ilya's initial idea was too complex for a
subplot, and she was given her own film instead. In April 1982,
before Richard Lester's *Superman III* even went into production,
the producers announced it would be followed by *Supergirl*.

"Her first great adventure."

Trailer tagline

When Lester declined to direct, Spengler and the Salkinds
turned to Jeannot Szwarc. Although he had primarily worked
in television (*Kojak, Night Gallery*), he had directed *Jaws 2* (1978)
and Christopher Reeve in 1980's *Somewhere in Time*. Given
a glowing testimonial by Reeve himself, Szwarc started his sixth
motion picture, and also agreed to helm the producers' next venture
Santa Claus: The Movie. Firmly embracing her comic book roots,
Supergirl went into preproduction. Plans for Superman to make a
cameo never materialized due to Reeve's scheduling conflicts, but
a line of dialogue about his being on "a peace-seeking mission to a
distant galaxy" inspired Bryan Singer's 2006 film *Superman Returns*.

PAGE TO SCREEN

Kara Zor-El debuted on the cover of *Action Comics* #252 (May 1959),
and in a solo series in that issue. A tag-along to her superstar cousin
at a time when female superheroes barely existed, Supergirl became
a solo star in her own title—as well as a creative way to protect DC's
trademark. She would die heroically in 1985's landmark limited
series *Crisis on Infinite Earths*, only to be officially resurrected in the
Post-*Crisis* DC universe years later.

With Szwarc at the helm, the next job was finalizing her story
for movie audiences. After viewing five very different scripts,
he selected a screenplay by David Odell (*The Dark Crystal, Masters
of the Universe*). During preproduction, the ever diligent Szwarc
consulted *Superman* director Richard Donner on technical issues.
Principal photography took place at Pinewood Studios from
April 18 to August 11, 1983.

Hundreds of young actors and top stars—like Melanie Griffith
and Demi Moore—auditioned for the title part, but Alexander
Salkind wanted Brooke Shields for the role. Salkind was convinced
otherwise by Ilya and Szwarc, who strongly advocated going with
an unknown as they had with Christopher Reeve. A compelling
factor was that at 6 feet (1.83 m), Shields was too tall to play
"average-sized" Supergirl, towering over her co-stars and making
shot-framing a huge challenge.

The first movie poster caused more excitement than
expected and no one on the production noticed the
Statue of Liberty held the torch in her left hand.

In 1985, DC featured Helen Slater in *Fifty Who Made DC Great*: a
50th-anniversary publication celebrating George Reeves, Lynda Carter,
Christopher Reeve, and others who had popularized the company's stars.

PRODUCTION: "SUPERGIRL"

"SUPERGIRL STRUGGLE FOREWARD AGAINST THE FORCE"

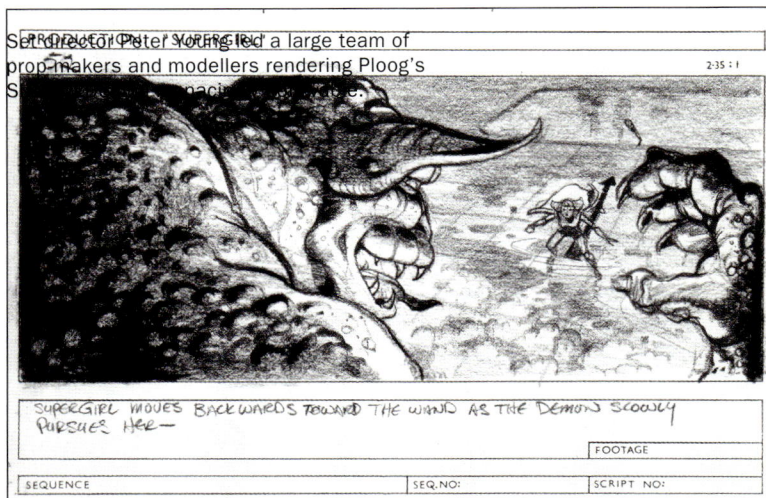

Art director Peter Young led a large team of prop-makers and modellers rendering Ploog's

"SUPERGIRL MOVES BACKWARDS TOWARD THE WAND AS THE DEMON SCOWLY PURSUES HER—"

Peter O'Toole's role as Zaltar comprised father figure; playful mentor; accidental tempter; and, ultimately, self-sacrificing savior.

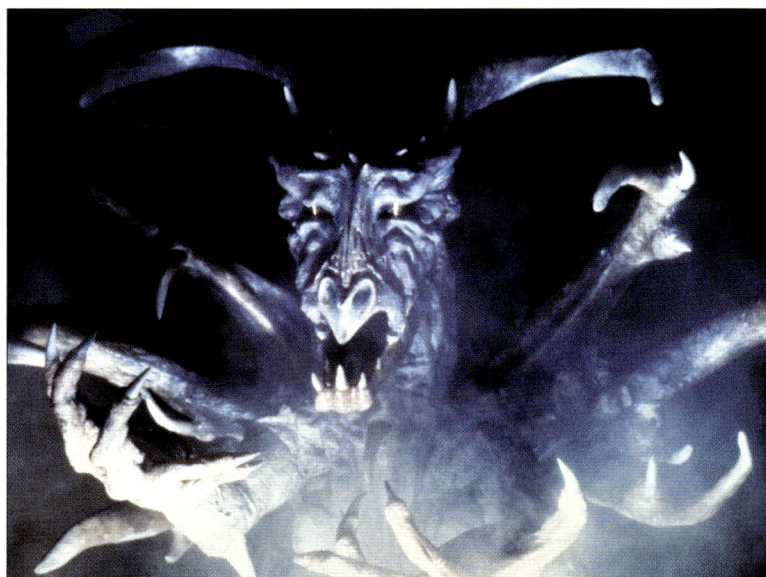

Supergirl in her human identity as Linda Lee, a student at Midvale High School. It was a name the comic book incarnation had also used.

Fresh from graduating high school, Helen Slater was signed to a three-picture deal as the producers anticipated at least two more *Supergirl* films. Once she got the job, stuntman Alf Joint (*Goldfinger*, *Lifeforce*) stepped in. He had been with the franchise since *Superman*, and was tasked with toning, toughening, and building up Slater. This involved daily running and other exercises—plus crash courses in gymnastics, rowing, and swimming. Slater also spent three hours a day for three months working on outdoor flying scenes, suspended on wires from a 200-foot (61-m) tower crane.

Supergirl's costume was designed by designer Emma Porteous (*Aliens*, *Judge Dredd*) who had to do the job twice. In early test filming, Slater's outfit—based on the then current comic book iteration—included hot pants and a headband. Unsuited to the producers' vision, DC changed their version, referencing a classic miniskirt look, which Porteous modified.

LEGENDS

As with *Superman*, star power rested with the supporting cast. When Dolly Parton, Goldie Hawn, and Jane Fonda were unavailable to play evil witch Selena, Ilya's partner and co-producer Alyssa Cartegna convinced Faye Dunaway to take the role. The star of *Bonnie and Clyde* and *The Thomas Crown Affair* had recently relocated to London, so was on hand and available when the offer came.

Peter O'Toole, fresh from bravura performances in *The Stunt Man* (1980), *My Favorite Year* (1982), and television triumphs like *Sherlock Holmes* and *Svengali*, signed on to play the scientist Zaltar, while British comedy great Peter Cook (*The Princess Bride*, *Bedazzled*) took on the role of the Warlock, Nigel.

Animator, production illustrator, and comics legend Mike Ploog (*The Thing*, *The Dark Crystal*) storyboarded *Supergirl*, working very closely with Szwarc on stunt details. The director had a reputation for overseeing every aspect of a production, and expressed concern

Helen Slater needed various harnesses for flying, with foam-padded fiberglass casts of her torso taken to help their creation.

for his actors' safety, particularly as one was a 19-year-old novice and the other an aging, frail, and occasionally unpredictable film icon. As a result, all potentially hazardous scenes—like Kara and Zaltar toiling through oily bogs and windblown wilds in the Phantom Zone—were carefully mapped out in advance. Szwarc's concerns led to a scene with Supergirl erupting from a lake being shot with cardboard cutouts and photographic effects rather than using actors or stunt doubles.

The small town of Midvale was custom-built from scratch, and its destruction by a rogue bulldozer took 22 days to film. In 1989, the same backlot became Gotham City's prime street location in Tim Burton's *Batman*. Apart from limited location shooting at a Scottish loch and Black Park Country Park, Buckinghamshire, the majority of filming—more than 85 percent—was on soundstages. The chief cinematographer was veteran cameraman, director, and technician Alan Hume, who worked on *Supergirl* in between filming Bond movies *Octopussy* (1983) and *A View to a Kill* (1985).

THE ACTION BEGINS

The story opens in the extradimensional "Survival Zone," where Kryptonians thrive in Argo City—a utopian paradise sustained by a reality-shaping orb named the "Omegahedron." Among the Argo City denizens are Zor-El (Simon Ward), his wife Alura In-Ze (Mia Farrow), and a daughter born long after Krypton died. Kara Zor-El (Helen Slater) is a bright, forceful teenager who inadvertently endangers everyone after tutor Zaltar (Peter O'Toole) lets her handle the Omegahedron.

Her playfulness causes a tear in Argo's life-sustaining membrane and the Omegahedron falls into interdimensional space. As Argo goes dark and begins to die, guilt-ridden Kara follows the orb in an AI-enabled escape pod, The Traveler. Pursuit brings her to Earth, where she is programmed with knowledge of the planet and dressed in garments that resemble those worn by her long-lost Kryptonian cousin, Kal-El. She knows

The argonaut

After her film debut, the Girl of Steel's screen time was limited to animated guest shots until television series *Smallville* introduced the mysterious "Kara" (Adrianne Palicki) in 66th episode "Covenant" (Season 3, May 19, 2004). She was a devious narrative red herring to blindside comics-savvy viewers over the actual debut of a Kryptonian Supergirl (Laura Vandervoort) in season 7 There, Supergirl was introduced as Kal-El's cousin, dispatched to Earth to protect the infant but diverted by cosmic misfortune for decades. Victimized by the Luthor family, Jor-El, and Brainiac, she ultimately found a home in season 10, joining the 31st-century Legion of Super-Heroes.

Kara Zor-El became a star in her own right and on her own terms in October 2015. Developed by Greg Berlanti, Ali Adler, and Sarah Schecter for Warner Bros. Television, *Supergirl* ran for six seasons, totaling 126 episodes, plus crossovers into other "Arrowverse" shows. Initially screened on CBS before shifting to The CW, the show brought many comic book concepts, heroes, and villains to the small screen before the epic run ended on November 9, 2021.

Melissa Benoist *(above)* played Kara Danvers/Supergirl with her supporting cast including many members of another Legion of Super-Heroes, Lex Luthor (John Cryer), other heroes of DC's Crisis-beset Multiverse, and a key mentor/partner role for a new J'onn J'onzz/Martian Manhunter—played by David Harewood. Early female role models Helen Slater (Supergirl) and Lynda Carter (Wonder Woman) both had recurring roles, and the series eventually reintroduced Kara's cousin Kal-El. Tyler Hoechlin played Superman in four episodes of *Supergirl* season 2 to such acclaim that the studio launched television show *Superman and Lois* in February 2021, just as Supergirl's own series was reaching its dramatic climax.

English satirist Peter Cook was warlock Nigel—a role created for him after his comedy partner Dudley Moore introduced him to the producers.

Kara's first full confrontation with Selena resulted in banishment to the Phantom Zone, echoing the exile of General Zod in the 1978 *Superman* movie.

The comic book Phantom Zone was an ethereal realm of intangible ghosts, but on film became a bleak wilderness of danger and imminent doom.

he reached Earth decades earlier; lives a double life as Clark Kent and Superman; and that, like him, yellow solar radiation has made her superhuman.

Reveling in Earth's abundant natural wonders, Kara also encounters poverty and crime before experiencing personal violence when two truckers try to assault the naive innocent. On discovering that Kal-El is off-world, Kara goes undercover to search for the Omegahedron, bluffing her way into Midvale Girls Boarding School as Linda Lee, and befriending Lois Lane's little sister Lucy (Maureen Teefy) and Jimmy Olsen (Marc McClure).

The orb is nearby, held by would-be sorceress Selena, who is impatiently studying magical lore from Midvale's math teacher and self-described warlock, Nigel. When Selena instinctively accesses the artifact's power, she misconstrues it as magic and—with fellow witch Bianca (Brenda Vaccaro)—gathers a coven. Playing increasingly deadly tricks and able to have anything she wants, Selena chooses to conquer humanity.

STAR CHILD

Initially clashing after innocent Linda develops a crush on school groundskeeper Ethan (Hart Bochner)—whom Selena wants for herself—Ethan is smitten with Linda (and Supergirl) when a "love potion" backfires. In retaliation, Selena attacks Supergirl, makes Midvale her kingdom, and razes it to the ground with a hexed bulldozer that is hunting Ethan.

Supergirl counterattacks, but is banished to the Phantom Zone, where she reunites with Zaltar, who had exiled himself to atone for losing the Omegahedron, Argo's lifeline. Powerless, they struggle to survive until Zaltar sacrifices himself to return Kara to Earth. As Selena seeks to become "princess of Earth," Supergirl strikes. Winning a fierce battle against Selena's demons, Kara bids a tragic farewell to Ethan, and sets off to find Argo City.

Although the Salkinds financed the film, it was made under Warner Bros. supervision for a scheduled launch in July 1984. However, challenging market conditions led to the producers request for it be shifted to year's end to avoid competition from

Brenda Vaccaro brought decades of experience and innate comedy timing to her roles as the pragmatic witch Bianca to balance the force and grand ambitions of Dunaway's Selena.

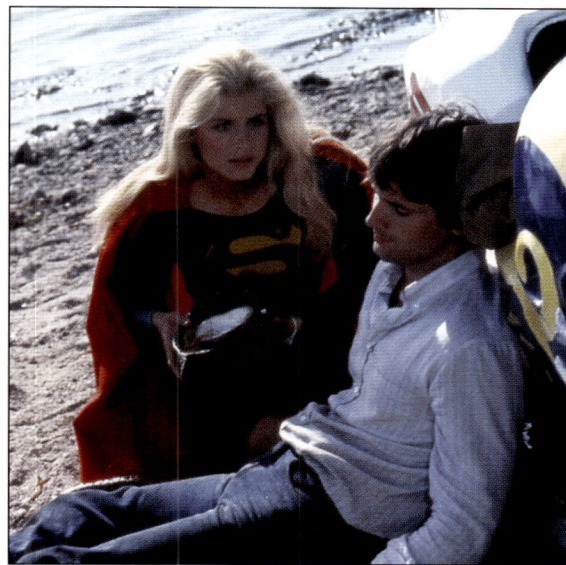

Supergirl's first love Ethan risks life, limb, and heartbreak for her, but thanks to Selena's schemes, she can never be sure if the passion is pure or potion-powered.

Supergirl's journey through the Phantom Zone wilderness with Zaltar symbolized her passage from reactive child to a powerful, responsible hero in command of herself.

other summer blockbusters and the inescapable distraction of the Los Angeles Olympic Games. Instead, Warner Bros. decided to shelve the finished feature.

It was subsequently picked up by Tri-Star/Embassy Pictures to distribute, making it and *Batman* (1966) the only DC Super Hero films not released under Warner Bros.' aegis. American test screenings saw Tri-Star edit the initial 123-minute *Supergirl* down to 105 minutes, although international versions (released months before the US premiere) retained the approximate two-hour length. *Supergirl*'s North American theatrical premiere came in November 1984, a relatively calm period prior to the hectic Christmas release schedule. Completing its US cinema run in February 1985, it was on sale as a home video by May 30. This was partially to counteract bootlegging issues caused by earlier releases in Japan and the UK.

The movie incarnation of *Supergirl* was absent for nearly 40 years, until reinvented in 2023's parallel Earths saga *The Flash*, but is now scheduled for a major return in *Supergirl: Woman of Tomorrow*, based on the comics miniseries by Tom King and Bilquis Evely.

Supergirl returns and returns

Supergirl was originally created during the Silver Age of American comic books after a "backdoor pilot" was published in *Superman* #123 (August 1958). Otto Binder, Dick Sprang, and Stan Kaye's "The Three Magic Wishes" had a mystic totem conjuring up "Super-Girl" to aid the Man of Steel: merely one request made by Jimmy Olsen. The strip made an instant impact. Such was the response that within a year a new version joined the Superman Family. Sixteen years previously in *Captain Marvel Adventures* #18 (December 1942), Binder and artist Marc Swayze had created Mary Marvel as a younger female version of the hero we know today as Shazam!.

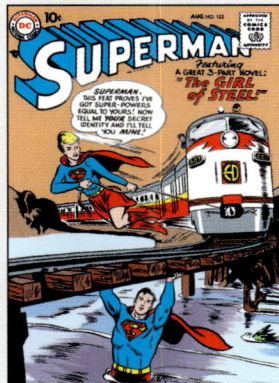

Superman's cousin Kara was born on a fragment of Krypton, hurled intact into space when the planet exploded. Eventually, Argo City turned to Kryptonite like the rest of that world's debris, and her dying parents, observing Earth through their scopes, sent Kara to safety as they perished. Landing on Earth, she met Superman, who created the cover identity Linda Lee and hid her in Midvale Orphanage.

After a lengthy heroic career, her epic demise in *Crisis on Infinite Earths*, and John Byrne's rationalization and reboot of Superman's comic continuity, led to numerous variations of Supergirl until the original was reintroduced to the comic book canon in *Superman/Batman* #8 (February 2004).

SUPERMAN IV: THE QUEST FOR PEACE

Release date: July 23, 1987 (premiere), July 24, 1987 (US/UK)
Starring roles: Christopher Reeve, Gene Hackman, Margot Kidder, Jackie Cooper, Marc McClure, Jon Cryer, Sam Wanamaker, Mariel Hemingway, Mark Pillow
Director: Sidney J. Furie

Screenplay: Lawrence Konner, Mark Rosenthal, Christopher Reeve
Cinematography: Ernest Day
Music: John Williams, Alexander Courage
Running time: 90 minutes
Box office: $36.7 million

Superman's first feature-film franchise closed in a headline-grabbing manner as the Man of Steel diverged from fantastic fiction into the dangerous arena of realpolitik. By the mid-1980s, similar to real world concerns being addressed in contemporary comic books, Christopher Reeve had become a passionate activist and commentator on a number of issues. He had officially retired his Kryptonian cape and costume, but agreed to return to highlight a global emergency—the spiraling nuclear arms race between the US and USSR, sparked in October 1986 by a breakdown of the Reykjavik Arms Limitation Summit.

REAL ACTION HERO

The film reunited the classic cast and hinted at renewed romance between Superman and Lois Lane. Reeve was enticed back by the largest fee of his career, story control, script input, a chance to direct, a producer credit, and—crucially—promised full-funding of his next project *Street Smart* (1987). Reeve requested Ron Howard to direct, but he was in preproduction on *Willow* (1988). He next asked Donner to return and Tom Mankiewicz to write, but his old mentors suggested Reeve should pick a meaningful story based on human conflict that superpowers could not fix and write it himself.

Despite contributing story plot and consulting on the screenplay, Reeve declined to helm the project or script himself, but did direct some second-unit work, such as a battle with Nuclear Man on the Moon, during which Mark Pillow (Nuclear Man) broke his foot.

In those tense times, money was tight everywhere. Following the less than successful *Santa Claus: The Movie*, negotiations at 38th Cannes Film Festival led to The Cannon Group gaining the rights for Superman from the Salkinds. However, Cannon Films had 30 other films in production and were quickly overstretched. An agreed budget of $36 million was slashed to $17 million before filming began on September 27, 1986.

To facilitate economy, filming was restricted to England, at Cannon Elstree Film Studios rather than the prestigious Pinewood facilities used by Donner and Lester. Milton Keynes and its rustic environs doubled for New York, as well as all external shots. The Kent family farm in Smallville was reconstructed at Baldock in North Hertfordshire.

SETTING THE SHOOT

For preproduction, most of the close-knit SFX team who worked on the first three *Superman* films and *Supergirl* returned, but gradually left over salary disputes, to be replaced by a more cost-effective Israeli crew. Only Special Effects/Visual Effects supervisor Roy Field (*Labyrinth*, *The Dark Crystal*) stayed until completion, as did stunt coordinator Alf Joint and many of his associates. Most crew were British, including production designer John Graysmark (*Lifeforce*, *Flash Gordon*) and John Bloomfield (*Doctor Who*, *The Mummy* franchise), who created new costumes.

Seasoned comics illustrator Martin Asbury did triple duty—working as concept designer, matte artist, and storyboarding the film for acclaimed Canadian director Sidney J. Furie (*The Young Ones*, *The Ipcress File*). Cinematographer Ernest Day (*A Clockwork Orange*, *Rambo III*) was an occasional director and passionate camera operator who David Lean called once called "my eyes."

"This is Superman's greatest battle. And it is for all of us."

Poster tagline

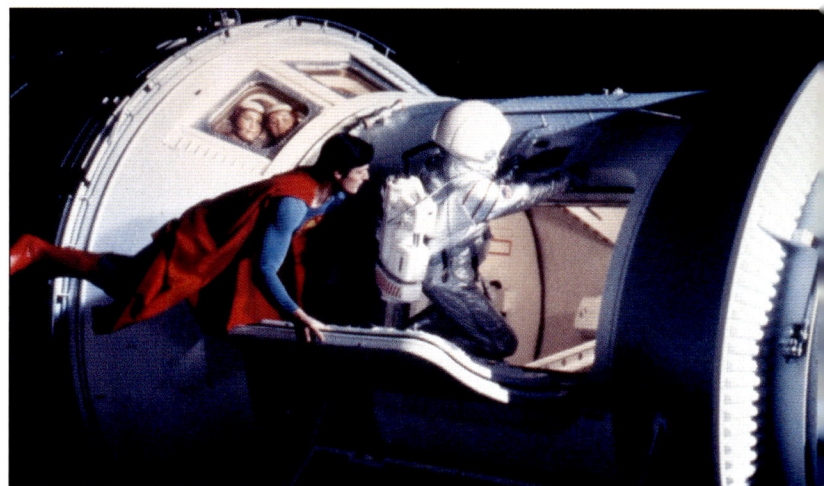

In the era of glasnost and perestroika, Superman's saving Soviet Russian cosmonauts served to emphasize that he was a friend and protector of the entire planet.

One of the film's most striking images saw Superman flying with Lacy Warfield (Mariel Hemingway), having saved her from the villainous clutches of Nuclear Man.

Superman IV saw Luthor gleefully devise a new way to counter Superman's awesome strength—by duplicating it.

Margot Kidder got to add sly comedy to her role as Lois tried to work out what the most glamorous woman in America saw in "her" Clark.

Gene Hackman was 56 when filming took place, making him the oldest person ever to play Lex Luthor on the big screen.

Nuclear Man evolved from an intention to use a character based on the comic book Bizarro. Played by Clive Mantle, the warped proto-being was cut from the final edit.

Working his way up from clapper loader in 1944 to director of photography in 1968, Day was the first British technician to use a 70mm film camera.

Budget limitations meant embarrassment for super-fit Reeve. His flying harnesses were concealed under his red shorts, but the setup always thickened his waistline. Previously, rapid cuts, creative camera angles, and carefully draping his capes concealed this, but now the look was obvious, leading many reviewers to remark unfairly that he had gained weight!

Initially, it was hoped Reeve would also play Nuclear Man as a debased doppelgänger, akin to comic character Bizarro. That proved unworkable and the rampaging villain role went to relative newcomer Mark Pillow. Reeve, Lawrence Konner, and Mark Rosenthal's original storyline had two bombastic brutes—a flawed prototype played by Clive Mantle (*Sherlock*, *Game of Thrones*) and a seemingly humanoid monster played by Pillow.

A heavy media promotional campaign ultimately worked against the film, as numerous prerelease articles hyped key film scenes that Cannon subsequently trimmed from the 134-minute epic to produce a final 90-minute US feature. Overseas versions were longer, but Cannon insisted that at 90 minutes, US theaters could screen it more times per day.

FIGHT FOR LIFE

The film sees Superman saving a damaged Russian space station before returning to his childhood home in Smallville. He's there to sell the farm, but also retrieves a Kryptonian crystal. A recording of his biological mother Lara (Susannah York) tells him it is the last of his Kryptonian birthright and can only be used once. Back in Metropolis, he learns unwelcome change is everywhere and the *Daily Planet* has been acquired by unscrupulous media tycoon David Warfield (Sam Wanamaker).

Appointing his spoiled daughter Lacy (Mariel Hemingway) as publisher over Perry White's (Jackie Cooper) head, Warfield exploits international tensions and an escalating arms race to sell papers, manipulating one boy's fears to provoke Superman. Ignoring his father Jor-El's teachings, Superman listens to his conscience. Taking control of humanity's destiny, he informs the United Nations he will remove atomic weapons from Earth.

Repeatedly hurling them into the Sun, he accidentally aids a diabolical scheme of old enemy Luthor (Gene Hackman). Sprung from jail by his nephew Lenny, Lex uses a strand of Superman's hair to create genetic plasma, and gathers frustrated, soon-to-be impoverished arms dealers in a ploy to enrich himself and end all opposition. Attaching the bio-matrix to a hijacked test missile,

Lex lets Superman throw it into the Sun.

Clark is distracted by rekindled feelings for Lois (Margot Kidder) and inexplicable amorous advances from Lacy Warfield, until an impossibly powerful hybrid clone born in the Sun and genetically programmed to obey Lex ambushes him. In a titanic battle across Metropolis and the world, Superman is viciously clawed by the monster and apparently dies—a situation that the *Daily Planet* tastelessly trumpets.

Superman is in fact fatally irradiated and increasingly powerless, but when Lois finds him and professes her love, he uses the Krypton crystal to repower himself—going after the monster and its master. When Nuclear Man takes a shine to Lacy and abducts her, revitalized Superman duels him in space and on the Moon. Realizing his foe becomes inert when deprived of sunlight, Superman moves the Moon, causing an eclipse. Ending the threat by dumping his defeated, decomposing enemy in a power plant's nuclear core, Superman recaptures Lex and commits Lenny Luthor to a Boys' Home, and celebrates when Perry finds a way to regain control of the *Daily Planet*.

WHAT MIGHT HAVE BEEN

Superman IV: The Quest for Peace is regarded by many comic fans as the most faithful movie verison of Superman—combining evil geniuses with monsters and costumed Super-Villains while also displaying Superman's incredible power and mighty heart.

A comic book adaptation of the film was produced by writer Bob Rozakis and illustrators Curt Swan (who had drawn the Man of Steel's exploits since *Superman* #51, April 1948) and inker Don Heck. Deadlines meant they based their version on an intermediate shooting script, providing readers a glimpse at what might have been. Scenes cut or altered after the comic went to print include a different origin for the Krypton crystal; Jor-El, not Lara advising Clark; a clash with the prototype Nuclear Man based on Bizarro; a globe-girding extended battle with the second—superior—atomic adversary; and a different ending with Superman and Jeremy (whose fears sparked the war against nukes) observing a pacified, safer Earth from space.

When Cannon Films collapsed, Superman's rights reverted to the Salkinds. A year later, they launched the television show (*The Adventures of ...*) *Superboy*. With its showrunners Cary Bates and Mark Jones, Ilya Salkind wrote fifth movie treatment *Superman Reborn*, in which he dies and is resurrected in the Bottled City of Kandor. The idea died in 1993 when the Salkind's sold Superman's rights back to Warner Bros.

Far left: Nuclear Man is the franchise's only costumed Super-Villain, fighting Superman across the world and on the Moon. As originally envisioned, he could also shapeshift and grow into a giant.

Left: In a rarely seen example of utopian idealism, the nations of Earth generally approve of Superman's crusade: similar unilateral actions in comic books and later DC movies usually meet concerted resistance.

Lois & Clark: The New Adventures of Superman

Superman—in various formats targeting differing age groups—has been a fixture of television since the 1950s. Arguably the most successful and well-remembered was a domestic drama that saw him fully partnered with his true love. Their exploits captivated viewers and even saw the eternal lovers finally wed—an event dutifully mirrored in comic books of that time and coordinated to occur at the same time as the TV nuptials. The episode "Swear to God, This Time We're Not Kidding!" aired as copies of bumper edition *Superman: The Wedding Album* hit stores—the culmination of decades of "will they-won't they?" comics stories.

With the movie franchise a memory and Superboy's TV show cancelled, DC President Jenette Kahn had been working to bring another aspect of Superman's mythology to small screens. Her idea was "Lois Lane's *Daily Planet*," but after writer/producer Deborah Joy DeVine became involved the drama was retooled as an adventurous romantic comedy.

Based on DC's rebooted 1988 continuity in the wake of *Crisis on Infinite Earths, Lois & Clark: The New Adventures of Superman* debuted on ABC on September 12, 1993. Starring Dean Cain as Superman and Terri Hatcher as Lois, it ran for four seasons and 88 episodes, ending on June 14, 1997. Blending laughs with love and action, it reintroduced a host of concepts and characters, especially Super-Villains like Lex Luthor, Mr. Mxyzptlk, Toyman, Metallo, Prankster, and Intergang.

THE RETURN OF THE SWAMP THING

Release date: May 12, 1989
Starring roles: Louis Jourdan, Heather Locklear, Dick Durock, Sarah Douglas, Ace Mask, Monique Gabrielle
Director: Jim Wynorski

Screenplay: Neil Cuthbert, Grant Morris
Cinematography: Zoran Hochstätter
Music: Chuck Cirino
Running time: 88 minutes
Box office: $274,928

Other than *Superman*, *Swamp Thing* was DC'c only movie presence after the world turned away from comic book superheroes in the 1960s. However, although fantastical adventure plunged in popularity, other types of films thrived.

In the years between Wes Craven's horror-romance *Swamp Thing* and its sequel, *The Return of the Swamp Thing,* scary movies evolved a new subgenre: gory, gross-out, cathartic satires emphasizing humor—very much as the 1966 *Batman* had parodied its own action-packed precursors. When *Swamp Thing* returned to the big screen, it was in this lighter mode, tapping into a trend for schlock horror as seen in *The Toxic Avenger.* Audiences still loved being scared, but even pure genre movies now had devotees looking for nostalgia, cheap shocks, and tongue-in-cheek silliness. All these were in play for Swamp Thing's celluloid second outing, whose impact created a screen icon of extraordinary longevity.

Beginning with *The Lost Empire* (1984) and *Chopping Mall* (1986), veteran B-movie screenwriter/producer/director Jim Wynorski had 150 films to his credit and was infamous for a certain kind of filmmaking—rude, funny, popular, and profitable. Wynorski personified the zeitgeist and was given $7 million by Lightyear Entertainment and distributors Miramax to revive DC's swamp hero. He was also given 30 days to film it all and completed the job three days under deadline.

"The beauty and the beast have fled!"

Anton Arcane

Wynorski started with a complete—uncredited—rewrite of the original script created by Neil Cuthbert (*Pluto Nash*, *Mystery Men*) and Grant Morris (*Dead Dog*, *The Shrimp on the Barbie*), realigning it with his distinct vision and instincts. Fortunately, he had returning stars and a popular actress heading his cast. Although the director seemingly disregarded the classic source material, the script embraced some of Alan Moore's comic book innovations,

acknowledged by the striking, mood-setting title sequence— a montage of comic book artwork set to Creedence Clearwater Revival's "Born on the Bayou."

HIDDEN HISTORY

The first sensation of comic books' Bronze Age, Swamp Thing had deep pulp-fiction roots. Theodore Sturgeon's 1940 novella "It!" revealed how swamp vegetation that aggregated around a skeleton became sentient, curious, and unintentionally deadly. "It!" inspired the monster antihero The Heap (*Air Fighters Comics* #3, December

While the comic series *Saga of the Swamp Thing* was revolutionizing horror stories, the muck-encrusted monster's second cinematic outing embraced the lighter side of terror.

The revised look of Swamp Thing was designed by Vicki Graef (*Witchblade*, *Dick Tracy*) and built and maintained by six of the 14 makeup technicians.

1942) and DC's Solomon Grundy (*All-American Comics* #61, October 1944). In 1971, Skywald Publishing revived The Heap just as the concept manifested with DC's Swamp Thing and Marvel's Man-Thing—all created within weeks of each other.

RETURN OF THE CREATURE

The film sees Federal Agents go on a field trip intent on taking out moonshiners, but fail to anticipate swamps being so wet and muddy and filled with danger. Agents are exterminated by mercenaries led by the psychotic Miss Poinsettia (Monique Gabrielle) or consumed by a "leechman" (Chris Doyle). Only agent Harry Dugan (Anthony Sears) survives and is restored to civilization by legendary "Swamp Thing" (Dick Durock). The story draws reporters, who offer $10,000 for a photo of the mossy messiah. Meanwhile, in Los Angeles, New Age florist Abby (Heather Locklear) gives up on finding true love and opts to finally confront her stepfather, Anton Arcane. She has 10 years of questions about her mother's unexplained death and the part he played in it.

Venturing to Louisiana—in reality the Oatland Island Reservation Wildlife Center of Savannah, Georgia—Abby finds him and his mistress Dr. Lana Zurrell (Sarah Douglas) strangely welcoming. It was Douglas's third outing as a glamorously wicked DC villain, having already played Kryptonian terror Ursa in *Superman: The Movie* and *Superman II*.

Interior scenes were shot at Mercer Williams House, while a false porch was built onto the Oatland Mansion, designed to explode in the climactic end scene. As it turned out, the stunt malfunctioned and the three rigged windows of the ancient edifice that were intended to detonate wrecked all the glass in the historic frontage.

WICKED GAMES

Years ago, scientists Dr. Rochelle (Wesley "Ace" Mask) and Dr. Zurrell had restored what remained of Arcane after the previous movie. Now, their efforts are faltering and all Arcane's resources are dedicated to rejuvenating himself, while their failed animal-human hybrids, the Un-Men, are running amok in the swamp. If Abby has the same pristine genetic code as her departed mother, the geneticists' task just got much easier.

When Abby discovers her stepfather's true intentions, she escapes into the bayou. Assaulted by outlaws, she is saved by the plant-man of her dreams. However, Arcane's mercenaries, led by Gunn (Joey Sagal), recapture her and blow Holland to fragments. By gathering the scraps, Arcane now has the last element necessary for success.

Despite reconstituting himself to rescue Abby, Swamp Thing's valiant attempts fail and she is imprisoned in the plantation house's basement laboratory. With precious time left, Arcane uses Lana as genetic fodder, too. She retaliates by trying but failing to help Abby escape. When Swamp Thing strikes, Zurrell vengefully injects Rochelle with mutagenic formula, triggering a horrific transformation.

Ultimately, Arcane is restored. Murdering Zurrell, he unleashes Rochelle when Swamp Thing comes too late for Abby. An explosive

The Un-Men were one of Swamp Thing's earliest and most persistent threats, having been created by Anton Arcane, by way of comic creators Len Wein and Bernie Wrightson, in *Swamp Thing* #2 (January 1973).

Multi-Golden Globe nominee Heather Locklear brought star power and celebrity glamour to the B-movie gothic proceedings. She was hugely popular thanks to television shows like *Dynasty*, *T.J. Hooker*, and *Melrose Place*.

Carl Fullerton and Neal Martz crafted a full-body latex suit for Durock. It took two hours to apply and caused so much sweating that the lip and eye prosthetics continually detached. The suit was modified for the TV series, with makeup substituting for facial attachments.

Deranged thug Gunn was played by multifaceted Joe Sagal, who wrote, produced, and acted in 2016's *Elvis and Nixon*.

clash ensues, killing Anton again and, as his empire burns, Holland brings Abby's body into the swamp—resurrecting her with his bio-restorative touch.

Durock's performance was far stronger and more believable here—bolstered by better makeup, more convincing costuming, and his own late flowering as an actor. Despite this, the studio overdubbed his voice for the final release without Durock's or Wynorski's knowledge.

For a low-budget film, *The Return of the Swamp Thing* boasted a substantial SFX team, indicating where Wynorski's focus lay. Rochelle's mutated stand-in was famed stuntman Rex Pierson (*Another 48 Hours*, *Darkman*), made unrecognizable by makeup and prosthetics. And the Un-Men alone commanded a 13-strong squad of specialists from The Todd Masters Company, led by Masters himself. In comparison, the entire stunt team was only nine strong.

Given its humorous, irreverent edge, it's not surprising that in-jokes pepper the production. Wesley Mask plays Dr. Rochelle—a name and role he used in other Wynorski films, including 1988's *Not of This Earth* and 1994's *Ghoulies IV*. When Miss Poinsettia catalogs her scars to rival mercenary, Gunn, she claims one of them came from a fan at a Mötley Crüe gig. At the time of the shoot, Heather Locklear was dating the band's drummer, Tommy Lee. Moreover, back in LA, Abby's plants are fans of *T.J. Hooker*—a cop show where Locklear played officer Stacy Sheridan.

Return of the Swamp Thing was released in May 1989 and by year's end was released for home viewing by RCA/Columbia Pictures Home Video. The theatrical version remained popular, playing in cinemas across America for 137 weeks. If the first *Swamp Thing* movie was hindered by preconceptions of movie monsters and film tropes, the fun sequel played right into them, and its surprise success has translated into various small-screen incarnations ever since. Indeed, Swamp Thing is slated to return in a major motion picture from DC Studios as part of James Gunn and Peter Safran's rebooted DCU continuity Gods and Monsters.

Silver screams

Following *The Return of the Swamp Thing*, Joseph Stefano (*Psycho*, *Outer Limits*) developed a television series, ditching the comedic angle to reclaim the tortured humanity at the heart of the comics incarnations. Launching on July 27, 1990, on USA Network, *Swamp Thing* ran 72 episodes over three seasons. Frequently the network's top-rated show, it was filmed at Universal Studios Florida site, a facilities and soundstages complex constructed by their MTE division. Initially, scenes were shot in real swamps, but that proved unworkable. Lighting was uncontrollable and transportation problems mounted, so an indoor bayou was built, which Dick Durock described as "ten times better than a real swamp."

Durock personally benefitted from technological advances. Carl Fullerton and Neal Martz's latex suits had electronic voice modulators and solutions for profuse sweating caused by earlier outfits, and were easier to don. "In the first feature, it took close to four hours," explained Durock. "(The) second was close to two hours. By the time we did the series—which ironically was by far the best makeup and costume—we had it down to about 45 minutes."

Heavily advertised in contemporary DC comics, the show began by appealing to young audiences before adopting a darker tone and abandoning comic continuity for generic horror themes. Additionally, Fox launched an animated kids series in 1991, but it ended after only five episodes.

A 2019 reboot *(below)* embracing the comics' sophisticated terror was created by Gary Dauberman (*Annabelle*) and Mark Verheiden (*Falling Skies*), premiering on May 31, 2019, but, despite a positive reception, only lasted one season.

MODERNIZING THE MYTHOLOGY

With Tim Burton's *Batman* in 1989, a new chapter in DC movie-making opened. Much as Richard Donner's *Superman* had revolutionized the perception of superheroes in 1978, compelling a generation to believe a man could fly, Burton's *Batman* represented a thrilling new approach to the genre— a visionary director channeling his wild imagination and idiosyncratic sensibilities into a highly stylized, gamechanging movie that became a blockbuster phenomenon.

Over the ensuing two decades, a succession of filmmakers would bring their particular visions to DC, from the arresting occult imagery of Francis Lawrence's *Constantine* (2005), to the heightened realism of Zack Snyder's *Watchmen* (2009), to Christopher Nolan's expansive quest for authenticity in his powerful *Dark Knight Trilogy* (2005–2012).

At the same time, technical advances in everything from computer-generated visual effects to costumes and cameras would make for ever more convincing takes on the fantastical subject matter. The leaps in technology allowed filmmakers to set their passions and artistry free.

BATMAN

Release date: June 19, 1989 (Los Angeles), June 23, 1989 (US), August 11, 1989 (UK)
Starring roles: Jack Nicholson, Michael Keaton, Kim Basinger, Robert Wuhl, Pat Hingle, Billy Dee Williams, Michael Gough, Jack Palance

Director: Tim Burton
Screenplay: Sam Hamm, Warren Skaaren
Cinematography: Roger Pratt
Music: Danny Elfman, Prince
Running time: 126 minutes
Box office: $411.6 million

Batman was first seen in March 1939 on the pages of *Detective Comics* #27, and quickly became DC's second big multimedia star. Following a brief, intense period of global popularity in the mid-1960s as a comedic parody for adults, he returned to his comic book roots, where he was gradually rehabilitated as a grim avenger haunting the night.

However, even 20 years after the *Batman* television show ended, to the wider world the Caped Crusader remained a figure of fun and camp hijinx. Then, in his 50th year of continuous publication, everything changed—thanks to the passion of a devotee-turned-producer. No one laughed when Batman's second feature film was unleashed on a largely unsuspecting public.

"Do I look like I'm joking?"
The Joker

The movie had been a long time coming. DC and Hollywood had both abandoned all hope of major screen revivals. In the late 1970s, DC was considering CBS's suggestion of "Batman in Outer Space," when occasional DC comics scriptwriter Michael Uslan (*The Shadow*, *Beowulf*) partnered with television producer Benjamin Melniker (*American Playhouse*, *Dinosaucers*) to form Batfilm Productions, Inc. On October 3, 1979, they bought the film rights to Batman. Dedicated Batman fan Uslan had a dream "to make the definitive, dark version of Batman. The way Bob Kane and Bill Finger had envisioned him in 1939. A creature of the night stalking criminals in the shadows" (*Batman-on-Film*, September 2013).

THE REAL DEAL
In November, 1979, Batfilms partnered with cinema hit-factory The Guber-Peters Company (*An American Werewolf in London*, *The Witches of Eastwick*), who immediately grasped the project's potential and provided fresh impetus.

With studios like Universal locked into the notion of a kid-friendly spoof and still rejecting the project, the producers publicly announced their serious Batman movie—with a proposed budget of $15 million—to fans attending the July 1980 New York Comic Art Convention. This bold move launched an avalanche of word-of-mouth anticipation and galvanized Warner Bros. to sign on,

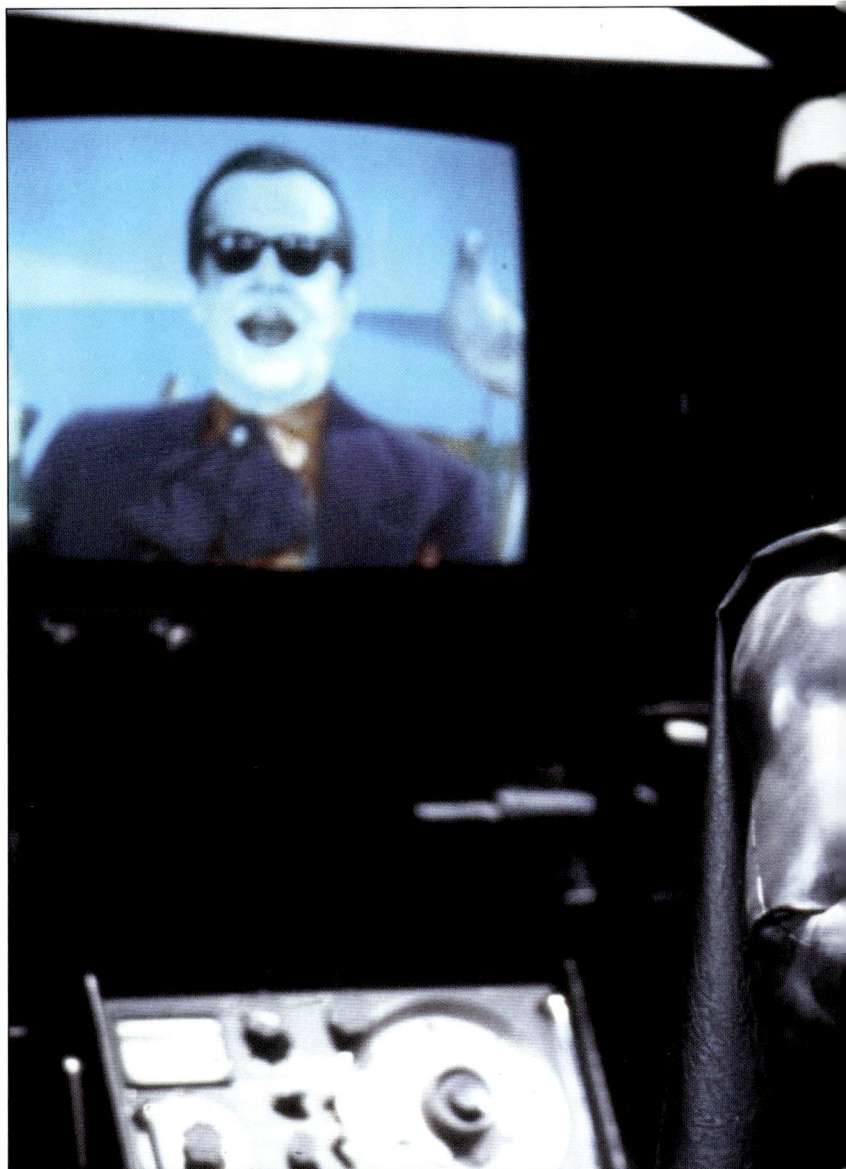

Past met future and stone met metal and plastic in the Batcave—where its dark master utilized surveillance technology to keep tabs on foes, friends, and lovers.

Far left: The Joker's relationship with Vicki was built on style, crazy laughs, and the constant threat of sudden death.

Left: Hertfordshire's Knebworth House has seen everything from war to rock festivals and been featured in 40 films—including a stint as Wayne Manor.

as the owners of Superman were not prepared for another studio to capitalize on one of their personal properties.

The search for screenplay, cast, crew, and director began with Guy Hamilton, Joe Dante (*Gremlins*), and Ivan Reitman (*Ghostbusters*) as early candidates. Wes Craven was also considered after his success with *Swamp Thing*. In June 1983, Tom Mankiewicz delivered a script based on Steve Englehart and Marshall Rogers's highly regarded 1970s comic book stories (collected as *Batman: Strange Apparitions*). These had successfully repositioned a retro-1940s Batman as a dark figure of justice and vengeance, and Rogers was subsequently hired to create concept art, with Englehart as a story consultant, alongside original creator Bob Kane. Englehart and Julie Hickson wrote full treatments

Terrifying top mobster Gus Grissom was utterly certain of his power and dominance … right up until Jack Napier killed and replaced him.

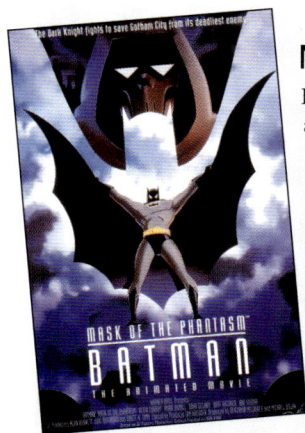

Man behind the curtain

It took Michael Uslan and Benjamin Melniker almost a decade to bring their heroic vision to the screen. They also produced two films starring Swamp Thing (February 1982 and May 1989) and subsequent television incarnations.

Uslan and Melniker remained credited as executive producers on every Warner Bros. Batman film until Melniker's death in 2018, while Uslan continues to be credited as "Executive Producer." Their influence extended to Will Eisner's *The Spirit* movie, Disney's *National Treasure,* and award-winning *Where on Earth is Carmen Sandiego?* Despite their original contract with DC specifically excluding television, they also produced *Batman: The Animated Adventures* and numerous animated Batman feature films, such as *Batman: Mask of the Phantasm.*

Trained as a lawyer, Uslan has been a dedicated comic book fan his entire life, and taught America's first university course in comics, before turning it into a textbook—*The Comic Book in America* (Indiana University, 1971). After initially scripting comics, he turned his attention to comics in mass media, securing film rights from DC, brokering deals, editing and bringing Stan Lee to DC with 2001's *Just Imagine* ... comic series.

before Sam Hamm (*Never Cry Wolf*) was eventually hired to create the first official screenplay. His biggest and best decision was to forgo a formal origin story and allow Bruce's secret to unfold in classic mystery novel fashion.

Batman and The Joker's comic book reclamation had begun even before the TV show was cancelled in 1968. Incrementally over decades, talented creators toiled to restore the hero to the spooky, relentless human weapon cloaked in secrecy he had been at the start. In 1973, a succession of superb stories featuring the hero's grinning antithesis culminated with Denny O'Neil and Neal Adams's classic "The Joker's Five-Way Revenge!" (*Batman* #251) sparking a renaissance for the Clown Prince of Crime and his descent into terrifying psychosis. In the 1980s, the ongoing process resulted in landmark stories completely revitalizing the hero. Frank Miller's *The Dark Knight Returns* and *Batman: Year One* (the latter with artist David Mazzucchelli) completely redefined the hero for a generation. Jim Starlin and Jim Aparo's *A Death in the Family* saw The Joker murder second Robin, Jason Todd, while Alan Moore and Brian Bolland's *Batman: The Killing Joke* finally gave the villain an origin of sorts. These, more than any other stories, shaped the new film franchise.

GREAT EXPECTATIONS

The most crucial piece of the puzzle was a director, and in 1986, fresh hot property Tim Burton joined the production. Studio executives were delighted by his proven ability to make popular, profitable movies on low budgets. He was also celebrated for his artistic, quirky style, as seen in early animation work, short film *Frankenweenie,* and recent feature film hits *Pee-Wee's Big Adventure* and *Beetlejuice.*

Burton admitted to not having preexisting emotional connection to Batman, but was fascinated by The Joker and intrigued by the gothic nature of their conflict. In a contemporary interview, Burton claimed he could never understand how comics even worked until he read *The Killing Joke,* with Moore and Bolland's rigorously structured storytelling directing the reader's gaze. Much of *The Killing Joke*'s tone informs Burton's film. After top billing and stealing every scene he's in, it is arguable that *Batman* could be described as the first true Joker movie.

The project also afforded Burton a chance to work with the talented and forthright production designer Anton Furst, who had first intrigued Burton with his work on *The Company of Wolves* and *Full Metal Jacket.* Furst was a philosophically minded designer who based his visual concept of Gotham City on industrial decline and gothic expressionism, and his work (with set decorator Peter Young) was a revelation. Its bleak and chilling appearance became as much a character in the movie as the cast, becoming the perfect milieu for their antic actions, particularly that of Batman's nemesis. "I starved Gotham City of color to exaggerate The Joker's look," explained Furst in the arts magazine *Bomb* in April 1990.

Crushed and twisted for decades by organized crime, Gotham City is gripped by terror. The scum of the earth—led by aging mob boss Gus Grissom (Jack Palance)—rule the dystopian city, but are now being picked off by a frightening batlike monster that strikes from the shadows. As this entity preys upon the predators, decent citizens prepare for the approaching bicentennial, but the cash-strapped authorities are helpless in the face of institutionalized corruption. New District Attorney Harvey Dent (Billy Dee

Far left: Always hands-on and open to new ideas, Tim Burton had initial questions about the story but no doubts over how the movie should look and feel.

Left: Keaton played against audience expectation in both his roles—a stoic, hyper-efficient, mysterious manhunter and an intense charmer armed with a ready smile and a sharp suit.

Vicki Vale is inventive and cool under fire. She manages to ride out and capitalize on The Joker's obsessive behavior and lethal lack of impulse control.

A true majordomo, Alfred aids and abets Bruce Wayne's two lives while also acting against his master's wishes when it's in Bruce's own best interests.

Williams, a set up to play Two-Face in the anticipated sequel) and Mayor Borg (Lee Wallace) promise change, but no one believes them. When reporter Alexander Knox (Robert Wuhl) meets photojournalist Vicki Vale (Kim Basinger), fresh from filming a war in Corto Maltese, he convinces her to help him prove "the Bat" exists. First, though, there's an easy gig snapping rich people at the home of reclusive socialite Bruce Wayne. The camera-shy billionaire is bankrolling a gala fundraiser for the bicentennial fund. He is young, charming, a little strange, and hiding a tragic secret.

BATMANIA RETURNS

Anticipation was already at fever pitch thanks to a growing fan community and Uslan's marketing savvy even before the age of social media. A second dose of "Batmania" exploded in 1988, decades after the TV show, when the man who would be Batman was revealed. Casting the damaged playboy had proved tough. The studio proposed many prominent leading men, including Mel Gibson, Kevin Costner, Charlie Sheen, Tom Selleck, Bill Murray, Harrison Ford, and Dennis Quaid, while Burton's dream choice—the unknown Willem Dafoe—was unavailable.

When the dust settled, Michael Keaton ended up playing Bruce Wayne/Batman. The actor was recommended by legendary producer Jon Peters on the strength of a bravura performance in *Beetlejuice* and his "edgy, tormented quality" in the addiction drama *Clean and Sober*. Burton agreed, but had to defend the decision, especially after *The Wall Street Journal* ran a front-page headline screaming "What a ridiculous choice!" and Warner Bros. received 50,000 protest letters from fans convinced the film was going to be another comedy mocking their hero.

However, as the villainous lead, Jack Nicholson was inarguably born to play The Joker, and wanted to. A number of actors such as Tim Curry, James Woods, Brad Dourif, Ray Liotta, John Lithgow, and even David Bowie were considered for the role, but producers and director soon settled on the only man for the job. Jack Nicholson

Bob Ringwood's eye-bending Joker chic and flamboyant wardrobe changes made the Clown Prince of Crime's scenes unforgettable on every level.

Gotham City ended its modern Dark Age and embraced its new champion by building and lighting a Bat-Signal.

Like every true visionary, The Joker embraced popular technology, using classic advertising tactics and television broadcast to get his message across to the masses.

commanded the biggest fee, top billing, a portion of earnings, and control of his shooting schedule, and in return would give one of the most memorable performances of his career.

FACE THE PRESS

Kim Basinger (*9½ Weeks*) was a near last-minute choice to play Vicki Vale. Sean Young (*Blade Runner, Dune*) had signed on for the part but was injured in a riding accident days before shooting started. Following frantic phone calls, Basinger flew to London, splitting her time between Pinewood Studios and Knebworth House (doubling for the Wayne Estate). As assistant director/co-producer Chris Kenny remarked about casting, every day ended with someone asking "Who is available tomorrow?" Shooting ran from October 1988 to January 1989.

Progress was made in the midst of much creative chaos. Shooting scripts changed daily, especially after the 1988 screen writers' strike ended Hamm's participation. Burton brought in Warren Skaaren, who reworked the third act, boosting characterization, cutting the debut of Robin, making Vicki privy to Batman's secret, and retrofitting young Jack Napier/The Joker as the murderer of Thomas and Martha Wayne. Although uncredited, Charles McKeown and Jonathan Gems also worked on the final shooting script.

British costume designer Bob Ringwood (*Excalibur, The Shadow*) assiduously avoided referencing the 1960s television show when creating outfits for the film. Like Jerry Hall, who played Alicia Hunt, he had narrowly missed joining the Bond film *Licence to Kill* and was conveniently available when co-producer Chris Kenny needed someone to dress his new production, *Batman*, in a hurry. Never having read the comics as kid, Ringwood based his look on 1940s gangster threads, while Napier/The Joker's double-breasted suits also employed the character's signature color livery. After studying the screenplay and rush-reading over 400 Batman back issues, he also took a cue from various Neal Adams stories and Marshall Rogers's depictions from the now legendary "Joker-Fish" storyline in *Detective Comics* #475–476 (February and April 1978).

Far left: Constructed from Lycra with foam rubber on top, it took four Batsuit prototypes to find a system that allowed Keaton to move convincingly.

Left: Built by John Evans, the speargun grappling hook Batman employs to save Vicki from The Joker's goons was a fully functional prop with twin motors.

Anton Furst's gothic vision

Anton Furst was born in London in May 1944. He studied at the Royal College of Art and, after designing award-winning television films *Just One Kid* and *It's a Lovely Day Tomorrow*, he worked in special effects on Ridley Scott's *Alien* before settling on production design. His preferred method was to dictate descriptions to chief draftsman Nigel Phelps and then modify and finish the pencil and charcoal images that Phelps generated. His studio sets for Neil Jordan's *The Company of Wolves* (1984) led to recreating Vietnam's Hué in England for Stanley Kubrick's *Full Metal Jacket* (1987).

Tim Burton wanted Furst for *Beetlejuice*, but the artist instead realized the look of 1988's *High Spirits* before at last linking up with his visionary soul-brother. "Tim Burton and I inevitably got together because he is firm in his opinion that film must have its own reality," he explained in *Bomb* magazine, April 1990. "I work on metaphors and parables of situations. Gotham City is all the elements of Manhattan exaggerated ... I imagined what it would have been like if it had been run by a criminal organization for a long time and had been allowed to become what you saw in the film."

In that same issue of *Bomb*, Furst outlined his approach to creating *Batman*'s distinctive milieu and the role of the designer: "The bottom line is always the script. But there are certain movies that require a whole reality, a world (where) the design and visual aspect becomes as significant as any other element." The result was a shared production design Academy Award (with Peter Young) for realizing Gotham City's industrial hellscape and the terrifying new Batmobile.

Gotham City skyline looking west across the Gotham River.

The 46th St. promenade looking south to the Gardner Overpass.

The Old Gotham City Police Headquarters.

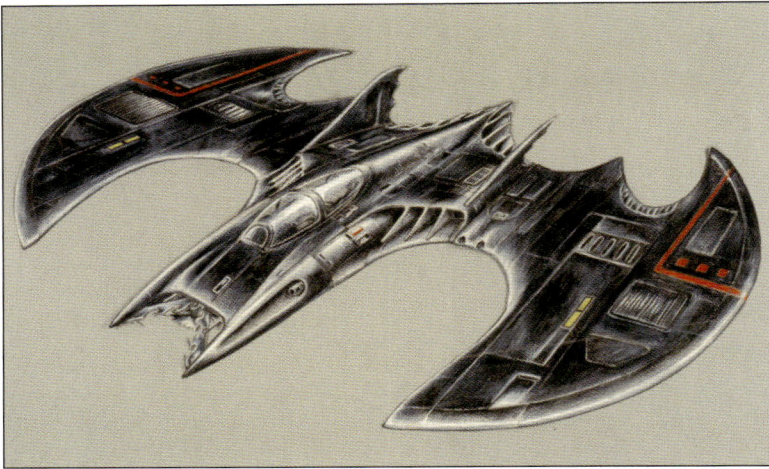

Anton Furst's design for the sickle-shaped Batwing mini-jet was based on Batman's chest symbol and realized by specialists working under Visual Effects Supervisor Derek Meddings.

Gotham City's overwhelmed leaders Mayor Borg, DA Dent, and Commissioner Gordon issue another empty, placatory statement nobody believes.

KNIGHT OF TERROR

Into Gotham City's slowly escalating crisis, a wild card is thrown. Gang boss Grissom, under pressure from DA Dent's investigation and incensed that his sociopathic right-hand man, Jack Napier, is sleeping with his girlfriend, Alicia Hunt, sets up his second-in-command at Axis Chemicals plant. Ordering his bought cop Max Eckhardt (William Hootkins) to kill Jack, Grissom's plan is foiled by honest Police Commissioner James Gordon (Pat Hingle) and the mysterious "Bat."

Stalking the abandoned complex like a ghost—and mimicking many of Bela Lugosi's poses and movements from Tod Browning's gothic masterpiece *Dracula* (1931)—Batman easily disposes of Napier's men and fights their leader to a stalemate. Suddenly, the mobster's face is struck and damaged by a ricocheting bullet and he falls into a vat of bubbling chemicals. Sometime later, as Vicki Vale gets closer to Bruce Wayne, Knox uncovers the story of the

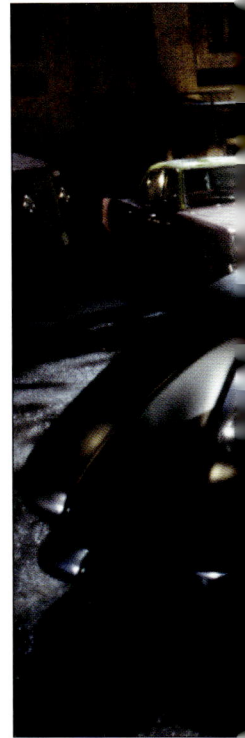

The Joker elevates himself from a jack to a king as he and his goons prepare to annihilate the hordes of greedy Gotham City denizens with Smylex gas.

Wayne murders, as a green-haired, chalk-faced maniac takes over Grissom's enterprises. Afflicted with a rictus grin, Jack Napier, now known as The Joker, attempts to switch the syndicate's business model from profit to aesthetics, in pursuit of the muses of terror and death.

LAST LAUGH

The Clown Prince's campaign includes random murders, brutal battles with authorities, and contaminating makeup and other shopping products with "Smylex," which causes victims to die laughing and leave a grinning corpse. He also forms a delusional fixation on Vicki, almost killing Wayne in the process of abducting her and repeating the phrase uttered by the man who shot Bruce's parents and left their boy alive and broken. Vale is eventually taken to the Batcave by faithful retainer Alfred Pennyworth (Michael Gough), who wants a normal life for his troubled charge. Bruce, however, cannot quit until he has stopped his parents' killer and leaves for another clash at Axis Chemicals, where his foe is preparing tons of Smylex.

The Joker lures a terrified populace to the bicentennial parade with promises of handing out millions of dollars, but is actually intent on effecting the largest mass-murder in history. When the Batwing destroys his poison-gas-filled blimps, The Joker shoots down Batman's minijet and climbs the crumbling Gotham Cathedral for a savage, fatal showdown, where he finally realizes that his enemy is his creation—young Bruce Wayne all grown up.

Homages to classic gothic landmarks such as *The Hunchback of Notre Dame* abound at the movie's end and Burton was happy to allow his players a high degree of autonomy. One such last-minute change occurred in the climactic Gotham Cathedral duel—sparked

Far left: The Batmobile was hell on wheels. Made from fiberglass, it was 19 feet long x 8 feet wide (5.9 m x 2.4 m), based on a Grand Prix racer frame, and equipped with specially imported 24-inch (60 m) drag-racer wheels. As production designer Anton Furst outlined to *Bomb* magazine (April 1990), "You're designing visual drama. The Batmobile was more like a knight in armor, an extension of Batman's costume—an intimidating, furious war machine."

Left: Derek Medding's son Mark was responsible for maintaining model buildings—ranging from Gothic to Brutalism to Art Deco—of Gotham City until they were destroyed in their final scenes.

by Nicholson and Peters attending musical *The Phantom of the Opera* in London while the scene was being shot and bringing back notes to enhance the final confrontation. In the aftermath, as Gordon cleans up the dregs of crime, the Commissioner unveils a special Bat-Signal to alert the city's new guardian, acting on Batman's promise to return if he's needed.

YEAR OF THE BAT
The film's mood and tone were amplified by an enthralling musical score from Burton's old ally Danny Elfman (*Pee-Wee's Big Adventure, Edward Scissorhands*), and enhanced by songs written and performed by Prince. Guber had originally wanted Prince to score The Joker's scenes with Michael Jackson doing romance songs, but the deal never closed.

With Anton Furst devising a gothic steampunk city, visual effects supervisor Derek Meddings (*Superman*, six Bond movies) creating astonishing models such as the Batwing, and special effects supervisor John Evans (*Moonraker, Raiders of the Lost Ark*) building the Batmobile and Batman's arsenal, Burton stuck to his brief, making a film never intended for children. Ultimately, *Batman* proved to be a monster hit with all demographics.

Box office topped $411.6 million, making it the fifth-highest-grossing film in history to that point. Critics and fans were positive, praising performances and Elfman's moody score. The film received a mountain of award nominations, with Furst winning an Academy Award for production design. It also triggered a new film franchise and an animated TV series that would become just as celebrated, and made Batman a global merchandising phenomenon, relaunching DC as a leader in licensed merchandise. Moreover, the film returned the favor to its source material—with interest—sparking a commercial and creative comics renaissance that added new Batman titles for readers of all ages.

Keaton unmasked
Michael Keaton's career is as mercurial as the roles he chooses, and he is wholly committed to each one. He began in children's television (on *Mister Roger's Neighborhood* in 1975) and by 1988 had gravitated from sitcoms like *Working Stiffs* (with Jim Belushi) to film comedies like *Night Shift* and *Mister Mom* to serious dramatic roles in *Clean and Sober* and eccentric exuberance in *Bettlejuice,* where he met Tim Burton.

For the production studios, he was a tricky choice for *Batman*, but spectacularly proved everyone wrong. Slight in build, his padded Batsuits restricted movements—particularly the cowl—necessitating short shots and dramatic cuts to convey the illusion of a human powerhouse in martial-arts action. Digging deep into his characters, Keaton made Bruce Wayne utterly compelling, while paring back Batman's dialogue to monosyllabic utterances and moody looks.

It was as Bruce Wayne that he won the world over—a charismatic if wounded and guarded soul, either lashing out or suppressing loss and fury from behind a mask of suave sophistication and boyish charm. As casting director Marion Dougherty said: "The eyes got him the job."

Keaton's depiction remains definitive, with his portrayal forming the basis of a modern comic book continuation in *Batman '89.* In 2023's *The Flash*, Keaton's Batman plays a significant role, extending the legend as an aging hero in the manner of Frank Miller's *The Dark Knight Returns.*

BATMAN RETURNS

Release date: June 16, 1992 (Hollywood), June 19, 1992 (US)
Starring roles: Michael Keaton, Danny DeVito, Michelle Pfeiffer, Christopher Walken, Michael Gough, Pat Hingle, Michael Murphy
Director: Tim Burton

Screenplay: Daniel Waters, Sam Hamm
Cinematography: Stefan Czapsky
Music: Danny Elfman
Running time: 126 minutes
Box office: $266.8 million

When Tim Burton was finally cajoled into making another Batman movie, it was very much on his own terms and—for him at least—a continuation but not a sequel. Despite colossal critical and financial response to the breakthrough 1989 film, the director preferred to pursue other projects and rejected studio bosses' entreaties to come back for more.

Other than creative control, his own staff, a co-producer credit (with long-term associate Denise Di Novi), and more money, what convinced him to return the Dark Knight was a script by Daniel Waters (*Heathers*, *Hudson Hawk*). However, as production began Waters's script was modified—ad hoc and uncredited—by Wesley Strick (*Cape Fear*, *Man in the High Castle*), who became on-set writer. Retaining the Christmas setting, Burton tasked Production Designer Bo Welch with reimagining Gotham City as a brutalist Soviet-styled urban enclave, and rejected most of two drafts supplied by *Batman* writer Sam Hamm. These involved Harvey Dent/Two-Face; Bruce Wayne engaged to Vicki Vale; Robin's debut; a lower body count; and—after urgings from Warner

Bros.—a very different Penguin and Catwoman hunting lost treasure and framing Batman for multiple murders.

Filming from September 1991 to February 1992 in Burbank on Warner Bros. lots and soundstages, Burton's new Gotham City took up half of the studio's total resources (over 13 sites) before spreading onto Universal Studios facilities.

Strick excised Robin, recharacterized The Penguin (with whom Burton most empathized), and "normalized" dialogue, but although credited in promotional material was excluded from the final credits. Waters's script had been gritty and bleakly verbose, moving Michael Keaton to reject many of Batman's lines. Already adamant that the hero should not speak much when in costume, he rejected "bitter and cynical" utterings like "Gotham doesn't deserve protection." Burton agreed, declaring Batman a wounded soul, not a nihilist.

EMPEROR PENGUIN

Once upon a Christmastime in Gotham City, a prestigious socialite couple had a deformed baby. Unable to face the shame and gossip, they secretly threw him away. Cast into a sewer, infant Oswald Cobblepot was found and raised by the cleverest creatures inhabiting the darkest depths—abandoned black-footed, king and

"I am Catwoman. Hear me roar."
Catwoman

Prop Master Bill Petrotta's team provided numerous weaponized umbrellas for Cobblepot to use. DeVito kept one of the "bumbershoots" once filming ended.

The mutual attraction of Selina and Bruce was enigmatically summed up by Tim Burton as "There's four great eyes there between the two of them."

Tim Burton described the feral chemistry of Cat and Bat as "There's a split to all these characters. What they want to be versus what they are."

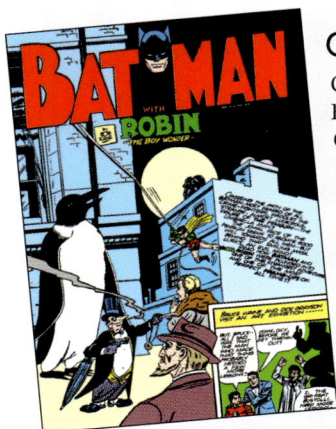

Cat calls and bird calls

Catwoman and The Penguin are among Batman's most persistent comic book foes. Created by Bob Kane with Bill Finger, "The Cat" crept into *Batman* #1 (Spring 1940)—a jewel thief on a cruise liner, falling afoul of a vacationing Dynamic Duo and later adding "Woman" to her title.

As "Mr. Boniface," The Penguin debuted in *Detective Comics* #58 (December 1941, also Kane, Finger, Robinson), making Batman and Robin victims of "One of the Most Perfect Frame-Ups."

While the Cat evolved into a conflicted antihero defending the poor underclass and the Dark Knight's unobtainable true love, the bird bandit is now an ostensibly legitimate presence in Gotham City. He was the 1940s Batman Sunday strip's most used villain, kicking off the feature in "The Penguin's Crime Thunderstorms" (Don Cameron, Kane, and Charles Paris, November 7–December 12, 1943). Thanks to Alvin Schwartz, Jack Burnley, and Paris, we learned his real name—Oswald Chesterfield Cobblepot—in sequence #21, "Oswald who?" (February 10–March 10, 1946).

Batman Returns was supported by a comic adaptation and prestige one-shots. *Batman: Catwoman Defiant*, by writer Peter Milligan and artists Tom Grindberg and Dick Giordano, sported a gold prismatic foil cover logo and *Batman: Penguin Triumphant* (John Ostrander, Joe Staton, and Bob Smith) similarly had one in silver. Although stand-alone stories, Brian Stelfreeze's covers form a single composite image.

Michelle Pfeiffer's portrayal of Selina Kyle became a symbol of female empowerment to many feminist critics and historians.

emperor penguins left behind when an Arctic-themed zoo closed. It would be 33 years before he surfaced again in Gotham City.

Paul Reuben and Diane Salinger from Burton's breakout film *Pee-Wee's Big Adventure* (1985) played atrociously snobbish, abusive parents Tucker and Esther Cobblepot. Reuben was a last-moment choice, inheriting the role originally offered to Burgess Meredith before he fell ill.

Bruce Wayne has settled into being Batman's mask and civilian appendage, waiting for the Bat-Signal to recall him into action, but he also fights for Gotham City in his civilian guise. However, after clashing with unscrupulous financier and faux philanthropist Max Shreck over an unnecessary power plant project, Wayne becomes increasingly distracted by the vulnerable, wounded charm of the retail tycoon's mousy personal assistant, Selina Kyle.

As Shreck attends his annual civic Christmas celebration, the event is overrun by outlaw circus performers the Red Triangle Gang. Abducted and taken below ground to meet their boss, he meets true evil face to face.

Oswald wants to reenter civilized society and as king of the sewers he's got evidence of all the dirty crimes Shreck believed shredded and flushed away. Embracing the unavoidable, Max arranges kidnapping the Mayor's baby and has bestial, birdlike Oswald publicly rescue the innocent. Feted by rich and poor alike, malformed orphan The Penguin only desires human contact—and access to all the city's records. Oswald says his dream is to find the parents who discarded him, but he has another, darker motive ... identifying the firstborn sons of Gotham City.

Reimagining a suave conman as an avian monstrosity came from Burton's animation training. Using his sketches, special Penguin makeup effects Stan Winston (*Aliens*, *Terminator 2*) devised Danny DeVito's astonishing daily transformations. He and his team also augmented animal actors with animatronic flightless birds to wear the more eccentric and dangerous weaponry envisioned by Burton and Waters.

The script called for modifications requiring true artifice, supplemented by early CGI from Boss Film Studio. Designs for flamethrowers were pragmatically replaced by nondetonating rocket launchers. Mechanical effects designers Richard Landon and Craig Caton-Largent supervised animatronics construction, requiring—per bird—over 200 moving parts to control head, neck, eyes, beaks, and wings.

Animal trainer Gary Gero wrangled flesh and blood waterfowl who lived like kings. In daily 100-degree heat, they enjoyed chilled sets, temperature-controlled trailers, swimming pool, tons of ice, and fish fresh from the docks every day. Sets were also chilled (to between 30–45 degrees). DeVito—who stayed in character as much as possible—found his heavy padded costumes came in very handy at those times. Cold sets also maintained the snow and ice of Gotham City at Christmas but took around three days to get down to target operating temperatures. As supervising art director Tom Duffield said in *The Making of Batman Returns* CBS special, "It worked as long as they kept the stage doors closed."

BIRDS OF A FEATHER

When Selina discovers her boss's project is a scam, he throws her out of his office window. Somehow, she survives—or is resurrected by alley cats. Gripped by long-suppressed anger and frustration, she wrecks all the trappings of her old life, cutting together a new

With Batman costumier Bob Ringwood supervising, co-costume designer Mary Vogt (*Looney Tunes: Back in Action*, *Men in Black I–III*) created her stitches and latex look, stating: "One thing about the black rubber, it almost looks liquid on the body."

look from rejected scraps and reinventing herself as a wild cat. Returning to work as if nothing happened, she toys with her horrified murderer like a cat with its prey.

Making the best of a bad deal, Max sponsors The Penguin's run for Mayor, hoping to quash opposition to his power plant by using the Red Triangle Gang to foment chaos and discredit the authorities. Batman tackles the thugs on the street and investigates them and Oswald. He finds links to child abductions across America. Meanwhile, his romantic interests are piqued by a strangely more vibrant and enticing Selina Kyle.

Almost killed by a wild, whip-wielding Catwoman prowling the rooftops and alleys, the hero's trials and tragedy mounts after she joins with Oswald. The wily bird frames Batman for murder at Shreck's grand Christmas tree lighting—a callous act severing the alliance. Terrible at dealing with rejection, The Penguin seemingly kills the Cat, too. Their clash also sparks a catastrophic battle in the streets as the Batmobile is telemetrically hijacked by The Penguin. In retaliation, Batman releases recordings of The Penguin's sick ranting about ordinary people and ends his bid for political power.

Pfeiffer beat many others for the role after original pick Annette Bening became pregnant. She trained for three months with whip trainer/choreographer Anthony DeLongis and did her own stunts. She nailed the scene where Catwoman decapitates four shop dummies in one take, prompting DeLongis to say in *The Making of Batman Returns* CBS special, "She is doing things with the whip that will make Indiana Jones green."

Deciphering the psychological drives of each participant, Burton summed up the movie's contribution: "Doctors have spent years trying to analyze all these characters. We'll do the best we can in two hours."

Pfeiffer constantly amazed the cast and crew by improvising wild acts for her character— such as popping the live caged songbird into her mouth during this off-the-wall "bedroom" scene.

Animal trainer Gary Gero schooled the bird actors to hit their camera marks with a whistle, explaining: "When they get to where they're going, they each get a fish."

Visually impressive and utterly unphased by on-screen dramatics, tame king penguins were flown in from a bird sanctuary in the Cotswolds, England.

Film historians regard *Batman Returns* as the centerpiece of Burton's "Unofficial Christmas Trilogy" between *Edward Scissorhands* and *The Nightmare Before Christmas*.

Even overwhelming and potentially lethal mutual attraction cannot make Batman and Catwoman let go of the traumas that made them.

At Max Shreck's Christmas Ball—which featured Siouxsie & the Banshees' "Face to Face," a song co-written by the Banshees and Danny Elfman—Selina tries to kill Max, but she and Bruce deduce each other's secrets. Their dilemma is forestalled when The Penguin attacks, having reverted to his original plan—destroying all firstborn sons of the city who got to live normal lives with real parents. He wants Shreck's heir Chip, but settles for Max instead, dragging him into his bird-infested underworld as the Red Triangles attack and a legion of radio-controlled, war-modified penguins unleashes a storm of missiles on all the city's children.

CAREFUL WHAT YOU WISH FOR

Faithful Alfred counters the command signal from the Batcave while Batman defeats the circus killers, before using his Bat-skimmer to breach The Penguin's lair. Catwoman is already there to kill Shreck and the bird beast who also took one of her nine lives. Unmasked in the battle that ensues and which claims

After realizing *Beetlejuice* and *Edward Scissorhands* for Burton, production designer Bo Welch (*The Lost Boys, Ghostbusters II*) redesigned Gotham City with the appearance of a chilling hell inside a snowglobe.

Even at the height of his Max Shreck-bought prestige and power, The Penguin remained a bestial monster inside and out.

Oswald's life, Bruce begs Selina to stop but in vain. After electrocuting Max—at the cost of four more lives—she flees as the returning penguins reclaim and despatch their former leader. As Alfred drives his battered charge home, a Bat-Signal lights up the sky and in an alley Catwoman stares up at it. That last shot was inserted after filming at the express wishes of Warner studio executives. It took three days to complete using a stand-in and animatronics, as Pfeiffer had moved on to her next project. Clearly, someone intended there would be more Catwoman to come.

Burton's signature dark whimsy and affection for the grotesque was fully unleashed in a film that was a huge midsummer hit. Autonomy bought his participation and resulted in a much more potent and personal movie, but also generated some controversy. A protest campaign from disgruntled parents who didn't realize that, despite its PG-13 rating, *Batman Returns* was not intended for kids, resulted in Joel Schumacher taking over the directorial reins for the next adventure. Nevertheless, Burton's masterpiece underpins the tone informing almost every modern superhero blockbuster, and in recent years, Michael Keaton's Batman was revived in the DCEU to play a key role in *The Flash* (2023).

Animal crackers

Despite initial popularity and acclaim, *Batman Returns* was overshadowed by its predecessor. However, in the light of subsequent Batman film franchises, the movie has been reevaluated by later generations and is now regarded by many fans and critics as perhaps the best Batman film of all.

That reassessment has sparked others to continue to expand the universe and characters as well as tap into that fan energy with new print projects. In 2022, DC released miniseries *Batman '89* with scriptwriter Sam Hamm at last concluding his long-deferred tale of Harvey Dent descending into Two-Face and the debut of Robin in a tense tale illustrated by Joe Quinones. The same year, Ivan Cohen crafted a seasonal tome celebrating the 30th anniversary in *Batman Returns: One Dark Christmas Eve*, and the Red Triangle Gang joined official comic book continuity the same year in *Robin* Volume 3, #15 (August 2022). Danny DeVito even wrote a skewed yarn of his landmark character for *Gotham City Villains Anniversary Giant* (January 2022). "Bird Cat Love" reveals how his slinky rival finally falls for him and how together they cure the COVID-19 pandemic.

BATMAN FOREVER

Release date: June 9, 1995 (Mann Village Theater LA), June 16, 1995 (US)
Starring roles: Val Kilmer, Tommy Lee Jones, Jim Carrey, Nicole Kidman, Chris O'Donnell, Michael Gough, Pat Hingle
Director: Joel Schumacher

Screenplay: Lee Batchler, Janet Scott-Batchler, Akiva Goldsman
Cinematography: Stephen Goldblatt
Music: Elliot Goldenthal
Running time: 122 minutes
Box office: $336.6 million

After Batman and Batman Returns categorically proved adults loved superhero movies, Warner Bros. felt it was time to officially open up the franchise to younger viewers. After stoking expectations over two movies, Two-Face (Tommy Lee Jones) finally debuted, but without Tim Burton directing, his plans for the compulsive coin-tossing psychopath went unrealized. Billy Dee Williams—who played Harvey Dent in prior Burton movies on the understanding he would ultimately be the District Attorney-turned-villain, was bought out of his contract when new director Joel Schumacher (*St. Elmo's Fire, Falling Down*) opted to explore Two-Face's manic rather than tragic side, introducing a far more crazed incarnation of the character.

RIDDLE ME THIS

Cinemagoers' attention was instead gripped by scene-stealing Edward Nygma a.k.a. The Riddler (Jim Carrey) who—his intellect augmented by brain-theft and an utter lack of scruples—was the true threat to Gotham City's guardian. Carrey co-designed many of The Riddler's outfits, but left crafting crime conundrums and killer clues to Will Shortz, the "puzzlemaster" on National Public Radio and editor of the *New York Times* crossword.

Prior to Schumacher signing on, The Riddler was to be the sole villain, until the director decided to resolve the hanging Two-Face plot thread. The disfigured, maniacal villain consequently brought Robin (Chris O'Donnell) into the franchise by murdering Dick Grayson's parents, the Flying Graysons. The brutal act moved Bruce Wayne, played by Val Kilmer, who replaced Michael Keaton in the dual lead role, to take the orphan acrobat under his wing.

Unlike Burton—who remained as producer for the third Bat-movie—Schumacher was a fan of the original comics, particularly the surreal noir settings, architectural landscapes, and mega-machinery of artist Dick Sprang. He had hoped to delve deep into the hero's psyche by adapting Frank Miller's epochal origin retelling *Batman: Year One* before bowing to studio pressure to make a fun, action-packed, "toyetic" movie.

However, Schumacher did populate his film with wildly anarchic streets, vertiginously tall buildings, and colossal Baroque public statuary. Award-winning production designer Barbara Ling (*The Doors, Falling Down*) crafted an outlandish urban milieu based on comics, 1930s New York City architecture, and modern Tokyo.

KILLER LOOKS

Detailed designs fell to set designer/visual effects model maker Kenneth A. Larson (*Batman Returns, Batman and Robin*), while special makeup designer/creator Rick Baker and his Cinovation Studios team returned to handle the many different appearances required to fulfill Schumacher's vision. Contrasts between opulent public spaces and underworld dystopias also needed chief set designer Elise "Cricket" Rowland (*Falling Down*) plus art directors Christopher Burian-Mohr (*Cowboys and Aliens*) and Joseph P. Lucky (*Terminator II: Judgment Day*) to complete. The overall look invoked biomechanical extravagance inspired by Swiss surrealist painter H. R. Giger (who had revolutionized cinema with his designs for *Alien* in 1979). That influence was most recognizably seen in the design of a new Batmobile and other vehicles.

The "Gigeresque" motif inspired set illustrator Tim Flattery to create two "biomechanical" supercars. The Batmobile's Chevy 350 ZZ3 high-performance engine, aluminum heads, and angled plugs delivered 350 horsepower inside a carbon fiber/epoxy fiberglass laminate shell. As a result, the vehicles were always piloted by trained stunt drivers—except when Chris O'Donnell insisted that he take the wheel for a joyride scene sparked by Dick Grayson rebelling against Bruce Wayne's efforts to deter him from killing Two-Face. O'Donnell crashed the wonder car into a curb and dented a fender.

"Was that over the top? I can never tell."
The Riddler

Attempting to convince orphan Dick Grayson to stay, Bruce shows him the Wayne auto collection. All vehicles are classic or vintage, with nothing built after the deaths of his own parents.

Batman Forever brought together four of the biggest stars of the decade, with Nicole Kidman playing criminal psychologist Chase Meridian, alongside Val Kilmer's Batman, Jim Carrey's The Riddler, and Tommy Lee Jones's Two-Face.

Giger's organic art motif echoed throughout the film, influencing a heightened anatomical appearance for Batman and Robin's costumes. Designed by Ingrid Ferrin (*The Client*) and Bob Ringwood (*Batman*, *Batman Returns*), these were looser and less constricting, allowing more athletic and lengthier fight sequences and recalling the frantic, extended choreography of Batman's television series. Produced in quantity (more than 100 each for senior and apprentice hero), the outfits were customized for specific stunts. Despite all modifications, though, Val Kilmer's primary Batsuit weighed so much, he lost 5 pounds (2.3 kg) just filming the opening fight scene.

The new direction came at a cost. Michael Keaton declined to play a lighter Batman and Leonardo DiCaprio passed on being Robin for much the same reason. The story went through many permutations before husband-and-wife screenwriting duo Lee and Janet Scott-Batchler delivered a script later revised by Akiva Goldsman.

Chris O'Donnell was first seen in *Batman Forever* as a circus acrobat wearing a fabric facsimile of Robin's 1940 comic book costume, now stored in the Batcave.

New Batman, fresh car, restyled lair. Val Kilmer was in a real bat cave in the Kalahari Desert in southern Africa researching a new role for a future film when he was offered the part.

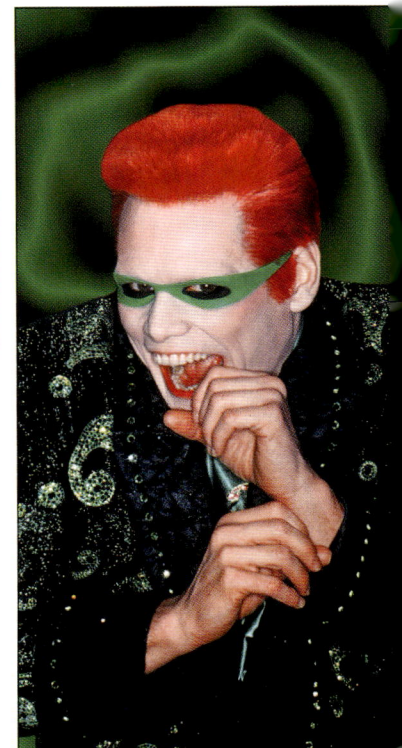

Jones only joined the movie because Two-Face was his son's favorite comic character, whereas Carrey was a huge fan of The Riddler.

Principal photography began on September 24, 1994, at Warner Bros.' Burbank soundstages and wrapped on March 5, 1995. Schumacher's desired look was accomplished via the artistry of cinematographer Stephen Goldblatt, who deployed his signature high-saturation symbolic color palette. Location work was shot at Alcatraz Island (doubling for Riddler's Claw Island fortress); the RMS *Queen Mary*; Figeroa Street, Los Angeles; and the US Customs House in New York City.

FAMILY-FRIENDLY

John Dykstra, Andrew Adamson, and Jim Rygiel were visual effects supervisors on a movie that was highly dependent on new CGI technology—supplied by Data Pacific Images, Acclaim Entertainment, and other third-party vendors—but traditional skills still dominated. Baker's first designs for Two-Face—featuring a bulging eyeball and exposed teeth on the scarred left side—were swiftly vetoed by studio execs, and a milder cosmetic construction was created. It took four hours every day to apply to Tommy Lee Jones before shooting could start.

In pursuit of commercially rewarding cross-marketing, the studio urged a more family-friendly venture to support maximized merchandising. Over 120 products were licensed, with Warner Bros. exerting greater oversight and control. Tie-in products included Kenner action figures, model vehicles, toys, games, clothing, cards, coins, jewelry, snack foods, and more. Crucially, conflating twin successes, much of the merchandise was designed not in the film's style but rather that of the hugely popular television series *Batman: The Animated Series*, which had been keeping Batman and Robin alive in the minds of kids, parents, and comics fans since 1992.

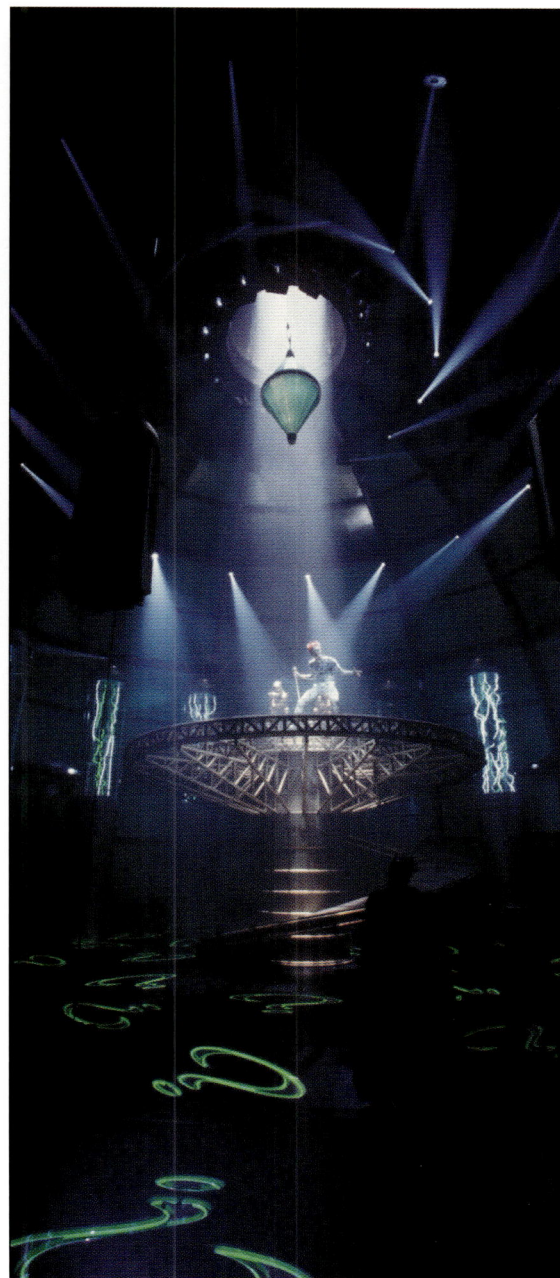

Far left: Producer Peter MacGregor Scott had 146 workers making over 100 costumes each for the heroes, customized for specific stunt functions like acrobatic combat, fire-fighting, or underwater filming.

It was the 100-pound (45-kg) primary Batsuit that made Val Kilmer understand the true, anonymous nature of the Dark Knight as a symbol in which others can see themselves, as he explained to the *New York Times* (May, 2020): "That's why it's so easy to have five or six Batmans. It's not about Batman. There is no Batman."

To comply with the studio's wishes, lifelong Batman fan Schumacher carefully, consciously, and conspicuously referenced not just comic books but also iconic moments from the 1966 *Batman* movie and television series. As well as upgrades to that film's Batboat, Batbike, and Batcopter—in the form of an awesome Batwing/Batsub designed by Matt Codd (*Men in Black*, *Shazam! Fury of the Gods*)—sly touches saw Batman punching thugs through drums, trapped on a sea buoy, and even driving the Batmobile up a building. The latter was a blistering upgrade of the Dynamic Duo's signature trick of climbing Batropes up walls every week in the classic TV show, often meeting a guest star of the week along the way. At one stage, Robin even exclaims "Holey Rusted Metal, Batman" in a verbal gag about the island fortress they are invading.

A product of constant change, compromise, and refinement, Joel Schumacher's stylish first Batman movie became the sixth-highest-grossing film of 1995.

Left: Originally using costume and posture to depict The Riddler, Carrey required Rick Baker's prosthetics and makeup for the climactic scenes on Claw Island as his stolen brainpower increasingly warped his skull and his mind.

Batman: The Animated Series

Despite an earnest quest for adult acceptance, the classic tone of Bob Kane and Bill Finger's noir-inspired Batman has never been better channeled than in a cartoon series for kids. Developed by Bruce Timm and Eric Radomski—with co-producers/head writers Paul Dini and Alan Burnett—three seasons of *Batman: The Animated Series* were made by Warner Bros. Animation and broadcast on Fox Kids (109 22-minute episodes spanning 1992–1995). In 1997, rebooted as *The New Batman Adventures*, a further 24 tales aired on Kids' WB (September 1997–January 1999), launching a DC Animated Universe of spin-off series including *Superman Adventures* (1996–1998) and *Justice League/Justice League Unlimited* (2001–2006), eight cinematic

releases beginning with *Batman: Mask of the Phantasm* (1993), video games toys, digital serials, and a host of comic book series. The groundbreaking, multi-award-winning series captivated young and old alike, breathing vibrant new life into a vintage concept. Adopting Tim Burton's iconic scenarios of Gotham City—and Danny Elfman's unforgettable theme music—the results shook up the public's image of the Dark Knight and fed new life back into print and filmic iterations.

Employing a mood-evoking visual style dubbed "Dark Deco," the show mixed elements from all Batman eras without diluting the power, tone, or mood of the premise, reinventing classic villains like The Joker and Man-Bat, creating new stars like Harley Quinn, and resurrecting forgotten foes like the Mad Hatter and Mr. Freeze.

BATMAN AND ROBIN

Release date: June 12, 1997 (Los Angeles), June 20, 1997 (US)
Starring roles: Arnold Schwarzenegger, George Clooney, Chris O'Donnell, Uma Thurman, Alicia Silverstone, Michael Gough, Pat Hingle, Elle McPherson

Director: Joel Schumacher
Screenplay: Akiva Goldsman
Cinematography: Stephen Goldblatt
Music: Elliot Goldenthal
Running time: 122 minutes
Box office: $238 million

After *Batman Forever,* Warner Bros. fast-tracked another film stressing child-accessible, toy-friendly action. While working on *A Time to Kill* (1996), director Schumacher and writer Akiva Goldsman devised a story of tragedy, revenge, ecoterrorism, and world-ending peril, packed with iconic, highly visual comic book villains and the birth of a new hero.

CASTING CHOICES

When Val Kilmer declined to return, many possible replacements soon narrowed to TV sensation George Clooney. Schumacher said in *E! Online,* that Clooney "brought real humanity and humor to the piece, an accessibility that I don't think anybody else has been able to offer." Michael Gough reprised his role as Alfred—albeit adding drama as his character secretly surrendered to a fatal medical condition—and Chris O'Donnell returned as Dick Grayson/Robin.

"Tonight, Hell freezes over!"

Mr. Freeze

Alicia Silverstone was the only choice for Batgirl. She played Barbara Wilson, the niece of Alfred, rather than Barbara Gordon, the original incarnation. Alicia's on-screen time was drastically edited after unwarranted media comments about her weight, prompting a spirited defense from Schumacher. In truth, the costumes were very unforgiving. Made from a new variety of foam rubber and largely based on Kilmer's third-act outfit in *Batman Forever,* the suits were lighter, but fragile and easily torn. Clooney and his doubles went through 50 suits, and he needed one further modified after injuring his leg playing basketball, with one boot cut off and replaced with a cast while filming the ice rocket scenes.

GREEN WITH ENVY

Poison Ivy was originally scheduled for *Batman Forever* with Nicole Kidman in the role, but the character was cut due to an abundance of villains already in play. Transferring to Schumacher's sequel, Ivy was portrayed by Uma Thurman—

Uma Thurman landed the much-coveted role of Poison Ivy, in part because Schumacher believed she was, at the time, convincingly seductive as "the most beautiful woman in the world."

In an example of the movie's close relationship with merchandisers, Mr. Freeze's lethal ice-blaster was designed by a toy manufacturer.

who beat Demi Moore, Sharon Stone, and Julia Roberts to the part thanks to an ethereal performance as Venus in Terry Gilliam's *The Adventures of Baron Münchhausen* (1988).

Created by writer Robert Kanigher and artist Sheldon Moldoff, the seductive, floral-themed felon Poison Ivy debuted in *Batman* #181 (June 1966), before eventually evolving into a plant/human hybrid at war with humanity. On screen, her ever-evolving look and outfits represent a plant's life cycle through a year. Her murderous, overmuscled minion, Bane, was conceived by Chuck Dixon, Doug Moench, and Graham Nolan as Batman's nemesis for comic book publishing event "Knightfall"—beginning in *Batman: Vengeance of Bane* #1 (January 1993). Here, professional wrestler/actor Jeep Swenson fills his mask and boots.

The other major villain that made his live-action debut in Batman and Robin was Mr. Freeze. Devised by writer Dave Wood and Moldoff, the character started life as the chilly criminal Mr. Zero in *Batman* #121 (February 1959)—his only appearance until

Robin's on-screen acrobatics benefitted from gold-medal-winning Olympic gymnast Mitchell Gaylord as a stunt double, while Brad Martin, who doubled for O'Donnell in *Batman Forever*, returned as Clooney's stuntman in *Batman and Robin*, and stunt coordinator Alex Field taught Alicia Silverstone to ride her Batbike with confidence and flair.

German entertainment/automotive product designer Harald Belker conceived and oversaw construction of the first single-seater Batmobile.

George Clooney's primary Batman outfit was mostly rubber: a 50-pound (22.6-kg) bodysuit attached to a 40-pound (18-kg) cape and headpiece. The Robin and Batgirl costumes each weighed 50-pound (22.6-kg).

Batgirls on page and screen

The *Batman* television show ended in March 1968, having triggered a huge shakeup in comic books, most notably the emergence of a whole new Caped Crusader—memorably played by Yvonne Craig *(left)*—who would become an integral part of DC's universe. Daughter of the Police Commissioner, Barbara Gordon was introduced in "The Million Dollar Debut of Batgirl" (*Detective Comics* #359, January 1967) by writer Gardner Fox and artists Carmine Infantino and Sid Greene. She was, in fact, the second Bat-Girl, replacing teenager Betty Kane (niece of the 1950s Batwoman), who was first seen in *Batman* #359 (April 1961), created by writer Bob Finger and illustrator Sheldon Moldoff.

Barbara Gordon became a mainstay of comics and animation both as Batgirl and Oracle—even occasionally stepping from the shadows to the spotlight. Batgirl has featured in every Batman animated series since 1968's *The Batman/Superman Hour,* including *The New Adventures of Batman* (1977), *Batman: The Animated Series* (1992), *The New Batman Adventures* (1997), *Batman Beyond* (1999), *The Batman* (2004), *Batman: The Brave and the Bold* (2008), *Young Justice* (2010), *The Lego Batman Movie* (2017), and adult animated series *Harley Quinn* (2019).

In live action on TV—and frequently wearing Alicia Silverstone's remodeled costume from *Batman and Robin*—Dina Meyer was paraplegic hero handler Barbara Gordon/Oracle as well as Batgirl in *Birds of Prey* (2002). The character of Oracle also appears in *Titans* (2018) from season 3, played by Savannah Welch. Finally, a very young Barbara Gordon makes a brief appearance in the Batman prequel series *Gotham* (2014) as a newborn baby.

screenwriter Max Hodge revamped him for the 1960s *Batman* television show. He was revived as Mr. Freeze in *Detective Comics* #373 (March 1968) and revised by Paul Dini and Bruce Timm in *Batman: The Animated Series* episode "Heart of Ice" (September 7, 1992), who recast him as a scientist who made himself a freak in a desperate effort to save his dying wife. It was a version that would stick, and profoundly informed Schumacher and Goldsman's take on him. Subsequently, Freeze would star in DCAU feature film *Batman and Mr. Freeze: SubZero*, originally commissioned to tie in with *Batman and Robin* but delayed until 1998.

COOL OPERATORS

Stars considered for the key role included Christopher Lloyd, Ed Harris, and Sylvester Stallone, but Schumacher set his sights on Arnold Schwarzenegger, as Mr. Freeze should be "big and strong like he was chiseled out of a glacier." The *Terminator* star had no qualms about comic book movies. He had been offered the Hulk, played Conan the Barbarian twice, was linked to an unproduced Sgt. Rock feature, auditioned for *Superman* in 1977 and *Batman* in 1988, and was Schumacher's pick for Dr. Manhattan in Terry Gilliam's unfinished 1980s *Watchmen* film. Moreover, Schwarzenegger wanted to work with Schumacher.

Despite being paid Hollywood's largest fee ever at the time, he arguably earned every cent. Diagnosed with cardiac problems prior to signing, Schwarzenegger underwent preemptive open-heart surgery so insurers would clear him to work on an action movie. He then filmed for six weeks, and his stunt and body doubles were on set more often than he was.

Mr. Freeze's exo-suit was constructed by British armorer Terry English (*Excalibur, Aliens*) at a cost of $1.5 million. It weighed 75 pounds (34 kg), and was fitted with contact lenses; acrylic paint; and toxic, flammable substances—especially prosthetics and LED lights in the mouth cavity, face, and helmet. Donning it halved Schwarzenegger's working day, taking a team

Far left: Joel Schumacher was a lifelong Batman fan who used his passion for the characters and early training as a fashion designer and store window dresser to deliver a visually compelling, family–friendly feature film.

Left: Mr. Freeze's Ice-Truck was designed by vehicular concept illustrator Jacques Rey, who had contributed the Bat–skiboat and Bat-Missile to *Batman Returns*.

of 11 wardrobe and makeup technicians six hours to fit. They also fed and massaged the actor to keep his muscles limber.

Schwarzenegger also retained his own makeup artist, Jeff Dawn, who had led the actor's makeup teams on 19 films. Dawn told *Entertainment Weekly* in 1997, "When you put [LED lights] in Arnold's mouth, (his) saliva would creep into the seams and the batteries would immediately start disintegrating and start (leaking) battery acid into Arnold's mouth." Dress and makeup were applied by computer designer Michael Key, who finished Freeze's look in postproduction. Due to on-set noise and the muffling effect of the headgear, lead dialogue mixer Donald O. Mitchell had to loop almost 95 percent of the film. The sound technician also pitch-shifted Batman's voice—adding depth and resonance to differentiate the hero from his civilian self.

GOTHAM CITY ON ICE

Filmed primarily at Warner Bros. Burbank Studios, with locations work in Vienna, Montreal, Quebec, Ottawa, and Ontario—and with Greystone Manor, Beverly Hills, doubling for Bruce Wayne's ancestral home—principal photography ran September 12, 1996, to late January 1997. Despite delays, Schumacher actually finished two weeks early, scheduling the shoot to enable Clooney to fulfil ongoing commitments to the hit medical drama *ER*. The actor regularly delighted his small-screen co-stars by visiting the hospital sets in full Bat-costume.

Despite increasing dependence on CGI—led by digital effects supervisors John Dykstra and Andrew Adamson, with the help of third-party vendors Rhythm and Hues and Pacific Data Imaging—a majority of the 450 individual FX sequences were handled physically. Miniatures and full-scale sets were built, and many substances were tested to create Gotham City on ice before settling on a fiber resin mix. According to production designer Barbara Ling, the ice effects alone took six months to perfect. Motion-capture techniques allowed stunt double specialists— such as ice-skaters, sky-surfers, acrobats, drivers, and more— to seamlessly transfer their unique skills to the on-screen actors.

Domestically and internationally, *Batman and Robin* was Warner Bros.' top-grossing film of 1997, but changing tastes and Hollywood reshuffles made it the last Dark Knight outing for almost a decade.

Arnold Schwarzenegger considered Victor Fries to be inherently good, a characterization that is reinforced by the fact that, to date, Mr. Freeze is the only filmic Bat-villain to repent.

STEEL

Release date: August 15, 1997
Starring roles: Shaquille O'Neal, Annabeth Gish, Judd Nelson, Richard Roundtree, Charles Napier, Irma P. Hall, Ray J
Director: Kenneth Johnson

Screenplay: Kenneth Johnson
Cinematography: Mark Irwin
Music: Mervyn Warren
Running time: 97 minutes
Box office: $1.7 million

Sometimes all it takes for a movie to happen is the right fan. The sparks igniting *Steel* were music producer Quincy Jones and writer/producer David Salzman. Both were huge fans of the DC comic character created for "The Death of Superman" publishing event as one of four potential Superman replacements. Jones and Salzman also wanted to see heroes and role models for children of minorities—especially in blighted inner cities. They had previously approached sports legend/occasional actor Shaquille O'Neal to play DC/Milestone's Hardware, but the athlete told them he found Steel more personally relatable.

FIREPOWER

Speaking about kids he saw, Jones said, "Their perspective on the future has changed for the worse, and I hate seeing young people who don't believe in the future. Steel—and I don't want to use the word 'superhero' because he doesn't fly or anything like that—represents a role model. Let's just call him a 'super human being.'"

In 1993, DC had shaken the world by killing the Super Hero who started it all. In an epic spanning all Superman titles, Doomsday savagely rampaged across America and was only stopped by Superman, who died in the process. As Earth adjusted to a "World Without a Superman," rumors circulated that—just like Elvis—the Man of Steel was not dead. Soon, four very different individuals appeared, saving lives as only the departed defender could.

TIME TO SHINE

Steel made his debut in *Man of Steel* #22 (June 1993), written by Louise Simonson and illustrated by Jon Bogdanove and Denis Janke, which explained how bereaved construction worker "Henry Johnson" felt compelled to carry on Superman's mission. He had once been saved by Superman and now—revealing technical and engineering genius unsuspected by all who knew him—built a suit of armor to facilitate his crusade. He also reclaimed his real identity as weapons designer Dr. John Henry Irons. Steel found further impetus after super-guns he had designed in his previous life were wantonly used by Metropolis street gangs. To sooth his conscience after a kid was killed in crossfire, Irons began cleaning up the streets and searching for whoever sold the so-called "toastmasters" to petty criminals.

"I laugh at danger."
Sparks

That scenario informed the *Steel* screenplay by television writer/director Kenneth Johnson (*The Six Million Dollar Man*, *Alien Nation*) in his third theatrical feature following *Short Circuit 2*, another science-fiction exploration of contemporary future shock and tech gone amok.

Culturally, the time was also ripe for change. Two decades previously, cinematic diversity had taken a huge leap forward after Blaxploitation films appeared in mainstream movie houses, popularizing heroes like *Shaft* and *Foxy Brown*. The 1990s greeted another wave of important films, such as *Boyz n the Hood* and *Menace II Society*, addressing Black consciousness and achievement, radically resetting the playing field.

Director Johnson modeled the role of engineer, tech assistant, and computer researcher "Sparky" (Annabeth Gish) on another groundbreaking DC character—Barbara Gordon as paraplegic crimebuster Oracle, as seen in *Birds of Prey*.

The cinematic Steel was formally disassociated from Superman, but Shaquille O'Neal's "S-Shield" tattoo had to remain a part of his on-screen look.

Prior to his first leading dramatic role, sports icon O'Neal was no stranger to the screen, having appeared in *Blue Chips* (1994), *Kazaam* and *Space Jam* (both 1996), and *Good Burger* (1997), as well as music videos and TV shows.

Wesley Snipes (*New Jack City, Passenger 57*) was Johnson's preferred choice for Steel, but Warner Bros. wanted O'Neal because he was better known to the American public.

Judd Nelson, who played the villain Nathaniel Burke, went from being cute and charming as one of the original "Bratpack" in *The Breakfast Club* to deadly in edgy crime dramas like *New Jack City*.

Johnson dialed back the comic's fantasy elements, divorcing his star from Superman links, feeling *Steel* should not be overshadowed or prejudged against the Man of Steel's reputation. Instead, he focused on modern gangster movies, resulting in a stripped-down street warrior, echoing the director's previous technologically augmented but plausible troubleshooters *The Six Million Dollar Man* and *Bionic Woman*.

In pursuit of veracity and integrity, Johnson took his screenplay to South Central Los Angeles, asking local kids if the language and settings were believable. Once actress/scenic painter Sharon Compton (*Battle Beyond the Stars*) storyboarded the results, art director Gershon Ginsburg (*The Abyss, S.W.A.T.*) and production designer Gary Wissner (*Seven, The Abyss*) reconstructed distressed yet vibrant inner-city environments.

MACHINE LEARNING

The late 1990s was an age of technical fetishism—cars, guns, fashions, fancy rigs, and shiny gear all evoked potent audience responses that still resonate today. If it looked cool and precision-tooled, or made expressive sounds—like a pistol being cocked or a mechanized mallet powering up—cinemagoers enthused and wanted one, too. Costume designer Catherine Adair (*Babylon 5, The Man in the High Castle*), who worked with Johnson on *Alien Nation*, dressed the characters, but costume specialist Linda Benavente-Notaro (*Hook, Interstellar*) crafted Steel's urban-paladin look. Johnson rejected the impractical red cape, describing Steel as a "blue-collar Batman" and devising grounded contemporary threats to challenge him.

Filming took 51 days—32 of them at night in downtown LA—and was complicated by the sports star's commitment to the 1996 Summer Olympics. "Shaq" had one full readthrough before leaving to train for the Olympics in Hawaii. While competing, he worked with acting coach Ben Martin and returned to the film production word-perfect on the script but with only five weeks to shoot his scenes.

On screen, armaments designer John Henry Irons resigns his Army commission after a scandal. During a live weapons test, his immediate superior Nathaniel Burke (Judd Nelson) seeks to impress visiting politicians by boosting Irons's laser and sonic cannons beyond safety tolerances. The resulting catastrophe destroys the test site, killing many and crippling Irons's friend and assistant Susan "Sparky" Sparks (Annabeth Gish). An inquiry sees Burke dishonorably discharged but not imprisoned, and Irons quits in disgust. He is unaware that Burke has stolen the specs for everything he'd invented.

Home with his formidable Grandma Odessa (Irma P. Hall) and impressionable nephew Martin (Ray J), Irons has no idea that the disgraced Burke is nearby, mass-producing superguns for local thugs and using criminals to demonstrate his wares.

Readjusting to civilian life and coasting, Irons is shaken from inactivity after seeing young gangsters rob a bank with his tech. Failing to stop them and tormented by the realization that his ideas are harming innocents, Irons tracks down Sparky, saving her from her own slow slide to oblivion in a veterans' hospital. Equally gripped by renewed purpose, they remodel a junkyard owned by John Henry's mysterious Uncle Joe (Richard Roundtree) into a forge, foundry, and lair, where they transform Irons into a modern-day knight.

Far left: Working-class hero Irons bluffs his way in before having to blast his way out of Burke's supergun sale of the century.

Left: Charismatic Richard Roundtree (*Shaft*) had a scene-stealing supporting role, adding humor and mystery to the action-packed proceedings.

Armed, armored, and mounted on a motorbike, "Steel" patrols the streets hunting the guns, the gangs, and ultimately Burke, while the cops chase him. As he closes in, the unmistakable oversized vigilante is arrested just as Burke makes his move. Betraying his sponsor, Burke starts to sell off his inventory in a global internet bidding war. By the time Irons is free, all that's possible is a last-ditch assault on Burke's base. Triumphing more by luck than valor, Steel and co. escape when Burke accidentally kills himself and his arsenal explodes. Later, Irons and Sparky look toward a safer future, building positive technologies like "walking wheelchairs" for paraplegics.

Released in the US on August 15, 1997, *Steel* failed to find a large audience and was generally considered to be an efficient, if by-the-numbers action thriller. Comics fans saw the movie as a noncontinuity endeavor like *Catwoman* and *Constantine*, set in its own reality. However, John Henry Irons recently returned to active duty as Steel on The CW's television hit *Superman and Lois* (2021–2024).

Left: At 7 feet 1 inch (2 m 16 cm), O'Neal was so tall and well built that no body double could be found. Consequently, he did all his own stunts, and even contributed to the movie's soundtrack, alongside rappers KRS-One, Ice Cube, B-Real, and Peter Gunz.

Locked and loaded

As a supreme technologist specializing in ballistics, the comic book iteration of John Henry Irons is a master designer who constantly upgraded his suit and weapons, and ultimately even his own biology. However, on his debut, his personal armory was restricted to portable offensive and defensive capabilities, beginning with a full-body carapace and helmet, with a symbolic and decorative red cape, a copy of Superman's "S" shield, and rocket boots. The boots were capable of speeds in excess of 700 miles per hour (1,127 kph) and a range of 1,500 miles (2,414 km) before refueling.

Impact and temperature resistant, strength-enhancing, and airtight, Steel's armor carried sensors, antivirus software, and an inertial damping field, with his main weapon being wrist-mounted cannons that fired devastating

red-hot rivets as befitted his blue-collar origins. For heavy assault, Steel carried a Kinetic Hammer, the impact force of which increased the further it traveled. At 20 yards, it can stop a car; at 60, a tank. Beyond that, it hits with power equivalent to an angry Kryptonian.

By comparison, the movie hero is far less powerful. Although the body armor has full radiophonic connection to Sparky at base, amplifies Steel's strength, and can offset small arms fire and blades and reflect lasers, it leaves his lower face exposed. His hammer employs electromagnetic waves and functions as a bludgeon and rifle. It also houses a laser projector, sonic cannon, and pump-action tear gas grenade launcher. Crucially, he doesn't fly, as a customized motorcycle replaces his comic counterpart's rocket boots.

CATWOMAN

Release date: July 2004
Starring roles: Halle Berry, Benjamin Bratt, Lambert Wilson, Frances Conroy, Sharon Stone
Director: Pitof
Screenplay: John Brancato, Michael Ferris, John Rogers

Cinematography: Thierry Arbogast
Score: Klaus Badelt
Running time: 104 minutes
Box office: $82,102,379

Filmed over the fall and winter of 2003–2004, *Catwoman* presented both challenges and opportunities for its director and lead star. The challenge for Pitof—the filmmaking alias of French director Jean-Christophe Comar—going into the movie was to launch a solo outing for a character whose screen appearances had previously been inextricably linked with Batman. While in comics Catwoman had sustained several series on her own merits—racking up nearly 100 issues of her own title from 1993 to 2001, followed by a stylish, noirish, second ongoing series in 2002 under the aegis of writer Ed Brubaker—in movies and TV, she had only ever been a supporting player.

"Own the night, live without fear, be more than human."

Trailer tagline

Feeling that the character deserved a movie origin story of her own, *Catwoman* producer Denise Di Novi had been trying to develop a solo outing ever since 1992's *Batman Returns*, which Di Novi had also co-produced. The intention was for that film's Selina Kyle, Michelle Pfeiffer, to reprise the role, with *Batman* (1989) and *Batman Returns* director Tim Burton helming—with the final scene of *Batman Returns,* showing Catwoman gazing up at the Bat-Signal above Gotham City, strongly hinting as much.

A decade on, with Burton and Pfeiffer out of the picture, and with Ashley Judd and Nicole Kidman both having been touted as stars in the interim (this despite Kidman playing a completely different character in 1995's *Batman Forever*), it fell to Pitof to finally bring the project to fruition.

In 2002, Ed Brubaker and Darwyn Cooke's *Catwoman* comics series featured a Selina Kyle whose leather outfit was closer to practical streetwear than a superhero costume, in a similar vein to Patience's outfit in the *Catwoman* movie.

Costume designer Angus Strathie used a combination of leather and a newly created silicone fabric to make Catwoman's outfit, which Halle Berry also had a hand in designing.

Far left: Forty-three domestic cats were employed under animal coordinator Boone Narr and lead trainer Mark Harden—including three to portray the Egyptian Mau that resurrects Patience.

Left: Angus Strathie and Sharon Stone worked together to create Laurel Beauty CEO Laurel Hedare's look—a stylish mix-and-match of high-fashion designer brands.

Patience's apartment is her refuge where she can paint abstract pictures in solitude—until her life is interrupted by an Egyptian Mau named Midnight.

Halle Berry spent hours with whip master Alex Green in order to fully master wielding a whip, which became an extension of her character as Catwoman.

GRAPHIC DESIGNER

With a background in visual effects, Pitof was no stranger to the level of CGI and VFX required to realize his vision, and neither was the film's star, Halle Berry. Fresh from *X-Men* sequel *X2* (2003), Berry was seeking a role that would offer a greater challenge after the ensemble work of the X-movies. With its themes of empowerment, transformation, and finding one's true self, *Catwoman* offered Berry that chance as the film's lead character, Patience Phillips. A talented but timid graphic designer working for cosmetics company Hedare Beauty, Patience inadvertently learns that an age-preventing product has unfortunate disfiguring side effects. On the orders of the company's ruthless CEO, Laurel Hedare (Sharon Stone), Patience is flushed out of the company's factory in a torrent of chemical waste, falling to her death in the bay far below. However, she is mysteriously resurrected by an Egyptian Mau cat she had earlier rescued from her apartment ledge, gaining catlike powers in the process, and sets out on a hunt for answers to her own murder.

HIGH STYLE

A pioneer in digital visual effects in his native France, Pitof had broken ground with his 2001 feature directorial debut *Vidocq*, the first film to be made in high definition. But just as important as his technical wizardry was his heightened, adrenalized filmmaking style, an approach he channeled into *Catwoman*. After she's washed ashore, Patience begins to experience her astonishing new feline abilities in the form of dizzying visual zooms to seagulls circling in the night sky above and crabs skittering in the mud below, achieved via digital VFX. Later fight scenes between Patience in her new Catwoman costume and Laurel Hedare make liberal use of camera whip pans and zooms, while the sets and lighting bring to mind music videos as much as action sequences.

   Those frantic fight scenes saw Halle Berry undertake a tremendous amount of tough physical training, at her own insistence, as the actor wanted to perform as many of the stunts as possible herself. Her training regime began three months before the start of principal photography under the guidance of trainer Harley Pasternak and continued under the tutelage of stunt coordinators Steve Davison and Jacob Rupp and fight coordinator Michael Gunther.

   For his part, Pitof, recognizing that Catwoman would not be a typical martial-arts fighter, wanted to find a style of combat that would be more appropriate for the character. Director and star settled on capoeira, a Brazilian combat technique incorporating dance and gymnastics, which Pitof felt captured the animalistic feel he was looking for. Studying capoeira allowed Berry to build her upper body strength to develop a style of fighting that was very catlike and close to the ground, involving spins, kicks, and acrobatics. That feline grace extended to all of Berry's movements as Catwoman to underscore her remarkable rebirth. Working with movement coach Anne Fletcher, Berry learned to move like a cat, shading her capoeira kicks and flips with catlike nuances.

OUTFIT FOR A FELINE

Aiding Berry in all her scenes as Catwoman was her costume. Where previous celluloid superhero costumes had frequently been restrictive affairs, the makers of *Catwoman* wanted to avoid

cladding Berry in a head-to-toe bodysuit. Costume designer Angus Strathie tried to give Catwoman's outfit a contemporary, urban texture that allowed for greater freedom of movement while also protecting her from assailants. In addition, the outfit afforded offensive capabilities with diamond-tipped claws on the fingertips of the gloves, and was accessorized with a bullwhip that Berry was trained to use by whip coach Alex Green. The final addition of leather pants and halter top reflected the film's narrative, which sees Patience creating her own costume partly from an unused outfit intended for a date that never happened. It also symbolized her fully embracing her newfound abilities and accompanying increased confidence.

For Berry, the way the costume revealed her spine and sinews was key to her building the character's growing sense of independence and sensuality. The ensemble was completed by a black catlike mask, which, in the movie, is provided by Ophelia Powers (Frances Conroy), a former professor who turns out to be the owner of the Egyptian Mau—named Midnight—that resurrected and remade Patience. From the cat-loving Ophelia, Patience learns about the lineage she is now a part of, a legacy of Catwomen (foreshadowed in the film's opening credits, which include newspaper clippings of costumed cat burglars, crimefighters, and circus performers) stretching back to ancient Egypt and the goddess Bast. According to Ophelia, Bast "represents the duality in all women—docile yet aggressive, nurturing yet ferocious." It's a neat encapsulation of Patience's transformation into Catwoman and the film's themes of escaping the confines of society and following one's own desires.

Far left: The *Matrix Reloaded* actor Lambert Wilson plays George Hedare, ruthless owner of Hedare Beauty and husband of the even more ruthless Laurel Hedare (Sharon Stone).

Left: Studying the 43 cats employed on the set of *Catwoman* helped Halle Berry develop a catlike style of movement, further bolstering the feline training Berry received from choreographer Anne Fletcher.

Nine lives

While *Catwoman* is set in a different milieu to its title character's previous big-screen outing in Tim Burton's *Batman Returns*—utilizing locations in Vancouver and Los Angeles, the unspecified city in which the action takes place is clearly not Gotham City—the movie does not reside in an entirely separate universe. Shortly after Patience gains her powers, her new mentor, Ophelia, shows her pictures of previous wielders of the Catwoman mantle—and there among the photographs is the version of Catwoman played by Michelle Pfeiffer in Burton's 1992 sequel.

In fact, beyond the confines of the history outlined in *Catwoman*, both Halle Berry and Michelle Pfeiffer belong to a lineage of screen felines that, while not stretching back as far as Catwoman's fictional one, still boasts a fine pedigree. The first actor to bring Catwoman to life on celluloid was Julie Newmar, who had found fame in 1964 playing an android on sci-fi sitcom *My Living Doll*. Newmar portrayed

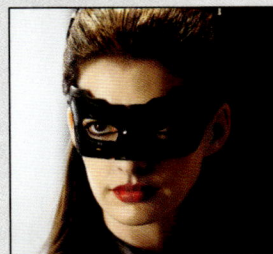

Miss Kitka, alias Catwoman, in 13 episodes of the *Batman* TV show from 1966 to 1967, but other commitments prevented her from reprising the role in the 1966 *Batman* movie, leading *The Time Tunnel*'s Lee Merriwether to step into the role instead. *Batman*'s 1967–1968 final season saw a third performer, singer Eartha Kitt *(top left)*, take on the role, which marked the first time a Black actor had played Catwoman.

Following Michelle Pfeiffer and Halle Berry's 1992 and 2004 turns, Anne Hathaway *(bottom left)* played Selina Kyle in *The Dark Knight Rises*—Christopher Nolan's 2012 finale to his Dark Knight Trilogy—who was rooted both in the movie's reality and in comics interpretations of the character. Zoë Kravitz, too, walked a similar line in Matt Reeves's *The Batman* (2022), while on the small screen, Camren Bicondova played a younger Selina in five seasons of *Gotham* from 2014 to 2019.

CONSTANTINE

Release date: February 7, 2005 (Paris), February 18, 2005 (US)
Starring roles: Keanu Reeves, Rachel Weisz, Shia LaBeouf, Tilda Swinton, Djimon Hounsou, Peter Stormare, Pruitt Taylor Vince, Gavin Rossdale
Director: Francis Lawrence

Screenplay: Kevin Brodbin, Frank Cappello
Cinematography: Philippe Rousselot
Music: Brian Tyler, Klaus Badelt
Running time: 121 minutes
Box office: $230.9 million

In the 1980s, comics expanded and diversified into niche markets dictated by genre, age, and personal interests and—like movies—adopted a ratings system. Comics weren't just for kids anymore, many containing extreme violence and explicit romantic situations. Stories also broached political, social, and gender-diverse issues outside a traditionally conservative mainstream.

Into this charged environment came John Constantine. He was no hero, but a troubled soul dancing on the edge of damnation. A disreputable, inveterate meddler, he inserted himself in whatever situation chance brought him to. The Hellblazer shrewdly manipulated events, people, and even devils, before—coolly dragging on an ever-present cigarette—standing back to let chaos happen around him.

That seductive scenario led producer Lauren Shuler Donner (*Pretty in Pink*, *X-Men* franchise) to pursue a Constantine film. Married to Richard Donner (*Superman*) since 1986, Shuler Donner was a pioneering force in Hollywood. She began work on

Constantine keenly aware of contemporary comics trends for outsider heroes. Her stated intention was to make a modern horror movie in the classic style—something like *The Exorcist*, that would stand the test of time, something "frightening, but not overpowering."

ANCIENT EVIL, NEW MAN

When proposed director Paul Hunter (*Bulletproof Monk*) dropped out in 1999, replacement Tarsem Singh (*The Cell*) began preliminary work with Nicolas Cage as lead, but by 2002, both had also moved on. At that time, Keanu Reeves was completing *The Matrix* trilogy, but on reading Kevin Brodbin's (*The Glimmer Man*, *Mindhunters*) script and some of the graphic novels, agreed to play Constantine, attracted by the antihero's compelling character journey.

After viewing Francis Lawrence's (*I am Legend*, *Hunger Games*) showreel, Reeves was instrumental in the music-video director landing his debut feature film, brought aboard with the brief to make the film "young and hip." Lawrence's enthusiasm was infectious. He even had himself suspended from harnesses to better view the project from every angle.

Unlike Vertigo comics series targeting older, more educated audiences, studio bosses wanted the cinematic *Constantine* to reach a broader fan base. When the Motion Picture Association of America

> # "Hi. My name's John ..."
> **John Constantine**

Constantine, Papa Midnite, and Chas leave the neutral bar catering to the forces of Heaven and Hell.

Rachel Weisz pulled a rare horror film triple play in *Constantine*—playing tough-fisted action hero, innocent victim, and the diabolical monster at the heart of the madness.

In a rare but evocative contemplative moment, Constantine weighs his options before again choosing the most dangerous and self-destructive path.

Gavin Rossdale, English rock singer and frontman for the band Bush, took on the role of the half-demon facilitator Balthazar.

Stan Winston's denizens of Hell were electrifying scene stealers, combining live actors, animatronics, puppetry, and early computer-generated imagery.

Born in a bayou

After a cameo in *Swamp Thing* #25, (June 1984), John Constantine made his official debut in *Swamp Thing* #37 (June 1985), by Alan Moore, Rick Veitch, and John Totleben. His look was based on musician Gordon "Sting" Sumner. Making regular appearances in *Swamp Thing*, he eventually won his own title. *Hellblazer* premiered in September 1987, during the dying days of the Reagan administration and the height of Thatcherite rule in Britain. The series reimagined traditional horror tales, boasting a proudly antiestablishment stance established by DC talent Jamie Delano, John Ridgway, and Richard Piers Rayner.

rejected their proposed "PG-13" certification—rating it "R" (Restricted to under-17s unless accompanied by an adult)—Lawrence attributed the decision to concerns over religious context and content, rather than any overtly shocking material in the final cut.

Constantine's anarchistic nature and Liverpudlian background didn't survive Hollywood prerequisites, and it was as an American exorcist that Reeves met troubled Angela Dodson, as she investigated the "suicide" of her devoutly Roman Catholic twin sister Isabel. Both were played by Rachel Weisz, as was demonic antagonist Mammon, whose minor role expanded once Lawrence saw the fantastic puppet/animatronic of Lucifer's son created by the Stan Winston Studio (Stan Winston School of Character Arts). The final screenplay—loosely based on *Hellblazer* comic story arcs *Dangerous Habits* and *Bloodlines*—was by Brodbin with rewrites by Frank Cappello (*American Yakuza*).

The story dealt with God and Lucifer's eternal war over Earth, with angels, demons, and half-breeds of both maintaining a truce allowing humanity to decide its own destiny. The balance is covertly steered by beings like demi-angel Gabriel (Tilda Swinton) and half-demon Balthazar (Gavin Rossdale) shaving odds on "the great wager," advancing personal agendas while waiting for the End of Days. Now Lucifer's son, Mammon, seeks to usurp Hell's throne and destroy everything.

In Los Angeles, an exorcist short on faith and time struggles to save a possessed girl. The demon almost makes her a portal to freedom on the mortal plane. Renowned for in-depth preparation, Reeves consulted an actual exorcist to learn the processes involved—using what he learned in the scene to extract the demon and trap it in a mirror. Reeves did most of his own stunts (as did the supporting cast) and said he didn't really have the character nailed down until he found the "right raincoat."

WAGERS OF SIN

Afflicted with supernatural visions and damned to Hell for attempting suicide as a teenager, the occult detective will soon die again—from smoking-induced lung cancer. Seeking a miracle from Gabriel, he instead meets LAPD detective Angela Dodson, who wants the Church to allow her sister a Catholic burial. Isabel's last word was "Constantine" ...

Angela is the key to the apocalypse, targeted for psychic abilities she's suppressed all her life and which made Isabel Mammon's ideal earthly host. Angela and Constantine are at the heart of a diabolical storm that engulfs and ultimately destroys John's apprentice Chas (Shia LaBeouf), Father Hennessy (Pruitt Taylor Vince), and occult nerd Beeman (Max Baker).

Revisiting Hell—only originally escaped thanks to first responders reviving 15-year-old John—Constantine learns the Dodsons are powerful psychics, and a hidden player intends housing Satan's malignant son in the surviving twin to destroy mankind and end the celestial ceasefire. Moreover, Isabel took her life for humanity's sake, damning her soul, which now burns forever ...

Hell was originally imagined as a cold, dark void, but Lawrence wanted something more intrusive and active. Consulting visual-effects supervisor Michael Fink (*X-Men*, *The Golden Compass*), they jointly conceived the underworld as a place of ceaseless burning turmoil, like ground zero of an atomic bomb detonation. It became a far bigger part of the film, with makeup, prosthetics, puppets, actors, and cutting-edge CG (computer graphics) techniques

Multi-award-winning actor Tilda Swinton brought style and gravitas to the role of Gabriel with her stunning portrayal of evil done in the name of good.

redefining the horrors there. The complex end result was a blazing analogue of rush-hour Los Angeles, with "particle animation" and wind machines adding a feeling of constant churning heat, choking erosion, and decay carried on scourging hellwinds.

Constantine convinces mystic Papa Midnite (Djimon Hounsou) to abandon an oath of neutrality and join the fight to postpone armageddon and liberate Isabel's soul from unjust damnation. No stranger to DC's properties or magical roles, Hounsou plays the Wizard in the *Shazam* and *Black Adam* films and voiced the Fisherman King in 2018's *Aquaman*.

With Angela possessed by Mammon, Constantine and Chas rush to rescue her, tearing through assembled half-demons until Gabriel ambushes them. The half-angel despises mortals and will purge humanity before creating something worthier of God's attention ...

Salvation, victory, and redemption come with supreme sacrifice as Constantine kills himself again, luring Lucifer (Peter Stormare) to Earth to take his soul. Not yet done with humanity, Lucifer crushes Mammon and Gabriel before turning to his true obsession and ultimate foe. In a feature packed with innovative effects and designs, Stormare boldly opted to play Lucifer without enhancements. Basing his performance on Fagin from Charles Dickens's *Oliver Twist*, the Swedish star used expression, posture, and an overlarge greasy white lounge suit to create a creepily bravura performance. As he later stated, "I asked the director to let me use my face instead. Let the audience use their imagination."

Exterminating plot and plotters, Lucifer gloatingly grants Constantine a favor and is stunned when the dead man begs for Isabel's freedom rather than renewed life—a noble act that unexpectedly saves his soul. As Constantine rises redeemed to Heaven, Lucifer hastily returns him to healthy life, refusing to let him escape more chances to fail and fall ...

Despite impressive commercial results, the film was disliked by critics and dismissed by comics fans. Deviations from the beloved source material may also have contributed to the film's undeserved reputation, but have not prevented it from becoming a cult classic whose fans eagerly anticipate an imminent sequel.

Universal presence

Devotees of the comic book *Hellblazer* received far more consideration when the obnoxious occultist starred in a TV series developed by Daniel Cerone and David S. Goyer for NBC. Firmly focused on more mature audiences, *Constantine* ran 13 episodes between October 24, 2014, and February 13, 2015, with Matt Ryan compellingly capturing the nuances and complex seedy charm of the crafty conman wizard from Liverpool.

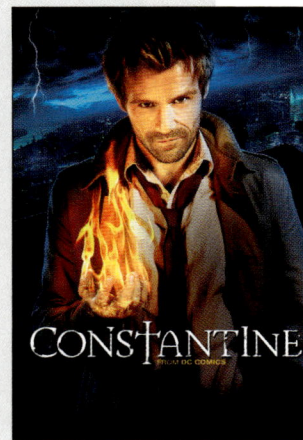

Working with magic-touched allies Zed (Angélica Celaya), Chas (Charles Halford), and Manny (Harold Perrineau), the chain-smoking conjuror crisscrossed America hunting supernatural threats to Earth and humanity sparked by a mysterious "Rising Darkness."

Although cancelled after one season, Ryan reprised his character for The CW's "Arrowverse" franchise, starting in season 4 of primary series *Arrow* ("Haunted"), with *Batwoman* and *The Flash* installments of multipart, multiseries crossover event "Crisis on Infinite Earths."

Constantine became a fixture of DC's *Legends of Tomorrow* (seasons 3 through 6) as writers and producers affirmed his most controversial comic book characteristic, with the bisexual warlock having affairs with teammates White Canary and Zari and enduring seeing his true love Desmond condemned to Hell because of him.

Ryan revisited the rogue mage in DC animated features *Justice League Dark*, *Justice League Dark: Apokolips War* and *Constantine: The House of Mystery*, which led to miniseries *Constantine: City of Demons* and the *Harley Quinn* episode "It's a Swamp Thing."

Below: The pivotal moment of the movie comes when Constantine returns to Hell and claws his way out of the pit to save humanity and redeem unjustly damned Isabel.

BATMAN BEGINS

Release date: June 2005
Starring roles: Christian Bale, Michael Caine, Liam Neeson, Katie Holmes, Gary Oldman, Cillian Murphy, Tom Wilkinson, Rutger Hauer, Ken Watanabe, Morgan Freeman
Director: Christopher Nolan

Screenplay: Christopher Nolan and David S. Goyer
Story: David S. Goyer
Cinematography: Wally Pfister
Music: Hans Zimmer
Running time: 140 minutes
Box office: $373,672,993

As its title suggested, *Batman Begins* was a new beginning for DC movies, but it also marked the beginning of the end of an era. In story, tone, and execution, Christopher Nolan's film was a marked departure from previous DC cinematic efforts, signaling a new way of looking at comic book characters. The director would follow it with two sequels that moved even further away from the stylized superhero films of the past and toward, if not reality, then an action-movie form of realism, in the process bringing one chapter of DC movie-making to a close. Back at the start of 2003, however, when Nolan embarked on his journey, Batman was very much beginning.

IN THE BEGINNING …

In the years following 1997's *Batman and Robin*, a number of attempts were made to engineer a follow-up, spearheaded by, in turn, that film's director, Joel Schumacher; *Remember the Titans* (2000) director Boaz Yakin with *Batman Beyond* (1999–2001) co-creators Paul Dini and Alan Burnett; *Pi* (1998) director Darren Aronofsky with *Batman: The Dark Knight Returns* (1986) creator Frank Miller; and *The Perfect Storm* (2000) director Wolfgang Petersen with *Se7en* (1995) writer Andrew Kevin Walker and, later, *A Beautiful Mind* (2001) writer Akiva Goldsman (this last attempt a Batman versus Superman story). Other names in the frame included *The Matrix*'s Wachowskis and *Buffy the Vampire Slayer*'s Joss Whedon. One by one, each attempt faltered and fell.

"The Legend Begins."
Marketing tagline

In 2002, director Christopher Nolan, who two years before had turned heads with his nonlinear thriller *Memento*, delivered his third film, the Al Pacino/Robin Williams psychological drama *Insomnia*. Pondering what he wanted to do next, the British expat had a notion of making something on a grand scale, along the lines of the blockbusters he had enjoyed as a child, such as the James Bond movies, or Richard Donner's *Superman: The Movie* (1978). As a boy growing up in London in the 1970s, Nolan had

Hallucinating after receiving a dose of The Scarecrow's fear toxin, Batman sees maggots writhing out of the villain's mask, as animated by visual effects company BUF Compagnie.

Top: London's St. Pancras Chambers was the location for Batman's dramatic plunge down the stairwell of Arkham Asylum, performed by Christian Bale's stunt double Buster Reeves.

Above: Christian Bale as Bruce Wayne descends the steps of Wayne Manor, filmed on location at Mentmore Towers, a 19th-century country house in Buckinghamshire originally built for the Rothschild family.

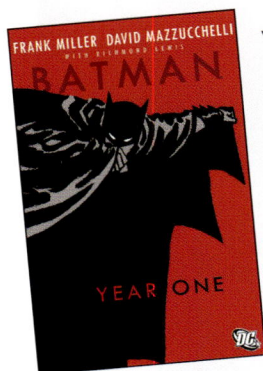

Year One and beyond

Batman Begins has an obvious comics antecedent in the shape of Frank Miller and David Mazzucchelli's *Batman: Year One*. Originally published in four parts in *Batman* #404–407 (February–May 1987), *Year One* was a stark departure from Batman comics of the past, delineating the character's origins and first fumbling attempts to fight crime in a far more grounded and realistic manner than had ever been seen before. Miller, who had already helped revolutionize comics in 1986 with his groundbreaking dystopia *Batman: The Dark Knight Returns*, redefined the character with a down-to-earth, downbeat script, while Mazzucchelli's instinctive storytelling and naturalistic artwork were the finest of his career to that point.

The start of a revamp of Batman in comics in the late 1980s and into the 1990s, *Year One* was certainly an influence on *Batman Begins'* second act, along with elements of Jeph Loeb and Tim Sale's 1996–1997 series *Batman: The Long Halloween*. But a shorter, lesser-known story was more important for the first act. Published in the 1990 trade paperback *Secret Origins of the World's Greatest Super-Heroes*, Denny O'Neil and Dick Giordano's "The Man Who Falls" comprised vignettes of Bruce Wayne's life between the death of his parents and his becoming Batman. A mixture of newly created scenes and moments taken from *Year One* and subsequent stories like Sam Hamm and Denys Cowan's "Blind Justice" and Denny O'Neil and Ed Hannigan's "Shaman," the story was a big influence on Bruce Wayne's voyage of self-discovery in *Batman Begins'* first third.

The deaths of Bruce Wayne's parents (played by Linus Roache and Sara Stewart) comes after Bruce (Gus Lewis), terrified by batlike creatures in the opera *Mefistofele,* asks to leave.

Constructed at Shepperton on a gimbal to simulate movement, the monorail train carriages would be used by Rā's al Ghūl to transport a microwave emitter to Gotham City's heart.

loved the 1966–1968 *Batman* TV show (which was shown on repeat on ITV in the UK), unaware of the camp nature of the enterprise and thrilling instead, as most kids did, to the sheer excitement of the thing. Looking back years later, Nolan recognized how he had responded to the archetypal nature of Batman, the notion of an individual dedicating themselves to a cause through self-discipline, and the allure of the double life and themes of duality inherent in a secret identity.

Aware of the problems the studio had experienced getting a new Batman movie off the ground, Nolan wondered if there was room for a new interpretation, both in approach and story. While he had found Tim Burton's *Batman* (1989) fascinating, that film and its sequels had been highly stylized affairs, treating Batman and his world as fantastic. Nolan wondered if there was scope for a more realistic take on the character, exploring how such a remarkable individual might work in a recognizably real world. Furthermore, while the deaths of Bruce Wayne's parents had been depicted many times, the subsequent events that led Bruce Wayne to put on a costume and fight crime had never been fully explored in film. In short, Nolan wanted to fill in those gaps in the mythology and create a believable origin for Batman.

WRITE THE LEGEND

Nolan pitched his ideas to Warner Bros. executives, who were impressed enough that they gave him the green light on the spot. Aware that while he was a Batman fan he was no comics expert, Nolan reached out to David Goyer, professed comic book aficionado and writer of *Blade* (1998) and *Blade II* (2002). As a child, Goyer had told his mother that one day he would go to Hollywood and make a Batman film, so in that sense Nolan's call was one he'd been waiting most of his life for. Unfortunately, he was in pre-production on *Blade: Trinity* (2004), which he was also directing, and didn't think he had the time—but still spent an hour telling Nolan what he would do if he did write the film, namely either look

Production designer Nathan Crowley produced a succession of models of the Batmobile to help realize Christopher Nolan's vision for *Batman Begins* of a heightened realism, including this 14-inch scale model.

forward to Batman's future, or back to his beginning. A few days later an insistent Nolan called again, and Goyer relented.

Nolan and Goyer began meeting in Nolan's garage, down the driveway at Nolan and his wife and producer Emma Thomas's Los Angeles house, working in the first instance on what they saw as moments for a potential teaser trailer—Bruce Wayne as an 8-year-old after his parents have been murdered, an image inspired by a photograph of a young John F. Kennedy Jr. at his father's funeral; Bruce's childhood friend, Rachel Dawes, waving at the lonely figure of Bruce framed in an upper story window of Wayne Manor; young Bruce falling into an abandoned well and being swarmed by bats. That last idea had its basis in a scene in Frank Miller's 1986 graphic novel *Batman: The Dark Knight Returns*, expanded on in Denny O'Neil and Dick Giordano's 1990 short comics story "The Man Who Falls." To Nolan and Goyer, it seemed a more plausible explanation for why a traumatized boy might later choose to wear a bat costume, rather than the original 1939 explanation of a bat crashing through Bruce Wayne's study window.

BUILDING A BETTER BATMOBILE

Formulating the story was one thing, but for Nolan the key to conveying his intentions with the film would be the Batmobile. If his Batman were to be a realistic, functional, utilitarian figure, so should his vehicle be: possessing the armor and weight of a tank but with a sloping, low profile—a fusion of a Hummer and a Lamborghini Countach. As he and David Goyer worked, Nolan showed the writer what he meant by shaping a ball of clay. The form may have been fairly crude, but it would bear a remarkable resemblance to the finished vehicle.

To help him realize his vision, Nolan brought on board his friend, fellow Brit, and production designer on *Insomnia*, Nathan Crowley. Over the summer of 2003, in the months before the art department was officially set up at Shepperton Studios outside London, Crowley joined Nolan and Goyer in the director's garage and set about conceiving a Batmobile and an array of other mockups, from the Batcave to Gotham City, all of which fed back into

Early model of the Tumbler clearly showing Nathan Crowley's technique of taking elements of model cars and aircraft and kit-bashing them together in an effort to find the form.

To produce the effect of the Tumbler blasting into the Batcave, a full-scale vehicle was launched on a nitrogen catapult through the waterfall on the Shepperton Batcave set.

Michael Caine and Christian Bale amid the flames on the Wayne Manor interior sets at Shepperton, used to film the scene where Rā's al Ghūl sets fire to the mansion.

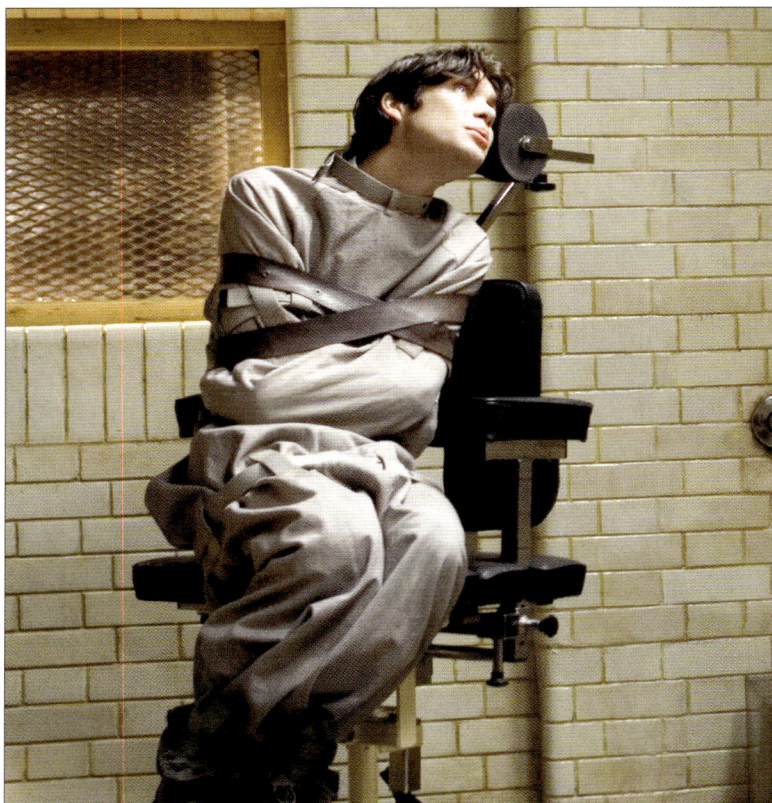

For Christopher Nolan, Arkham Asylum was as much a character in the story of *Batman Begins* as its administrator, Dr. Jonathan Crane, alias The Scarecrow.

A character from *Batman: Year One* and *Batman: The Long Halloween*, Carmine Falcone symbolizes the corruption consuming Gotham City—and his capture by Batman the start of the city's salvation.

the writing. For the Batmobile, Crowley kit-bashed thousands of dollars' worth of car and airplane model hobby kits until he arrived at the desired design—the Tumbler, as it was nicknamed. When Nolan showed that model to studio executives to communicate his utilitarian vision, they were so enthusiastic that they financed the building of a full-size prototype.

To enhance the sense of realism, Nolan intended to shoot as much of his film as possible "in camera," rather than relying on postproduction and visual effects. Unlike previous Batman movies, where Batmobiles were beautiful but limited props, the Tumbler would have to perform at speeds of up to 100 miles per hour (260 kph) in chase scenes rivaling those of *The French Connection* (1971), something that had never been attempted before. Despite the fact that Crowley's model had no front axle, special effects supervisor Chris Corbould worked with engineers and fabrication experts to build multiple full-scale, functional, matte black Batmobiles, each with a speciality, whether that be hydraulics for the sequences where the vehicle would jump across rooftops, or a practical flame that erupted from the exhaust like a jet as the Tumbler barreled through the streets of Gotham City.

THE WAYNE FOUNDATION

While the production effectively began with the Batmobile, the film itself begins with Bruce Wayne. Writing the script, Nolan and Goyer reasoned that if they could get the audience to care about Bruce, rather than merely anticipating him donning the Batsuit, they would have succeeded in their mission of making a more realistic movie. Unfolding in a nonlinear fashion (a signature of Nolan's work), and powered by Hans Zimmer's rumbling, gradually crescendoing two-note theme, the first third of the film cuts between scenes of Bruce as a boy, as a vengeance-consumed

Concept art of Gotham City's haphazard skyline, showing the modernist monorail built by Thomas Wayne counterposed against the smokestacks of the city's older architecture.

college dropout intent on confronting his parents' killer, and as a young man traveling the world and training for a mission he doesn't yet comprehend.

Playing the adult Bruce Wayne was Christian Bale (the young Bruce was played by Gus Lewis). Casting Bruce/Batman, Christopher Nolan knew that whoever played the part should be able to embrace both the duality and complexity of the character and his physical presence and power. The first actor the director met was Bale. Known for taking on dark and challenging roles, from Patrick Bateman in *American Psycho* (2000) to Trevor Reznik in *The Machinist* (2004), the British actor had become interested in potentially portraying Batman after reading Frank Miller and David Mazzucchelli's 1987 revisionist origin story *Batman: Year One,* and had become more intrigued after learning of Nolan's involvement. Just as intrigued, Nolan screen-tested Bale, who packed on the weight he'd lost for *The Machinist*— and more—and delivered an intense Bruce Wayne and feral Batman that won him the part.

Taking a leaf out of Richard Donner's *Superman: The Movie,* Nolan filled out the rest of the cast with big names: Michael Caine as Alfred (the start of a long working relationship between Caine and Nolan); Katie Holmes as Bruce's childhood friend Rachel Dawes, now Gotham City's Assistant District Attorney; Gary Oldman as Gotham City Police Sergeant Jim Gordon, who would become Batman's key ally; Cillian Murphy as Arkham Asylum administrator Dr. Jonathan Crane, alias the villainous The Scarecrow (again, the beginning of a long association with Nolan, culminating in 2023's *Oppenheimer*); Tom Wilkinson as mob boss Carmine Falcone; and Morgan Freeman as Lucius Fox, the mothballed head of the Applied Sciences Division (shades of Bond's Q Branch) at Wayne Industries, Bruce's inherited company.

Reinventing Gotham City

In summer 2003, three months before the *Batman Begins* art department was set up at London's Shepperton Studios that September, production designer Nathan Crowley joined Christopher Nolan and David Goyer in the director's garage and began creating models and mock-ups for the film. Crowley was very much a part of the creative conversation from the production's earliest days, his constructions both informed by and informing the writing in what Nolan termed a parallel process.

Among the mock-ups he put together were models of Gotham City, Crowley taking architectural elements from real cities and combining them to create Gotham City's distinctive look. From Tokyo, he took the idea of an elevated freeway and combined it with streets from New York, from where he also made interpretations of buildings like Grand Central Station and the Grand Hyatt. One important area of Gotham City for the story was the Narrows, the city's crime-riddled slum area. For this, Crowley looked to Kowloon Walled City, which before it was demolished in 1994 was a densely populated, ungoverned enclave within Hong Kong. To symbolize the divide between Gotham City's underbelly and the glittering city above, Crowley constructed a model of the Narrows around a monorail. Built in the narrative by Bruce Wayne's billionaire father, Thomas, as a gift to Gotham City, with Wayne Tower at its center, the monorail would serve as the site of the climactic fight for the survival of Gotham City between Batman and his former mentor/father figure Rā's al Ghūl.

The daughter of Wayne Manor's housekeeper, Rachel Dawes—played by Katie Holmes—was created by Christopher Nolan and David Goyer to be Bruce Wayne's oldest friend.

The Narrows descends into madness after being engulfed by The Scarecrow's hallucinogenic compound, in a sequence filmed on the Cardington sets and involving high-wire work by stunt performer Buster Reeves.

In keeping with the filmmakers' push for plausibility, it's from Fox's department that Bruce acquires the basis of his Batsuit—a "Nomex survival suit for advanced infantry," which Bruce informs Fox he wants to borrow "for spelunking"; a Kevlar climbing harness, which becomes his Utility Belt; a grappling gun; and memory cloth, which becomes his cape. He also acquires the Tumbler; after putting the camouflaged military bridging vehicle through its paces, he memorably inquires, "Does it come in black?"

THE HERO'S QUEST

As they were breaking the story, David Goyer had shown Christopher Nolan his photos of Tibet, taken when Goyer, on the advice of his writing mentor Nelson Gidding, had traveled the world in order to gain some lived experience. Those pictures formed the basis of Bruce Wayne's globetrotting quest for purpose, Nathan Crowley using them as the inspiration for Bruce's journey to Bhutan, and ultimately to the lair of the League of Shadows in a Himalayan monastery. While the Bhutan prison scene at the start of the movie was filmed at Coalhouse Fort on the banks of the River Thames in Essex, the monastery exteriors were filmed in Iceland, as was the sword fight on a frozen lake at the edge of a glacier between Bruce and his mentor, Ducard—one of a number of surrogate father figures for Bruce in the film, and later revealed in a twist as the leader of the League, Rā's al Ghūl—played by Liam Neeson. The first scene to be shot when principal photography began in February 2004, the fight, previously practiced by Bale and Neeson on ice rinks, was a race against time to finish before the warming weather melted the ice, the loud cracking sounds unnerving cast and crew.

From Iceland, the production moved to Shepperton, where Nathan Crowley's team built the monastery interior, Wayne Manor interiors, and most impressive of all, the huge Batcave, filling the studio's biggest soundstage and boasting running streams and a waterfall. Even more gargantuan, however, were the sets for Gotham City, which Nolan dubbed New York on steroids, including the Narrows, the slum area which Crowley based in part on Hong Kong's Walled City of Kowloon. Housed in one of the Cardington Sheds—former World War I dirigible hangars in rural Bedfordshire, near where Emma Thomas had grown up—the set comprised full-scale buildings and streets, and was ideal for shooting stunts and, on a practical level regarding Batman's M.O., nighttime scenes, which otherwise would have meant weeks of night shoots.

MIGHTY REAL

While the Cardington Sheds served the production well, Christopher Nolan was adamant that actual city locations would be vital in reinforcing the film's feel of reality. The towering spires of Chicago would stand in for Gotham City, lending the city a greater scale than even the Cardington sets could convey, and providing

Overseen by stunt coordinator Paul Jennings and fight arranger David Forman, the monastery training session, like all of *Batman Begins*' brawls, was based on the Keysi Fighting Method, a melding of martial arts and street-fighting techniques.

Below: During a training session, Bruce Wayne hides among the League of Shadows to evade detection by Ducard, in a scene filmed on the monastery interior set at Shepperton.

the locations for the film's biggest action set piece, in which Batman barrels along Gotham City's freeways and across rooftops in the Tumbler, pursued by cops and with a hallucinating Rachel Dawes, infected by the The Scarecrow's gas, in the passenger seat. Shot over three weeks on the double-decker highway of the Chicago Loop, in a parking garage, and on a disused section of freeway, the chase sequence saw cinematographer Wally Pfister making use of a robotic crane arm mounted on a Mercedes camera car. While the Tumbler was driven by stunt performer George Cottle, among those inside the Mercedes as it raced along at 100mph in pursuit of the Batmobile was Nolan himself—a perfect illustration of the director's desire to get as close to the action as possible in order to deliver the most realistic experience achievable.

The Demon's Head and The Scarecrow

The choice of Rā's al Ghūl and The Scarecrow as the primary villains of *Batman Begins* arose from a determination on the part of Christopher Nolan and David Goyer not to use any villains who had appeared in previous Batman movies. After listing characters from Batman's Rogues Gallery who hadn't yet been used, Goyer arrived at one of his favorites: Rā's al Ghūl. Created by Denny O'Neil and Neal Adams in 1971, the Demon's Head, as his name translates to in comics lore, was a criminal mastermind who sought to bring balance to the world by exterminating much of mankind. As well as not appearing on screen before, Rā's—or Ducard, as he's initially known in *Batman Begins*—also filled a role Nolan and Goyer had been discussing of a mentor for Bruce Wayne who becomes a villain. In the comics, Ducard did help train Bruce Wayne, but was an entirely separate character from Rā's.

As for Dr. Jonathan Crane, alias The Scarecrow, although he had been around in comics since 1941, he too had not made the leap to cinema. For Nolan, the character's background as a psychiatrist who manipulates people through fear made for an interesting comparison to Bruce Wayne's adoption of the Batman persona, while structurally his addition would keep the plot moving until the reappearance of Rā's. One thing Nolan disliked, however, was the comics The Scarecrow's mask (see right from *Batman* #189, February 1967). He and Goyer eventually reasoned it could act as a gas mask to protect Crane from his own toxin while instilling fear into his victims, a notion made manifest by costume designer Lindy Hemming's translation of the mask into a misshapen burlap sack.

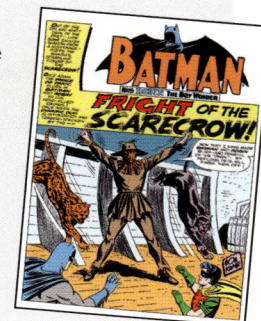

SUPERMAN RETURNS

Release date: June 21, 2006 (LA), June 28, 2006 (US)
Starring roles: Brandon Routh, Kate Bosworth, James Marsden, Frank Langella, Eva Marie Saint, Parker Posey, Kal Penn, Sam Huntington, Kevin Spacey
Director: Bryan Singer

Screenplay: Michael Dougherty, Dan Harris
Cinematography: Newton Thomas Sigel
Music: John Ottman
Running time: 154 minutes
Box office: $391.1 million

In July 2004, when an opportunity to extend the legacy of one of his favorite childhood characters arose, Bryan Singer (*The Usual Suspects*) didn't hesitate to take the helm. Taking his trusted team—writers Michael Dougherty and Dan Harris, production designer Guy Hendrix Dyas, cinematographer Newton Thomas Sigel, costumier Louise Mingenbach, and composer John Ottman—the director stepped away from his current commitments for his passion project: *Superman Returns*.

DREAM JOBS

Warner Bros. had been trying to regenerate their Superman franchise for 12 years. Kevin Smith, Tim Burton, J. J. Abrams, McG, Brett Ratner, and others had come and gone when Singer signed on. At the time, he was in a three-picture contract with 20th Century Fox, working on *X-Men: The Last Stand* and preparing to remake sci-fi thriller *Logan's Run*. Ultimately, Singer would retire from those tentpole movies to work on *Superman Returns*.

Dougherty and Harris crafted six scripts to reach the pre-production stage, but Brandon Routh (Superman), Kate Bosworth (Lois Lane), and Kevin Spacey (Lex Luthor) all signed on without reading any of them. After working with him on *The Usual Suspects*, for which Spacey picked up an Academy Award for Best Supporting Actor, Singer had no one else in mind for the villain—even tailoring Spacey's six-week shooting schedule around his role as Director of London's Old Vic Theatre. Spacey, in turn, recommended Bosworth, having directed her in 2004's *Beyond the Sea*.

Like his movie-making idol, director Richard Donner, Singer chose star power for supporting cast and an unknown for the lead. In 2000, Brandon Routh's amazing resemblance to Christopher Reeve had almost landed him the part of Clark Kent in hit TV show *Smallville* but, like Reeve, he needed intense exercise and a revised diet to bulk up for Superman. Moreover, costume designer Louise Mingenbach (*K-PAX, Shazam! Fury of the Gods*) had a design problem to fix before shooting could begin. Superman's suits were made from camera-friendly spandex-derivative Milliskin, but it restricted movement and sagged after use. To counteract this, she had to make 80 suits, 100 capes, 30 pairs of boots, and 90 belts for the shoot.

"On June 30, 2006! Look Up In The Sky!"
Tagline

Her design required screen printing dark areas for texture. In 2005, she told *Dreamwatch* magazine, "I wanted something tight fitting but sleek, and didn't have the constant wrinkle problems that beset Chris Reeve's outfit," adding, "Poor Brandon can't gain or lose any weight, because the suits have been computer mapped to his peak body type."

The triumvirate of Jimmy Olsen (Sam Huntington), Lois Lane, and Perry White (Frank Langella) have backstopped Superman in every media incarnation of his life of action and adventure.

Although impressive and authentic-looking, the eight-barreled "BFG XP/50 Mk. II" was completely fictional. Experts assessed its rate of fire at 25,000 rounds per minute.

Just like his predecessor Christopher Reeve, Brandon Routh had to undergo strenuous and continual bodybuilding training to "beef up," adding 20 pounds (9 kg) of muscle to his lean frame.

A large proportion of the vast Art Department's job was creating physical printed props and digital periodical pages to embody and emphasize the nonstop output of the *Daily Planet*.

Krypton lives again and Jor-El bestows more words of wisdom, as Marlon Brando is digitally resurrected through archive footage, clever editing, and pioneering CGI manipulation.

To keep in character, during shooting, Kevin Spacey drove around the sets in a golf cart labeled "Lex's Super Buster," dragging an effigy of his hated enemy and screaming, "Super must die!" into a megaphone.

Codified as "Red Sun" to thwart news snoopers, filming the 60 set pieces took place at Fox Studios, Sydney, Australia, requiring nine soundstages and two workshops over eight months in 2005. Principal photography ran from late March to November, with cinematographer Sigel (*The Usual Suspects*, *Bohemian Rhapsody*) initially using 65mm film for its "glossy" look, before switching to cutting-edge methods. *Superman Returns* was the first film to use Panavision Genesis HD cameras—eight in all.

IMAX EXPERIENCE

The Kent farm was built at Fox and shipped to rural Tamworth, New South Wales, where the crew motto became, "There's no detail too small for this production." Set construction started in January. After beating the entire area to drive out snakes, at the height of a seven-year drought, the crew constructed nearly 4.5 miles (7 km) of road, all properly garnished with telephone poles, and shipped in tons of water and fertilizer to grow 37 acres (15 hectares) of corn. It had to be 6.5 feet (2 m) tall before Superman's crystal pod could crash into it.

When Warner Bros. ordered 3D added, Singer cut 30 minutes of story and converted 20 minutes of 2D material into four spectacular augmented scenes (Clark's Kansas boyhood, rescuing a spaceplane and sinking ship, and the conclusion's flyover in space). *Superman Returns: An IMAX 3D Experience* premiered simultaneously in 111 modified theaters across the globe, and Singer devised an on-screen cue for viewers—a corner icon of Clark's glasses flashing green when a 3D scene began and obscured by a red circle with a strikethrough when it ended.

Ever more technically complex, movies had graduated to designated teams for storyboarding. *Superman Returns* employed CG animator/director Marc Messenger, Tani Kunitake (*Black Panther*), and titles sequence specialist Simon Clowes (*Aquaman*) to map out the story processes. With Donner's film as an

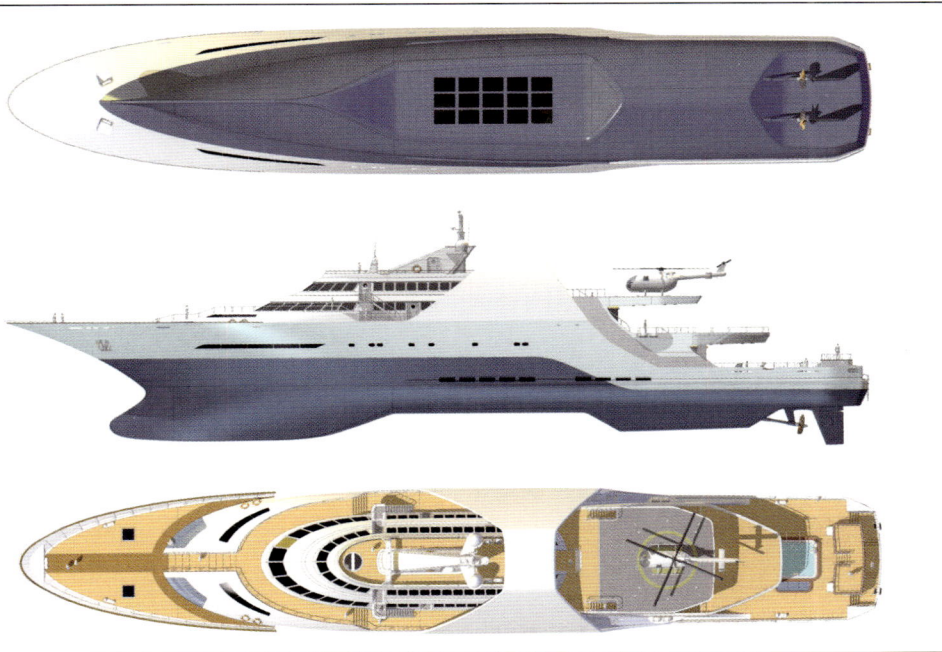

Far left: Luthor's nearly 300-foot (90-m) mega-yacht "Gertrude" was constructed in the Fox workshops. The two full-scale sections included a gourmet galley, gym, jacuzzi, glass floor, palatial library, and stained-glass windows.

Left: According to production designer Dyas, the Daily Planet Building was inspired by "the work of Frank Lloyd Wright, Hugh Ferris, and William Van Allen, who built the Chrysler Building, and Raymond Hood's Daily News Building, which doubled as the Daily Planet in Richard Donner's film."

inspirational template, *Superman Returns'* title sequence channels the original's opening with a flight through space to Earth.

The spectacle required 1,400 visual-effects shots, outsourced to specialist teams like Rhythm and Hues—who digitally resurrected Marlon Brando as Jor-El—Sony Pictures Imageworks, Framestore, Rising Sun Pictures, and The Orphanage each contributing set sequences, making the film a patchwork quilt of action and imagination. Despite Warner Bros.'s trimming, at 154 minutes, *Superman Returns* is the longest film in the franchise and the first to be categorized PG-13 (by the Motion Picture Association of America) rather than a family-friendly PG rating.

DOWN TO EARTH

Five years after he vanished, Superman's story resumes with his return, crashing in the same Kansas cornfields that first welcomed him as an infant. Reunited with adoptive mother Martha Kent (Eva Marie Saint), he shares his disappointments and doubts before trying to restart his stalled civilian life in Metropolis.

Although duty called him away for so long, he still loves Lois Lane, but she has moved on. Engaged to Richard (James Marsden), the nephew of Perry White (Frank Langella), Lois has a son, Jason (Tristan Lake Leabu), and seemingly has no fondness for someone who so abruptly abandoned everything.

Elsewhere, Superman's archfoe is on top of the world. Avoiding prison, Lex Luthor beguiled wealthy octogenarian Gertrude Vanderworth (Noel Neill) and, on her inevitable death, used her money in his long game to control everything. With a gang of thugs and new paramour, Kitty Kowalski (Parker Posey), Lex invades Superman's deserted Fortress of Solitude, removing Kryptonian memory crystals to facilitate another elaborate and genocidal property scam.

Insights into how this all occurred are alluded to, but never seen. An excised subplot had *Daily Planet* science writer Stamford (Kal Penn) bribed by Luthor to deceive Superman with stories that Krypton had survived. Lex's ultimate victory was tricking his enemy into leaving Earth. With no hero to testify against him,

Smalltown hero

On October 16, 2001, Superman returned to television with a new vision of his formative years. Developed by screenwriters Alfred Gough and Miles Millar (*Lethal Weapon 4*, *Shanghai Noon*), *Smallville* merged comic book fantasy action with compelling teen drama.

The pilot—setting ratings records for The WB with 8.4 million viewers on October 16, 2001—saw baby Kal-El arrive on Earth in a shower of Kryptonite meteors that, over his childhood, irradiated, mutated, and empowered dozens of potential foes.

Blending Clark Kent's coming-of-age story and evolution (Clark played by Tom Welling) into the ultimate superhero with weekly threats and menaces, the show ran for 10 seasons (217 episodes). The finale—broadcast on May 13, 2011—ended with *Daily Planet* cub reporter Clark donning Superman's uniform for the first time. That costume was one originally worn by Brandon Routh in *Superman Returns*; Routh had been a close contender for the lead in *Smallville* back in 2000.

Taking its lead from Richard Donner's film mythology, the series introduced many DC characters to a wider world: Green Arrow, Brainiac, Doomsday, Kara Zor-El, Darkseid, Aquaman, Booster Gold, Blue Beetle, Cyborg, J'onn J'onzz, Doctor Fate, the Legion of Super-Heroes, and more. It also returned many previous Superman Family screen stars to fans' attention. Terrence Stamp (Zod) voiced Jor-El, and Annette O'Toole (Lana Lang) was Martha Kent, with cameos from Christopher Reeve, Margot Kidder, Helen Slater, and Marc McClure. The show spawned spin-offs—*Smallville: Chloe Chronicles*, and *Vengeance Chronicles*—YA novels, soundtrack albums, and a comic book tie-in that evolved in 2012 to a continued series (*Smallville: Season 11*, #1–22, April 2012–November 2013).

Girl reporter

The first big-screen Lois Lane was Noel Neill (November 25, 1920–July 3, 2016). Her parents—dancer Lavere Gosbroth and *The Minneapolis Star Journal* journalist/news editor David Holland Neill—had enrolled 4-year-old Noel at a school for aspiring performers, and by her teens she was modeling, singing, dancing, acting, and playing banjo across the Midwest. Following her first film *Mad Youth* (1940), Neill signed to Paramount and worked in short features, westerns, comedies, and more.

In 1945, producer Sam Katzman gave her a recurring role: go-getting school reporter Betty Rogers in *Junior Prom*—first in Monogram Pictures' Teen Agers film musical series—before she graduated to thrillers and early television shows. Playing Betty Rogers made her Katzman's choice for Lois Lane in serial *Superman* (1948)—a role she reprised two years later in *Atom Man vs. Superman*. She used all she had learned from her dad and regularly consulted him during filming. Phyllis Coates played Lois in *Superman and the Mole Men* (1951) and season 1 of *The Adventures of Superman* television show, but was unavailable for subsequent series, and Neill stepped into the iconic role once again.

While Neill appeared in over 80 films and TV series over the course of her career, she was always associated with the Superman family. In her later years, she appeared in *Superman* (1978), *Superboy* (1991), and—with Jack Larson—*Superman Returns*. In June 2010, in Metropolis, Illinois, she was immortalized as a statue of 1950s Lois Lane.

Lex Luthor's train set took 14 weeks to construct. Supplied by German specialist Märklin, its 306 yards (280 m) of track had to accommodate any shooting angle Singer (pictured) or Sigel needed.

The film is loaded with fan-targeted tableaux recreating iconic moments, like reenacting *Action Comics* #1's cover (above), and referencing Superman saving a spaceplane in John Byrne's 1986 reboot *Man of Steel* #1.

Lex avoided prosecution and imprisonment. Those cuts included Superman in Krypton's star system, exploring what really remained. Shooting the scenes cost $10 million—the most expensive in film history to be left on a cutting-room floor.

Only Martha knows Superman is back, but when Luthor tests the seemingly living crystals, their energy blacks out the East Coast and Clark must act to save an airplane-launched space shuttle from crashing. One of the journalists aboard is Lois. With Superman back, Lex uses Kitty as a distraction to steal Kryptonite from a museum, and has the crystals create a new continent off the coast. As Superman battles catastrophic geological damage the landmass inflicts, Lois goes snooping. When she's captured and Jason reacts to Kryptonite, Luthor deduces who his father is.

Superman confronts Luthor, but is weakened by Kryptonite infusing the landmass. Brutally beaten and stabbed by Lex's Kryptonite shard he is left to die. Indomitably unyielding, Superman saves Lois and Jason, heaving the new continent into space. Fleeing, Lex is betrayed by Kitty who, horrified by his actions, dumps the control crystals into the sea, before their escape helicopter runs out of fuel and leaves them stranded on a deserted island. Later, Superman lies near death in Metropolis Hospital,

but miraculously rallies after Lois and Jason sneak in to whisper a secret in his ear. Superman reassures Lois that he is back to stay and flies above the Earth and gazes down at his adopted planet once again.

THE RISE AND RISE OF LEX LUTHOR

Superman Returns is an epic, elegiac end-point to the hero's mythology, but is in many ways a "villain's film" resembling The Joker's show-stealing turn in *Batman* (1989). Here, Luthor is the main attraction—sardonic, sadistic, and totally compelling. Comics' most recognizable villain, Luthor is the quintessential "mad scientist," epitomizing mind over muscle and an indicator of what each new generation deems evil.

As conceived by Superman's creators, Joe Seigel and Jerry Shuster, Lex Luthor debuted in *Action Comics* #23 (April 1940) as a red-headed, modern Genghis Khan using super-science for profit by fomenting war. Thanks to confusion with one of the Superman newspaper strip's villains though, Luthor soon appeared with his more famous bald countenance. Lex appeared in newspaper strips from November 1940 onward and made his live-action premiere in 1950's *Atom Man vs. Superman*, where he was played by Lyle Talbot. But TV would be where the villain seemed to find his home.

After *Crisis on Infinite Earths,* Luthor morphed from technocrat to merciless capitalist and even the US president. That storyline resurfaced in TV's *Smallville* (2001-2011), in which Michael Rosenbaum played Lex. Other small-screen incarnations included James Scott Wells and Sherman Howard, who shared the role in *Superboy* (1988–1992), John Shea in *Lois and Clark: The New Adventures of Superman* (1993–1997), Jon Cryer in "Arrowverse" series *Supergirl* (2015–2021), Titus B. Welliver in *Titans* (2002), and Michael Cudlitz in *Superman and Lois* (2021–2024).

In 2006, *Superman Returns* was the second-highest-grossing DC film to date (behind *Batman*), but although a sequel was announced, continued postponements and delays like the 2007–2008 Writers Guild of America strike led to cast and team individually finding other projects. In 2013, Superman would be rebooted for a very different, new lease of life.

Above left: Routh and Spacey don't share screen time until the 112th minute, but once they finally meet, the intensity of their feeling was electric.

Above: Kate Bosworth has one blue and one hazel eye, meaning—unlike here—she often requires at least one colored contact lens when working.

Left: In keeping with a messianic leitmotif, key scenes reference classical Christian art tropes, such as this pieta allusion as mother Martha Kent cradles her wounded yet resurrected son.

THE DARK KNIGHT

Release date: July 2008
Starring roles: Christian Bale, Michael Caine, Heath Ledger, Gary Oldman, Aaron Eckhart, Maggie Gyllenhaal, Morgan Freeman
Director: Christopher Nolan
Screenplay: Jonathan Nolan and Christopher Nolan
Story: Christopher Nolan and David S. Goyer
Cinematography: Wally Pfister
Music: Hans Zimmer and James Newton Howard
Running time: 152 minutes
Box office: $1,003,045,358

Although the sequence of films that came to be known as *The Dark Knight Trilogy* was never intended as a trilogy, right from the first film in the series director Christopher Nolan had an inkling that the story of Bruce Wayne and Batman was bigger than one movie. As they collaborated on *Batman Begins* (2005), Nolan and his co-writer David Goyer had worked out roughly where Bruce's story could go next, while the final scene of *Batman Begins*, as well as unveiling the Bat-Signal (inspired by an earlier scene where Batman chains mob boss Carmine Falcone to a spotlight), features Lieutenant Jim Gordon showing Batman the calling card of a homicidal robber with "a taste for the theatrical, like you"—a Joker playing card. Even so, there were no guarantees of a sequel, let alone a trilogy. But after audiences embraced Nolan's vision and *Batman Begins* became a success at the cinema, a continuation of the director and the Dark Knight's journey became much more of a certainty.

BEGIN AGAIN

Before he could begin *The Dark Knight*, Christopher Nolan had another project to pursue, along with Bruce Wayne/Batman actor Christian Bale and Alfred actor Michael Caine: director and stars followed up *Batman Begins* with *The Prestige* (2006), a crafty tale of rival Victorian magicians, with another comic book movie star, Hugh "Wolverine" Jackman, playing opposite Bale. Once that film was completed, Nolan turned his thoughts fully to Batman again.

"Out of the darkness … comes the Knight."
Marketing tagline

An obvious thread for Nolan and David Goyer to follow was the iconic villain intimated at the end of *Batman Begins*, and how The Joker might derail Bruce Wayne's efforts to cleanse Gotham City of crime and corruption. As with Batman himself, Nolan and Goyer wanted to delineate a more realistic Joker—a genuinely scary agent of chaos, as in the character's earliest appearances in *Batman* #1 (Spring 1940), whose origin was shrouded in

Peter Robb-King, John Caglione Jr., Conor O'Sullivan, and the rest of *The Dark Knight* makeup team utilized medical research to ensure The Joker's scarring looked realistic.

Far left: Already scheduled for demolition, Chicago's Brach's candy factory stood in for Gotham City General Hospital, rigged to blow up (by The Joker in the film) as if it were exploding outward rather than inward.

Left: To ensnare The Joker, Lieutenant Jim Gordon (Gary Oldman) of the GCPD Major Crime Unit dons a SWAT uniform to drive the armored truck containing Harvey Dent as bait.

127

Basing himself once more in Christopher Nolan's garage, production designer Nathan Crowley filled the walls with reference, concept art, and designs.

For Christopher Nolan, Aaron Eckhart was able to embody Harvey Dent's Robert Redford-esque air of decency, and convincingly portray his descent into darkness.

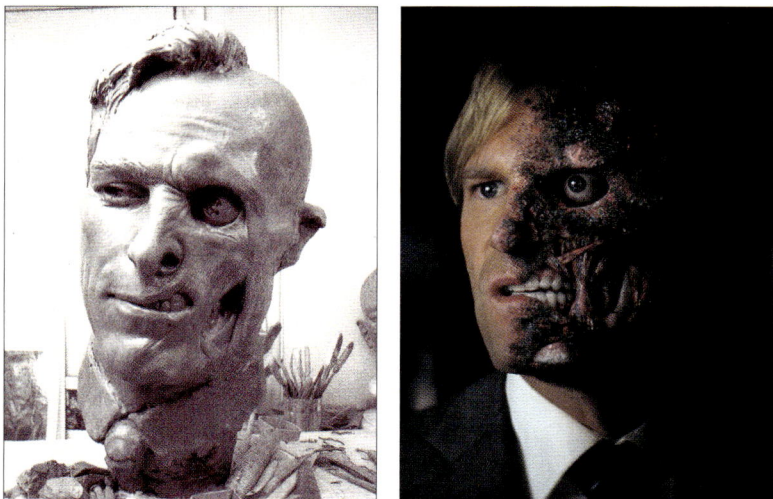

Harvey Dent's gruesome appearance as Two-Face was created via concept sketches, clay sculptures, and VFX, assisted by Aaron Eckhart wearing a half-bald skullcap marked with tracking dots.

obfuscation and misdirection in Alan Moore and Brian Bolland's acclaimed graphic novel *Batman: The Killing Joke* (1988).

Playing The Joker, who the filmmakers viewed as an unknowable, anarchic force of nature akin to Alex in *A Clockwork Orange* (1971) or the shark in *Jaws* (1975)—someone who, in the words of Alfred (Michael Caine), just wants to "watch the world burn"—would be Heath Ledger. In his fearlessness and willingness to go to the extremes required, the *Brokeback Mountain* (2005) actor, who tragically died shortly after completing filming, helped Nolan, Goyer, and Nolan's brother Jonathan—who came on board to write the first-draft screenplay—shape the story. Moreover, Ledger worked with the wardrobe and makeup departments to achieve The Joker's terrifying, scarred appearance, his look inspired at Christopher Nolan's suggestion by Francis Bacon's paintings, notably 1953's *Study After Velázquez's Portrait of Pope Innocent X*.

TWO'S TROUBLE

Another comics character from Batman's Rogues Gallery who intrigued the writers was Harvey Dent, the Gotham City District Attorney who became the unhinged, coin-flipping villain Two-Face after half his face was scarred by acid in *Detective Comics* #66 (August 1942). For the film, Dent's face was disfigured in an explosion after he is taken hostage by corrupt cops under the sway of The Joker. Discussions about including Dent in the narrative dated back to *Batman Begins*, when Jeph Loeb and Tim Sale's 13-issue comics series *Batman: The Long Halloween* (1996–97) had been an influence on the writing. The almost operatic tragedy of Harvey Dent's downfall dovetailed with Nolan and Goyer's notions for *The Dark Knight*, the pair seeing not Bruce Wayne as the protagonist of the film, but Dent, with the struggle for his soul between Batman and The Joker coalescing as the film's theme.

Playing Dent would be *Thank You for Smoking* (2005) actor Aaron Eckhart, who Nolan believed could embody the duality of Dent's charm and underlying anger. Unlike with Ledger, whose look was created with makeup and prosthetics, Eckhart's burnt face was achieved via VFX, Nolan and his team reasoning that was the best

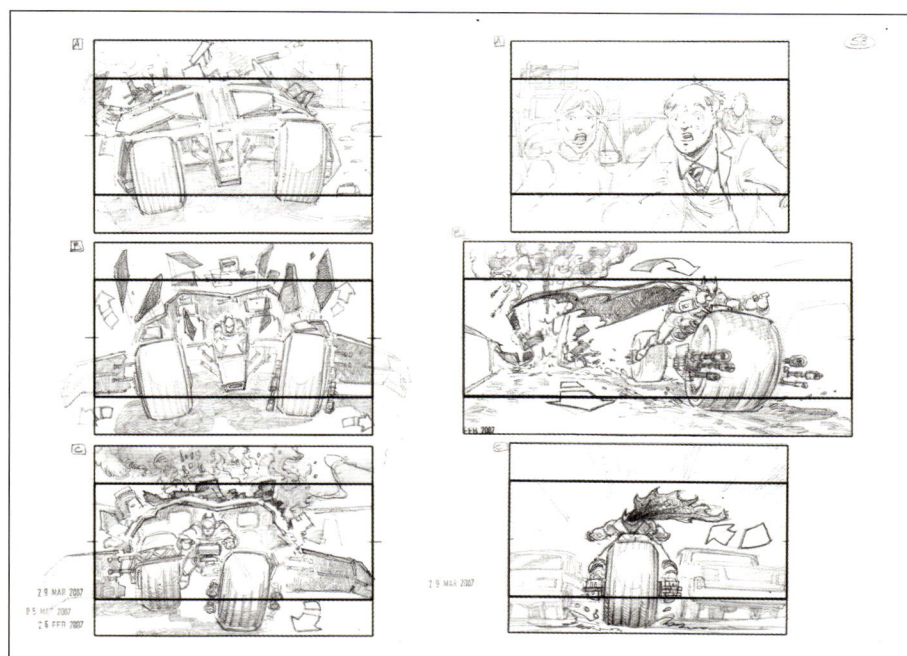

Far left: The only person able to ride the Bat-Pod was stunt performer Jean-Pierre Goy, who trained on the vehicle for months to master its idiosyncrasies.

Left: Gabriel Hardman's intricate storyboard sequence depicting how the Bat-Pod breaks free of the wrecked Tumbler, emerging to the surprise of motorists as the Batmobile explodes in the background.

way to give the actor freedom to perform and to produce the desired skeletal appearance. The effect was accentuated by cinematographer Wally Pfister lighting Two-Face more moodily than the clean-cut Dent.

REAL ZEAL

Where on *Batman Begins* Christopher Nolan and production designer Nathan Crowley had felt somewhat constrained by the established look and feel of Batman's world, even as they stretched the boundaries of the mythos in their search for veracity, on *The Dark Knight* director and designer felt free to pursue their reality with greater zeal. As he had on *Batman Begins*, Crowley started the design process in Nolan's garage—which in the interim had been transformed by Nolan into offices and a screening and art room—kit-bashing together a bizarre two-wheeled vehicle christened the Bat-Pod. In the narrative of the movie, the Bat-Pod is ejected from the Batmobile/Tumbler after the vehicle is wrecked during a chaotic armored car chase with The Joker and his henchmen, a set piece that climaxes with an 18-wheel truck flipping over head to tail. (The Tumbler, incidentally, was originally set to be destroyed in *Batman Begins*, until Nolan and co. fell in love with the vehicle.)

That stunt, designed and overseen by special-effects supervisor Chris Corbould and performed by flipping a full-sized truck with a piston, was filmed in the streets of Chicago, the city once again standing in for Gotham City. This time, however, the filmmakers made even greater use of Chicago, wherever possible eschewing the theatricality of soundstage sets for real-world locales. Even so, some sets were deemed necessary. With Bruce Wayne having relocated to Gotham City after Wayne Manor burned down at the hands of Rā's al Ghūl, living an isolated existence in a penthouse, a new underground base of operations in the city was required for Batman. Built at the Cardington Sheds in Bedfordshire—formerly the site of *Batman Begins*'s Gotham City sets—the concrete Bat-Bunker's rectangular, boxlike shape, suspended illuminated ceiling, and hidden compartments

Gotham City via Chicago

Although *The Dark Knight* is set mostly within the confines of Gotham City, the filmmakers largely eschewed the soundstage sets of *Batman Begins*, instead preferring to shoot wherever possible on the streets and in the buildings of Chicago. That commitment to keeping it real began with the start of principal photography in April 2007, when the prologue bank heist was filmed—using IMAX cameras—at the Old Chicago Post Office. The climax of the scene, where a school bus reverses through one of the bank's walls, required special effects supervisor Chris Corbould's crew to build a false wall within the building and then pull a full-sized bus through it, which they had to dismantle and reassemble in order to bring it inside.

Other Chicago locations included One Illinois Center, which was used for Bruce Wayne's penthouse, where his fundraiser for Harvey Dent is interrupted by The Joker, leading to the first confrontation with Batman. The later scene where The Joker has rigged two ferries to explode was filmed at Navy Pier alongside Lake Michigan—which also stood in for the Bahamas in the scene where Bruce Wayne leaps into the ocean from his yacht—although the ferries themselves had to be custom built atop barges. Away from Chicago, one notable location was London's then-deserted Battersea Power Station, which doubled for the warehouse where Rachel Dawes—played by Maggie Gyllenhaal, assuming the role from Katie Holmes—is killed in a Joker-rigged explosion. The blast was so loud that some local residents believed a terrorist attack was underway, despite the production sending out advance notice.

The Victorian-era Farmiloe Building in London stood in for GCPD headquarters, where Batman's brutal interrogation of The Joker takes place.

For the Hong Kong sequence where Batman swoops from the city's tallest skyscraper, a digital double of the Dark Knight was composited onto IMAX footage.

Maggie Gyllenhaal replaced Katie Holmes as Rachel Dawes for *The Dark Knight*.

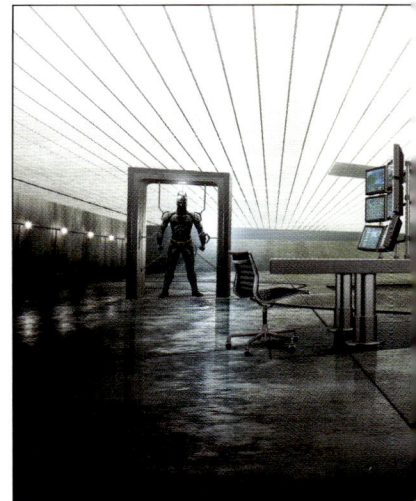

Concept art for the Bat-Bunker, a base accessed via a freight container on the outskirts of Gotham City.

for added security reflected the film's modern urban feel and the production's quest for authenticity and logic.

Among the compartments that rise from the floor of the Bat-Bunker is Batman's armory, housing his equipment, his weaponry, and his Batsuit, which underwent a redesign for *The Dark Knight*, both for practical and narrative reasons. After a run-in with The Scarecrow (Cillian Murphy making a cameo return) and Chechen mobsters, plus a bunch of Batman copycats, in a scene filmed at the same Chicago parking garages where part of *Batman Begins*'s rooftop Tumbler chase was shot, Bruce Wayne asks Wayne Industries CEO Lucius Fox (Morgan Freeman) if he can assist with a more functional and flexible suit, one where turning his head is easier. Following that story logic, costume designer Lindy Hemming designed a segmented Batsuit with separate cowl and neck pieces that both served the narrative and was more comfortable for Christian Bale to wear.

HONG KONG CALLING

One feature Hemming wanted to incorporate into the new suit was a backpack that Batman's cape could retract into. The costume designer envisioned that function coming into use during the sequences where Batman rides the Bat-Pod, but in the event stunt rider Jean-Pierre Goy was able to ride the vehicle with a cape billowing safely and cinematically behind him. Instead, the backpack was used in the scene where, on a sojourn to Hong Kong in pursuit of crime lord Lau (Chin Han), Batman leaps from one skyscraper and glides to another. The scene gave Christian Bale the opportunity to outdo the moment during filming in Chicago when he stood in Batsuit costume at the precipice of the Sears Tower, a hundred stories up, by standing in costume atop Hong Kong's International Finance Center, at the time the tallest building in Hong Kong at over 1,300 feet.

The Bat-Pod chase and elements of the Hong Kong sequence were examples of perhaps Christopher Nolan's biggest innovation with *The Dark Knight*. The director had been considering utilizing large-scale IMAX film cameras, previously the preserve of documentaries, in narrative filmmaking, fascinated by the bigger canvas the format afforded. After *Batman Begins* visual effects

supervisor Janek Sirrs had secured some IMAX shots of Chicago for use as VFX background plates, Nolan issued 80 prints of that film to IMAX cinemas, enlarging the footage from 35mm to IMAX's 70mm. Stunned by how well the film translated to the massive IMAX screen, Nolan and cinematographer Wally Pfister used IMAX for an effect in *The Prestige* as a test for Nolan's next Batman movie.

EXPLOSIVE

To do justice to the epic nature of *The Dark Knight*, Nolan decided to shoot 40 minutes of the film with IMAX cameras. Besides the Bat-Pod and Hong Kong scenes, these sequences included The Joker's destruction of Gotham City General Hospital, which involved the demolition of an actual building as Heath Ledger walked away from it, and Batman's final fight with The Joker and his henchmen. But the most prominent example is the film's six-minute prologue, a bravura bank robbery by The Joker's henchmen wearing clown masks, with Hans Zimmer and James Newton Howard's atonal strings ratcheting up the tension as each twist unfolds, culminating with the reveal of The Joker himself. Released in select IMAX theaters six months ahead of *The Dark Knight*'s cinema debut, it signaled the scope and ambition of Nolan's film, and hinted at how much grander the director's ambitions were for the future.

Shot in Chicago's LaSalle Street Canyon, the truck-flip involved stunt driver Jim Wilkey driving an 18-wheeler as a piston on the back of the vehicle propelled the truck over.

Gordon's law

One of many highlights of *The Dark Knight Trilogy* is Gary Oldman's portrayal of Sergeant-turned-Lieutenant-turned-Commissioner Gordon as a decent, compassionate family man and something of a father figure to Bruce Wayne. Intriguingly, these qualities were quite at odds with other characters and figures Oldman had played prior to the trilogy, among them Sid Vicious in *Sid and Nancy* (1986), Lee Harvey Oswald in *JFK* (1991), Count Dracula in *Bram Stoker's Dracula* (1992), and a rather different sort of cop, deranged DEA agent Norman Stansfield in *Léon: The Professional* (1994). For his Gordon—a character who had been a constant in comics since his appearance in the first panel of Batman's debut story in May 1939's *Detective Comics* #27—Oldman took visual

inspiration from David Mazzucchelli's depiction in 1987's celebrated *Batman: Year One*, written by Frank Miller.

Oldman's warm and sensitive performance was markedly different than previous screen Gordons. In the 1966–1968 *Batman* TV show, Neil Hamilton's Commissioner Gordon (left) is a stalwart supporter of the Caped Crusader, continually calling on his services via the red Batphone in his office, while in Tim Burton's *Batman* (1989) and its sequels, Pat Hingle's bluff Gordon initially dismisses Batman as a rumor. Subsequent performers have delivered more nuanced takes on the character, more in keeping with Gary Oldman's version, including Ben McKenzie in the 2014–2019 Fox TV show *Gotham*, and Jeffrey Wright in Matt Reeves's 2022 film *The Batman*.

WATCHMEN

Release date: March 2009
(February 2009 UK)
Starring roles: Malin Åkerman,
Billy Crudup, Matthew Goode,
Jackie Earle Haley, Jeffrey Dean
Morgan, Patrick Wilson
Director: Zack Snyder

Screenplay: David Hayter,
Alex Tse
Cinematography: Larry Fong
Music: Tyler Bates
Running time: 163 minutes
Box office: $185,382,813

For two decades after Alan Moore and Dave Gibbons's *Watchmen* was first published—initially as a groundbreaking 12-issue comic book maxiseries in 1986–1987, then as a perennially best-selling graphic novel—a variety of filmmakers tried to turn the intricate and multilayered comic into a movie. The roll call of directors who attempted to film *Watchmen* in the years following publication included Terry Gilliam (*Brazil*), Darren Aronofsky (*Pi*), and Paul Greengrass (*The Bourne Supremacy*). While Gilliam worked from a screenplay by *Batman* (1989) and *Batman Returns* (1992) writer Sam Hamm, the screenplay that both Aronofsky and Greengrass worked from was by actor-turned-director David Hayter, whose previous scripts included 2000's *X-Men* (he would also co-write 2003 sequel *X2*).

> ## "Justice is coming to all of us. No matter what we do."
> ### Marketing tagline

Hayter had been hired in 2001, producing a screenplay that even Alan Moore, whose antipathy toward movie adaptations of his work was legendary, conceded was as close as he could imagine anyone getting to his and Gibbons's original. The intention had originally been for Hayter to make his feature film directing debut with *Watchmen*, but by 2006 he, Aronofsky, Greengrass, and a number of other directors had come and gone.

ZACK SNYDER'S DC DEBUT

Step forward director Zack Snyder (*Dawn of the Dead*). In June 2006 news broke that Snyder had been hired to direct *Watchmen* largely on the strength of another film he was making for WB Pictures at the time, *300*, his Spartan action epic, which was set to be released that December. Adapted from *Batman: The Dark Knight Returns* creator Frank Miller's 1998 graphic novel, Snyder's *300* adhered closely to the original work, the director using comics panels as the basis for his storyboards and employing chroma key compositing—a visual-effects technique whereby image layers are streamed together based on color hues—to replicate the distinctive

Watchmen co-creator Dave Gibbons, on set for the filming of this scene, was struck by the way the characters' personalities shined through in their poses for this photo op.

Far left: This shot of the Comedian being thrown through his apartment window is a faithful recreation of a panel from early in the first issue of *Watchmen*, published in September 1986.

Left: Flashback sequence depicting the lab accident that disassembled Dr. Jon Osterman, transforming him into Dr. Manhattan—played in both cases by Billy Crudup.

Reading Watchmen

Trying to encapsulate Alan Moore and Dave Gibbons's multiple-award-winning *Watchmen* is akin to attempting to explain the gigantic, fantastically intricate machine Dr. Manhattan is working on in the first chapter of the series—such is its complexity that the more one describes it, the more elusive it becomes. Originally published as a 12-issue comic book maxiseries from September 1986 to October 1987, *Watchmen* astonished even its creators with its layers and meanings, each issue revealing additional depths to Moore and Gibbons themselves as they worked on it. Their discovery of themes and significances is reflected in the reading experience, *Watchmen* rewarding repeated readings with a seemingly bottomless bounty of accreting details.

Ostensibly a postmodern deconstruction of superhero archetypes, *Watchmen* reveals itself as a meditation on life, physics, reality, nuclear destruction, and time—less a superhero story and more, as Dave Gibbons realized while drawing it, a science-fiction alternate history. Moreover, its themes are more than matched by its formal innovations, from the series' covers, a succession of close-ups which act as the first panel of each chapter; to Gibbons's nine-panel grid and precise storytelling; to the *Tales of the Black Freighter* comic-within-a-comic; to the seemingly supplementary but in actuality intrinsic articles at the back of each issue. These innovations are exemplified by the fifth chapter, "Fearful Symmetry," in which each of the 14 pages which comprise the first half of the comic has a corresponding "mirror" page in the second half, reflecting the storytelling, layout, and John Higgins's coloring.

Jeffrey Dean Morgan, the Comedian, would be cast by Zack Snyder again as Bruce Wayne's father, Thomas, in *Batman v Superman: Dawn of Justice.*

look of the comic. Snyder's work on *300* convinced the studio that he was the right person to take on *Watchmen*, but Snyder himself, fully aware of how complex the original comic was, was hesitant.

Ultimately the prospect proved too tantalizing to pass up, and Snyder set about bringing a work many had deemed unfilmable to the big screen, utilizing many of the techniques he had honed during the making of *300*. Once again David Hayter's screenplay provided the basis for the project, except this time reworked by Alex Tse—writer of Spike Lee's 2004 TV movie *Sucker Free City*—who combined elements of Hayter's previous drafts with his own. One decision made was to set the movie largely in the 1985 of the original comic, rather than make it contemporary, though again in keeping with the original, flashbacks would span the years 1938 to 1985.

As he had with *300*, Snyder used the comic itself to draw shot-by-shot storyboards for the entire film. Though drawn in a simple style, Snyder's storyboards were packed with information, and would prove invaluable in particular when creating the film's title sequence.

CREDIT WHERE IT'S DUE

A slo-mo montage of vignettes both drawn directly from the original comic and newly envisioned for Snyder's cinematic version, in many ways *Watchmen*'s title credits sequence sets the tone for what follows. As Bob Dylan's "The Times They Are a-Changin'" plays on the soundtrack, the visuals trace the history of superheroes in the skewed universe of *Watchmen*, from the emergence of Nite Owl, Silk Spectre, Comedian, and the other masked adventurers who banded together as the Minutemen during World War II; to the ignominious end many of them met in the years following the war; to the advent of a genuinely super-powered individual at the end of the 1950s, in the shape of Dr. Manhattan; to the role the Comedian played in the assassination

Far Left: In a title sequence vignette, the Minutemen—Silhouette, Mothman, Dollar Bill, Nite Owl, Captain Metropolis, Comedian, Silk Spectre, and Hooded Justice—gather for a photo.

Left: As in the original comic book, when Rorschach visits Dr. Manhattan at the latter's military research center base, Manhattan is working on an elaborate machine.

With his facial features covered by a mask, Jackie Earle Haley had to use his physicality in his performance, as when Rorschach visits the Comedian's grave.

Jackie Earle Haley in his character's civilian guise as Walter Kovacs, consigned to jail after being set up by the killer of the Comedian.

of President John F. Kennedy; to the emergence of a new generation of heroes in the 1970s, and the riots that ensued in the wake of President Nixon's election to a third term. Moreover, the sequence is the first taste of the film's visual style, a mixture of live action and computer-generated VFX, the real and the unreal blending into something that Deborah Snyder—one of *Watchmen*'s producers, and Zack Snyder's wife—dubbed stylized realism.

Zack Snyder himself felt strongly that, stylistically and visually, his film should treat the comic book *Watchmen* almost as if it were a sacrosanct illuminated text. Accordingly, the production would respect the visual style of the graphic novel while also using it as a bible, a template from which to extrapolate. Where typically on movies directors and production designers will look at multiple reference sources, here there was one main reference. Designers, technicians, and actors would frequently refer to the graphic novel on set. Snyder even engaged Dave Gibbons and *Watchmen*'s colorist, John Higgins, to draw new pages to give a taste of how the altered climax created for the movie—which differs from the original comic in making Dr. Manhattan complicit in the catastrophe that consumes New York—might have looked as comics pages. (The pair also created new illustrations of key shots for marketing purposes.)

This quest to remain true to the comic saw production designer Alex McDowell—whose previous work included such visually striking films as David Fincher's *Fight Club* (1999) and Steven Spielberg's *Minority Report* (2002)—utilizing the perverse color palette of the original comic, from the costumes to the sets and props. For McDowell, using a controlled palette inspired by John Higgins's unusual (for the time) palette of secondary colors—purples, greens, and oranges, as opposed to the more traditional primary comic book colors of reds, blues, and yellows—would signal to the audience that this was a parallel world they were witnessing, allowing them to be drawn in. Higgins himself had been inspired by the New York of the 1980s in his color choices, and so in their pursuit of fidelity to the source material the filmmakers also looked at reference material of the city of that era, not least because with so many flashbacks, it was important for the milieu and outfits to reflect each era so the audience knew where they were in the film.

The interiors of Ozymandias's Antarctic base made use of the biggest set built for the film, while exteriors were created using computer-generated imagery.

Filmed on New York sets built on a Vancouver backlot, the flashback where the Comedian and Nite Owl attempt to pacify rioters made use of the Owlship for a dramatic entrance.

Once again echoing the imagery of the graphic novel, Nite Owl experiences a nightmare where he and Silk Spectre kiss against the background of a nuclear blast.

ATTENTION TO DETAIL

When he visited the set during filming, Dave Gibbons was amazed by the level of detail he witnessed, right down to seemingly incidental props in the background that would barely be seen on screen. Much as the graphic novel reveals additional layers and nuances on successive readings, so viewers would need to watch Snyder's *Watchmen* multiple times in order to spot all of the Easter eggs, from the genetically engineered (thanks to Dr. Manhattan's existence) four-legged chicken served in the restaurant where Dan Dreiberg—the second Nite Owl—and Laurie Jupiter—the second Silk Spectre—meet, to the hairspray the outlawed vigilante Rorschach uses as a weapon against a SWAT team—branded Veidt, after billionaire businessman Adrian Veidt, alias retired costumed crimefighter Ozymandias.

But though highly stylized, all of this would still be grounded in a form of realism that the audience could buy into—for despite the comic book origins of *Watchmen*, it was important to director and crew that the movie feel real to audiences. A touchstone for Zack Snyder was Martin Scorsese's classic *Taxi Driver* (1976), a film which was both stylized and yet grounded in a visceral reality (it didn't hurt, either, that the New York of *Taxi Driver* is aptly seedy and decrepit). Wherever possible, the filmmakers created physical sets, props, and costumes. Though the production used the source material as their guide, there was still room for interpretation in how that would translate to such aspects as costumes, where costume designer Michael Wilkinson—who had worked with Zack Snyder on *300*—and his team used suitably antiquated costuming techniques to create the outfits for the Minutemen, and more detailed, textured techniques for the modern superheroes.

Far left: For actor Matthew Goode, Ozymandias is less a villain than a practical man who comes up with a cold and mechanical solution for the world's ills.

Left: Back in costume, Nite Owl and Silk Spectre rediscover their mojo—and their passion for one another—after rescuing a group of tenants from a blazing building.

THE MANHATTAN PROJECT

As the actor playing the only genuine superhuman in *Watchmen*, Billy Crudup had to wear less a costume and more a tracking device. Crudup's performance as the atomically altered, blue-glowing Dr. Manhattan was captured on set in order that he could interact with the other actors, but to assist John "DJ" DesJardin and his visual effects team, who would create the final computer-generated Manhattan, Crudup wore a special suit coated in LEDs, the brightness of which could be increased or decreased depending on the scene. Not only did these cast a diffused blue light that reflected off the surroundings and the other actors—even creating sparkle in their eyes to add to the illusion—but they could be used as motion-capture markers, to translate the actor into the VFX version of Manhattan.

Visual effects were also used to assist with Jackie Earle Haley's performance as Rorschach. The vigilante's mask, with its iconic "ink blots," was developed by Michael Wilkinson and his team using a special printing process on four-way Lycra. However, to make the blots move and change shape, as in the comic, Hadley wore a mask covered with tracking markers and with large eyeholes through which he could emote, which DesJardin's team then used to replicate his emotions in the form of animated blots, utilizing expressive patterns created by Alex McDowell's art department.

As inventive as all this digital wizardry was, it all served to enhance the practical, physical elements in order to create the desired stylized reality, whether it be the second Nite Owl's full-size Owlship, which Nite Owl actor Patrick Wilson was blown away by when he first walked into the vessel's cockpit (Wilson subsequently worked with the designers to determine which buttons and switches did what in the ship); or the split-level jail set from which Nite Owl and Silk Spectre spring Rorschach; or Ozymandias's Antarctic lair Karnak, with its custom-built, museumlike interior set—a mixture of the modern and the ancient—and digitally created exterior. Above all, Zack Snyder and his crew never lost sight of their primary mission—to bring *Watchmen* to life as accurately and vividly as possible.

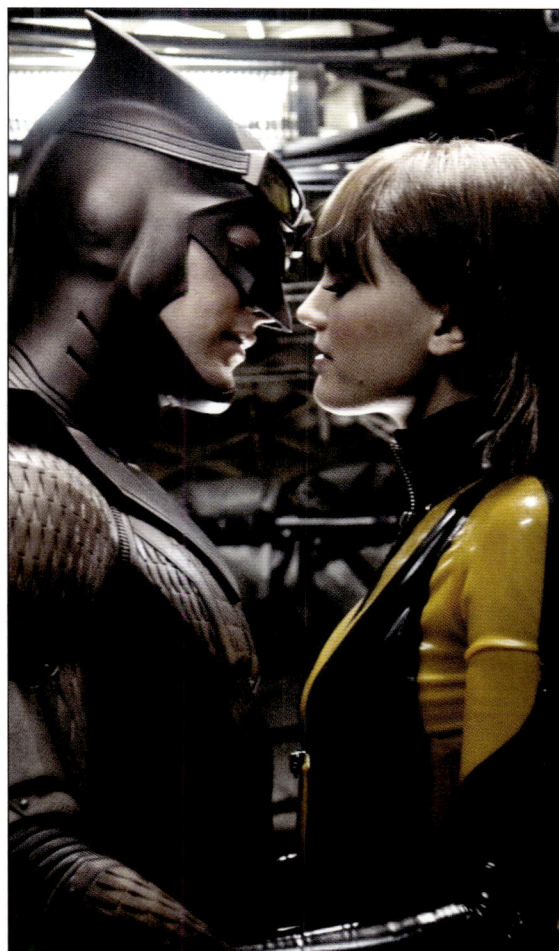

Made for television

When writer David Hayter, whose screenplay formed the basis of Zack Snyder's 2009 *Watchmen* movie, first pitched for the project in 2001, he originally pitched it as an HBO miniseries. At the time the projected cost of $100 million nixed that notion, but nearly two decades later a version of *Watchmen* was brought to the small screen by *Lost* co-creator and showrunner Damon Lindelof. This iteration would be contemporary, set in 2019, 34 years after the events of the original story, and would deal with racial rather than Cold War tension, though in common with the comic it would make liberal use of flashbacks.

First broadcast across the fall and winter of 2019, Lindelof's *Watchmen* initially seemed to bear little relation to its namesake. As the nine episodes unfurled, however, the links with the original comic became clearer, Lindelof weaving the dangling narrative threads of the graphic novel into a new tapestry, while also interweaving new elements into the original, notably the identity of Hooded Justice, the first masked vigilante in the alternate world of Watchmen. Rapturously received by critics, the show was praised for the way it built on the source material to address contemporary themes, and went on to win 11 Emmy Awards, including Outstanding Limited Series; Outstanding Writing for a Limited Series, Movie or Dramatic Special; and Outstanding Lead Actress in a Limited Series or Movie for Regina King, who played masked police detective Sister Night.

JONAH HEX

Release date: June 18, 2010
Starring roles: Josh Brolin, John Malkovich, Megan Fox, Michael Fassbender, Will Arnett, Michael Shannon, Wes Bentley
Director: Jimmy Hayward, Francis Lawrence (reshoots)
Screenplay: Mark Neveldine, Brian Taylor, William Farmer
Cinematography: Mitchell Amundsen
Music: Marco Beltrami, Mastodon, John Powell
Running time: 81 minutes
Box Office: $11 million

Western movies were a hugely popular sector of cinema and TV, peaking between 1945 and 1965 when the genre comprised a full quarter of Hollywood's entire output. DC capitalized on gunfighters from the start, with cowboy Jack Woods on the cover of *New Fun* #1 (January 11, 1935). Westerns were a major strand of DC's output until the peak of the Silver Age superhero explosion. Despite this, DC's only screen venture in the genre was 1948's *Vigilante* movie serial (see page 27). The company's most successful Western hero was Jonah Hex, who first ambushed an unsuspecting readership in July 1971.

"Revenge gets ugly."
Promotional tagline

RISKY BUSINESS

While Jonah Hex was often mentioned as a potential movie or series, real progress only began in 2000 with a proposed TV special linked to screenwriter/producer Akiva Goldsman (*Batman Forever*) and producer Robert Zappia. When it stalled, Warner Bros. paired Goldman with producer Andrew Lazar (*Space Cowboys*) and writers Mark Neveldine, Brian Taylor, and William Farmer. The production gained momentum when A-lister Josh Brolin signed on as Hex in October 2008. Throughout this preproduction process Thomas Jane (*The Punisher*) had lobbied hard for the role, having makeup artists recreate Hex's ruined face for him to wear while petitioning producers. Fate had other plans, though Jane eventually voiced the hero in an animated adventure.

Thanks to the prestige garnered by multi–Oscar winning *No Country for Old Men*, Brolin was afforded a high degree of creative control, including choice of co-stars and crew. John Malkovich was lined up to play villain Quentin Turnbull, backed up by Michael Fassbender as Turnbull's philosophically sadistic fixer Burke. They were joined by Will Arnett as US Army liaison Lieutenant Glass and Michael Shannon as Doc Cross Williams, organizer of gladiatorial death matches in a fight circus. Shannon was slated as lead villain for the planned but never realized Hex sequel. Comic book fan Megan Fox—fresh from starring in the hit Transformers movies—played combative romantic lead Lilah.

Part of an acting dynasty including father James and daughter Eden, Josh Brolin arrived on a wave of critical acclaim generated

In *Jonah Hex*, history
and the laws of physics
give way to action,
spectacle, and cool visual
beats in the pursuit of
audience satisfaction.

Far left: Lilah and Hex's
intimate yet casual
romantic relationship
provided much of the
film's glamor and most
of its earthy humor.

Left: Michael Fassbender
proved memorably manic
as sadistic chief flunky
Burke, equally adept at
murdering innocents,
maiming heroes, raiding
forts, and robbing trains.

139

Brolin and director Jimmy Hayward kept a close eye on detail, maintaining the film's internal integrity while staying true to the nature of Westerns.

Hex erupted back to life after learning Turnbull had faked his own death. Hex's tracking skills soon brought him into explosive conflict with the killer.

by the Coen Brothers's epic, Ridley Scott's *American Gangster* (both released in 2007) and Gus Van Sant's *Milk* (2008). He was keen to play a classic antihero in the manner of his childhood influences Clint Eastwood and Charles Bronson, and a great fan of the genre-changing westerns of Sergio Leone and Sam Peckinpah that had equally inspired Jonah Hex's comic creators.

Josh Brolin was an admirer of cinematic chameleon Lon Chaney, whose legendary makeup skills and powerful performances as tragic monsters and grotesques like *The Phantom of the Opera* (1923) and Quasimodo in *The Hunchback of Notre Dame* (1925) earned him the title of "The Man of a Thousand Faces." He appreciated him even more after enduring grueling daily fittings of the prosthetic recreating Hex's monstrous disfigurement. It took three hours every day to assemble, and Brolin had to eat and rehydrate through a straw until shooting ended. He claimed at a Gizmodo *Jonah Hex* roundtable that after 46 days of shooting, "We figured ... that I had spent five and a half full days in the makeup chair."

However, as reported by Megan Fox in an interview with Canada's tribute.ca, getting the look right nearly cost Brolin an eye, as early attempts to mimic Hex's ocular damage dried out the eye and brought on an infection within an hour. The search for a director took longer, with several linked to the project. These ranged from cutting-edge TV and advertising newcomers like McG to Brolin's list of foreign luminaries like Park Chan-Wook (*Oldboy*) and Takashi Miike (*Ichi the Killer*). Brolin was ultimately swayed by an impassioned email from animator Jimmy Hayward (*Horton Hears a Who*, *Toy Story*, *Finding Nemo*) who took on the job—his first live-action feature—determined to preserve as much of the comic's integrity as possible. With Hayward in place, an intense location shoot began in Louisiana on April 20, 2009. The production was slowed by rewrites and reshoots (directed by *Constantine* director Francis Lawrence) before final filming ended in February 2010.

Jonah Hex hit the big screen in mid June 2011. Blending horror tropes with steampunk visuals, it depicted a world-weary former Confederate soldier back from the dead on a mission of vengeance, while saving America from terrorism.

SOLDIER BLUES

Sporting a heavy metal/ambient music soundtrack by Tony Sanders and his band Mastodon, and pared down to 81 minutes, the final cut emphasizes eye-catching action and wicked black humor. It also employs a sequence of comics-style illustrations by DC artist Eduardo Risso (*100 Bullets*, *Batman*) and colorist Alec Sinclair, to cover the years between Hex's immolation and the return of Turnbull. Left behind on the cutting-room floor were atmospheric worldbuilding scenes such as a ghost-ridden hunt through a New

Orleans graveyard, moody establishing shots, and a subplot of Hex being followed by dead people. One late addition that did find general favor was giving Jonah a narrated internal monologue, enhancing his humanity and isolation.

The comic book Jonah Hex debuted in *All-Star Western* #10 (March 1972) by writer John Albano and illustrator Tony DeZuniga. Hex was a restless, utterly ruthless gunslinger who killed for pay.

Malkovich's portrayal of Quentin Turnbull is a masterclass in barely restrained obsession and suppressed passion that is perfectly complemented by Fassbender's crazed performance.

As initially conceived by John Albano and illustrated by Tony DeZuniga, Jonah Hex is arguably the most memorable Western comic star ever created. His dark comic book background was changed for the movie, where he was portrayed as an honorable soldier who once rejected an illegal order. His refusal to set fire to a Union hospital cost the life of his best friend Jeb Turnbull and earned the eternal enmity of their commanding officer Quentin Turnbull. In retribution, Turnbull has Jonah's family burned alive as Hex helplessly watches, before branding Hex's face. Traumatized, Hex completes the facial disfigurement himself and dies, only to be magically revived by the enigmatic Native American Crow People. He comes back able to converse with the dead.

Learning Turnbull had died, Hex becomes a bounty hunter, roaming the west in a violent haze until President Ulysses S. Grant compels his cooperation in hunting down terrorists sworn to destroy America in its centennial year. Hex's search is punctuated by Turnbull's atrocities across the country, drawing in relative innocents like Jonah's companion Lilah, and brings him savage conflict with Turnbull's enforcer Burke (Fassbender) who joyously set the blaze that took Hex's wife and daughter. Thanks to his spectral gifts, Hex and Lilah—real name Tallulah Black—catch up to the terrorists, but he almost dies again, before escaping to intercept and destroy Turnbull as he bombards Washington, D.C. from a customized ironclad warship on the Fourth of July.

Not one to hang up his spurs, Jonah Hex remains a popular character and, with Westerns a perennial live-action favorite, Hex's web series and frequent appearances in DC's TV and animation divisions may see him back on the big screen.

Iconic imagery from the comics informed much of the film's look. Movie ally Lilah was based on vengeful bar-girl-turned-bounty-hunter Tallulah Black, but focused on her life before her disfiguration in the comic continuity.

Lonesome Cowboy ...

Jonah Hex had dramatic guest appearances in *Batman: The Animated Adventures* ("Showdown," 1995, voiced by William McKinney) and *Justice League Unlimited* ("Weird Western Tales," 2005, with Adam Baldwin). These led to lighter episodes in *Batman: The Brave and the Bold*, and even the *Teen Titans Go!* movie.

In 2010, the *Jonah Hex* Vertigo comic Two Gun Mojo was adapted as a seven-episode motion comic and, in the same year, actor Thomas Jane achieved

his lifelong ambition, playing Hex in the animated feature *DC Showcase: Jonah Hex*.

The grim gray gunslinger became a live-action regular across The CW's "Arrowverse" franchises, notching up nine appearances over five seasons of DC's *Legends of Tomorrow*, (left) with a cameo in *The Flash* and *Batwoman*. As sheriff of Salvation as well as a bounty hunter, he was played by Johnathon Schaech, and revealed to be a close ally of maverick time master Rip Hunter.

GREEN LANTERN

Release date: June 15, 2011 (premiere), June 17, 2011 US (general release)
Starring roles: Ryan Reynolds, Blake Lively, Peter Sarsgaard, Mark Strong, Angela Bassett, Tim Robbins
Director: Martin Campbell

Screenplay: Greg Berlanti, Michael Green, Marc Guggenheim, Michael Goldenberg
Cinematography: Dion Beebe
Music: James Newton Howard
Running time: 114 minutes
Box office: $220 million

Despite being a linchpin of their comic book continuity since 1960, Green Lanterns have barely appeared outside DC's printed publications, and then only in animated versions. This changed when "Emerald Gladiator" Hal Jordan finally hit cinema screens in 2011.

Created by John Broome and Gil Kane (for *Showcase* #22, October 1959), the saga of the light-wielding Green Lantern Corps was partially inspired by author E.E. "Doc" Smith's "Lensman" pulp science-fiction stories. An unfolding pictorial epic, the worlds of *Green Lantern* filled DC's growing shared universe, ultimately linking all its heroes.

"Fearless is the job description."

Hal Jordan

CALL OF DUTY

Development on a feature-length Green Lantern movie began in 1997 but stalled until October 2007 when Greg Berlanti (*The Broken Hearts Club*, *Dawson's Creek*) was hired to write and direct. When he stepped down in February 2009, Martin Campbell (*The Mask of Zorro*, *GoldenEye*) signed on to realize a constantly evolving script by Berlanti, Michael Green, Marc Guggenheim, and Michael Goldenberg.

Campbell had firm ideas about the science-fiction epic. He wanted its action scenes to feel like a fight in a phone booth—"quick and fast and dirty ... (with) big, grand sweeping movements"—and based his main villain Parallax on footage of disasters on TV news, mixed with monumental religious festivals. Campbell felt that his all-consuming fear-monster should blend with "fantastic images of (a) writhing mass of living beings." The results—by Oscar-winning production designer Grant Major (*The Lord of the Rings*) and conceptual creature designers Neville Page (*Watchmen*) and Arron Ingold (*Star Trek Into Darkness*)—saw the hero spectacularly battle the carnivorous, screaming cloud Parallax across Coast City.

The filmmakers' drive to make light-based uniforms mirrors comic book evolution, with Hal Jordan originally wearing a fabric mask and costume before switching to a light-construct in the 1970s.

Far left: When Abin Sur (Temuera Morrison) passed the Green Lantern ring to Hal Jordan, it was in prosthetic makeup that took five hours to put on and a loose gray suit that would be transformed by CGI magic.

Left: Everything had to be exactly right for director Martin Campbell. Beyond the intense physical training for Carol Ferris's action scenes, Blake Lively's blonde hair was dyed 14 times to create the exact shade desired.

143

Unlike the movie, in the early comics Hal Jordan's green light constructs were simplistic tools like shovels, swords, or boxing gloves, but evolved into any device he could conceive of and understand.

Two comic villains were merged for the film, with Guardian Krona corrupted by the yellow light of fear to become Parallax. In comics, fear's avatar was independently sentient and Krona's dogged research accidentally introduced evil into the universe.

Peter Sarsgaard loved the continually mutating appearance of Hector Hammond and dubbed himself the "king of the prostheses!"

Hal Jordan is a lost soul seeking purpose, scarred from childhood by witnessing the death of his test pilot dad. Candidates for the nuanced, tragic, yet devil-may-care role included Bradley Cooper, Sam Worthington, Justin Timberlake, Chris Pine, Henry Cavill, and Jared Leto. Ryan Reynolds won the part on July 10, 2009, with future wife Blake Lively playing his on-screen love interest, Carol Ferris. During shooting, Lively improvised one of the best lines in the movie when—facing the masked hero—she quipped, "I've seen you naked! You think I wouldn't recognize you because you covered your cheekbones?"

Lively (*Gossip Girl*) landed her role against stiff opposition from Eva Green, Diane Kruger, Keri Russell, and Jennifer Garner. Warner Bros. greenlit sequels before the first film was released, commissioning Berlanti, Green, and Guggenheim to script another movie while Campbell was still shooting the initial outing. Lively keenly anticipated becoming Super-Villain Star Sapphire, but the studio abruptly killed the plans. This also deprived the world of seeing Mark Strong's Sinestro descend from revered celebrated hero to the ultimate enemy of life. His transition was foreshadowed in a midcredits teaser when Sinestro dons a power ring channeling the yellow essence of fear rather the green force of willpower—the primordial energy funneled by the Guardians of the Universe to their interstellar peacekeeping agents for billions of years.

GREEN GUARDIANS

With preproduction and character/concept design underway, by March 2010, most of the live cast were signed, and principal photography took place from March 15 to August 6. Shooting should have started the previous November at Fox Studios in Sydney, Australia, but only began once the production had relocated to Louisiana, with New Orleans becoming Coast City, California.

New Orleans's art deco Lakefront Airport was physically and digitally remodeled to be the Ferris's Aircraft complex—ground zero for alien incursions and birthplace of a unique Super Hero. Concept artist Fabian Lacey (*Black Panther*) designed the site and his final painting hung in CEO Carl Ferris's office during filming.

Roles were still being cast after filming began and—like *Superman Returns* in 2006—the studio later decreed it should have 3D sequences. Angela Bassett was hired for the big-screen debut of Amanda Waller nine days after shooting started. Her character's paranoid diligence endangers Earth when she compels xeno-biologist Hector Hammond (Peter Sarsgaard) to perform an alien autopsy on Green Lantern Abin Sur's corpse and he is infected with Parallax's power to become Jordan's first super-foe.

Expectation was high that Hal Jordan's path to becoming an intergalactic super-cop would carry at least three pictures and pave the way for the expansion of DC's cinematic Super Hero pantheon. *Green Lantern* was released carrying plans to later reintroduce Superman and debut the Justice League. Ultimately, however, everything was scaled back to Jordan's witnessing cosmic majesty and terror when he's brought to Oa, the Guardians' homeworld, for training under Sinestro, Kilowog, and Tomar-Re.

Postproduction work and key reshoots started at Warner Bros. Studios, Los Angeles, in January 2011, coinciding with hiring voice actors for CGI-generated alien GLs. Geoffrey Rush (Tomar-Re), Michael Clarke Duncan (Kilowog), and others filled the ranks of the Green Lantern Corps as Campbell faced the daunting nature

Far left: The immortal overseers of the Green Lantern Corps were designed by committee and based on the look of Israeli statesman David Ben-Gurion.

Left: The projected multifilm story arc of Sinestro was intended to take actor Mark Strong from cosmic hero to universe-wrecking ultimate Super-Villain. However, his plans were never realized.

of digital finessing. Completion required 1,300 visual shots, with Warner Bros. contributing an additional $9 million to the budget for 3D conversion costs and enlisting more digital-effects workers.

LIGHT FANTASTIC

As befits heroes whose weapon of choice is light, *Green Lantern* pioneered innovative and much-copied visual effects, using computers to generate digital uniforms that convincingly mapped to the actors' movements. Wishing to avoid extensive use of spandex, rubber, and leather, the filmmakers rejected physical materials and fittings enhanced by CGI. Instead Campbell and Oscar-winning costume designer Ngila Dickson (*Lord of the Rings*) opted for garments made of light and pixels.

The complex, digitally produced feature demanded an enormous amount of preplanning. Harnessing resources from cinema's ever-growing CGI industry, a veritable army of artists was enlisted to imagine every facet of the film's look in pencil, paint, digital art, and 3D models. They conceived a limitless universe and all its wonders, a host of alien races and individuals, plus the stunning sequence that showed how rookie Green Lantern Hal Jordan saves Earth by luring Parallax into the Sun.

A huge team of concept illustrators including Rudolpho DaMaggio, Seth Engstrom, Fabian Lacey, Michele Moen, Paul Ozzimo, Justin Sweet, Criss Ross, and Alex Laurant concentrated on evoking mood, while dozens of storyboard artists were assigned specific scenes, such as Hal battling Parallax in Coast City (Collin Grant) or flying into space (Eric Ramsey). Michael Anthony Jackson, Ed Natividad, Chris Buchinsky, and others storyboarded specific shots that were eventually assembled into an enormous walking gallery that stretched down the studio corridors.

Despite failing to find a large audience on its initial release, the film and its heroes have enjoyed a recent reassessment and renaissance. As has the concept of ring-powered, galactic space cops, with DC's plans for the TV series *Lanterns* set to bring back Jordan alongside partner John Stewart, and with fan-favorite Nathan Filion set to play Guy Gardner in James Gunn's forthcoming *Superman*.

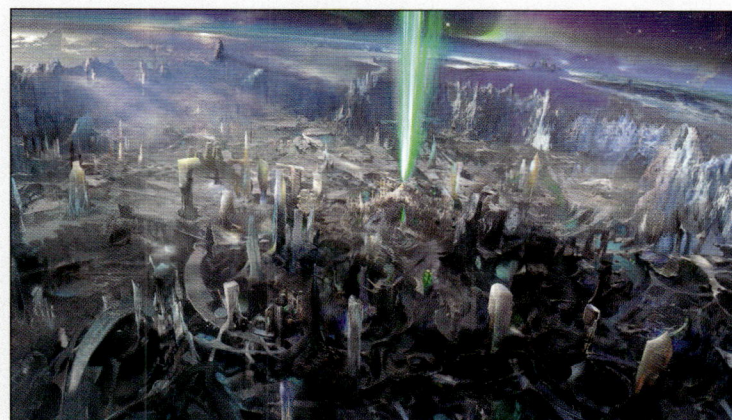

High concept

Leading his own stellar corps of concept illustrators, Grant Majors gave them a broad but inspirational working brief for realizing the vast, ancient but largely civilized cosmos that the Oan Guardians of the Universe police.

As Majors elaborated to Syfy in 2010, "I looked to the comics (for design concepts for Oa). I also wanted to give it a sort of broader aspect. I really wanted to make it the sort of place where, just from the glimpse that we have of it, that you'd really want to go back there and have a big look around, and in the interest of the film, maybe give birth to subsequent films.

"Oa (pictured above), of course, is at the center of the Universe, and is also an extremely old place. It's been around since not too long after the Big Bang. And with its function as a sort of U.N.-cum-military-compound in the middle of space, you'd imagine that with 3,600 different sectors, it must have a lot of influence on a lot of different cultures and time.

"So what I've tried to do is to introduce a plethora of different types of architectural styles and a feeling that, over the millennia, it's just been building on and building on [itself], and there's this huge history of culture that's been there."

THE DARK KNIGHT RISES

Release date: July 2012
Starring roles: Christian Bale, Michael Caine, Gary Oldman, Anne Hathaway, Tom Hardy, Marion Cotillard, Joseph Gordon-Levitt, Morgan Freeman
Director: Christopher Nolan
Screenplay: Jonathan Nolan and Christopher Nolan

Story: Christopher Nolan and David S. Goyer
Cinematography: Wally Pfister
Music: Hans Zimmer
Running time: 165 minutes
Box office: $1,081,041,287

Christopher Nolan and David Goyer had the ending of *The Dark Knight Rises*, the third installment in *The Dark Knight Trilogy*, before they even knew for sure whether the film would exist.

In the fall of 2008, shortly after Nolan and Goyer's second Batman movie, *The Dark Knight*, became the biggest film of the year (and one of the biggest in history), director and writer met for lunch to discuss where a third and final (Nolan was adamant about that) film might go. Nolan's preference on any project was not to start before he had a strong sense of the ending. But given the tremendous financial and critical success of *The Dark Knight*, and the resultant heightened expectations for any third film, it was more important than ever that the finale be satisfying. As the pair talked, an idea for the final scene arose—Bruce Wayne, retired from his life as Batman, enjoying lunch with a beautiful woman.

Four years later, when *The Dark Knight Rises* debuted in cinemas, that scene remained essentially unchanged from the one Nolan and Goyer had discussed.

A LIFE LESS ORDINARY

As far back as the earliest days of formulating *Batman Begins* (2005), Christopher Nolan and David Goyer had discussed in outline how Bruce Wayne's life might unfold over three films. In the first he would become Batman; in the second he would become consumed by Batman's world; and in the third he would draw a line under his time as Batman. But as Nolan and Goyer talked about a third film in the wake of *The Dark Knight*, Nolan was uncertain if there would even be one. Without a compelling story, driven by character and theme, he couldn't conceive of a third chapter.

As they had before, Nolan and Goyer set up shop in Nolan's garage and wrote down notes for characters and plots on index cards, bringing in Nolan's brother Jonathan at various junctures for insights and ideas and to write the first draft of the screenplay, as he had on *The Dark Knight*. The story the three hatched had its roots in the end of the previous film, where Batman had taken the

"The legend ends."
Promotional tagline

Many of *The Dark Knight Rises*'s action scenes were shot in broad daylight, with the embellishment of simulated snow in the case of Batman and Bane's final battle.

In Joseph Gordon-Levitt, the filmmakers saw an actor who could embody GCPD cop John Blake's idealism and hold his own in scenes with Gary Oldman.

Beginning training as soon as he agreed to play Bane, Tom Hardy gained a lot of body mass but was still intimidated the first time he saw Christian Bale as Batman.

Its design based on an Indian stepwell, the prison pit set was built at Bedfordshire's Cardington Sheds, refurbished after being used for *Batman Begins*.

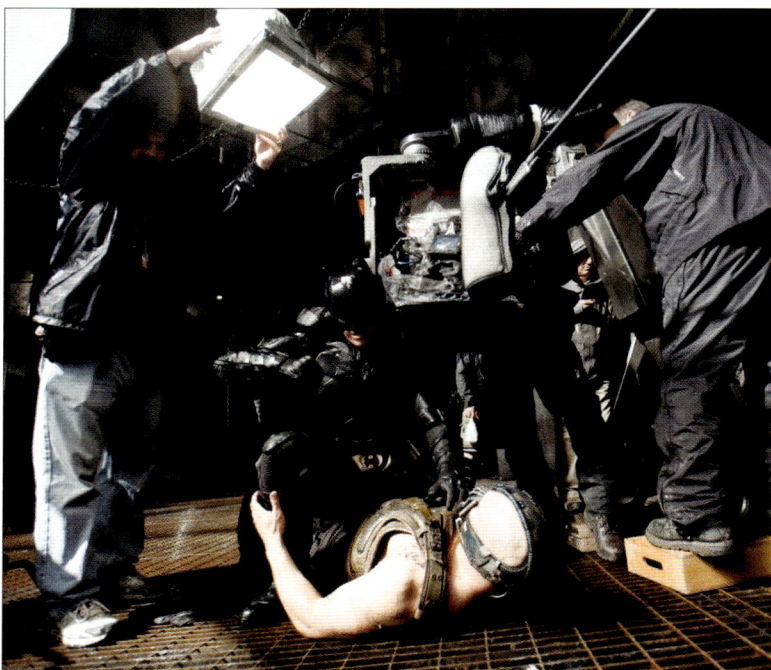

Choreographed by stunt coordinator Tom Struthers, the brutal battle between Batman and Bane was filmed on a huge set in the Cardington hangar.

Commissioner Gordon almost exposes the lie about Harvey Dent's heroism, in a scene shot outside Wollaton Hall in Nottingham.

blame for the murders Harvey Dent had committed as Two-Face, in order that Dent's mob prosecutions and standing as Gotham City's heroic white knight remain intact. Eight years later, Dent's heroism has inspired Gotham City to lift itself out of the mire without the aid of Batman, who has vanished; but the lie at the heart of this transformation—perpetuated by a complicit Commissioner Gordon (Gary Oldman)—has manifested in a malignant hidden underworld of crime and corruption, one ripe for exploitation by external forces.

VENGEANCE OF BANE

Where *Batman Begins* had been the story of a hero going on a great journey to find himself (in a similar vein to 1962's *Lawrence of Arabia*, a film Christopher Nolan and co. discussed as an antecedent), and *The Dark Knight* had been a crime movie dealing in escalation and terror (along the lines of 1972's *The Godfather*, another forerunner film discussed), *The Dark Knight Rises* would be an epic war movie: a struggle for survival against forces set on destabilizing and bringing down Gotham City—and, by extension, civilized society (a theme that has only gained greater significance in the years since). Even so, Christopher Nolan and David Goyer were clear that the story should develop from the characters, rather than be led by the action.

For the themes Nolan and Goyer wanted to explore, the comic book character Bane seemed entirely apposite. Created in 1993 to serve as the lead villain in that year's "Knightfall" event—a comics crossover which saw Bruce Wayne replaced as Batman by the vigilante Azrael—the musclebound, fiercely cunning, wrestling-mask-wearing Bane broke Batman's back in that summer's *Batman* #497, a moment that would be replicated in *The Dark Knight Rises*. With his imposing physique, keen mind, and defined backstory of a hellish boyhood growing up in prison, Bane stood in marked contrast to the mercurial, chaotic, enigmatic Joker.

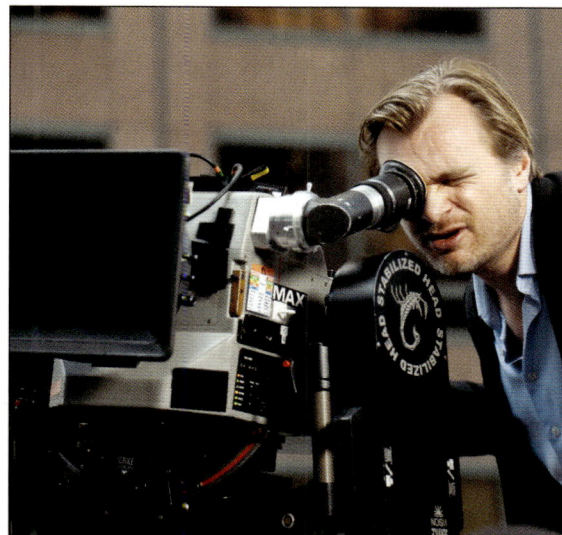

Far left: Pared back from its initial full-head look to differentiate it from Batman's, Bane's mask, with its spider-like mouthpiece, aided Tom Hardy in his powerful performance.

Left: For Christopher Nolan, the larger scale and increased quality afforded by IMAX suited the operatic scale of *The Dark Knight Rises*, with its spectacular action set pieces.

Knowing that whoever played Bane would have to convey their performance through a mask, Christopher Nolan cast British actor Tom Hardy. Having worked with Hardy on *Inception* (2010), Nolan knew the versatile actor could draw on every facet of his body and deliver the physicality required. Hardy began training immediately after accepting the role to gain the necessary body mass, and looked to actor Richard Burton and boxer Bartley Gorman to formulate Bane's loquacious vocal manner. For Bane's mask, which in the narrative performs the function of delivering anesthetic to ease Bane's constant pain, costume designer Lindy Hemming referenced gorillas and spiders to create an animalistic look, and jet engines to convey the idea of the mask being an injection system.

BACK TO IMAX

Bane's powerful introduction comes during *The Dark Knight Rises's* thrilling six-minute prologue, accompanied by Hans Zimmer's thunderously pulse-pounding score. Like *The Dark Knight*'s exciting Joker bank robbery prologue, the sequence was filmed entirely with IMAX cameras, with the same intention of unveiling it in select IMAX cinemas six months prior to the film's release. Shot in the skies above Inverness, Scotland, with plane interiors filmed in a fuselage rig outside Bedfordshire's Cardington Sheds, the sequence sees Bane's men enacting a daring midair abduction —of Bane himself, who has allowed himself to be captured by the CIA, along with nuclear physicist Dr. Leonid Pavel (Alon Aboutboul). Filming in the Scottish skies involved parachutists wing-walking on the CIA plane and four aerialists on lines flying

The world of Batman

Continuing the precedent he set with *Batman Begins* and pursued to a greater degree on *The Dark Knight*, for *The Dark Knight Rises* Christopher Nolan shot as much of the film on location as possible. Principal photography began in May 2011 at Jaipur in India, the walled city forming the backdrop to the scene where Bruce Wayne emerges from the prison pit where he was banished after his back was broken by Bane, and where Bane himself was once confined. From there the production moved to the UK, where Nottingham's Wollaton Hall stood in for Wayne Manor in place of the unavailable Mentmore Towers in Buckinghamshire, which had served as the house in *Batman Begins*.

While Bane's lair in the sewers beneath Gotham City—the location of his back-breaking battle with Batman—was built in Bedfordshire's Cardington Sheds (as was the interior of the prison pit, with its Indian stepwell-like walls), Pittsburgh stood in for many of Gotham City's exteriors. Among these, Heinz Field became the home of the Gotham Rogues for the scene where explosions under the field bring a football game to a deadly end. The production filled the stadium with 12,000 extras, who watched the spectacle of special effects blasts and stunt performers disappearing into holes in the field. Extras also played a part in Batman's final fight with Bane on the steps of Gotham City Hall, in reality Pittsburgh's Carnegie Mellon Institute. Away from that city, one of the film's final scenes, depicting John Blake reaching a waterfall-hidden cave entrance after receiving a mysterious map reference (and a spelunking harness) in Bruce Wayne's will, was shot at Henrhyd Falls in Wales.

149

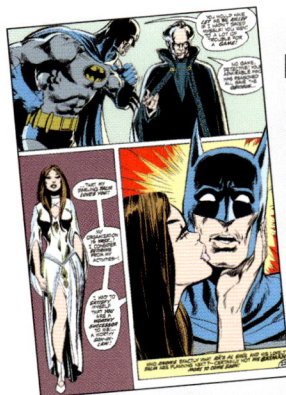

Daughter of the Demon

Following the demise of Bruce Wayne's childhood friend and lost love Rachel Dawes in *The Dark Knight*, *The Dark Knight Rises* finds Bruce still mourning her passing eight years later. He is shaken out of his torpor by one potential love interest, cat-burglar Selina Kyle, but it's in the arms of Wayne Industries board member Miranda Tate, played by Marion Cotillard, that he finds solace. Unfortunately, Tate is actually Talia al Ghūl—daughter of Rā's al Ghūl and leader of the League of Shadows—who is intent on finishing her father's work vis-à-vis Gotham City.

In the narrative of the movie, Talia grew up in prison, protected by Bane until she could escape, but in comics she had a different background. Created by Denny O'Neil and Bob Brown and debuting in 1971, a month before her father, her first story saw her rescued by Batman from the clutches of the League of Assassins's Doctor Darrk. Talia and Batman swiftly became lovers, and her subsequent appearances over the decades have seen her loyalties torn between the Dark Knight and Rā's al Ghūl. In Mike W. Barr and Jerry Bingham's 1987 graphic novel *Batman: Son of the Demon*, Talia gave birth to Batman's child; the boy would grow up to be Damian Wayne, the fifth Robin.

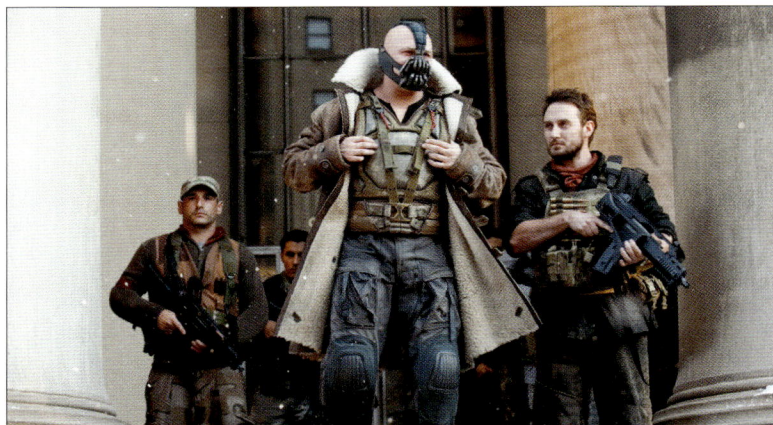

Playing on Bane's mercenary background, costume designer Lindy Hemming created a costume composed of different military elements.

Filmed in Pittsburgh, the sequences of the Bat flying low through Gotham City streets involved a full-scale Bat mounted atop a tow truck, which was digitally removed.

Heinz Field doubled for Gotham Stadium, with real-life wide receiver Hines Ward and his fellow Pittsburgh Steelers dressed in Gotham Rogues uniforms.

behind the pursuing C-130 Hercules—more than stunt coordinator Tom Struthers believed had ever been attempted even by the military.

Among the other scenes shot with IMAX cameras were a number featuring Selina Kyle, played by Anne Hathaway, including Selina stealing Bruce Wayne's Lamborghini and petulantly partnering with Batman in a rooftop bust-up with Bane's henchmen. Better known in comics and previous Batman movies and TV shows as Catwoman, in *The Dark Knight Rises* she is never actually referred to as such. The character's inclusion was advocated for by Jonathan Nolan, who convinced his skeptical brother that there was a place for Selina in the movie as a conwoman and grifter who could add shades of gray to Batman's stark worldview. As ever, the filmmakers formulated a practical, logical explanation for her catlike countenance, Selina's cat-burglar goggles flipping up to form "ears" atop her head.

Another character new to the "Nolanverse" was Gotham City cop John Blake, played by Joseph Gordon-Levitt, who had featured alongside Tom Hardy in *Inception*. An orphan like Bruce Wayne, Blake represents the vulnerable members of society, those most impacted by the corruption slowly rotting Gotham City's core. By film's end he is positioned to carry on protecting Gotham City in Batman's stead, after the Dark Knight seemingly dies preventing the city from being destroyed in a cleansing nuclear fire brought about by Bane and the resurgent League of Shadows, led by Rā's al Ghūl's daughter, Talia (Marion Cotillard).

BEHOLD THE BAT

Batman's final sacrificial act of transporting Bane's nuclear device out to sea (somewhat reminiscent of the scene in the 1966 movie spin-off from Christopher Nolan's childhood-favorite *Batman* TV show, where the Caped Crusader "just can't get rid of a bomb") is performed with the aid of the Bat, the latest in the trilogy's line of Bat-vehicles. Once again, during the writing, production designer Nathan Crowley joined Christopher Nolan and David Goyer in

Right: A new addition to Batman's arsenal of Batarangs, grappling gun, mini-mines, and sticky-bomb gun, the EMP rifle emits an electromagnetic pulse that disables electronics.

the director's garage offices, which by now also encompassed the garage belonging to the house next door, which Nolan had bought. As usual, Crowley's first task, and his way into the world, was to design a new vehicle, in this case an airborne craft.

Aesthetically in keeping with previous Bat-vehicles, the Bat may have been more fantastical than its forebears, but it was still rooted in reality, based on various troop-carrying vertical takeoff and landing craft, such as the Harrier jet and helicopters. As before, Crowley's designs were translated into full-scale versions by special effects supervisor Chris Corbould and his team, though in this instance the practical Bat would not be capable of actual flight, and instead would be driven around the streets of Pittsburgh on a tow-truck rig, suspended from cables in a New York skyscraper canyon, and recreated via miniatures and visual effects.

From the Bat, Crowley moved on to designing sets, among them Batman's base of operations. With Wayne Manor rebuilt—and Bruce Wayne living a reclusive life within it, until Bane's assault on Gotham City brings him back to the world—Batman is based once more in the Batcave. This time, the design team fused visual elements from *Batman Begins* and *The Dark Knight*, as both films were relevant to *The Dark Knight Rises's* story, which was both global and Gotham-specific. Built at Sony Studios in Culver City, the set was a mixture of the original Batcave and the Bat-Bunker, featuring modernist cubes containing vehicles and equipment which rose up from the water.

BATMAN ENDS

Writing *The Dark Knight Rises*, Christopher Nolan had Charles Dickens's revolutionary epic *A Tale of Two Cities* in mind, exemplified by the film's climactic snowbound battle on the steps of Gotham City Hall between Batman and the Gotham City police on one side and Bane's forces on the other. With themes that have only become more relevant since, *The Dark Knight Rises* is both a war movie on a massive scale and a more personal story of one man's struggle to free Gotham City from the forces of chaos and tyranny and find peace for himself. As such, it's a grand and fitting finale to one of the most distinctive and celebrated cinematic superhero sagas ever filmed.

Left: The rationale for the form-hugging black suit worn by Selina Kyle—played by Anne Hathaway— could be found in the character's nocturnal cat-burgling activities.

EXPANDING THE UNIVERSE

The 2010s represented a fresh start for DC's movies. Where the previous two decades had been characterized by distinct films existing independently of one another, or in the cases of Tim Burton's *Batman* movies and Christopher Nolan's *Dark Knight Trilogy* residing within their own distinctive continuities, for the first time DC's cinematic endeavors would be set within a shared universe.

The first tentative steps were taken with Zack Snyder's *Man of Steel* (2013), but it was three years later with Snyder's follow-up, *Batman v Superman: Dawn of Justice* (2016), that DC's pantheon of heroes and villains began to coalesce, leading to such varied visions as *Suicide Squad* (2016), *Wonder Woman* (2017), *Justice League* (2017), *Aquaman* (2018), *Shazam!* (2019), *The Flash* (2023), and more.

But there was still room for experiments—idiosyncratic films able to find their own niches and flourish, whether that be Todd Phillips's searing character study *Joker* (2019), or Matt Reeves's intense and psychological *The Batman* (2022).

MAN OF STEEL

Release date: June 2013
Starring roles: Henry Cavill, Amy Adams, Michael Shannon, Diane Lane, Russell Crowe, Antje Traue, Harry Lennix, Richard Schiff, Christopher Meloni, Kevin Costner, Ayelet Zurer, Laurence Fishburne
Director: Zack Snyder

Screenplay: David S. Goyer
Story: David S. Goyer, Christopher Nolan
Cinematography: Amir Mokri
Music: Hans Zimmer
Running time: 143 minutes
Box office: $668,045,518

It was to be the start of a new era for DC's cinematic endeavors, the beginning of a shared movie universe for DC's characters the likes of which had never been attempted. But though *Man of Steel* did indeed represent a new beginning for DC movies, the film's origin also had its roots in the previous era of DC cinema, specifically in Christopher Nolan's Dark Knight Trilogy.

RISE OF SUPERMAN

As director Christopher Nolan and writer David Goyer—who co-wrote all three of Nolan's Batman movies (later with the director's brother, Jonathan)—worked on the story for the finale to their epic series, *The Dark Knight Rises* (2012), the pair reached an impasse on the third act. After Nolan suggested taking a break from the writing to clear their heads, Goyer began thinking about Superman instead, inspired by some old comics he had lying around his office. Noting his ideas down, Goyer shared with Nolan his concept for a new Superman movie. As children, writer and director had both loved Richard Donner's *Superman* (1978), in Nolan's case especially its presentation of Superman as an aspirational character, but he was skeptical that a creation as fantastical as Superman could be made to work for a contemporary audience. Goyer's concept convinced him that there was a way.

"Accomplish wonder."
Marketing tagline

Goyer's idea took a science-fictional approach to Superman, updating him in a way that would make sense to modern viewers. In 1986, comics writer and artist John Byrne had done something similar with his million-selling *The Man of Steel* miniseries (and subsequent *Superman* and *Action Comics* relaunch), in which he had revamped and updated the Superman mythos, in the process reenvisioning Krypton as a highly advanced but cold and sterile civilization. Goyer's concept went further. His notion was to make a realistic Superman story: a story of the biggest event in human history—first contact with an alien species, Superman's arrival on Earth—grounding the character in a world that felt real, even though he himself, with his extraordinary abilities, might stretch the bounds of credibility.

Midway through writing of Man of Steel, David Goyer decided to lean into the the story's themes of fatherhood, embodied by Jor-El (Russell Crowe, here with Ayelet Zurer as Lara).

David Goyer also became a stepfather while writing the story, reinforcing the film's father-son themes in the shape of Jonathan Kent (Kevin Costner).

Laurence Fishburne based his performance as *Daily Planet* editor-in-chief Perry White on the late *60 Minutes* reporter Ed Bradley, who he greatly admired.

As conceived by the filmmakers, Superman's Kryptonian suit, with its chainmail-like motifs, was designed to protect the wearer from the vacuum of space.

After Zod demands the handing over of the Kryptonian hiding on Earth, Superman surrenders, letting the military decide what should happen.

Amy Adams was struck by the juxtaposition between her character, the grounded Earth reporter Lois Lane, and the more fantastical Man of Steel.

As portrayed by Michael Shannon, General Zod's ruthlessness is fueled by his overwhelming desire to save his people, whatever the cost.

Zod's ship, the *Black Zero*, was conceived by the filmmakers as a jerry-rigged prison ship with a disorganized interior, replete with dangling cables.

TAKING FLIGHT

Within days, Nolan and Goyer got the go-ahead from the studio to begin work. Utilizing the same index-cards-on-boards method they had on the Batman movies, the pair spent the next few months working on the story, meeting two or three times a week. However, with *The Dark Knight Rises* about to go into production, Nolan and his wife, producer Emma Thomas, were adamant that while they could produce the film—working once more with Dark Knight Trilogy producer Charles Roven, who worked on most of the DC movies from *Batman Begins* onwards—Nolan could not himself direct it.

After considering a number of names, Nolan and Thomas encountered the ideal candidate at, aptly enough, 35,000 feet. Flying to Las Vegas to present *Inception* (2010) at ShoWest, the national convention of cinema owners, the Nolans met another husband and wife producing pair, Zack and Deborah Snyder, who were on the same flight on the way to present *Legend of the Guardians: The Owls of Ga'Hoole* (2010). That first meeting prompted the Nolans to invite the Snyders to lunch in order to discuss Superman.

Any misgivings the Snyders had about taking on such an iconic character were dispelled during that lunch, as Nolan outlined his vision for the film. Shortly after, the Snyders read an early draft of Nolan and Goyer's screenplay and recognized that the pair had come up with a way to make Superman work. In order to realize that concept, however, Zack Snyder would need to adopt a filmmaking style that was less like the stylized realism of *Watchmen*, and closer to a handheld, vérité form of filmmaking, especially for the Earthbound sequences.

Before Superman could make first contact with the people of Earth, there was the small matter of Kal-El's costume and heritage

Lois follows the borehole in the ice created by Clark's heat vision, descending to the Kryptonian scout ship buried below, and her first fateful encounter with the Man of Steel himself.

to deal with—for in *Man of Steel*, the two would be inextricably intertwined. Despite being presented with a range of redesigns, Zack Snyder felt no urge to discard the fundamentals of Superman's suit, from the primary red, blue, and yellow color scheme, to the cape and triangular chest emblem. Initial costume designer James Acheson began the development of the suit and the Kryptonian costumes, before passing the baton to Michael Wilkinson, Zack Snyder's costume designer on *300* (2006), *Watchmen* (2009), and *Sucker Punch* (2011). Wilkinson developed those designs further, turning them into physical costumes using digital body scans and 3D computer modeling, drawing on medieval chainmail and Celtic and Japanese influences to create a sci-fi Superman suit whose narrative purpose was to protect its wearer from the vacuum of space.

LAST DAYS OF KRYPTON

One key component was Superman's chest insignia, which in *Man of Steel* would be both a family symbol, denoting the House of El, and a symbol of family status within the caste system of Kryptonian society. Depicted as an ancient, decaying civilization looking inward after millennia of interstellar expansion, Krypton was the result of a phenomenal amount of world-building, starting with the history David Goyer developed as he wrote the screenplay.

His vision of a planet and people that had depleted their natural resources and adopted population control and a rigid, hierarchical society flowed through to the designs developed by Alex McDowell's production design department. The surface of Krypton was envisioned as furrowed and scarred from strip-mining, reflected by interiors such as the aged, decrepit Council Chamber, with its ancient inscriptions carved into the walls, while, with no metal to use, Kryptonian technology, armor, and weaponry would be crafted from arthropods and invertebrates. On every

The Krypton factor

Not content with helping to bring a bold new vision of Superman to the big screen, in 2018 David Goyer brought Kal-El's birth-world to the small screen with the TV show *Krypton*. Goyer began developing the show the year after *Man of Steel*'s cinematic debut in 2014, with British newcomer Cameron Cuffe cast two years after that in the lead role of Seg-El, Superman's grandfather, and fellow Brit Georgina Campbell as military guild member Lyta-Zod.

Set two centuries before the destruction of the eponymous planet, *Krypton* was less a prequel to *Man of Steel* than its own entity: drawing on the same comic book mythology, but presenting a Krypton that was quite different than that seen in Zack Snyder's film, although in common with *Man of Steel* the show adopted a sci-fi approach. With the benefit of the additional time afforded by 10 episodes per season, the show was able to introduce live-action versions of a number of Superman-associated characters, including interplanetary adventurer Adam Strange (played by Shaun Sipos), galactic despot Brainiac (Blake Ritson, *above*), and in the second and final season, broadcast on Syfy in 2019, perennially popular extraterrestrial bounty hunter Lobo (Emmett J. Scanlan).

Costume designers James Acheson and Michael Wilkinson worked with production designer Alex McDowell to make the Kryptonian armor look alien.

Martha Kent (Diane Lane) endures a close encounter with a different sort of Kryptonian—Sub Commander Faora, played with ice-cold menace by Antje Traue.

Coupled with the Kryptonian World Engine over the Indian Ocean, the *Black Zero* begins the terraforming process above Metropolis, causing untold destruction.

level, the doomed planet Krypton was conceived as an ecological cautionary tale.

To further enhance the veracity of this vision, a Kryptonian language was developed by linguistic anthropologist Christine Schreyer, which was then turned into both utilitarian and ornate ceremonial fonts by graphic designer Kirsten Franson. In addition, each Kryptonian house or guild would have its own symbol, in the form of an insignia worn on the chest. For the infant Kal-El, propelled from Krypton as the planet ruptured—the result of drawing power from the planet's core—that insignia denoted not just the House of El from which he originated, but was also the Kryptonian symbol of hope.

CASTING CALL

All this extraordinary world-building would be for naught without the figure at the center of the film—Kal-El, alias Clark Kent, alias Superman. At the start of 2011, following an exhaustive international search, British actor Henry Cavill—best known at that point for historical drama series *The Tudors*—was cast in the coveted lead role. For creators Zack Snyder and Christopher Nolan, Cavill embodied both Superman's strength and dignity and Clark's vulnerability and relatability. But as central as Cavill was to the film, the filmmakers were intent on ensuring the movie had a deep cast, taking a lead from Richard Donner's *Superman* in filling out even supporting roles with big names, whether that be Russell Crowe and Kevin Costner as Kal-El/Clark's natural and adoptive fathers, Jor-El and Jonathan Kent, Diane Lane as his adoptive mother, Martha, or Laurence Fishburne as Perry White, editor-in-chief of the *Daily Planet*.

The investigations of Perry White's star reporter, Lois Lane (Amy Adams), drive the plot, as an assignation to a Kryptonian scout ship buried in the Canadian Arctic ice sets her on the trail of Clark, who has come to the ship seeking answers to his alien, superpowered heritage. In a nonlinear narrative recalling Bruce Wayne's voyage of discovery in *Batman Begins*, and shot in a documentary style, Clark has been roaming the Earth trying to find his place in the world, leading him eventually to the Kryptonian ship, which provides answers in the form of a holographic Jor-El, and a uniform that will symbolize his mission on Earth—to protect the planet and act as its denizens' guardian.

DOWN TO EARTH

No sooner has Clark taken on this mantle than a threat originating from his lost homeworld manifests in the shape of General Zod (Michael Shannon) and his Kryptonian insurgents. Having escaped confinement in the Phantom Zone, the Kryptonians have been seeking Kal-El, prompting Superman to reveal himself to the world.

Where the Krypton segment of the film was about world-building, on Earth the emphasis was on story-building. Accordingly, although Zack Snyder and his team used visual effects to tell that story, it was important that the Earthbound sequences feel real to the audience. Wherever possible, real locations were used. To stand in for Clark's childhood home of Smallville—also the site of one of the film's biggest action set pieces, when Superman fights both the Kryptonian insurgents and the US military (with whom

Zod's Kryptonian drop ship arrives at the Kent farmhouse, which was built from scratch by the production on a farm property near Plano, Illinois.

the production cooperated to ensure credibility and enhance the sense of realism)—supervising location manager Bill Doyle picked Plano, Illinois. Chosen from over 50 towns around Chicago, which would stand in for Metropolis (with its skyline digitally altered), besides its proximity to the city Plano possessed the unique feature of missing three blocks in its main street. This allowed the crew to erect storefronts which could then be destroyed during the battle, both practically and digitally.

Even that confrontation would be overshadowed by the climactic one between Superman and Zod in Metropolis, home of the *Daily Planet*. With Chicago's geography and skyline already digitally altered, the destructive battle would require more extensive visual effects on the part of John "D.J." DesJardin and his team, and the construction of partial studio sets. Storyboarded, like the rest of the film, by Zack Snyder, and making heavy use of bobbing-and-weaving handheld camera movements—additionally complicating DesJardin's work—in many ways the fight was the ultimate expression of Snyder's intent with *Man of Steel*—to root the action in a veracity earned from working through concepts, backstories, and implications, in order to make the unreal feel real.

A formative scene depicting the young Clark—played by Dylan Sprayberry—rescuing a school bus full of his classmates from a watery fate.

Family of steel

Spinning out of the 2015–2021 CBS/CW *Supergirl* TV show, *Superman and Lois* made its debut in March 2021, shortly before *Supergirl*'s final season began airing. Developed by Todd Helbing—who would also act as showrunner—and Greg Berlanti, a veteran of the CW "Arrowverse" who had worked with Helbing on *The Flash*, the show starred Tyler Hoechlin and Elizabeth Tulloch as the eponymous couple, with Jordan Elsass as Jonathan (said role inherited by Michael Bishop as of 2023's season 3) and Alex Garfin as Jordan, their teenage sons. Although not linked to *Man of Steel*, like Zack Snyder's movie *Superman and Lois* aimed for

a reality that audiences could relate to. In *Superman and Lois*'s case, that reality had its basis in the family drama aspect of the series, the show's creators looking to small-town sports drama *Friday Night Lights* (2006–2011) for inspiration in their efforts to make their series grounded and relatable—albeit still with a healthy slice of superhero action. Renewed for a fourth season in 2023, *Superman and Lois* has won praise and plaudits for its portrayal of super-powered family life, and in 2022 beat both *The Flash* and *Supergirl* to win the Saturn Award for Best Science Fiction Television Series.

BATMAN v SUPERMAN: DAWN OF JUSTICE

Release date: March 2016
Starring roles: Ben Affleck, Henry Cavill, Amy Adams, Jesse Eisenberg, Diane Lane, Laurence Fishburne, Jeremy Irons, Holly Hunter, Gal Gadot
Director: Zack Snyder

Screenplay: Chris Terrio, David S. Goyer
Cinematography: Larry Fong
Music: Hans Zimmer, Junkie XL
Running time: 152 minutes
Box office: $873,634,919

In a way, there was an inevitability to it. No sooner had *Man of Steel* arrived in cinemas in June of 2013 than a sequel was announced, with Zack Snyder and David Goyer set to reprise their roles as director and writer (this time with Christopher Nolan in a more advisory capacity as an executive producer). With an eye on further DC movies down the road, all concerned knew that as well as continuing the story of Superman, the sequel should introduce other characters from the DC universe. Discussions about direction and story ranged far and wide, but one idea about Kryptonite being delivered to Bruce Wayne brought up Batman— and once that notion had been raised, there was no escaping it.

"Who will win?"
Marketing tagline

The story that would bring Superman and Batman together— with, as it would transpire, the third member of the DC Trinity— had its roots in the climactic battle between Superman and Zod in *Man of Steel*, and the consequences of that conflict. As established at the start of *Batman v Superman: Dawn of Justice*, one of the Metropolis buildings demolished during the fight—now known as the Black Zero Event, after the renegade Kryptonians' ship—was Wayne Tower, witnessed by Bruce Wayne himself. Eighteen months after the battle, Superman's activities have seen him called before a US Senate committee, while his acts of heroism have become the subject of debate, with the world divided between those who see him as humanity's savior, and those who view him as its greatest threat (much as his adoptive father, Jonathan, foresaw in *Man of Steel*).

In the latter camp is Bruce Wayne, alias Batman. Played by Ben Affleck, this older, more seasoned Batman has been the protector

Shot partly at Michigan Central Station, the battle between Batman and Superman saw Ben Affleck donning a practical Mech Suit made of foam and nylon under a fiberglass shell.

Far left: Heroes Park, a memorial to those who died in General Zod's attack, has been established in the ruins of central Metropolis, complete with a statue of Superman.

Left: Bruce Wayne (Ben Affleck) encounters Diana Prince (Gal Gadot) at Lex Luthor's fundraiser—both of them there with the intention of accessing Luthor's mainframe.

Vance Kovacs's concept art for Batman's Mech Suit, showing the influence of Frank Miller's *Batman: The Dark Knight Returns* in the armor's analog, prototypical appearance.

Kovacs's powerful concept art helped establish the tone of key sequences in the film, not least the atmospheric fight between Batman and Superman at Gotham City's Wayne Station.

Reflecting Batman's state of mind, the Batcave is an oppressive, brutalist space where the weight of the rock overhead is ever-present, as in Ed Natividad's concept art.

of Gotham City, Metropolis's downtrodden neighbor, for two decades, but his methods have become increasingly brutal—a state of affairs sardonically commented on by his butler and technical assistant Alfred, played by Jeremy Irons—as his war on crime has come to seem increasingly and frustratingly futile. With Superman as scornful of Batman's activities as the vigilante is of his, the stage is set for a confrontation between the two, exacerbated by the manipulations of billionaire tech genius Lex Luthor (Jesse Eisenberg), a narcissistic sociopath whose hatred of his late father fuels his loathing of Superman.

DESIGNING THE BATMOBILE

Much as Christopher Nolan's production designer on the Dark Knight Trilogy, Nathan Crowley, began the work of visualizing their films by creating their version of the Batmobile, so Zack Snyder's production designer on *Batman v Superman: Dawn of Justice*, Patrick Tatopoulos, began their movie with the Batmobile. When Snyder—with whom Tatopoulos had wanted to work since seeing *Dawn of the Dead* (2004)—first reached out to the production designer following his work on *300: Rise of an Empire* (director Noam Murro's 2014 sequel to Snyder's *300*), Tatopoulos enquired whether the movie would be Man of Steel versus The Dark Knight. Informed by Snyder that while the film would be a sequel to *Man of Steel*, Batman would be newly conceived, Tatopoulos stopped at a coffee shop on the way home and sketched a Batmobile design on a napkin.

That first sketch of a car, with its side profile akin to that of a motorcycle (a passion of the production designer's), proved remarkably close to the final version, a full-sized working vehicle of which was built by picture car coordinator Dennis McCarthy, who had previously driven the Batman Begins Tumbler. In fact there were two Batmobiles—one with a full interior cockpit, the

othera stripped-back version for stunt driving. When not in use the Batmobile and its aerial counterpart the Batwing—a combination of a custom-built cockpit and canopy and computer-rendered wings—would be housed within the Batcave beneath the minimalist glass lake house Bruce Wayne lives in on the Wayne estate. A huge set constructed by Tatopolous's team, the cantilevered, split-level Batcave, its elements suspended from the ceiling, was a brutalist extension of this Batman's hard, bold personality.

Also within the cave was the armory, housing Batman's array of weapons, notably his grapnel gun. Put together by property master Doug Harlocker, originally the gun was all metal with a carbon fiber handle, until Zack Snyder determined the grip should be wooden: distressed and nicked, but polished, as if it were a trusted tool. In addition, again at Snyder's suggestion, a return was added to the grip so that Batman could use it as a blunt weapon.

From Patrick Tatopoulos's initial sketch of the Batmobile and Snyder's direction that this Batman would be rugged and real,

Above: Called before the Senate committee investigating his activities, Superman is confronted by a sea of both supporters and protesters.

Left: In the Batcave, Bruce Wayne stands before his Batsuit, which bears the scars of decades spent fighting crime on the streets of Gotham City.

World's Finest team

Superman and Batman have been teaming up, or at least appearing together, for almost the entire lengths of their respective comics careers. While *World's Finest Comics*, which launched in 1941 (titled *World's Best Comics* for its first issue), was established as the title in which readers could thrill to both Batman and Superman's exploits, spotlighting the two heroes together on its covers—invariably with Robin in tow—for the first dozen or so years of its existence they only ever appeared separately in their own stories. Their first appearance in a story together actually came during a Justice Society of America adventure in *All-Star Comics* #7 (October–November 1941), though that tale implied they had

known each other for a while. A decade on, "The Mightiest Team in the World!" in *Superman* #76 (May 1952) detailed how the pair discovered each other's secret identities when Bruce Wayne and Clark Kent wound up sharing a cabin during a cruise, while two years after that the two belatedly featured together in a *World's Finest* story ("Batman—Double for Superman!" in #71, July–August 1954).

In the decades since, Batman and Superman have teamed up in multifarious comic books—some form of team-up title has long been a staple of DC's publishing output—and animated series. But their meetings haven't always been on friendly terms, as exemplified by Frank Miller's 1986 dystopia *Batman: The Dark Knight Returns*, the climactic battle of which between Batman and Superman was a major influence on Zack Snyder's movie, in storytelling and design.

To play Lex Luthor, Jesse Eisenberg dialed up the theatricality of his performance, in order to convey the histrionic, narcissistic nature of the character.

While the Doomsday of the movie bears a resemblance to the comics version, the film's Doomsday is created from General Zod's corpse.

"Is she with you?" Superman asks Batman as Wonder Woman joins the fray, followed by Batman's surprised response, "I thought she was with you."

the tone for the project as a whole was established. In pursuit of his vision, Snyder wanted a Batsuit that was true to both the comics and his conception of this Batman as older, bigger, more muscular. Above all, he decreed it should define the man wearing it, rather than enhance him. Costume designer Michael Wilkinson and his team came up with a fabric suit that skimmed the body, showing off Ben Affleck's musculature (the actor having trained for more than a year before filming) but was also aged and battle-worn, with a distressed cape made from a specially created, layered and laminated textile, reflecting this Batman's hard years of fighting crime.

Wilkinson's team was charged with creating other Batman costumes besides. Falling asleep in the Batcave, Bruce Wayne has a vision of a dystopian future where Superman has overthrown the world and Batman leads the insurgency against his despotic regime. This Knightmare Batman wears a visually striking costume, with a worn trench coat and combat trousers, reflecting Snyder's notion of the outfit evolving over time in the postapocalyptic world—a lived-in Batsuit cobbled together from multiple practical elements.

The Knightmare sequence, which takes place in the blasted ruins of Gotham City overlooking the desertlike basin of the bay between that city and a crumbling Metropolis, features a fight scene that required over a hundred moves on the part of Ben Affleck's stunt double Rich Cetrone, as Batman battles dozens of opponents, some real, some digitally added. Directly following that fight, a captured Batman is confronted by a vengeful Superman, who blames him for the loss of Lois Lane—a premonitory foreshadowing of the conflict to come in the present day.

THE BIG FIGHT

That heralded titular brawl between Batman and Superman featured a further iteration of the Batsuit. Inspired by the armor Batman wears fighting Superman at the climax of Frank Miller's influential 1986 graphic novel *Batman: The Dark Knight Returns*, the Mech Suit was a bulky, heavily armored affair that in Zack Snyder's mind was likely created for a different reason—perhaps to deal with riots—but repurposed to bring down an alien demigod. Echoing the prototypical, analog nature of the original *Dark Knight Returns* version, Michael Wilkinson made the Mech Suit oversized and brutish, while Batman's weaponry, too, recalled *The Dark Knight Returns*, from ear-disrupting sonics to Kryptonite gas.

While some of the Mech Suit's moments during the fight scene were achieved via motion capture and VFX, Wilkinson and his team created an actual practical Mech Suit costume that Ben Affleck could wear. To enhance the reality of the sequence, the filmmakers determined that the physical Mech Suit should be used wherever possible, not least because it allowed them to capture on camera Henry Cavill's reactions to the imposing figure of Affleck in the costume.

WONDER WAIL

Following Batman's bruising rescue of the captive Martha Kent (Diane Lane)—a complicated stunt sequence storyboarded, like the rest of the film, by Zack Snyder and choreographed by stunt coordinator Damon Caro—the film's final action set piece introduces a third combatant alongside Batman and Superman. Making her debut earlier in the movie as antiquities expert Diana

Director Zack Snyder gets up close to the action, as Batman emerges from the Batmobile to confront Superman for the first time.

Bruce Wayne's fears about Superman are realized in a vision of a bleak future where Batman leads an insurgency in a postapocalyptic landscape.

Prince, Gal Gadot's first appearance as Wonder Woman comes as Lex Luthor unleashes a genetically engineered Kryptonian monster he dubs Superman's Doomsday. Accompanied by Hans Zimmer and Junkie XL's unforgettable "Is She With You?" theme—inspired by Led Zeppelin's "Immigrant Song," and featuring an indelible electric-cello banshee wail performed by Tina Guo—Wonder Woman takes her rightful place in the Trinity.

It was a moment all involved in the production felt the historical significance of—bringing such an icon to life on the big screen. Cast at the end of 2013 following a showstopping audition with Ben Affleck, Gal Gadot embodied the character for all concerned, but there were still challenges to surmount in introducing her, not least in creating her costume. Michael Wilkinson designed a gladiator-style armor that bore the influence of ancient Greece and told a story of 3,000 years of use, yet was still engineered to allow Gadot ease of movement, utilizing a specially created material that resembled metal, and a sectioned breastplate. To complement the armor, Doug Harlocker's team created a sword engraved with an ancient, extinct—but in reality, newly created—script, along with an aged and textured shield, and a lasso made of a distressed gold braid, with fiber-optic cable interweaved for lighting effects that could then be enhanced by VFX.

DIRECTION OF TRAVEL

As soon as the filmmakers had made the early decision to put Batman in the movie, Zack Snyder knew that could only point in one direction. That direction was further cemented by the addition of Wonder Woman, and with Diana, other signs and portents, decrypted by Batman from Lex Luthor's mainframe—a photo of Wonder Woman with a band of soldiers seemingly dating from World War I; snatches of video of other metahumans: The Flash, Aquaman, Cyborg. There could be only one ultimate destination: Justice League.

The Death of Superman

More than two decades before Superman's death at the hands of Doomsday in *Batman v Superman: Dawn of Justice*, the Man of Steel hit the big one in comic book form, in a blockbuster crossover event that introduced the character of Doomsday and made headlines around the world. Directly influencing Zack Snyder's film, "The Death of Superman" was conceived in 1991 by the creative teams of DC's various Superman titles when the idea of a wedding between Clark Kent and Lois Lane was shelved by DC president Jenette Kahn, who wanted to coordinate any wedding with the in-development *Lois & Clark* TV show for maximum publicity. Instead, *Adventures of Superman* writer Jerry Ordway jokingly suggested they should kill Superman—unexpectedly, the assembled creatives and DC's executives agreed to go for it.

Published across the Superman titles in the winter of 1992–93, the first phase of the story culminated with the Man of Steel's demise in January 1993's *Superman* #75. Driven by a media frenzy, the issue sold out its three million first printing in a day. But that was only the beginning of the bigger storyline. Over the course of 1993, a succession of wannabe Supermen, from armor-wearing Steel to teen clone Superboy, jostled to replace Superman, leading to the real Man of Steel's eventual, inevitable resurrection and return.

SUICIDE SQUAD

Release date: August 2016
Starring roles: Will Smith, Jared Leto, Margot Robbie, Joel Kinnaman, Viola Davis, Jai Courtney, Jay Hernandez, Adewale Akinnuoye-Agbaje, Cara Delevingne
Director: David Ayer

Screenplay: David Ayer
Cinematography: Roman Vasyanov
Music: Steven Price
Running time: 123 minutes
Box office: $746,846,894

To date, DC's cinematic endeavors in this brave new world of interlinked movies had been led by the comic book Trinity: Superman, Batman, and Wonder Woman. With cameos from Aquaman, The Flash, and Cyborg in *Batman v Superman: Dawn of Justice* (2016), and with a Wonder Woman solo outing in the works, the goal was clear—to bring DC's big guns together for a Justice League movie. Before then, however, a collection of DC's lesser known—one might even say criminally unknown—characters would take their turn in the spotlight, joining forces for a walk on the wild side ...

LEADER OF THE SQUAD

As a boy, David Ayer had spent countless hours at the library reading comic books, losing himself in the world of heroes and villains, sometimes poring over the pages to examine how the various elements—lines, dialogue, coloring—combined to create the whole. Years later, he would see the similarities between creating comics and creating movies—of beginning by roughly sketching out a story, then elaborating with designs in frames, then constructing a world with brushes or tools. In film, as in comics, almost everything needed to be created, from story to sets, costumes to props.

"Justice has a bad side."
Marketing tagline

So it proved when Ayer, now a writer and director, got the chance to turn one of the comics he'd read as a kid into a film. A Suicide Squad movie had been hinted at even before *Man of Steel* (2013) kicked off the modern era of interrelated DC cinema, with the focus falling on the Super-Villain incarnation of the comics team (rather than the Silver Age scientists version). Put together by writer John Ostrander in 1986 during that year's *Legends* comics crossover event, the Suicide Squad comprised hardened super-criminals such as Deadshot and Captain Boomerang, recruited by Amanda Waller, head of covert government agency Task Force X, to carry out often deadly assignments under the field command of Colonel Rick Flag.

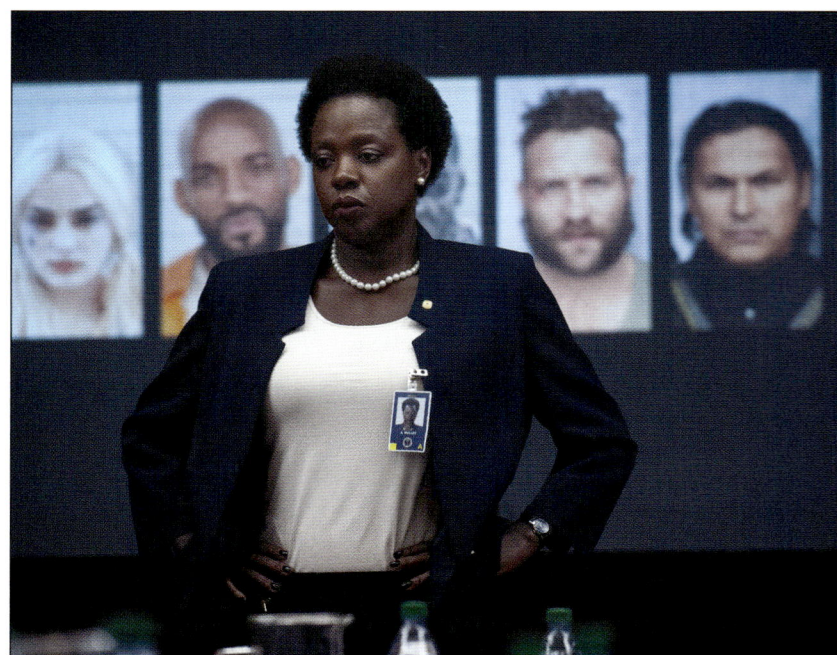

The Squad assembles: Adam Beach as Slipknot; Jai Courtney as Boomerang; Cara Delevingne as Enchantress; Karen Fukuhara as Katana; Joel Kinnaman as Rick Flag; Margot Robbie as Harley Quinn; Will Smith as Deadshot; Adewale Akinnuoye-Agbaje as Croc; Jay Hernandez as El Diablo.

Far left: For Viola Davis, the power of her character, government intelligence operative and Suicide Squad chief Amanda Waller, lay in her fierce intelligence and complete absence of guilt.

Left: The costumes worn by Margot Robbie as Harley Quinn often included callbacks to the character's original look, such as the checkered diamond pattern on the dress worn by Harley in The Joker's club.

167

Deadshot's costume incorporated practical wrist-Glocks operated by pneumatic actuators, and a military chestplate designed by the director himself.

David Ayer and crew filming in the yard of the Belle Reve set, where, as well as directing the movie, Ayer also made a cameo as one of the prison's guards.

Jared Leto and Margot Robbie on the helicopter cargo hold set, filming the scene where The Joker rescues Harley from the Suicide Squad, only to lose her again.

When Ayer signed on to direct in 2014 in the wake of *Man of Steel*, planning started in earnest. Ayer's résumé as the writer of *Training Day* (2001) and writer/director of *End of Watch* (2012) suggested he had the necessary understanding of morally ambiguous characters who straddle the line between right and wrong—or simply stride straight over it. Following his war film *Fury* (2014), Ayer found his appetite had been whetted for bigger-scale movies and the attendant opportunity to create whole worlds. In *Suicide Squad*, he saw a way of combining comics and conflict in a Super-Villain version of Robert Aldrich's 1967 convict war movie *The Dirty Dozen*—a character-driven ensemble piece with a straightforward plot.

RECRUITMENT DRIVE

With Ayer on board to both write and direct, the task of casting the Squad—a combination of characters hailing from the 1980s *Suicide Squad* comic book series and later recruits—began in earnest. Headlining would be Will Smith as Deadshot, alias Floyd Lawton. A mercenary marksman, Deadshot's only appearance had been in 1950 wearing top hat and tails before writer Steve Englehart and artist Marshall Rogers gave him a more modern countenance in 1977. Their modern incarnation came complete with wrist-mounted guns and a mask incorporating a targeting sight. It was this version who formed a part of not only the 1980s Suicide Squad but most comic book versions since, and who would be the basis for Will Smith's character.

David Ayer and costume designer Kate Hawley adapted Deadshot's comics costume in a recognizable but realistic fashion, distilling elements like the mask and the signature red hue into a more practical outfit, the designer following the director's dictum to avoid anything that looked like a Super-Villain suit. In preparing to take on Deadshot, however, Will Smith looked

Far left: Harley escapes her cage-within-a-cage in Belle Reve, an athletic sequence that made use of the months of gymnastic training Margot Robbie undertook prior to filming.

Left: Not only did Jared Leto lose his beard and long hair to become The Joker, but the actor agreed to have his eyebrows shaved off as well.

beyond the confines of comics. In order to get into the mindset of a contract killer, someone who murders for money, the actor read *The Anatomy of Motive* (1999) by Mark Olshaker and FBI profiler John Douglas, whose earlier book, *Mindhunter* (1995), would in 2017 inspire the eponymous Netflix series.

Although he undertook his own research, Smith wasn't working in a vacuum. From his first movie as director—2005's *Harsh Times,* starring Christian Bale, who became Batman the same year— Ayer's method was to engage his actors in an intensive three-to six-month preproduction period of not only physical training, but character exploration. For the latter, Ayer would gather Smith and the rest of the cast and probe and discuss not just their characters but their personal life experiences in an effort to draw out parallels between the two.

DEADLY DUO

Though it served to bond the cast, the process of revealing personal details wasn't always a comfortable one, as Australian actress Margot Robbie later admitted. But having that preproduction period allowed all of the actors to truly inhabit their characters. Robbie, who had not read comics growing up and thus was unfamiliar with Harley Quinn, immersed herself in her character's comics backstory. The daily process of being physically transformed into Harley also aided the actress, who was painted white from head to toe and had makeup, cosmetic bruises and cuts, and 20 tattoos applied. Indeed, most of the film's characters sported tattoos, from Deadshot to The Joker, all of them created by tattoo designer Rob Coutts.

One thing Robbie struggled to comprehend at first was how such a willfully strong character as Harley could be in thrall to a twisted individual like The Joker, until the actress realized the relationship was akin to an addiction. Though The Joker would not be a member of the Suicide Squad itself, he would play a role in the movie as a chaotic fly in the ointment, played in unnerving fashion by Jared Leto. Remarkably, Leto remained in character

Harley and Mr. J

From her first appearance in the 1992 *Batman: The Animated Series* episode "Joker's Favor," Harley Quinn was inextricably linked with Mr. J, as she called the Clown Prince of Crime. Originally envisioned as essentially an adjunct to The Joker, Harley was created by writer-producers Paul Dini and Bruce Timm to serve as his henchwoman, as opposed to his usual henchmen, but her popularity led to her making multiple returns in *Batman: The Animated Series* over the next two years and

emerging as a compelling character in her own right. By late 1993, Harley was featuring in the spin-off comic book series *Batman Adventures,* too, and by the end of the decade had made the leap over to the regular DC universe, debuting in the 1999 one-shot *Batman: Harley Quinn.*

Harley's red-and-black harlequinlike costume in comics initially matched her animated one, but in 2011, as part of DC's radical line-wide New 52 revamp, she received a makeover more akin to her corseted and pigtailed appearances in the video games *Batman: Arkham Asylum* (2009) and *Batman: Arkham City* (2011). That new look was unveiled in the New 52 Suicide Squad series, marking the first time Harley had been a member of the team, accompanied by an altered origin in which her transformation from Dr. Harleen Quinzel into Harley Quinn was achieved by The Joker throwing her into a chemical vat, similar to his own origin. Two years later, artist-writer team Amanda Conner and Jimmy Palmiotti further refined Harley's look and characterization, setting the stage for her appearance in *Suicide Squad.*

Freed from Amanda Waller's control, Enchantress, played by Cara Delevingne, attempts to take over the Earth aided by her brother, Incubus, played by Alain Chanoine.

As played by Jay Hernandez, El Diablo proves decisive in the battle against Incubus, detaining the mystical being long enough for the Squad to blow him—and El Diablo—to bits.

Costume designer Kate Hawley researched real-life criminals to create Harley's signature look and took inspiration from rock stars like Debbie Harry.

throughout filming, immersing himself to the extent that cast and crew referred to him on set as Mr. J or Smiley, only meeting Leto himself after the film had wrapped.

CRIMINAL MINDED

Like Will Smith, Margot Robbie, and Jared Leto, the rest of the main cast were encouraged by David Ayer to use their own feelings to drill down into their characters. In the case of Jai Courtney, who would be playing scuzzball thief Digger Harkness, a.k.a. Captain Boomerang, the director instructed the actor to get into the criminal mindset by scouting his own street for a house he would like to break into, while fellow Squad members Jay Hernandez as Diablo and Adewale Akinnuoye-Agbaje as Killer Croc were similarly encouraged.

Whereas all of Croc's teammates had been Suicide Squad members in comic books prior to the movie, the atavistic, reptilian Croc, alias Waylon Jones, only became a team member in comics the same year as the film. Introduced in 1983 as a brutal but cunning opponent for Batman, Croc had become ever more bestial over the decades, but David Ayer's drive to root *Suicide Squad* in reality led the movie Croc to hew closer to his original comics incarnation. Even so, while the makeup team used Akinnuoye-Agbaje's own skin tone to give the impression that Croc was suffering from a skin condition rather than being an out-and-out monster, Akinnuoye-Agbaje was still required to wear layers of prosthetics, so much so that the prosthetics team had to invent a cooling system to regulate the actor's body temperature.

Like Croc, Deadshot had originally been a member of Batman's Rogues Gallery in comics, reflected in a scene early in the film where Batman apprehends the mercenary while Floyd Lawton is out with his daughter. Briefly returning to the role of Batman for the cameo, Ben Affleck also appeared in the subsequent scene, capturing Harley Quinn, while Affleck's soon-to-be teammate Ezra Miller made an even more fleeting cameo as The Flash, collaring his comics nemesis, Captain Boomerang, mid-robbery.

WIDER WORLD

The presence of Batman and The Flash served to tie *Suicide Squad* into DC's wider cinematic milieu, but further reinforcing the ties between films was the iconic character who, despite being dead, drives the formation of the team. In the narrative, Superman's demise in *Batman v Superman: Dawn of Justice* is the impetus for Amanda Waller to activate Task Force X, although it's a member of the Squad itself who convinces the US military brass to give the green light after demonstrating her arcane powers, and who provokes the Squad's first mission when she goes rogue. Playing the twin roles of Dr. June Moone and her malevolent mystical counterpart Enchantress, Cara Delevingne had to embody both a buttoned-down archaeologist—not to mention romantic interest of Task Force X field team leader Rick Flag—and a full-blown witch. To bring Enchantress to life, Delevingne was advised by David Ayer to tap into her animal side and connect with nature, in order to display an organic, flowing physicality when Enchantress was using her powers.

The actors behind June Moone's lover, Rick Flag, and his bodyguard, Katana, had to come to grips with a different sort of physicality, both Joel Kinnaman and newcomer Karen Fukuhara undergoing rigorous training regimes. In the case of Kinnaman and his Navy SEAL cohorts Scott Eastwood (playing Edwards) and Alex Meraz (playing Gomez), that entailed entering a military immersion program involving carrying heavy backpacks and tracking in the woods on virtually no sleep. As for Fukuhara, as well as drawing on her own martial arts background, the actress received training in the use of the deadly katana sword from fight choreographer Richard Norton. For all concerned, it was just another intensive aspect of David Ayer's process of bringing the Suicide Squad to visceral life.

The Wall

The lineup of the various comic book versions of the Suicide Squad may have changed over the decades, but one thing most modern incarnations have in common is Amanda "The Wall" Waller. Created by John Ostrander and debuting in the first issue of DC's 1986 comics crossover *Legends*, Waller was a strikingly unusual team leader—not a svelte, superpowered hero, but a heavy-set Black widow from the projects. Knowing that an unruly team like the Suicide Squad would need someone tough in charge, Ostrander decided to base Waller on some no-nonsense women he knew from Chicago, conceiving her as someone who had muscled her way out of the ghetto and was prepared to get the job done no matter the cost. For Ostrander, Waller's size represented her power.

Academy Award winner Viola Davis's commanding portrayal of the Wall in *Suicide Squad* and subsequent DC movies is remarkably close to the character's original incarnation, but other actors have delivered convincing takes on Waller, too. In 2010, *Jackie Brown* (1997) actress Pam Grier played Waller in the ninth season of *Smallville*, while a year later, Golden Globe winner Angela Bassett *(above)* brought Waller to the big screen in *Green Lantern* (2011). Two years after that, Cynthia Addai-Robinson, who would go on to play queen regent Míriel in *The Lord of the Rings: The Rings of Power* (2022), portrayed Waller across three seasons of *Arrow* from 2013 to 2016.

WONDER WOMAN

Release date: June 2017
Starring roles: Gal Gadot, Chris Pine, Connie Nielsen, Robin Wright, Danny Huston, David Thewlis, Saïd Taghmaoui, Ewen Bremner, Eugene Brave Rock, Lucy Davis, Elena Anaya
Director: Patty Jenkins
Screenplay: Allan Heinberg

Story: Zack Snyder, Allan Heinberg, and Jason Fuchs
Cinematography: Matthew Jensen
Music: Rupert Gregson-Williams
Running time: 141 minutes
Box office: $821,847,012

Just over a year after making her big-screen debut in 2016's *Batman v Superman: Dawn of Justice*, Wonder Woman stepped into the spotlight in her first solo cinematic outing. Whereas her debut the previous year had merely hinted at Diana's origins, *Wonder Woman* would explore her history more fully, from her childhood on the Amazon island of Themyscira to her emergence into Man's World. All involved felt the weight of responsibility in bringing such an iconic character to the big screen, but for director Patty Jenkins, the project was especially personal; the inspiration for her making the film lay in her own childhood experiences.

Various versions of a *Wonder Woman* script had been in development for decades by the time *Man of Steel* arrived in cinemas in 2013, but it was Zack Snyder's reinvention of Superman that gave the project added impetus. By the time *Batman v Superman:*

Dawn of Justice was in postproduction in 2015, Snyder and writer Allan Heinberg—who as well as writing and producing for such television hits as *The O.C.* and *Grey's Anatomy* had penned a well-received comic book run of *Wonder Woman* in 2006—had come up with a story that pointed the way forward for the character, utilizing elements of other writers' scripts (although only one of those writers, Jason Fuchs, ended up receiving a screen credit).

TOUCHSTONE
Ultimately, it wasn't until Patty Jenkins came on board as director in 2015 that the various versions of the script coalesced, Jenkins working with one of the film's executive producers, Geoff Johns—who at that point was DC's chief creative officer, having written for DC for 15 years—to bring it all together. An early touchstone for Jenkins—for whom *Wonder Woman* would be her first film as director since her cinematic debut, the award-winning *Monster* (2003)—was Richard Donner's *Superman* (1978). Jenkins had seen Donner's movie as a child shortly after her father (a US Air Force

"Power. Grace. Wisdom. Wonder."
Marketing tagline

Queen Hippolyta (Connie Nielsen) and her Amazon guard protected Diana's home of Themyscira, an island of powerful warrior women.

Charlie (Ewen Bremner), the Chief (Eugene Brave Rock), Steve Trevor (Chris Pine), and Sameer (Saïd Taghmaoui) take a breather in No Man's Land.

In the war-ravaged town of Veld, Wonder Woman wields her Amazonian shield and God-Killer sword against the invading Germans, to devastating effect.

The Legend of Wonder Woman

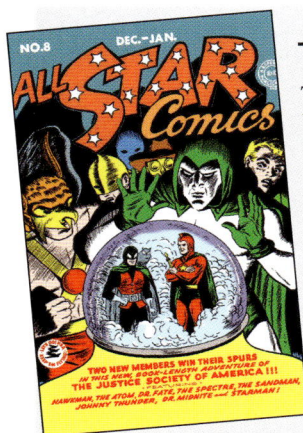

The core elements that would come to define Wonder Woman as not only the most famous female Super Hero on the planet, but also a figurehead for feminism, were in evidence right from the start. The two-part tale which introduced the character in *All-Star Comics* #8 and *Sensation Comics* #1 at the end of 1941 details how Diana, princess of the Amazons of Paradise Island, rescues Captain Steve Trevor from his wrecked plane, and then against the wishes of her mother, Queen "Hippolyte" (as the queen's name was originally spelled), competes in an Amazonian contest to determine who should accompany him back to America to "fight the forces of hate and oppression." Transporting Trevor back to the US in a "transparent plane," Wonder Woman uses her superhuman strength and speed and bulletproof bracelets "to save the world from the hatreds and wars of men in a man-made world!"

Later interpretations would refine or alter her origins, abilities, and place in popular culture—strengthening her mythological roots at the end of the 1950s; depriving her of her powers at the end of the 1960s; positioning her as a feminist icon on the cover of *Ms.* magazine in 1972, and, at the other end of that decade, redesigning her costume; repositioning her as an ambassador in the late 1980s; and reinventing her as a demigoddess in the 2010s. Yet Wonder Woman's essential belief in the power of love and compassion has remained constant throughout.

The armor Wonder Woman takes with her from Themyscira includes a tiara that belonged to her aunt, Antiope (Robin Wright), and the protective Bracelets of Submission.

After German soldiers pursue Steve Trevor onto Themyscira's beach, a battle ensues, resulting in the deaths of the troops and a number of Amazons, including Antiope.

fighter pilot) had been killed during a training exercise, and had been powerfully affected by the film, vowing to become a filmmaker herself in order to inspire in others the kinds of emotions she had experienced watching *Superman*.

Jenkins recognized in *Wonder Woman* the opportunity to do just that. For the director, Wonder Woman the character represented the kinds of attributes that she hoped would inspire audiences in the same way she had been inspired all those years ago: love, forgiveness, strength, and power—attributes that could help make sense of a complicated world.

THE WONDER OF HER

In order to go forward with the project, Jenkins and her collaborators first needed to look back—to the original incarnation of Wonder Woman. Created in 1941, Wonder Woman was the brainchild of psychologist William Moulton Marston, who, witnessing the explosion of superheroes in the wake of Superman's comics debut in 1938, set about creating a character who would embody his belief that women had the power to eradicate violence in the world of men. It was this primordial version of Wonder Woman that Jenkins and co. wanted to honor and stay true to, while also incorporating more modern comics interpretations, such as George Pérez's 1980s reinvigoration of the character, or Brian Azzarello and Cliff Chiang's 2011 reimagination (published as part of that year's DC New 52 revamp).

In one respect, a lot of the work had already been done. Although Gal Gadot had already been cast by the time Patty Jenkins joined the production, the director couldn't have been happier about the choice. For Jenkins, Gadot embodied everything the director was looking for in a portrayal of Wonder Woman: a youthful spirit combined with a wisdom born of her decision to remain open to the world, despite its harshness. Gadot, too, found Wonder Woman's values of understanding, love, forgiveness, and

Concept art for Themyscira, displaying many of the aspects that would feature in the final version: stone arches, waterfalls, lush foliage, and buildings rising from the rocky facade.

the proper wielding of power entirely relevant for the modern world.

This film, however, would largely be set in the past—not World War II raging when William Moulton Marston had first created his character—but an earlier, and in many ways more apposite conflict: World War I. For the filmmakers, the industrial nature of the Great War, with its attendant attritional trench warfare, was a modern, visceral form of conflict never before seen, and certainly never experienced by Diana of Themyscira.

NO MAN ON AN ISLAND

Before Diana could join that deadly conflict in her quest to kill the God of War, however, the contrast of her life on Themyscira needed to be established and explored. Patty Jenkins was keenly aware that whereas international travel was not common when Wonder Woman's Paradise Island home was first delineated in her debut appearance in 1941's *All-Star Comics* #8, today the notion of an ancient, yet fantastically advanced, Greek city on a remote island was not as exotic as it once was. The challenge, then, was to create an environment that would conjure a sense of wonder in a jaded audience, yet still feel as if it could exist.

Jenkins and production designer Aline Bonetto—best known for her lyrical work with visionary French director Jean-Pierre Jeunet on films like *Amélie* (2001) and *A Very Long Engagement* (2004)— set about determining what an island established by gods and inhabited by Amazon warriors would look like. Reasoning that the women would work with the existing landscape rather than against it to create their city, Bonetto envisioned an environment where dwellings were carved into the stone edifices of the island. While realizing much of this in physical form would require a mixture of custom-built sets and CGI, such as with Queen Hippolyta's majestic throne room, the production was fortunate in that location scouting turned up a real-world locale in which to shoot exterior scenes: Matera, an ancient city in southern Italy where the urban core was cut out of the rock canyons.

Though her home of Themyscira is literally an island paradise, as she grows up the young Diana still bristles against her overprotective mother, Hippolyta. Events are brought to a head when a male interloper upsets the Amazons' island idyll. The character of Steve Trevor has been an intrinsic part of Wonder Woman comics lore since her first appearance, when the US Army intelligence captain's plane crashed on Paradise Island. Broadly speaking, Jenkins's Wonder Woman would adhere to that origin

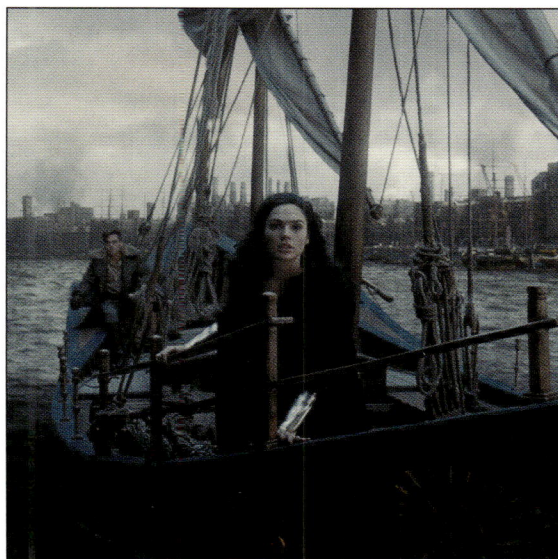

The boat in which Diana and Steve sail into London was a full-size set which was floated on a barge on the River Thames, with abackground buildings digitally altered.

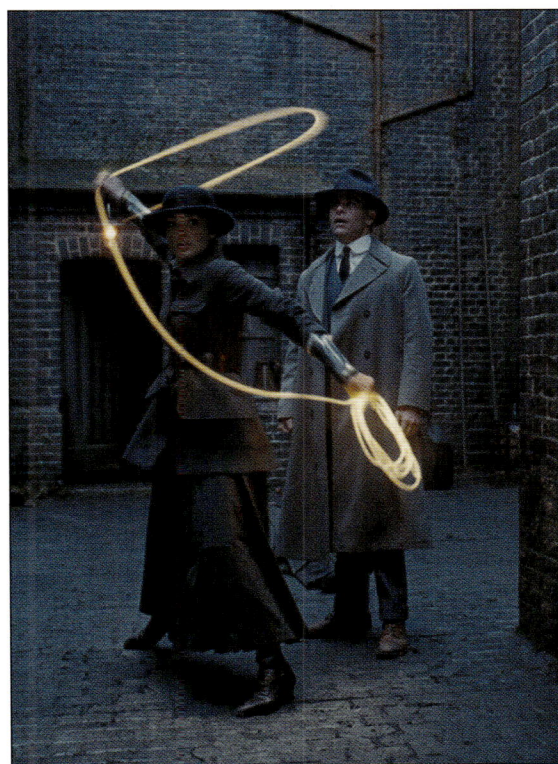

As well as a method of learning the truth from anyone bound by it, the Lasso of Hestia is an effective weapon, as Diana demonstrates against German spies in London.

175

Having worn a cloak during her journey to the front lines, Diana discards it as she emerges from the trenches, revealing her armor to the awed soldiers.

For Wonder Woman's momentous dash through No Man's Land, a mixture of real explosions and VFX work was used, aided by Gal Gadot wearing sneakers instead of boots, which were digitally added later.

Constructed on a British studio backlot in winter, the No Man's Land set was so authentic that actors and crew spent a lot of time covered in mud.

Sameer, Steve, Diana, Chief, and Charlie pose for the photo that, decades later, will be discovered by Bruce Wayne, alias Batman, and returned to Diana.

story, with Trevor played by *Star Trek* (2009) actor Chris Pine, who was able to embody the qualities that Jenkins and producer Zack Snyder were looking for—someone with a tremendous spirit who could both act as a parallel to Diana and be inspired and changed by her.

But where in the original comics Steve Trevor was embroiled in World War II, here the conflict his plane spirals down from into the sea off the coast of Themyscira was World War I. The grinding trench warfare of the War to End All Wars, as it was dubbed at the time, would act as a brutal awakening for Diana as she emerged into Man's World, bringing home the cruelty of modern conflict. An early taste of this horror comes as Diana, Steve, and their motley crew of n'er-do-wells Sameer (Saïd Taghmaoui), Charlie (Ewen Bremner), and Chief (Eugene Brave Rock) set out from Dover docks in England on their mission to prevent German General Ludendorff (Danny Huston)—whom Diana believes is Ares, the God of War—from unleashing a deadly new form of mustard gas. Filmed at the port of Tilbury in Essex, the scene finds Diana witnessing returning soldiers, shellshocked, gravely

Concept art depicting the young Diana running through the streets of Themyscira shows the influence of many different cultures and traditions on the city's design.

injured, or dead. Such was the level of authenticity that the production strove for that set decorator Anna Lynch-Robinson and her team outfitted the traumatized troops with World War I packs containing such items as letters from loved ones, even though they would barely be glimpsed on screen.

INTO BATTLE

When Diana and her group reach the front lines in Belgium, they are confronted by the full horror of life in the trenches. Vividly recreated on a studio backlot in the freezing cold of a British winter, No Man's Land is the setting for the dramatic unveiling of Wonder Woman's costume, as she leads the Allied troops out of their trenches, drawing the German gunfire onto herself so that the British soldiers can advance. The armor that Diana wears had already been designed by Michael Wilkinson for her appearance in *Batman v Superman: Dawn of Justice*, but Wonder Woman costume designer Lindy Hemming and her team worked to make it as comfortable and practical as possible, given that Gal Gadot had so much more action to perform this time.

Case in point: Wonder Woman's perilous, superhuman dash across No Man's Land at speeds far beyond those of a mortal. Surrounded by practical explosions, wreathed in blue smoke

Island Paradise

When Themyscira was first introduced on the first page of Wonder Woman's debut story in 1941's *All-Star Comics* #8, it was named simply Paradise Island. Depicted in that tale as a fertile isle on which the Amazons had settled after fleeing the oppressive world of men, building a city akin to an ancient Greek metropolis, Paradise Island would retain that name and origin for the next 45 years, in comics and on the 1975–1979 *Wonder Woman* TV show. It was only when *New Teen Titans* and *Crisis on Infinite Earths* co-creator George Pérez relaunched the Wonder Woman comic book series in 1987, ramping up the Greek mythology, that Paradise Island took on the name Themyscira.

As with much comics lore, Themyscira has gone through many changes in the decades since, often as the result of conflict. In 1995, Darkseid, ruler of Apokolips, laid waste to the island, killing half its Amazon population, while six years later the cosmic villain Imperiex destroyed Themyscira completely. Subsequently rebuilt, the island was relocated to the Bermuda Triangle, and then later removed from Earth completely for a time. Yet Themyscira has always returned as an essential part of Wonder Woman's mythos, as enduring a concept as the character herself.

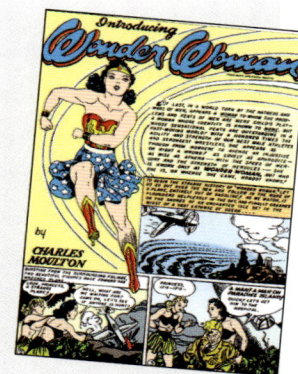

Taken off guard, Diana dances with Ludendorff at the general's gala, the interiors for which were filmed at Hatfield House, Queen Elizabeth I's former residence in Hertfordshire.

Elena Anaya plays Dr. Isabel Maru, alias Doctor Poison, the disfigured chemist who creates a deadly new poison gas for her associate, General Ludendorff.

Posing as a German, Steve Trevor steals Doctor Poison's notebook of formulae and escapes on a plane, leading him to eventually crash in the water off the coast of Themyscira.

to contrast with her costume, Gadot's run across the mud and debris was a combination of footage shot on set and elements filmed on a treadmill against green screen, allowing the actor to run at full speed. The subsequent battle in the town of Veld again saw Gadot running through a practical set in sub-zero temperatures, and included a scene where Wonder Woman hefts a German tank and throws it into a building—the tank in real life a small green box that visual-effects supervisor Bill Westenhofer weighted enough to sell the moment, which was then digitally transformed into a vehicle. In a further illustration of the film's marriage of CGI and practical effects, Westenhofer's team then embedded a custom-built tank into the set wall.

FINAL CONFLICT

While the movie's climactic battle between Wonder Woman and Ares—who it transpires has disguised himself as British politician and ostensible peace-seeker Sir Patrick, played by David Thewlis—was shot entirely on a green-screen stage, the airfield sequence just before that again was a combination of real-world locales, purpose-built sets, and VFX. Two separate airfields were used for location shooting—RAF Halton in Buckinghamshire, which was still in use, and RAF Upper Heyford in Oxfordshire, which had been closed for two decades—while Bill Westenhofer and his team built a control tower set for the fight between Wonder Woman and General Ludendorff.

That fight features a moment where Diana scissor-kicks Ludendorff through the wall of the tower's upper deck, something the stunt department declared had never been done on film before. In fact, the stunt incorporated two camera passes shot separately. In the first, Danny Huston's stunt double, Gary Kane, was pulled by a wire through a hole in the wall, while in the second, Gal

Left After Steve is killed destroying the poison gas, Wonder Woman unleashes her full furious power against Ares, in a sequence filmed against green screen and utilizing CGI.

Gadot's stunt double, Caitlin Dechelle, performed a scissor kick on a wire. The two elements were composited together with a built wall that was broken apart digitally to create the final effect.

LOVE AFTER ALL

For all its action and digital wizardry, *Wonder Woman* remains a movie about the power of love, and how it often requires courage and sacrifice. This is exemplified by one of the film's final scenes, in which jubilant crowds fill London's Trafalgar Square on Armistice Day. Shot on location in Trafalgar Square itself, which Aline Bonetto festooned with red, white, and blue Union Jack flags, the scene finds Diana alone in a crowd, while all around her there are tears of joy. As she contemplates all she has lost, Diana reflects on how love requires bravery and acceptance, and how she must remain strong even in the face of overwhelming darkness—an understanding that will serve her well in the dark times to come.

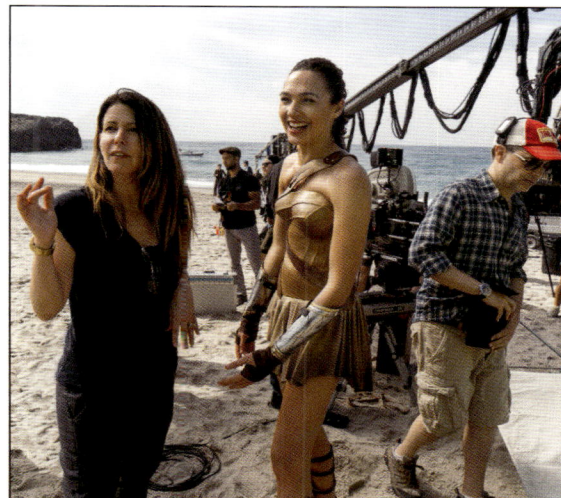

Patty Jenkins with Gal Gadot on Themyscira's beach—in reality the Italian Cilento Coast, chosen for its particular light and geography, and because it could accommodate around 30 galloping horses.

Right-hand man

Chris Pine's Steve Trevor hews relatively closely to the original conception of the character by William Moulton Marston and artist Harry G. Peter—albeit transplanted to World War I from World War II—even to the extent that he is rescued by Wonder Woman from his crashed plane, much as he is in *All-Star Comics* #8. That first comic book appearance established a pattern for the pair of Steve being rescued from peril by Wonder Woman (or, on occasion, vice versa); as early as the two characters' second appearance in *Sensation Comics* #1, Steve is again saved from certain death by Diana when he leaps from a doomed plane only to have his parachute ripped away.

After being killed off and returned to life repeatedly during the 1960s and '70s, Steve Trevor was reworked as an older man by writer/artist George Pérez in the 1987 relaunched *Wonder Woman* series, his backstory altered. No longer romantically entwined with Diana, this version of Steve eventually married his aide, Etta Candy (played in the *Wonder Woman* movie by Lucy Davis). But in 2011, DC's New 52 line-wide relaunch saw a younger version of Steve restored to continuity, and by the time of DC's 2016 Rebirth initiative, Steve's origin story had once more been restored to a version closer to Marston and Peter's original telling, while his and Diana's romance was rekindled.

JUSTICE LEAGUE

Release date: November 2017
Starring roles: Ben Affleck, Henry Cavill, Amy Adams, Gal Gadot, Ezra Miller, Jason Momoa, Ray Fisher, Jeremy Irons, Diane Lane, Connie Nielsen, J. K. Simmons
Director: Zack Snyder. Joss Whedon reshoots

Screenplay: Chris Terrio, Joss Whedon
Story: Chris Terrio, Zack Snyder
Cinematography: Fabian Wagner
Music: Danny Elfman
Running time: 120 minutes
Box office: $661,324,295

As the movies rolled out in this brave new era of interrelated DC cinema, from *Man of Steel* (2013), to *Batman v Superman: Dawn of Justice* (2016), to *Wonder Woman* (2017)—via a devious detour in the twisted shape of *Suicide Squad* (2016)—there was no mistaking the eventual destination, nor the momentum building toward it. In big-budget, multiplex cinema, however, nothing is certain. With multitudinous parts in play and multiple stages and challenges to surmount on any production before the cameras can roll—scripts, casting, production design, sets, costumes—any number of factors can prevent a film from being made. In the case of *Justice League*, there was even a precedent in the not-too-distant past of a previous attempt that had faltered and fallen.

"You can't save the world alone"
Poster tagline

In 2007, plans were hatched for a Justice League movie. With a Writers Guild of America strike looming, a script was put together and *Mad Max* (1979) director George Miller hired to helm, but as 2008 unfolded, problems with filming in Miller's preferred choice of his home country, Australia, pushed the production back to summer. Then, in July, Christopher Nolan's *The Dark Knight* debuted in cinemas, breaking box-office records and refocusing minds on the potential of Nolan's vision of Batman and for solo superhero movies in general. The decision was made to delay a League movie until the time was right—even if that meant waiting a decade.

ORIGINS OF THE LEAGUE

As it turns out, it would indeed be almost 10 years before *Justice League* reached the big screen, though thoughts again turned seriously toward such a venture even before *Man of Steel* reached cinemas in 2013. While the immediate priority once Zack Snyder's Henry Cavill–starring Superman reboot debuted in June 2013 was a sequel to that film, the notion of a League movie was a natural

The League assembled: Ezra Miller as The Flash; Henry Cavill as Superman; Ray Fisher as Cyborg; Gal Gadot as Wonder Woman; Ben Affleck as Batman; and Jason Momoa as Aquaman.

Far left: At the memorial to Superman in Heroes Park in Metropolis, Batman faces a resurrected Superman, who in his confused state has already defeated the rest of the League.

Left: During a rescue of S.T.A.R. Labs personnel at a Gotham Harbor facility, The Flash uses his speed to evade the blasts from a Parademon's Apokoliptian weapon.

Concept art depicting the moment when Steppenwolf uses a Boom Tube to breach the Penetralium, the fortress on Themyscira where the Amazons guard a Mother Box.

Zack Snyder's idea to have Aquaman covered in tattoos was inspired by a tattoo on Jason Momoa's left forearm, a shark fin design representing his family's ancestral guardian.

follow-on, especially once it was confirmed a month after *Man of Steel*'s cinematic debut that Batman would co-star in the sequel. Swiftly following that announcement was the news that Ben Affleck would play Bruce Wayne/Batman in the movie, while by the end of the year it had been confirmed that Wonder Woman, too, would play a part in the film, as portrayed by Gal Gadot.

With the DC Trinity in place, 2014 brought further additions to the cast of *Batman v Superman: Dawn of Justice*, as the *Man of Steel* sequel was now titled. Appearing in cameos would be newcomer Ray Fisher and Ezra Miller (*We Need to Talk About Kevin*). Fisher would be playing Victor Stone, alias Cyborg, a cybernetically enhanced hero who had debuted as a member of Marv Wolfman and George Pérez's *New Teen Titans* in 1980 but had been elevated to core membership of the *Justice League* as part of DC's New 52 comics revamp in 2011, while Miller would be playing Barry Allen, alias super-speedster The Flash. Already cast—having auditioned for the role of Batman back in 2013, but finally officially confirmed in October 2014—was Jason Momoa (*Game of Thrones*), playing Arthur Curry, alias Aquaman.

Their roles in *Batman v Superman: Dawn of Justice* may have been minor, but the implications of Fisher, Miller, and Momoa's casting, on top of Affleck and Gadot's, were anything but—a Justice League movie was about to become a reality.

REBUILDING THE HEROES

Marshaling *Justice League* would be the filmmaker who had directed both *Man of Steel* and *Batman v Superman: Dawn of Justice*, Zack Snyder. Joining him behind the scenes were a number of the names who had helped him make those movies—and worked with him to produce Patty Jenkins's *Wonder Woman* (2017)—among them his wife and producing partner Deborah Snyder, and producer Charles Roven. Where *Batman v Superman: Dawn of Justice* had been a deconstructive take on superheroes, for director and producers, *Justice League* represented the opportunity to build them up again. Moreover, it was a chance to further the character threads of the

Concept art for the underwater stronghold where the Atlanteans guard the Mother Box that was entrusted to them—until Steppenwolf arrives to take it away.

Concept art for the interior of S.T.A.R. Labs, the Metropolis facility where Silas Stone saved his son Victor's life by transforming him into Cyborg.

previous films—of Superman learning there was a cost to saving the world, and making the ultimate sacrifice as a consequence; of Batman learning through Superman's sacrifice that there was still good in the world, and that it was worth fighting for; of Wonder Woman, having previously closed herself off from the world, accepting the responsibility of being a hero.

Joining the Trinity were Aquaman, The Flash, and Cyborg. Though cinematic newcomers, each could lay claim to decades of comic book continuity, from which the filmmakers drew to craft characters who were all, in their own ways, searching for purpose. The catalyst that brings them together in *Justice League* is the death of Superman in *Batman v Superman: Dawn of Justice*, a devastating event which in turn has triggered the reactivation of three Mother Boxes, alien devices hailing from the planet Apokolips. Heeding their call, would-be conqueror Steppenwolf, voiced by Ciarán Hinds (*Game of Thrones*), and his army of Parademons descend on Earth via extradimensional portals known as Boom Tubes, with the intention of combining the Mother Boxes and remodeling the planet in the nightmarish image of Apokolips.

START THE ENGINE

Also on board was production designer Patrick Tatopoulos, who had filled the same role on *Batman v Superman: Dawn of Justice*. Where on the prior movie Tatopoulos's way into the film had been to design the Batmobile, for *Justice League* he instead needed to

In the Kryptonian scout ship's genesis chamber, The Flash uses the electrical energy generated by his super-speed to wake the Mother Box and bring Superman back to life.

Steppenwolf and the Parademons

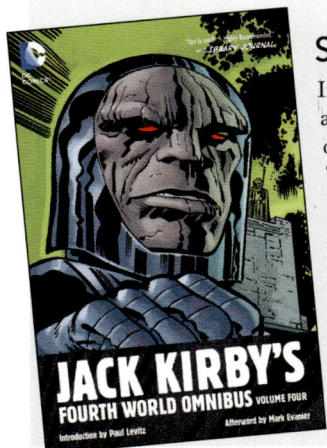

In 1970, creative powerhouse Jack Kirby returned to DC after a dozen years at Marvel, where he had co-created, among others, the Fantastic Four, the Avengers, and the X-Men. Turning his prodigious imagination to a bold new concept, Kirby unleashed the Fourth World saga, an interlinked series of comic book titles centering on characters hailing from the opposing worlds of New Genesis and Apokolips. The despotic ruler of the latter was Darkseid, a granite-faced cosmic dictator who sought to dominate all existence via the Anti-Life Equation and who over the ensuing decades rose to become one of the most feared Super-Villains in the DC universe.

It was this mythology that the makers of *Justice League* tapped into to bring Steppenwolf, one of Darkseid's military generals, to the screen, along with the Parademons, Darkseid's genetically altered shock troops, and the Mother Boxes. Using the characters' comic book incarnations as a jumping-off point, production designer Patrick Tatopoulos and his team of concept artists and designers conceived a look for Steppenwolf and the Parademons that was part technological, part organic. That biomechanical appearance extended to their base, an abandoned nuclear plant in the (fictional) Russian town of Pozharnov, the surrounding area of which was transformed by Steppenwolf into a horrific approximation of Apokolips.

Wonder Woman ensnares a terrorist at a London bank, using the Lasso of Hestia to compel him to reveal his group's aims in taking hostages.

A behind-the-scenes glimpse of Connie Nielsen as Queen Hippolyta as she fires an arrow at Steppenwolf, who has obtained the Mother Box.

Renderings and concept art of Steppenwolf, voiced and performed in the film by Ciarán Hinds, who wore a motion-capture suit and helmet for the role.

embellish it. Fortunately, Tatopoulos had had the foresight to originally design the car in such a way that it already had the appearance of being able to be altered or upgraded, which was precisely what was required for the new film, where Batman would effectively be going to war. While retaining the Batmobile's low profile, Tatopoulos gave the automobile more of a tanklike feel, removing the passenger seat and placing a cannon there instead, and positioning two machine guns on the top of the car, plus even more missile launchers on the back, all of the weaponry based on real-life weapons.

In a similar fashion to the way his first order of business on *Batman v Superman: Dawn of Justice* had been to design the Batmobile, on *Justice League*, Tatopoulos again tackled a vehicle first—one he was particularly excited about, as it was an opportunity to design a new aircraft. Able to carry the Batmobile in its hold, the Flying Fox was so huge that it could only be realized with CGI, much to the regret of Tatopoulos, who would have loved to have built the craft. Possessing the scale of a bomber, the Flying Fox was inspired by the designer's interest in Spitfires and World War II fighter jets, with a cockpit positioned toward the back, while its interior was influenced by a pipe-riddled, organic-looking steam engine Tatopoulos had seen in Detroit while working on *Batman v Superman: Dawn of Justice*.

In the narrative of *Justice League*, the Flying Fox transports the team—and the Batmobile—to Pozharnov, a derelict Russian city where Steppenwolf has established his lair. However, an earlier battle with Steppenwolf and his Parademons beneath Gotham City harbor required a rather different sort of Bat-vehicle—one closer

Academy and Golden Globe Award winner Jeremy Irons as Bruce Wayne/Batman's assistant Alfred, reprising the role he first played *Batman v Superman: Dawn of Justice.*

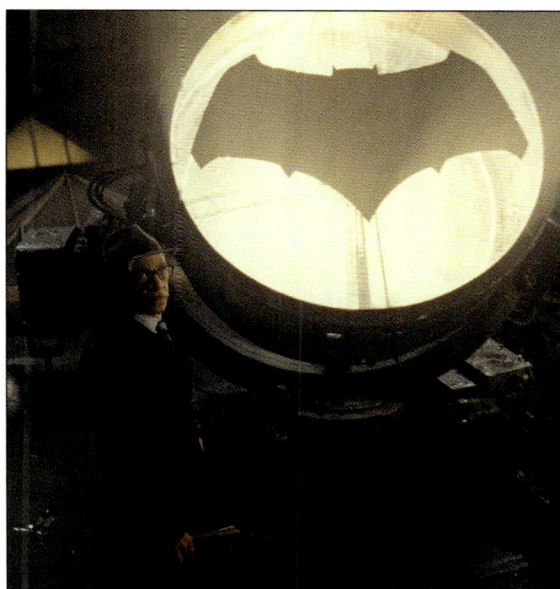

Making his debut as Commissioner Gordon, J. K. Simmons found lighting up the Bat-Signal on the roof of the Gotham City Police Department an iconic moment.

in appearance to a crab or a spider. Featuring four legs incorporating tank treads, the Knightcrawler could scale walls with the help of spikes in the sides of the legs—a useful attribute when escaping flooded tunnels. When the notion of the Knightcrawler was first discussed, Tatopoulos was concerned it veered too far into the realm of sci-fi, but as it turns out the vehicle was realized as a plausible part of Batman's armory.

BATCAVE RETURNS

As before, Batman's armory resided in the Batcave, the set for which had been scanned by the visual effects team during filming of *Batman v Superman: Dawn of Justice* so that it could be recreated later digitally. Inhabiting the cave in a more corporeal form was Jeremy Irons, making a return as Bruce Wayne's butler and chief of tech/security Alfred Pennyworth, this time interacting in amusing fashion with the superpowered individuals Bruce has chosen to bring together. Also making a return were Connie Nielsen as Queen Hippolyta, who leads the Amazons in battle when Steppenwolf arrives on Themyscira seeking a Mother Box; Amy Adams as Lois Lane, still mourning the passing of Clark Kent/ Superman; and Diane Lane as Martha Kent, who has to deal with losing the family farm on top of losing her adopted son—though in both cases, Bruce Wayne will ultimately provide redress.

New additions to the cast included Amber Heard (*London Fields*) as Atlantean princess Mera, who uses her aquatic powers to try and prevent Steppenwolf from obtaining the Mother Box guarded by Atlantis, and Academy Award winner J. K. Simmons as Gotham City Police Department Commissioner James Gordon. Having previously played J. Jonah Jameson in Sam Raimi's three Spider-Man films from 2002 to 2007—a role he would resume for two of Jon Watts's Spider-Man movies in 2019 and 2021—Simmons

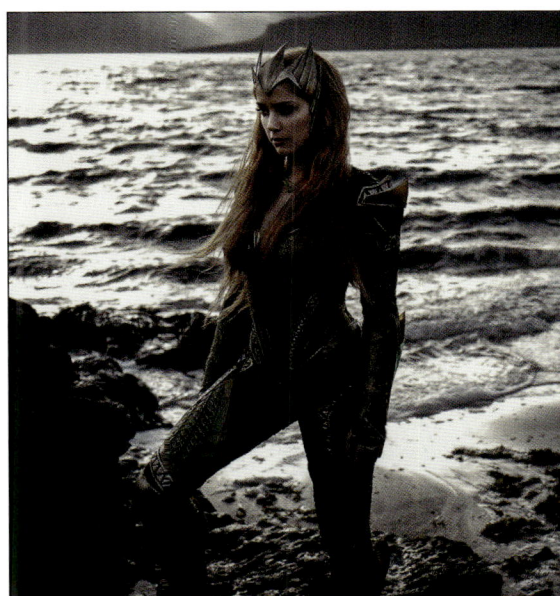

Costume designer Michael Wilkinson and his team researched fish scales and bioluminescent textures to create the armor worn by Mera, played by Amber Heard.

Arriving in the Russian town of Pozharnov, the Justice League prepare to make their assault on Steppenwolf's stronghold, while Batman clears the way in the Batmobile.

Taking to the air, Aquaman battles Parademons in the sky, spearing one with his trident and riding the creature back to earth as if on a surfboard.

Batman leaps into action in his tactical suit, joining the fray in the nuclear facility where Steppenwolf has established his base to bring about the Unity.

During the battle in Pozharnov, Batman in the Batmobile unleashes a volley of machine-gun fire against the hordes of Parademons protecting Steppenwolf's base.

was no stranger to inhabiting comic book characters. To bring Gordon to life, the actor adopted a wig and mustache that gave him the physical appearance of the comics Gordon.

SETS AND SUITS

A key scene for Gordon takes place on the roof of the Gotham City Police Department, when he lights up the Bat-Signal and is confronted not just by Batman, but by Wonder Woman, The Flash, and Cyborg as well. Patrick Tatopoulos sketched out the rooftop to envision the moment where Batman appears atop one of the building's gargoyles, framed against a stormy sky, and spent a lot of time with the production's sculptors ensuring the gargoyles turned out exactly as he had pictured. Just as satisfying was the realization of Barry Allen's pad, a haphazard riot of color, cluttered with books, equipment, and screens reflecting Barry's eclectic personality and put together with the input of Ezra Miller.

For Barry's Flash suit, Zack Snyder and costume designer Michael Wilkinson—who had worked on both *Batman v Superman: Dawn of Justice* and *Man of Steel*, as well as Snyder's previous films *Sucker Punch* (2011), *Watchmen* (2009), and *300* (2006)—conceived an outfit that was very much a prototype, put together by Barry with a 3D printer using aerodynamic, heat-resistant materials to protect him from the superhuman speeds and fierce temperatures his new powers entailed. For Barry's skater/punk civilian clothes, Ezra Miller again contributed ideas, as did Jason Momoa for Arthur Curry's outfits, a mixture of rock 'n' roll chic and tribal aesthetics that channeled Momoa's personal sense of style. Cyborg, on the other hand, was created with the help of computer-generated imagery, Ray Fisher donning a motion-capture suit that was then translated into the final mechanical look, with its layers of shapes, textures, and colors.

While Batman and Wonder Woman's costumes were already established, Michael Wilkinson and his team still tweaked them a little, and in the case of Batman added a tactical suit featuring

Filming on set in Barry Allen's pad, as Bruce Wayne (Ben Affleck) flings a Batarang, forcing Barry (Ezra Miller) to reveal his super-speed by evading the weapon.

a layer of protective armor for use during the final battle. Another costume Wilkinson was able to further develop with new fabrics was that of Superman. In the narrative of the movie, the newly formed League determines to resurrect Kal-El using the genesis chamber in the Kryptonian scout ship first seen in *Man of Steel*, in conjunction with one of the Mother Boxes. Though initially confused and vengeful, Superman is brought back to himself by the love of Lois, allowing him to decisively join the fight against Steppenwolf at film's end.

In spring 2017, with *Justice League* in postproduction, tragedy struck the Snyder family when Zack and Deborah's daughter, Autumn, took her own life. The Snyders withdrew from the production of *Justice League*, with *Avengers* (2012) director Joss Whedon stepping in to finish the film, adding his own touches to the completed movie.

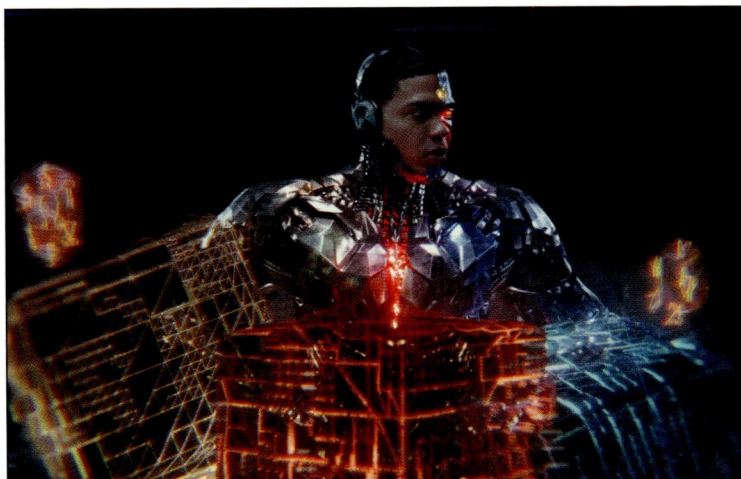

In an effort to prevent Steppenwolf from bringing about the world-destroying Unity, Cyborg pries the three Mother Boxes apart, allowing Superman to separate them completely.

The Snyder cut

Four years after the film's release, following an intensive fan campaign, Zack Snyder got to realize his vision for the movie in a revised and extended cut released on HBO Max in March 2021. With a much longer runtime, *Zack Snyder's Justice League*, as the recut film was called, was able to include more character work; a more prominent role in the narrative for Steppenwolf's Apokoliptian master, Darkseid; a reprise of the dystopian Knightmare sequence from *Batman v Superman: Dawn of Justice*—now also featuring Mera, The Flash, Cyborg, Joe Manganiello's Deathstroke, and Jared Leto's The Joker; and a cameo at the close of the movie from Martian Manhunter. Most importantly, the fan movement that led to *Zack Snyder's Justice League* also resulted in half a million dollars being donated to the American Foundation for Suicide Prevention. Dedicating his version of the movie to the memory of his daughter, Snyder closed the film with Autumn's favorite song, Leonard Cohen's "Hallelujah," performed by friend of the family Allison Crowe, who had sung it at Autumn's funeral.

Animated Leagues

Decades before the Justice League was realized in live-action form, the team was first rendered in animated form. Originally debuting in comics in anthology title *The Brave and the Bold* in 1960, the Justice League of America—to give the group its full name—first made the leap to animation just seven years later, in three segments as part of the *Superman/Aquaman Hour of Adventure* on CBS in 1967. But it was six years later that the JLA made a more sustained series of appearances on the small screen, when the League-inspired series *Super Friends* launched as part of ABC's Saturday morning cartoon lineup in 1973. Initially featuring Superman, Batman, Robin, Wonder Woman, and Aquaman, *Super Friends* ran in one form or another for the next dozen or so years.

The new millennium brought with it a fresh animated take on the League. Developed by *Batman: The Animated Series* and *Superman: The Animated Series* co-producer Bruce Timm, *Justice League*—later rebranded *Justice League Unlimited*—was effectively a sequel to those two successful shows, boasting some of the same voice cast—notably Kevin Conroy as Batman—and creative staff. Running for five seasons across the two iterations of the show, from 2001 to 2006, *Justice League Unlimited* is still ranked as one of the best animated shows of all time.

AQUAMAN

Release date: November 2018
Starring roles: Jason Momoa, Amber Heard, Willem Dafoe, Patrick Wilson, Nicole Kidman, Dolph Lundgren, Yahya Abdul-Mateen II, Temuera Morrison
Director: James Wan
Story: Geoff Johns, James Wan and Will Beall

Screenplay: David Leslie Johnson-McGoldrick and Will Beall
Cinematography: Don Burgess
Music: Rupert Gregson-Williams
Running time: 143 minutes
Box office: $1,151,961,807

"A tide is coming."
Marketing tagline

For years, James Wan had dreamed about which superhero he would most like to bring to the big screen if given the chance. Naturally, there were the big hitters to consider—the likes of Superman, Batman, and Wonder Woman—but what most excited the director was the thought of making a film about a hero who hadn't been seen on cinema screens before.

Of all the myriad comics characters Wan might have considered, he would never have guessed that Aquaman would be the one he would feature in a film. Yet the King of the Seas, embodied in charismatic fashion by Jason Momoa, would prove the perfect vessel for Wan's kinetic strengths as a filmmaker, resulting in a film which employed revolutionary effects in service of a story that had as much, if not more, in common with the action-adventure movies of the 1980s than the brooding superhero epics of more recent years.

TESTING THE WATER

Arguably a less familiar figure to the general public than DC's Trinity of Superman, Batman, and Wonder Woman—his most high-profile screen outings being the animated likes of *The Superman/Aquaman Hour of Adventure* in the late 1960s and *Super Friends* in the 1970s—Aquaman was nevertheless a prime candidate for a movie treatment in the wake of *Man of Steel* (2013), especially if a Justice League film were to become a reality. Certainly DC's then-Chief Creative Officer Geoff Johns was eager to see such a thing happen, a sentiment that was shared by DC's then-president Diane Nelson. Johns had already given the character a boost of popularity via the *Aquaman* comic book series that had launched in 2011 as part of DC's New 52 comics revamp. By the summer of 2014, scripts were in development for an Aquaman movie, but a more significant development had come the summer before, when an actor's unsuccessful audition had led to a rather different opportunity.

In 2013, Jason Momoa, whose star was on the rise following his 2011–2012 turn as Khal Drogo on the HBO sensation *Game of Thrones*, auditioned for the role of Batman in Zack Snyder's *Batman v Superman: Dawn of Justice* (2016). Though he lost out to Ben Affleck, a few weeks later Momoa was called in by Snyder, who told the surprised actor that he would like him to play Aquaman in the movie. When the announcement of Momoa's casting was made the following June, the implication was clear—big plans were afoot for the character.

MAN FROM ATLANTIS

By the time director James Wan signed on to direct *Aquaman* a year later in June 2015, Jason Momoa had been living with the idea of playing Aquaman for two years. He had also been keeping the role a secret for much of that time, something that Wan was cognizant of when he took the project on. A priority for the

Frequent James Wan collaborator Patrick Wilson could empathize with the aims of Orm, Aquaman's half-brother, if not the character's methods.

As Mera and Atlanna, Amber Heard and Nicole Kidman relished the opportunity to play strong, powerful women, with each character as formidable in their own ways as Aquaman.

Jason Momoa connected to the flawed nature of Arthur Curry,
with his blue-collar background, his reluctance to discuss
emotions, and his fondness for bars and drinking.

The Atlanteans employ a variety of sealife in a range of roles, from whales and giant turtles carrying cargo, to sharks acting as warriors' steeds.

Yahya Abdul-Mateen II saw his character Black Manta's vendetta against Aquaman as more about the seeking of justice rather than revenge.

As played by Willem Dafoe, it is Vulko, Aquaman's mentor and counselor, who sends Mera to Arthur, beginning the quest for Atlan's trident.

director was to get together with Momoa and talk about how they both viewed Arthur Curry—to give the half-Atlantean Aquaman his human name—and what they wanted to do with him. Momoa and Wan quickly realized they were on the same page, viewing Aquaman as a man of two worlds—Atlantis and the surface—who feels as though he belongs to neither, a characterization that Momoa, born in Hawaii but raised in Iowa, could relate to.

As the story for Aquaman developed, Momoa came to grips with the character in a more physical sense, playing him in *Justice League* (2017). But while that film firmly established his gruff, glowering take on Aquaman, the character's origins were barely hinted at. Aquaman would afford the filmmakers the opportunity to flesh out Arthur Curry's background and worlds, from his time growing up in a lighthouse in the working-class community of Amnesty Bay with his father, Tom, played by Temuera Morrison (*Star Wars: The Empire Strikes Back*), to his Atlantean heritage.

With over 70 years of comic book history to draw from, encompassing numerous interpretations and incarnations—from the original Aquaman dreamt up by writer Mort Weisinger and artist Paul Norris in 1941, to Peter David's bearded, harpoon-handed 1990s reinvention—the filmmakers looked to the more recent New 52 revamp as their guide, albeit still incorporating earlier elements. Moreover, as in *Justice League*, Jason Momoa's performance would incorporate elements of the actor's own personality and traits, Momoa's personification of Aquaman so complete that the dividing line between the two was often blurred.

DIVING IN

With Momoa making for a commanding presence as the title character, it was important that the rest of the film's cast be comprised of actors able to deliver similarly powerful performances. Cast early in 2016 was Amber Heard (*The Ward*) as Mera, who would also be making an appearance in *Justice League*. Reflecting the New 52 comics incarnation, the movie Mera is a princess of Xebel, one of the seven kingdoms or tribes that once comprised ancient Atlantis. Possessing water-manipulation powers that make her the equal of Aquaman, Mera assumes a central role in the narrative alongside Arthur.

Far left: Captured by Atlantean troops, Aquaman is held in chains and tortured, before being confronted by his half-brother, Orm, Atlantis's ruler, who Arthur challenges to the ritual duel known as the Combat of the Kings.

Left: Peaceful poets and philosophers who have evolved to become one with the marine life around them, the denizens of the Fishermen Kingdom keep themselves separate from Atlantis, until they are drawn into Orm's war.

Mera is betrothed to Orm, ruler of Atlantis and Arthur's half-brother, played by Patrick Wilson. Not just a DC movie veteran, having previously played Nite Owl in Zack Snyder's *Watchmen* (2009) and voiced the President of the United States in *Batman v Superman: Dawn of Justice* (2016), Wilson was the star of James Wan's *Insidious* and *The Conjuring* franchises, and as such was a natural to join the cast. In the mythology of the comics, Orm is the Aquaman nemesis known as Ocean Master, a title that in the movie Orm seeks to assume by uniting the Atlantean kingdoms and waging war on humanity.

Joining Heard and Wilson in Atlantean roles were Academy Award winner Nicole Kidman as Atlanna, Arthur's mother and the queen of Atlantis; Academy Award nominee Willem Dafoe as Vulko, Arthur's mentor and trainer; and action-movie veteran

With their fearsome fangs and claws, the Trench are among the most terrifying predators in the seas, their appearance the result of their isolated devolution in the darkest depths of the Mariana Trench.

Underwater world-building

In conceiving the Atlantis of *Aquaman*, James Wan, a big fan of world-building in storytelling, led production designer Bill Brzeski and visual effects supervisors Kelvin McIlwain and Charlie Gibson in first establishing how the underwater kingdom functioned. Wan wanted the production team to consider everything from how Atlanteans ate and used the bathroom to how they moved around. The result was a multilayered city without stairs or roads—aside from the Gateway Bridge, a remnant of the old Atlantis—lit by bioluminescent Portuguese men-of-war, a glowing technological wonderland achieved via a mixture of practical sets and cutting-edge visual effects.

The same approach was used for the other underwater kingdoms that comprised that wider world. Once a close political ally of Atlantis, Xebel was now an independent realm, with armor and weaponry that the production based on 1960s Asian sci-fi. The Fishermen were envisioned as having evolved beyond human form, Bill Brzeski referencing the work of 19th-century marine biologist and artist

Ernst Haekl to design a city that appeared as if it were made of coral. Most alien of all, the Trench, who had first appeared in the 2011 New 52 *Aquaman* comic book series, were conceived as having mutated to survive in the hostile environs of the Mariana Trench, with an attendant terrifying fanged-and-clawed appearance.

Concept art for Dead King's Island, final resting place of King Atlan and the location of the sacred trident that Aquaman seeks.

Concept art of Atlantis delineating the multilayered nature of the city, free from the constraints of gravity, lit by gigantic jellyfish.

Specialty costume sculptor Brian Wade of Fracture FX sculpting the prosthetics for Ricou, ruler of the Fishermen Kingdom, played by Andrew Crawford (voiced by Djimon Hounsou).

In the arid caverns of the Deserters Kingdom, Aquaman and Mera unlock a hologram of Atlan, who reveals the whereabouts of his trident.

Dolph Lundgren as Nereus, Mera's father and the king of Xebel. In each case, knowing that they would need actors who could bring gravitas and emotional weight to their parts, the filmmakers aimed high in casting, even using Kidman and Lundgren's likenesses in concept art. They were rewarded when each actor enthusiastically signed on and threw themselves into their roles.

WET SUITS

All of the Atlantean actors were clothed according to the parameters of the underwater realms from which their characters hailed. Costume designer Kym Barrett, whose previous credits included the *Matrix* trilogy (1999–2003) and *The Amazing Spider-Man* (2012), worked out what underwater denizens who had evolved over the course of 20,000 years from air-breathers to water-breathers would wear. Outfits and armor were designed to appear as if they utilized the living resources around them, reflecting the glistening scales of fish and intricate patterns and vivid colors of coral. Costumes were produced via a rubberized print process incorporating heat-pressed foil to replicate a wet look, Barrett and her team working in close collaboration with Bill Brzeski's production design department to determine what kind of fabrics and materials would align with the sets, even sampling textures from those sets in order to recreate them in the costumes.

Also of Atlantean origin were the armor and weapons utilized by David Kane, alias the mercenary Black Manta, played by Yahya Abdul-Mateen II. An implacable comic book foe of Aquaman, the Black Manta of the movie is driven to seek vengeance when Arthur prevents the piratical Kane and his father from hijacking a submarine, resulting in the death of Kane Sr. To further both David's aims and his own, Orm supplies David with a hydrostatic suit and experimental rifle, which the latter uses to transform himself into Black Manta, adopting a mantalike stolen Navy prototype as his underwater vessel.

The object of Manta's ire, Aquaman belatedly adopts his own Atlantean outfit when, at the urging of Vulko, and with the help of Mera, he retrieves the ancient Trident of Atlan from the center of the Earth and reclaims his birthright as King of the Seven Seas. Returning triumphant with the trident, Aquaman is clad in a golden and green armor that both recalls Aquaman's comics costume and reflects the filmmakers' desire that the outfit be spectacular but believable. Kym Barrett and her team created a chainmail tunic comprised of gold coins that resembled scales, the suit hugging Jason Momoa's muscular physique but also allowing room for stunt padding and hidden hooks for the harnesses used in dry-for-wet filming.

AQUATIC ADVENTURE

As a kid growing up in the 1980s and 1990s, James Wan developed a deep love and appreciation for the films of stylish directors like Steve Spielberg, George Lucas, and Tim Burton. Accordingly, Wan's intention with *Aquaman* was to make an old-school, swashbuckling, aquatic action-adventure movie akin to *Raiders of the Lost Ark* (1981) or *Romancing the Stone* (1984), complete with a synthesizer-heavy orchestral score by Rupert Gregson-Williams recalling such 1980s electronic pioneers as Vangelis, Jean-Michel Jarre, and Giorgio Moroder.

It was an approach that audiences responded to enthusiastically, propelling *Aquaman* to over a billion dollars at the worldwide box office and proving that in the right hands, with the right actor, and the right approach, Aquaman could become as familiar a figure to the general public as Superman, Batman, or Wonder Woman. No longer just the King of the Seas, Aquaman now presided over the land, too, and would return in *Aquaman and the Lost Kingdom*.

Aquaman and Mera's quest for Atlan's trident leads them to Sicily, Italy, where they're attacked by Black Manta, who demonstrates the destructive power of his hydrostatic suit by unleashing a blast at Aquaman.

Aquaman poster art, showing Jason Momoa as Arthur in his full Aquaman costume displaying the influence of the comics incarnation, complete with the trident of Atlan, and accompanied by Amber Heard as Mera.

Dry for wet

A film set in large part under the sea presents its own unique challenges, not least how to shoot those underwater sequences. On *Aquaman*, James Wan opted to shoot dry for wet, filming the actors against a blue screen, with the water added in postproduction. But that was only the start of a technological process which wouldn't have been possible even five years earlier.

To give the performers the appearance of buoyancy, a harness system dubbed the "tuning fork" by the crew was positioned at the actors' hips, so that they could hold their bodies in the correct position to appear as if they were underwater. For smaller moves, the fulcrums were fixed to weighted bases on the floor with wheels so they could be moved around, while for larger moves the tuning forks were hung from the ceiling, allowing 360 degrees of movement. Sequences were shot against blue screen rather than the more usual green, visual effects supervisor Kelvin McIlwain reasoning that blue would be psychologically easier to deal with for the actors for extended periods, and would also spill into their skin tones to help with visual effects in postproduction. In addition, the performers' hair was tied back, to be reproduced later in CGI form to simulate the way it would move underwater.

SHAZAM!

Release date: March 28, 2019
Starring roles: Zachary Levi, Mark Strong, Asher Angel, Jack Dylan Grazer, Djimon Hounsou, John Glover, Adam Brody, Grace Fulton, Michelle Borth, Faithe Herman, Meagan Good, Ian Chen, Ross Butler, Jovan Armand, D. J. Cotrona
Director: David F. Sandberg

Screenplay: Henry Gayden and Darren Lemke
Cinematography: Maxime Alexandre
Music: Benjamin Wallfisch
Running time: 132 minutes
Box office: $367.7 million

Although Superman is the undisputed pioneering primal force of superheroes, in 1940, Shazam's champion—originally named Captain Marvel—became his greatest rival. They never met or fought (back then, at least), but in terms of sales and media crossreach it was a no-holds barred-struggle for supremacy. Superman was first with a newspaper strip, on the radio, and on cinema screens (in astounding cartoon shorts by the Fleischer Studios), whereas, at the height of his popularity, Captain Marvel outsold the Man of Tomorrow on his own home turf: comic books. Crucially, in 1941, the mystically enhanced pretender was the first superhero to appear live on screen, thanks to landmark chapter-play *Adventures of Captain Marvel*.

NEW LINE OF HEROES

New Line Cinema had been developing *Shazam!* since 2000. Treatments involving director Peter Segal; actor/producer Dwayne Johnson; and writers such as William Goldman, John August, Alec Sokolow, and Geoff Johns (who wrote many of the comic books the eventual film was based on) came and went as studio executives vacillated between lighter or heavier interpretations.

This was especially the case after the success of Christopher Nolan's noir epic *The Dark Knight* (2008). In July 2017, New Line, which has operated as a production studio within Warner Bros. since 2008, announced that Daniel F. Sandberg (*Lights Out*, *Annabelle: Creation*) would direct *Shazam!*

With production designer Jennifer Spence (*Annabelle: Creation*) supported by *Aquaman* stunt coordinator Kyle Gardiner already hired, Zachary Levi was cast in October, joining Dwayne Johnson. The original script involved a modern novice hero battling his ancient predecessor Black Adam, with Johnson attached to play either role. When he polled his numerous fans, they chose the villainous "man in black," but Johnson's agreement brought fresh challenges. Concerned that his growing Hollywood profile could be harmed by playing the bad guy in someone else's story, studio bosses suggested dropping him from *Shazam!* and giving Black Adam his own feature and origin tale. As a result, *Shazam!*'s script was adjusted, Zachary Levi became Shazam!, and his oldest enemies were recruited as opposition.

Filling roles was complex for casting director Rich Delia. *Shazam!* has multiple actors sharing many single character roles. Mark Strong (*Stardust*) is the adult Dr. Sivana; with Ethan Pugiotto as his boyhood self, with his bullying brother, Sid Sivana being played by Wayne Ward; and Landon Doak as is his teen self. Shazam's young alter ego, Billy Batson, has many siblings, with their own mystically enhanced adult identities. Young Freddy is played by Jack Dylan Grazer, while Adam Brody (*The O.C.*) is his

"I seek a champion to inherit my magic!"
Shazam

After playing King Ricou in DCEU film *Aquaman* (2018) and Kree warrior Korath the Pursuer in *Captain Marvel* (2019), Djimon Hounsou found a home in *Shazam!*.

Chief Lighting Technicians Michael L. Hall and R. Scott Phillips led a large team tackling varying conditions, from the wizard Shazam's otherworldly cavern to cold winter daylight.

Zachary Levi stayed in gleefully juvenile character on set and between takes by playing video games with his young co-stars.

Shazam! on TV

In 1971, National Periodicals/DC licensed the dormant rights to Fawcett Comics' characters (only fully purchasing them in 1991). As America embraced national nostalgia across all media, in 1973, DC relaunched the Marvel Family in their own kinder, weirder, completely separate universe. To offset potential copyright confusion, their new title was *Shazam!*—a term that had already entered the American language. The whimsical tales readily translated to Saturday Morning TV.

Co-produced by Filmation and DC Comics Warner Bros. Television for three seasons and 28 live-action episodes, *Shazam!* (pictured above) premiered on September 7, 1974 (the year Sivana was rejected by the Wizard in the 2019 film's prologue). A year later, it became *Shazam!/Isis Hour*—continuing until October 16, 1976. Billy was played by Michael Gray—who cameos in *Shazam! Fury of the Gods*—with Les Tremayne as Uncle Dudley analog Mentor and Jackson Bostwick (and later John Davey) playing Captain Marvel in 22–minute, youth-oriented morality plays like "The Joy Riders," and concluding with an actual moral like "Do the right thing." When the show ended, NBC followed it with Filmation Studios' *The Kid Super Power Hour with Shazam!* (September 12, 1981, to September 11, 1982). This live-action variety anthology featuring the animated exploits of Captain Marvel, Mary, Junior, Uncle Marvel, and Tawky Tawny against comic book foes like Dr. Sivana, Mr. Mind, Black Adam, and more. Isis became part of the Freedom Force animation in 1978 and was eventually subsumed into DC continuity as Adrianna Tomaz, the wife of Black Adam, in weekly maxiseries *52* (2006–2007).

Director Sandberg probes the deepest, darkest corners of motivation to show the intrinsic differences between Sivana and Billy ... and who truly deserves the power of Shazam.

super-incarnation. Grace Fulton is Mary, with Michelle Borth her enhanced self. Faithe Herman is young Darla, and Meagan Good her older counterpart. Ian Chen is boy hacker Eugene, with Ross Butler his action-hero alternate, while Jovan Armand and D. J. Cotrona play Pedro as shy kid and super-hunk respectively.

Not counting stunt doubles, Billy Batson alone required three actors—Asher Angel as the 14-year old, Zachary Levi as the comical champion, and David Kohlsmith as the toddler abandoned by his overwhelmed mother. Even Daniel F. Sandberg got in on the act. Thanks to the marvels of modern technology and puppeteers Neil Morrill and Steve Newburn, the Swedish director is all three Crocodile-Men imprisoned in a subdimension, and also voices wicked worm Mister Mind and Marilyn Batson's obnoxious boyfriend Travis. Body doubles and stand-ins took the doppelgänger quotient well into double digits.

MIX AND MATCH

Cinematographer Maxine Alexandre (*The Hills Have Eyes*) started principal photography in Canada on January 29, 2018, mostly at Pinewood Toronto Studios, but also at specialist locations including the University of Toronto and Woodbine Shopping Centre, before concluding on May 11. Then, a vast postproduction army of CGI artists, modelmakers, puppeteers, and sound technicians began making their own magic, with reshoots taking place between November and December 2018. Still an executive producer but having withdrawn from the project, Dwayne Johnson agreed for his image to be used as a magical, context-establishing hologram in an early scene.

Costume designer Leah Butler (*Annabelle: Creation, Ray Donovan*) first clothed Levi in breakthrough TV show *Chuck*, but here she had to admit that fitting a thunderbolt into the triangular chestplate was her hardest job yet. Eventually—in conjunction with props and

Far left: In a turning point moment, Billy stops running from responsibility by accepting that the power demands he fight for others, not himself.

Left: In a sly in-joke reference, the derelict factory Billy and Freddy practice in carries signage for Ace Chemicals: the facility where The Joker was created in Tim Burton's *Batman* (1989).

SFX artists—the costume department took its design inspiration from 2014's *Justice League: War* animated movie and produced padded muscle suits and physical light-emitting chest regalia for the Marvel family, which would be augmented postproduction.

Another effects-heavy vehicle with a huge heritage to embrace, *Shazam!* also enlisted traditional storyboarders and animatic storyboard artists, including Monty Granito working on discrete sequences alongside numerous concept artists/illustrators like Laurent Ben-Mimoun, Vicki Pui, Jim Magdaleno, Henry Fong, and character designer Daniel Carrasco.

YOU CAN'T DO MAGIC

The key moment of the movie is actually its prologue—setting up events and potential future storylines while subtly introducing thousands of years of hidden history and a major villain to the unfolding DCEU. In 1974, coincidentally the year CBS began broadcasting the *Shazam!* TV show, 8-year-old Thaddeus Sivana vanishes from a car carrying his tyrannical father (John Glover) and bullying brother Sid (Landon Doak). A sequence of magical symbols displayed on his Magic 8-Ball toy opens a portal to power as Thad is spirited away to an extradimensional temple. Here, he is tested by a fearsome wizard (Djimon Hounsou) who has been abducting countless candidates for centuries in a desperate hunt for someone "worthy" to whom he can pass on his power.

His cavernous citadel, the Rock of Eternity, holds in petrified bondage the Seven Deadly Sins—eternal predators upon humanity—who are gradually breaking free. Already, their psychic temptations invade Thad's mind. Lured by promises of power, the boy fails and is dismissed. However, in his mind—and 8-ball screen—remains the Seven Sins's seductive command to find them.

Golden Age comics moderated and paraphrased the devilish Sins as the "Seven Deadly Enemies of Man." Cosmetic changes

Being a goofy, starstruck kid on screen—man and boy—was a major shift from comic book lore. In print from his 1940 debut onward, Billy Batson was a brilliant investigative journalist on radio and eventually television.

Despite its comedic tone, *Shazam!* explores issues of parental abuse, revealing how two kids respond to similar circumstances, innate differences between Sivana and Billy ... and who truly deserves the power of Shazam.

Despite Billy's rudely defensive manner, disabled Freddy and his foster siblings never stop trying to help the newcomer, and finally break through his emotional walls by finding his mother for him.

Family business

The size of Shazam's family of champions has waxed and waned with various DC reboots over the years, but began in *Whiz Comics* #2 (February 1940) in a tale by Bill Parker and Charles Clarence "C. C." Beck. When homeless orphan Billy Batson was selected by an ancient wizard to battle injustice, he was able to channel the powers of six mythical legends. By uttering the acronymic name, Billy transformed from scrawny boy to brawny adult Captain Marvel—briefly bestowed with the wisdom of Solomon, the strength of Hercules, the stamina of Atlas, the power of Zeus, the courage of Achilles, and the speed of Mercury: a noble but inherently immature boy in a superhuman body.

The Golden Age comic book Marvel Family included Billy, his sister Mary, and their friend Freddy Freeman (Captain Marvel Jr.); three Lieutenant Marvels (also all named Billy Batson and able to access Shazam's gift); Freckles Marvel; genial talking tiger Mr. Tawky Tawny; and affable fraud "Uncle Dudley Marvel" who tags along, pretending his powers were diminished by "Shazambago."

There was even an anthropomorphic iteration of the hero—Hoppy the Marvel Bunny—having amazing adventures in a cartoon wonderland. In those days, Mary Marvel's powers were tastefully provided by a group of goddesses endowing the plucky girl with Selene's grace, Hippolyta's strength, the skill of Ariadne, fleetness of Zephyrus, beauty of Aurora, and Minerva's wisdom. But when DC began relating their exploits in 1974, the patrons were standardized as Billy's benefactors.

turned "Sloth" into Laziness, "Wrath" into Hatred, "Gluttony" into Selfishness, and "Lust" into Injustice. On film, the Seven Sins were stunt doubles in motion-capture suits that enabled CGI technology to make them memorably monstrous. This was especially so when they were unleashed to kill Sivana's father and brother, and in the climactic battle against the newly empowered Shazam Family. Sandberg wanted the Seven Sins to evoke memories of the "Terror Dogs" in *Ghostbusters* (1984), and their character-enhancing voices were supplied by Steve Blum, Darin DePaul, and Fred Tatasciore.

The screen story, set in present-day Philadelphia, finds teen runaway Billy Batson hunting for his lost mother for the past decade—ever since he was separated from her at a carnival. Arrested again, he reluctantly joins a group home where Rosa (Marta Milans) and Victor (Cooper Andrews) Vásquez already care for five foster kids. Mary Bromfield, Freddy Freeman, Pedro Peña, Eugene Choi, and Darla Dudley all welcome and want to help Billy, but he's already planning his escape, because families are for losers who can't take care of themselves.

WHO ARE YOU?

Thanks to Sandberg dictating a kid-friendly approach and near reverential treatment of semicomedic source material, *Shazam!* is a thrilling, funny, buddy movie/coming-of-age drama that piles on laughs, but also shares a search for and redefinition of family and belonging. There's even a hilarious running gag on the search for a cool action identity, with Freddy vexing Billy with a cascade of dumb options—like Sir Zaps-a-Lot,

Left: The spectacular climactic battle between the newborn Shazam! Family facing off against Sivana and the Seven Deadly Sins more than doubled the film's original stunt list, adding a further 60 set pieces and subsequent CG enhancements to the shooting schedule.

Below: Mark Strong has played two DC villains subverted and warped by light: Thaal Sinestro beguiled by a yellow power ring in *Green Lantern* (2011) and Sivana, here possessed by the Seven Sins's Orb of Evil.

Thundercrack, and Captain Sparklefingers—in the crucial quest to find a fit and proper hero name.

This wickedly mirrors real life. When the Golden Age Captain Marvel ceased publication in 1953, copyright to the name passed through various publishing companies before Marvel Comics secured it in 1968. When DC revived the original in 1973, they had to navigate many permutations to publish their nostalgia-tinged title under his most well-known and sales-worthy designation. Eventually, just as in the movie, the hero simply calls himself Shazam.

Billy's journey from lost boy to newbie champion of humanity largely avoids dwelling on angst and tragedy, instead celebrating the collaboration as he willingly shares his gift of power with the siblings he initially rejected. Billy learns to enjoy being a part of something rather than apart from everyone: a trope almost universal in modern superhero films.

Shazam! embraces joy, wonder, and innate goofiness, looking at superheroes through the eyes of a child who is one. Moreover, laughter softens up audiences for surprises, like a blast of monster-terror or tragic shock, when Billy finally finds his mother and discovers she didn't lose him but left him behind.

Midcredits sequences offer tantalizing glimpses of what could be when Billy/Shazam meets Superman. However, Henry Cavill was unavailable, and Levi's stunt double Ryan Handley was the Man of Steel's costumed torso in a sequence cementing Freddy and Billy's reconciliation. Additionally, frenzied, jailed Sivana plotted revenge with evil genius Mister Mind—originally billed in comics as "The Wickedest Worm in the Universe!" Sadly, a real-world global pandemic derailed the plans, and when the spin-off and sequel finally arrived, they were very different from what was originally envisioned.

Costumer Heather Armstrong needed five official "Shazam suit wranglers" to ensure that the rigors of filming—especially the flying scenes—didn't wreck the look of the padded Shazam outfit.

JOKER

Release date: October 2019
Starring roles: Joaquin Phoenix, Robert De Niro, Zazie Beetz, Frances Conroy
Director: Todd Phillips
Screenplay: Todd Phillips and Scott Silver

Cinematography: Lawrence Sher
Music: Hildur Guðnadóttir
Running time: 122 minutes
Box office: $1,078,751,311

Todd Phillips always had a liking for bad guys. The director had begun his filmmaking career in 1993 with a documentary about controversial punk rocker GG Allin, while his feature films, from *Road Trip* (2000) to *The Hangover* (2009) and its sequels, frequently focused on scoundrels, ne'er-do-wells, or (in the case of *War Dogs* [2016]) a pair of arms dealers. Phillips had little interest in making a movie based on a comic book character, until he saw a different way of approaching such a subject: an intense, relatively low-budget character study—almost the antithesis in many ways of contemporary superhero movie-making—centering on a single protagonist, arguably the baddest bad guy of all. Given the character's iconic status and murky comics history, the movie would not claim to be a definitive origin story but an interpretation of his possible backstory, a rumination on how someone could become him—hence the movie's title *Joker* rather than The Joker.

CURTAIN RAISER

Todd Phillips started thinking about The Joker in August 2016. Standing outside the premiere of *War Dogs* on Hollywood Boulevard, Phillips pondered on what it was that audiences really wanted to watch. He knew that the kinds of films he had loved growing up, 1970s character studies like Martin Scorsese's *Taxi Driver* (1976), were tough to get made in the contemporary climate. Staring up at a poster for *Suicide Squad*, which had opened shortly before *War Dogs*, Phillips had an idea: What if he could make a lower-budget, street-level, urban character study like *Taxi Driver* or *Death Wish* (1974), but about a comic book character? Phillips had been offered comic book movies before, but had turned them down simply

"Put on a happy face."
Marketing tagline

because he didn't watch those kinds of movies. This would be different, however: less laser-eyed superhero bombast than a laserlike focus on a single individual.

The individual Phillips was drawn to was The Joker. There was something about the Clown Prince of Crime's innate mayhem and chaos that the director responded to—that, and the realization that The Joker's backstory had never been explicitly detailed on screen, despite the character appearing in multiple movies and TV shows across many decades, played by everyone from Jack Nicholson to Heath Ledger to, most recently, in *Suicide Squad*,

Joaquin Phoenix puts on a happy face as Arthur Fleck, pulling a smile that recalls The Joker's appearance in such classic comics as 1988's *Batman: The Killing Joke*.

Far left: In a theater bathroom, Arthur confronts billionaire Thomas Wayne—played by Bret Cullen—who tells him that he is not his father, sending Arthur into a maniacal rage.

Left: Arthur unveils his clown persona on *Live with Murray Franklin*, the talk show hosted by the eponymous Murray, played by Academy Award winner Robert De Niro.

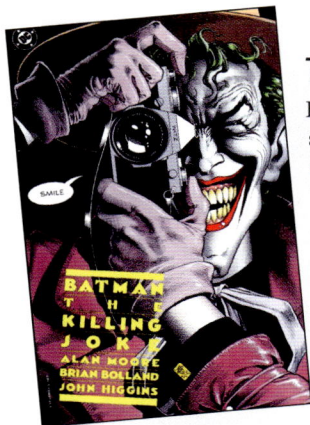

The Killing Joke

By the mid-1980s, following a string of spectacular covers and the *Camelot 3000* maxi-series, British artist Brian Bolland's star was very much on the rise at DC. Given carte blanche by the company as to what he wanted to do next, Bolland thought of his favorite writer of the moment, fellow Brit Alan Moore, and two of his favorite characters, Batman and The Joker. The result was the 1988 48-page prestige format one-shot *Batman: The Killing Joke*, a psychological examination of the twisted relationship and parallels between Batman and his arch-nemesis.

Hugely influential, the story has been cited as an influence not just by Todd Phillips, but by Tim Burton for *Batman* (1989) and Christopher Nolan for *The Dark Knight* (2008). Three decades after its initial publication, *Batman: The Killing Joke* was adapted into a 2016 animated movie by *Batman: Broken City* writer Brian Azzarello and *Superman/Batman: Public Enemies* director Sam Liu, in collaboration with *Batman: The Animated Series* co-producers Bruce Timm and Alan Burnett, and with that show's Kevin Conroy, Mark Hamill, and Tara Strong returning to voice respectively Batman, The Joker, and Batgirl. On TV, the story has been referenced in both the 2002 WB *Birds of Prey* show and the 2018–2019 Fox series *Gotham*, as well as in the animated shows *Young Justice* and *Harley Quinn*.

Unable to control his laughing fits, Arthur is violently assaulted on the subway, before retaliating by shooting his attackers dead.

Director Todd Phillips discusses the script on set with stars Joaquin Phoenix (Arthur/Joker) and Zazie Beetz (Arthur's neighbor, single mom Sophie).

Jared Leto. By his very nature mercurial, unpredictable, and unknowable, The Joker's true backstory has never been established in comics, though over the years one comic in particular had become widely recognized as coming closest. Published in 1988, Alan Moore and Brian Bolland's *Batman: The Killing Joke* provided an origin for The Joker in the form of flashbacks—the glaring caveat being that The Joker is the ultimate unreliable narrator.

KILLING JOKES

Nevertheless, it was to *Batman: The Killing Joke* that Phillips and his co-writer Scott Silver (*8 Mile*, *The Fighter*) looked for inspiration, particularly one element that Moore and Bolland had added to The Joker's mythology—that he had been a failed comedian. But just as important was the work of Martin Scorsese, especially the aforementioned *Taxi Driver* and a later film also starring Robert De Niro, *The King of Comedy* (1982), in which the actor had played a delusional wannabe stand-up comic.

From these touchstones, Phillips and Silver set about writing a new origin for The Joker that was distinct from the character's comics roots. They also endeavored to make their story as real and authentic as possible. Discarding some of the more fantastical aspects of The Joker's backstory, such as that he fell into a vat of chemicals and as a consequence was left with white skin and green hair, the pair tried to reverse-engineer what was known about the character in order to arrive at plausible explanations for his existence. The filmmakers' goal was not to make a state-of-the-nation polemic—though thematically the film couldn't help but comment on current affairs—but simply to ask why The Joker was the way he was. What made him that way?

Phillips and Silver talked about where The Joker's laugh came from; discussed why he would wear makeup; and explored notions of narcissism and ego, and what it would mean to go through life wearing a mask, only to eventually take it off and become your

Far left: The start of the movie sees Arthur employing his clowning in service of a music store's closing sale—until his "Everything must go" sign is stolen by street kids, who then beat him up.

Left: At comedy club Pogo's, Arthur attempts to deliver his stand-up routine in front of an audience which includes Sophie, but his efforts are derailed by a laughing fit and jokes that fall flat.

true self. Set in an alternate past—the year never explicitly identified, but in Phillips' mind a run-down, broken-down New York City of 1981—their tale would center on Arthur Fleck, a failed clown and aspiring stand-up comic whose mental deterioration leads him to commit a series of murders, climaxing with a televised killing that sends the city spiraling into chaos.

As important as the story and tone were, it would all be for naught without a leading man who could convincingly bring the character Phillips and Silver were creating to life. Coincidentally, years previously, the actor the pair were writing their movie for, Joaquin Phoenix, had spoken to his agent about the possibility of making a lower-budget film about a comic book character. At that point, Phoenix dismissed the idea of tackling The Joker, figuring the character had already been done, but years later, hearing of what Todd Phillips was planning, the actor was naturally intrigued and excited. Even so, it took months of meetings, calls, and emails for Phillips to persuade Phoenix to take the role on. The actor finally cast in summer 2018.

PHOENIX

Known as a committed performer who will go to extreme lengths in his pursuit of character, Phoenix had previously delivered powerful performances in a wide range of roles, whether it be Commodus in *Gladiator* (2000), Johnny Cash in *Walk the Line* (2005), or Freddie in *The Master* (2012). For Phillips, it was Phoenix's unpredictability as an actor that made him right for the role of The Joker, while Phoenix himself responded to Phillips' singular vision of Arthur and his challenges. Getting the character's wardrobe right was an intrinsic part of Phoenix's eventual performance; costume designer Mark Bridges found an organic way to arrive at the ultimate Joker outfit modeled by Arthur in the movie, an adaptation of the suit Arthur wears while doing his stand-up routines.

Strengthening the film's ties to the work of Martin Scorsese was not only Scorsese himself, who early on served as a producer before the demands of making *The Irishman* (2019) pulled him away, but Scorsese's frequent collaborator, Academy Award winner

Playing talk show host Murray Franklin, Robert De Niro could see the thematic connections between *Joker* and 1982's *The King of Comedy*, in which he played disturbed wannabe stand-up Rupert Pupkin.

Production designer Mark Friedberg wanted the interior of Ha-Ha's Talent Booking to look like a set from a Federico Fellini film.

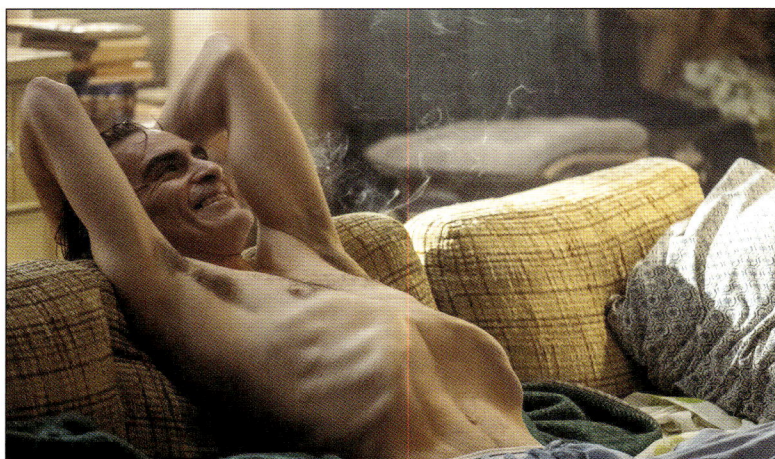

In formulating his performance as Arthur, Joaquin Phoenix started by losing a lot of weight, a process that affected his psychology.

In the narrative, Arthur's ailing mother Penny (*Six Feet Under/American Horror Story*'s Frances Conroy) once worked for Thomas Wayne.

Robert De Niro. In a role that mirrored his own in *The King of Comedy*, rather than playing a delusional comedian, here De Niro was playing a talk show host, Murray Franklin. Joining De Niro were Zazie Beetz as Sophie, a single mother with whom Arthur becomes fixated, and Frances Conroy as Arthur's ailing mother.

CITY OF REALMS

As much a character in *Joker* as the human players is the city in which they all reside. Having grown up on New York's Upper West Side, production designer Mark Friedberg vividly recalled what the city was like by the time he left to go to college in 1981—dirty, dysfunctional, rough, and torn apart by strikes and corruption, with piles of garbage lining the streets. For *Joker*, Friedberg and his team created a city that reflected all of that, as well as one that had distinctive realms, differentiating between where Arthur lives, the hospital he works at, or the comedy club he performs at. These regions were distinguished in different ways, whether it be styles of architecture or how garbage was dealt with—by the neighborhoods, by the municipal center, or by the wealthy areas. The production envisioned a city of bridges and islands related both to Gotham City and New York City, even creating a map so they could understand where Arthur traveled to in the film, and how each locale related to every other one. A transit version of the production's map can be glimpsed in the film itself on the walls of subway stations.

Shot in New York and New Jersey, the film opens in Gotham Square, essentially analogous to Times Square, which by 1981 had become arguably the most notorious neighborhood in New York. Seeking a suitable location, the production descended on Newark, which although a city on the rebound, still had at its heart an area that retained some of the architecture and grit of the New York of the early 1980s. As elsewhere in the film, as much as possible was captured in camera, with architecture and backgrounds altered in postproduction to add graffiti or change skylines. Originally, Friedberg wanted to locate Arthur's home in the projects of Brownsville—to his mind one of the toughest neighborhoods in New York—but Phillips opted in the end for the South Bronx, with its alleys and stairways that Arthur

Pulled from a crashed cop car at the close of the film, Arthur/Joker finds himself the focus of an insurrection on the streets of Gotham City.

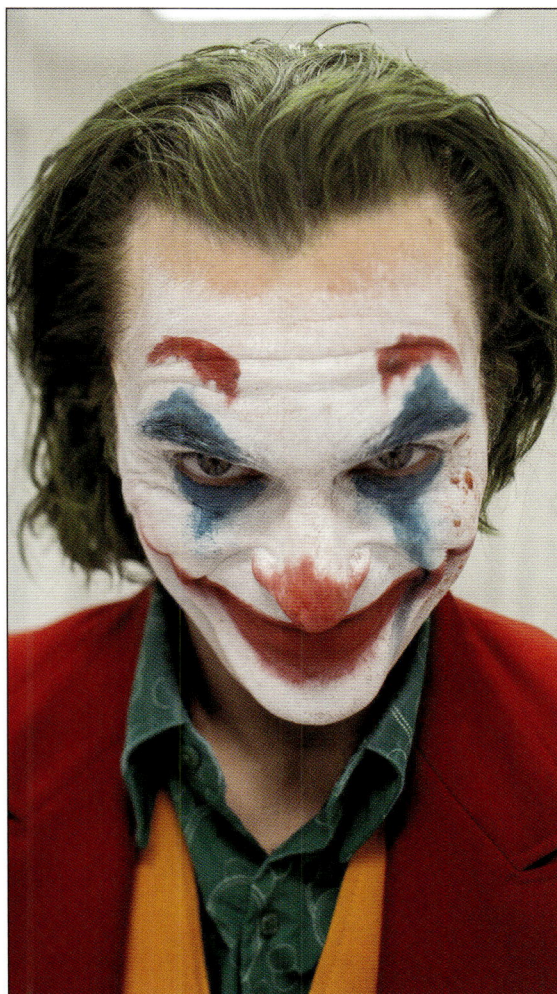

Far left: After murdering Murray Franklin live on air, Arthur is pursued by the police into the subway, where a bloody brawl breaks out between passengers wearing clown masks, bystanders, and the police.

Left: Makeup department head Nicki Ledermann wanted the final look Arthur adopts as Joker to be messy like Heath Ledger's Joker; classic like Jack Nicholson's and Cesar Romero's; but still original, organic, and realistic.

could trudge up and down, the locale serving to acutely underline what the character was experiencing and feeling.

LAST LAUGH

Though conceived as a low-key character piece, *Joker* belied its relatively low budget to become one of the biggest films of the year, bringing in over a billion dollars at the worldwide box office, much to the surprise of Todd Phillips. The film's themes of disaffection, alienation, nihilism, delusion, and transformation connected with audiences, but moreover, unusually for a film based on a comic book character, the movie connected with many critics, too.

At the 2019 Venice International Film Festival, *Joker* was awarded the festival's highest prize, the Golden Lion, while at the 2020 Academy Awards, it received 11 nominations, more than the previous comic book movie record-holder, *The Dark Knight* (2008). Recalling Heath Ledger's (posthumous) win for Best Supporting Actor for *The Dark Knight*, Joaquin Phoenix's performance as a very different kind of Joker earned him the Best Actor award.

A clown for all seasons

For almost as long as there has been Batman, there has been The Joker. The Clown Prince of Crime made his debut in the first issue of the *Batman* comic book series in spring 1940, a year after the Dark Knight's own debut in the pages of *Detective Comics* #27 in May 1939. He quickly became Batman's most popular nemesis, returning regularly over the next few decades, but by the mid-1960s The Joker had begun to fade from visibility—until the advent of the 1966 *Batman* TV show. Brought to vivid, cackling life by Cesar Romero, The Joker of the TV show boosted the popularity of the character in comics once again.

When the show ended in 1968, The Joker virtually vanished from comic books, until in 1973, Denny O'Neil and Neal Adams crafted a story that revolutionized the character. In September 1973's *Batman* #251, "The Joker's Five-Way Revenge!" returned the villain to his homicidal roots. O'Neil and Adams's characterization proved an enduring influence on the generations of writers and artists who followed in their footsteps, including Alan Moore and Brian Bolland with *Batman: The Killing Joke*. By the time *The Killing Joke* was published in 1988, The Joker's popularity had skyrocketed, reaching a crescendo the following year with Jack Nicholson's performance in Tim Burton's *Batman*, a level of fame and notoriety the Clown Prince has remained at ever since.

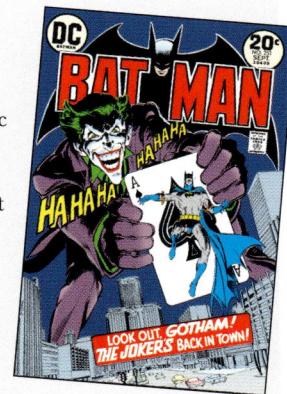

BIRDS OF PREY

Release date: February 2020
Starring roles: Margot Robbie, Rosie Perez, Mary Elizabeth Winstead, Jurnee Smollett, Ewan McGregor, Ella Jay Basco, Chris Messina, Ali Wong
Director: Cathy Yan
Screenplay: Christina Hodson

Cinematography: Matthew Libatique
Music: Daniel Pemberton
Running time: 109 minutes
Box office: $205,358,461

In 2015, with production proceeding apace on David Ayer's *Suicide Squad* (2016), one of the film's stars, Margot Robbie, had an idea for a follow-up featuring her character. Robbie's vision was of an R-rated girl-gang movie, unrestricted in its use of language or violence. Pitching her idea to the studio, the actor compared her proposal to previous female ensemble action films—what they had done well, what they had done less well—in the process making the point that there needed to be more such movies. By the following year, with *Suicide Squad* nearing its release date, Robbie had gotten the go-ahead to pursue her vision—a fantabulous female-fronted action film featuring the soon-to-be breakout star of *Suicide Squad*, one Harley Quinn.

TAKING FLIGHT

Although *Birds of Prey (and the Fantabulous Emancipation of One Harley Quinn)*, as the film would eventually be known, gained a writer early on in the shape of British screenwriter Christina Hodson, there was still a long way to go before the project could move into production. As Hodson and Margot Robbie worked on the story over the next two years, Robbie continued to present the project to the studio—noting that as a character Harley Quinn worked best when interacting with others; arguing that a girl gang would be an ideal setup for the film; and urging that if possible the film's director should be female.

"Mind over mayhem"
Marketing tagline

In April 2018, the actor got her wish when Cathy Yan, director of that year's indie comedy drama *Dead Pigs*, signed on to direct, in the process becoming the first female Asian director of a superhero film. With Robbie herself on board as one of the film's producers, *Birds of Prey* entered preproduction that summer. As the confirmed title suggested, however, and per Robbie's original proposal, this wouldn't be a Harley Quinn solo movie.

Casting for the characters who would comprise the rest of the eponymous Birds of Prey began in earnest in August 2018, with the filmmakers looking not just to the various incarnations of the

Playing Huntress in *Birds of Prey*, Mary Elizabeth Winstead found it liberating to be working on a film with so many other women in positions of power.

Harley Quinn tells Black Canary about her breakup with The Joker at the bar at Roman Sionis's Black Mask Club, where Dinah Lance works as a singer.

The Birds of Prey assemble for the final fight: Rosie Perez as Renee Montoya; Mary Elizabeth Winstead as Helena Bertinelli/Huntress; Margot Robbie as Harley Quinn; Ella Jay Basco as Cassandra Cain; and Jurnee Smollett as Dinah Lance/Black Canary.

For the *Birds of Prey* actors, the final fight in the carnival funhouse involved long days and long takes, with the stars doing many of their own stunts.

The hyena that Harley adopts, Bruce, was performed by a pair of German shepherds, before the visual effects team transformed them into the final creature.

Ewan McGregor saw his character, Roman "Black Mask" Sionis, as spoiled in his upbringing, thin-skinned, and with a desperate need to be the center of attention.

comic book team for personnel, but the broader Batman/Gotham City corner of the DC universe. Besides Harley, the girl gang would feature Dinah Lance, alias Black Canary, one of the original members of the comics Birds of Prey, who would be played in the film by Jurnee Smollett-Bell; Helena Bertinelli, alias Huntress, a crossbow-wielding Gotham City vigilante, played by Mary Elizabeth Winstead; Renee Montoya, a Gotham City Police Department detective, played by Rosie Perez; and Cassandra Cain, who in the comics had inherited the mantle of Batgirl but who in the movie would be a pickpocket, played by Ella Jay Basco.

BAD GUYS

Also hailing from the Gotham City corner of DC were the film's lead villain and his chief henchman, both of whom were fixtures of Batman's comics Rogues Gallery. Black Mask, alias Roman Sionis, was a Gotham City crime lord with a fixation on masks, while Victor Zsasz, created by Alan Grant and Norm Breyfogle in 1992, was a serial killer who kept a tally of his kills by carving his own skin.

In *Birds of Prey*, Black Mask would be portrayed by Ewan McGregor (*Star Wars* prequels), who seized on the opportunity to play a larger-than-life villain, building on the sadistic ruthlessness of the comic book incarnation to play a spoiled narcissist who loves nothing more than being the center of attention. Reflecting this characterization, costume designer Erin Benach and her team dressed McGregor in velvet and brocades, working with production designer K. K. Barrett to play Sionis's costumes off the interior lighting in his lair, the Black Mask Club. Benach even designed a personalized logo for Sionis which was used to monogram his handkerchiefs and scarves, and used McGregor's

Far left: Dispatched by Roman Sionis to find Cassandra Cain, Harley launches an assault on the Gotham City Police Department, freeing not only Cass but every other criminal locked up in the cells.

Left: For the scene where Black Canary sings "It's a Man's Man's Man's World" in the Black Mask Club, costume designer Erin Benach created an outfit that translated the character's comics costume into a haute couture dress.

own face to create a fabric pattern for Sionis's pajamas. As for Victor Zsasz, played by Chris Messina, Benach combined a street-urchin vibe with a more elevated sense of style, topped with a bleached-blond close crop.

SHE'S IN FASHION

Fashion figured prominently for the Birds of Prey themselves, too, chief among them the former Dr. Harleen Quinzel, who sports a succession of striking outfits throughout the film. Early on, in an effort to find herself after The Joker breaks up with her, Harley joins a roller-derby team, in a sequence inspired by a scene in Amanda Conner and Jimmy Palmiotti's 2013 *Harley Quinn* comic book series. For Harley's roller-derby outfit, Erin Benach designed a costume that utilized the red-and-black palette of the character's original harlequin costume but incorporated flames in the side panels.

Other Harley costumes included a jacket fringed with feather-like shredded police "caution" tape, signifying Harley's DIY approach to clothing and symbolizing her explosive, destructive nature, and a gold leather jumpsuit etched with a diamond pattern worn over a pink bandeau top. A touchstone for Benach was the 1980s *Days of Our Lives* fantasy sequence that later inspired writer Paul Dini to conceive the character of Harley Quinn, showing Arleen Sorkin (who would go on to voice Harley in *Batman: The Animated Series*) in a sparkly red-and-blue jester's costume.

As with Harley's outfits, the costumes Benach designed for Harley's girl-gang teammates took cues both from comics and from the characters' personalities and professions. The mesh dress worn by Jurnee Smollett-Bell when her character of Dinah Lance performs in the Black Mask Club reflected the fishnet stockings

Harley couture

The catalog of cool looks modeled by Margot Robbie as Harley Quinn in *Birds of Prey*, from roller-derby duds to the blue-patterned, flame-fringed blazer she sports by film's end, reflect the character's comics evolution. For the first few years after she made the leap from *Batman: The Animated Series* to the DC universe in 1999, Harley's costume remained relatively stable—a red-and-black, jester-hatted affair based by Harley's co-creator, Bruce Timm, on medieval harlequins. But after DC revamped their entire line of comics in 2011 under the banner of the New 52, the doors were flung wide for a succession of fabulous new looks for Harley.

Appearing in the New 52 as a member of the Suicide Squad, Harley's initial look took a lead from her appearances in the video games *Batman: Arkham Asylum* (2009) and *Batman: Arkham City* (2011), presenting a punky combination of colored pigtails and a red-and-black bodice. Two years later, artist Amanda Conner took inspiration from a group of roller-derby girls she'd met to concoct a new costume for Harley, launching her into a new series drawn by Chad Hardin and co-written by Conner's husband Jimmy Palmiotti. Conner's keen eye for what works for cosplayers saw Harley adopt all manner of costumes over the course of the series, from a cocktail dress to a nurse's outfit, a state of affairs that has persisted as successive creators have made their mark on the character.

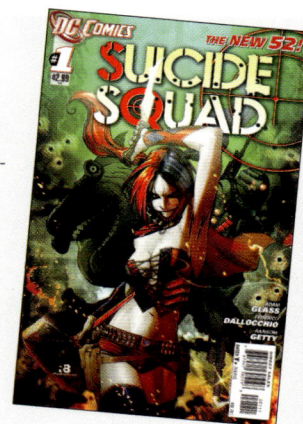

Birds of a feather

Birds of Prey's eponymous team has its basis in a comics concept conjured up in the mid-1990s by DC editor Jordan B. Gorfinkel, who had the idea of teaming Barbara Gordon—the former Batgirl, who after being consigned to a wheelchair by The Joker in 1988 had remade herself as computer whiz and information specialist Oracle—with Dinah Lance, alias costumed adventurer Black Canary. After a handful of *Birds of Prey* one-shots, at the start of 1999, writer Chuck Dixon and artist Greg Land launched an ongoing series, which in 2003 saw writer Gail Simone add Huntress to the team. The membership has waxed and waned in the years since to include, variously, Lady Blackhawk, Cassandra "Batgirl" Cain, Katana, Poison Ivy, and (in 2020, under the aegis of Amanda Conner and Jimmy Palmiotti) Harley Quinn and Renee Montoya.

In 2002, *Birds of Prey* made the leap to television, *(above)* albeit with a few changes from the comics incarnation. While the backstory of Oracle, played by Dina Meyer, closely resembled her comics counterpart, Huntress, played by Ashley Scott, had feline abilities inherited from her mother, Catwoman (her father being Batman, echoing the 1977 version of the character), while Rachel Skarsten as Dinah Redmond (née Lance) boasted precognitive and telepathic powers. *Birds of Prey* ran for just one 13-episode season from October 2002 to February 2003, but almost two decades later, Scott and Meyer reprised their roles in cameos in the 2019 CW Arrowverse crossover event "Crisis on Infinite Earths"—though only in the form of a voice over comms in Meyer's case.

Costume designer Erin Benach created distinct character-specific looks for each of the Birds of Prey, from Black Canary's chic dress to Cassandra Cain's teen streetwear.

of the comic book Black Canary, while Dinah's pantsuit similarly drew on the blue, black, and gold color scheme of the comics Canary. As the vigilante Huntress, Mary Elizabeth Winstead wore a costume that recalled the purple and blacks of the comics version while serving the purpose of camouflaging her in the shadows. As petty thief Cassandra Cain, Ella Jay Basco was outfitted in a custom windbreaker in which she could stash her ill-gotten gains, part of an ensemble that Benach put together with an eye on contemporary street culture.

MARTIAL-ARTS ACTION

As well as designing outfits that were visually arresting and in keeping with the characters, Benach and her team created articulated action versions of the costumes employing stretch fabric for use during fight sequences, of which there were many. Rather than referencing previous superhero films when formulating action set pieces, Cathy Yan and her stunt coordinator Jonathan Eusebio—whose credits included coordinating fights for *John Wick* (2014)—looked to martial-arts action movies, in particular the work of Jackie Chan and Gareth Evans's Indonesian action thriller *The Raid* (2011). The fight scenes, frequently involving the violent demise of various villainous men, also largely eschewed CGI in favor of in-camera action, enhanced by cinematographer Matthew Libatique's vibrant, visceral camera work.

Most spectacular of all is the climactic confrontation between the Birds of Prey—Harley Quinn, Renee Montoya, Huntress, Black Canary, and Cassandra Cain—and the forces of Roman Sionis inside an abandoned funhouse. Staged on an elaborate set boasting a mirror maze, undulating tongues protruding from walls, a tunnel slide, and a turntable floor, the battle spotlights each Bird of Prey's unique fighting style. In the case of Harley,

Concept art for Harley's costumes, utilizing the character's original comic book red-and-black color scheme and including designs for her roller-derby outfit.

Above: Margot Robbie's role as figure skater Tonya Harding in *I, Tonya* (2017) helped with the rollerskating required of her in *Birds of Prey*, though the actor still found certain aspects difficult.

Margot Robbie wanted to find the fun and joy of fighting, bringing an unpredictable, whimsical levity to even the most brutal bust-ups, while Rosie Perez channeled her personal love of boxing into Montoya's style of fighting, lending her the feel of a street brawler. In keeping with her character's background as a performer, Jurnee Smollett-Bell employed a lot of legwork in Black Canary's fight sequences, using her arms for defense and her legs for kicks, while to achieve Huntress's precision fighting approach, Mary Elizabeth Winstead's training with Jonathan Eusebio and his team involved learning aspects of judo, ju-jitsu, and karate.

PASSION FRUIT

For all of the actors, along with the entire crew, the final fight, with its multiple moving parts and complex set, encapsulated the experience of making *Birds of Prey*—enormously fun, but also incredibly hard work. For Margot Robbie in particular, the film was the culmination of her dedicated quest to realize a Harley Quinn girl-gang movie, a female-fronted and empowering action flick that discarded the rules in favor of a chaotic sense of fun. As writer Christina Hodson, director Cathy Yan, and the rest of the crew and cast acknowledged—not to mention Harley's co-creator, Paul Dini, who loved the movie—it was Robbie who had driven the project from the beginning, overcoming multiple challenges and obstacles over the course of five years in order to see the film come to fruition. The actor and producer poured her heart and soul into the movie in a manner that proved an inspiration to her creative cohorts; so while the film would not have been made without Robbie's tenacity and commitment, *Birds of Prey* became a passion project for all concerned.

Left: Harley's confrontational, anti-establishment attitude was encapsulated by costume designer Erin Benach in the T-shirt worn by Harley in the film's second act, emblazoned with the legend Harley ****ing Quinn.

211

WONDER WOMAN 1984

Release date: December 2020
Starring roles: Gal Gadot, Chris Pine, Kristen Wiig, Pedro Pascal, Robin Wright, Connie Nielsen, Lilly Aspel
Director: Patty Jenkins
Story: Patty Jenkins and Geoff Johns

Screenplay: Patty Jenkins, Geoff Johns, and Dave Callaham
Cinematography: Matthew Jensen
Music: Hans Zimmer
Running time: 151 minutes
Box office: $169,601,036 (dual digital/theatrical release during COVID-19 Pandemic)

Patty Jenkins was lying on her bed meditating when Gal Gadot called to tell her the reviews were in for the just-opened *Wonder Woman* (2017). Jenkins knew instantly that the reviews were good, (otherwise the film's star wouldn't have called), but she wasn't prepared for what happened next. The director started seeing photos of women posing with the film's posters, responding to the movie's empowering message of love, forgiveness, and hope.

Over the ensuing weeks, as *Wonder Woman* became a hit and a worldwide phenomenon, the conversations about a sequel began. But how to follow a film that had spoken to so many? Jenkins's answer was to couch a serious message in an ostensibly fun setting—the Washington, D.C. of the director's own 1980s youth.

BACK TO THE EIGHTIES

Patty Jenkins's first Wonder Woman film had dealt with Diana's Amazonian origins and her first encounters with humanity, not to mention her first real experiences with loss and grief. These losses came in the forms of her aunt and mentor, Antiope, played by Robin Wright—who would return in *Wonder Woman 1984* in a flashback sequence at the start of the film—and her lover, Steve Trevor, played by Chris Pine. With Diana only really becoming Wonder Woman in the latter stages of the first film, Patty Jenkins had a desire to make a movie about a Wonder Woman who was fully herself. Reflecting on the state of the world today, with its crises of disinformation, falsehood, and deception, Jenkins began to wonder how Wonder Woman, with her Lasso of Truth, might impact such a world.

"A new era of wonder begins."

Marketing tagline

To counterbalance a message that could have weighed the film down, Jenkins and her co-writer Geoff Johns (former DC executive) elected to set the film in the 1980s, an era that in its gaudy excess would offer both light relief and afford a window on

In *Wonder Woman 1984*, Gal Gadot returns as Diana, here wearing the golden armor once belonging to Asteria, the Amazons' greatest warrior.

Far left: In pursuit of Max Lord and the wish-fulfilling Dreamstone, Wonder Woman intercepts Max's convoy in Egypt, trying to bring it to a halt with the assistance of Steve Trevor.

Left: Wonder Woman finally manages to ensnare Max in the White House, leading to a confrontation with the Secret Service in the corridors of the iconic building.

For *Wonder Woman 1984* director Patty Jenkins, Gal Gadot's innate decency and kindness were intrinsic to the actress's portrayal of Diana.

The visual effects team endeavored to produce a refractory-like pattern when Wonder Woman spins the Lasso of Truth to generate a force field during the White House battle.

Wonder of television

For a generation who grew up in the 1970s and beyond, including Patty Jenkins, Wonder Woman is synonymous with the eponymous TV show first broadcast from 1975 to 1979. Starring Lynda Carter in the title role, the show was a relatively faithful take on the character's comic book incarnation. But it could have been so different ...

In 1967, *Batman* producer William Dozier and his Greenaway Productions staff attempted to capitalize on the Caped Crusader's success by producing short pilots for other superhero shows. As well as creating a Batgirl short starring Yvonne Craig—who would instead be incorporated into Batman's 1967–1968 third season—Dozier and co. filmed a portion of a pilot for a Wonder Woman show. Titled "Who's Afraid of Diana Prince?," and adopting a comedic tone akin to Batman's, it featured Ellie Wood Walker as a mousy, clumsy Diana Prince and oddly narcissistic Wonder Woman.

While that pilot was unaired, seven years later a more serious effort did make it to air. Written and directed by *Star Trek* veterans John D. F. Black and Vincent McEveety, and starring Cathy Lee Crosby (pictured above) in the title role, *Wonder Woman* was broadcast as a TV movie in March 1974. While more straight-faced than its unaired predecessor, the pilot was effectively a spy story rather than a superhero adventure tale, while Wonder Woman herself bore little resemblance to her comic book counterpart. However, the movie scored well enough with audiences for ABC to take another look at the character, with rather different results the following year.

today's obsession with power and money. The pair also zeroed in on Washington, D.C. as a location for the action, reasoning that as Wonder Woman was now based in the United States, the Amazon would naturally gravitate to the heart of the nation's power. More than 40 years before, Washington had been the setting for the Lynda Carter–starring *Wonder Woman* TV show, of which Jenkins was an avowed fan. But the Washington of the 1980s was also well known to Jenkins, who as a teenager had lived in the area for more than a year.

SHOPPERS' PARADISE

With the film set in the capital, Washington would naturally provide many of the movie's locations, not least for an early sequence in a shopping mall where Wonder Woman acrobatically ensnares a group of hapless robbers. Shot at Alexandria's Landmark Mall, which had closed at the start of 2017, the scene foregrounds the Lasso of Truth, signaling the movie's message and visually setting out the film's stall with a riot of consumerism and color. The location had been found by returning Wonder Woman production designer Aline Bonetto (*Amélie*), who dressed three floors of the defunct mall in 65 period-appropriate stores, accurate right down to their fixtures and fittings.

Bonetto and Patty Jenkins had early discussions about the film's vibrant color palette and tone with costume designer Lindy Hemming, also making a return from *Wonder Woman*. Hemming

The opening Amazon Games flashback sequence saw 13-year-old Lilly Aspell reprise her role as young Diana. Aspell trained for five months to perform most of her own stunts, alongside many of the professional athletes who portrayed Amazons in the first film.

researched 1980s patterns, fashion magazines, and events to come up with the look of the outfits worn both by Diana in her civilian guise and the movie's two chief antagonists: geologist and cryptozoologist Barbara Minerva, played by Kristen Wiig (*Saturday Night Live*), and failing, avaricious businessman Maxwell Lorenzano, alias Max Lord, played by Pedro Pascal (*Narcos*, *The Mandalorian*). Rather than taking inspiration from the comics incarnations of the characters (respectively perennial Wonder Woman nemesis The Cheetah, a form of whom would feature later in the film, and former Justice League financier Maxwell Lord), Hemming looked to the Armani, Ralph Lauren, and Calvin Klein clothes of the period, dressing Pascal in broad-shouldered suits and signaling Barbara's evolution from preppy bookworm to a fiercer, more feral countenance with Wiig's wardrobe of animal fabrics and shaggy fur coat.

GOING FOR GOLD

The item that brings about the transformation in Barbara, a wish-fulfilling ancient artifact called the Dreamstone, also brings about the resurrection of Steve Trevor, in the body of another man. Played once again by Chris Pine (with his unnamed physical host played by Kristoffer Polaha), Steve is baffled and delighted by a world he sees as almost unrecognizably futuristic, a bewilderment that carries through to his wardrobe. Lindy Hemming credited her assistant Nat Turner, a child of the '80s, with Steve's various brash and outrageous looks in the film, among them a memorable combination of a Members Only jacket with a fanny pack. Hemming may have been horrified by some of the creations, but the costume designer noted Patty Jenkins and Chris Pine's shrieks of laughter when the latter was trying the outfits on.

Wonder Woman's costume, too, underwent some revisions. In the previous film, Diana had spent much of her time in the trenches and behind the enemy lines of the World War I, with the consequence that her costume was often grimy. Here, Jenkins wanted the outfit to have more of a 1980s glowing feel, prompting

For the scene where Diana and Steve fly a jet through Fourth of July fireworks, Gal Gadot and Chris Pine were filmed in a cockpit on a gimbal against blue screen, with practical fireworks shot separately.

Diana meets Barbara Minerva (Kristen Wiig) for the first time, when the clumsy geologist drops her papers all over the Smithsonian Institute floor.

215

Wonder Woman's attempt to capture Max Lord at the White House goes awry when a Dreamstone-empowered Barbara intervenes—on the side of Max.

For the scene where Wonder Woman learns to fly for the first time, Gal Gadot was shot on a wire rig against a blue screen.

As played by Pedro Pascal, Max Lord appears in a TV ad accompanied by his catchphrase slogan, "Life is good … but it can be better."

Hemming and her team to make the costume more colorful and translucent, lending the ensemble more texture and depth.

A more radical design was the armor worn by Wonder Woman toward the end of the film. In the film, in order to defeat Max and Barbara—who has been transformed by Max, now merged with the Dreamstone, into a cheetahlike apex predator—Diana dons a golden suit of eagle-winged armor once worn by Asteria, the long-lost greatest warrior of the Amazons. In this instance, Hemming and her team did look to comics for inspiration—in particular Mark Waid and Alex Ross's 1996 near-future dystopia *Kingdom Come*, the climax of which sees an older Wonder Woman wearing a winged golden armor, and a 1999 sequence in Wonder Woman's own comic book series where Diana wears the armor in the present day draped in the American flag. Hemming also researched ancient pre-Greek armors and modern fashion icons like Alexander McQueen and Thierry Mugler to arrive at the final version, making sure that the 3D-printed armor gleamed but did not act like a mirror so it would not show the reflections of the film crew. From start to finish, the process took more than six months.

CONSUMER CULTURE

As well as presenting the opportunity to recreate some outrageous fashion crimes—not to mention bring to the screen a spectacular golden armor—*Wonder Woman 1984* afforded Patty Jenkins the chance to recreate the Wonder Woman she had loved as a kid and to contrast the 1980s setting with the world of today. Even though she had already made one *Wonder Woman* movie, Jenkins craved the Wonder Woman who had inspired her, in the form of Lynda Carter in the 1970s. Moreover, for Jenkins, 1984 was the quintessential peak of commercial capitalism, a time when excess was everything and little thought was given to the consequences of that excess. By setting the movie in the 1980s, Jenkins could comment both on that era and the modern one.

That commentary reaches its apotheosis in the movie's spectacular finale, in which the world is brought to the brink of annihilation after the Dreamstone-powered Max grants everyone

Far left: The armor of Asteria was created long ago during the war between the Amazons and the humans, when the Amazons merged all of their armors together in order to produce one suit capable of withstanding attacks.

Left: During the White House battle, Max is astonished when Barbara, who relishes the power that has been granted her by the Dreamstone, intervenes against Wonder Woman on his behalf, allowing him to escape.

on the planet their greatest wish. Inevitably, absolute power corrupts absolutely, until Diana, who has already renounced her wish and sorrowfully returned Steve to oblivion, convinces the world to do the same. But Jenkins has reserved one wish for herself—a midcredits scene reveals Asteria secretly living among humanity and committing the odd heroic deed still. Making a cameo as Asteria was none other than the Wonder Woman of Jenkins's youth, Lynda Carter.

Wonder Woman '75

A year after the 1974 Cathy Lee Crosby–starring *Wonder Woman* pilot aired, ABC broadcast a second TV movie pilot, this time to more enduring success.

Produced by former Paramount exec Douglas Cramer, *The New Original Wonder Woman*, as the TV movie was titled, aired in November 1975, starring little-known newcomer Lynda Carter. Just over a year before, Carter had auditioned for the lead in the 1974 pilot, bringing her to the attention of Cramer, who fought for her to star in this second try at turning Wonder Woman into a television success. With *The Carol Burnett Show* regular Lyle Waggoner stepping into the role of American Air Corpsman Steve Trevor, *The New Original Wonder Woman* took a much more faithful approach to the character's comic book roots, depicting Diana's time with the Amazons and detailing Steve's arrival on Paradise Island and Diana returning with him to Washington, D.C. Moreover, unlike Cathy Lee Crosby, in look and costume—the latter designed by noted TV and movie costume designer Donfeld—Carter bore a striking resemblance to her comics counterpart.

The pilot was a hit, and ABC ordered two more episodes, aired in April 1976, followed by another 11 episodes aired toward the end of the year. Like the pilot, the first season of *Wonder Woman* was set during World War II, prompting DC to follow suit with their *Wonder Woman* comic book, shifting the setting of the series to World War II at the start of 1977, just as the final episodes of the TV show's first season were airing. When the show returned for its second season in September of that year, however, now titled *The New Adventures of Wonder Woman* and airing on CBS, the setting had changed to the modern day, with Diana, after returning to Paradise Island for three decades, spinning back into action alongside Steve Trevor's son, Steve Trevor Jr.—still played by Lyle Waggoner.

The New Adventures of Wonder Woman lasted just one more season, coming to an end in September 1979. However, the show's impact was sizable, with Lynda Carter's warm and winning performance as Wonder Woman thrilling and inspiring a generation of women, Patty Jenkins among them.

217

THE SUICIDE SQUAD

Release date: August 2021
Starring roles: Margot Robbie, Idris Elba, John Cena, Joel Kinnaman, Sylvester Stallone, Viola Davis, David Dastmalchian, Daniela Melchior, Michael Rooker, Jai Courtney, Peter Capaldi

Director: James Gunn
Screenplay: James Gunn
Cinematography: Henry Braham
Music: John Murphy
Running time: 132 minutes
Box office: $168,717,425 (theatrical release during COVID-19 Pandemic)

When James Gunn signed on to write and direct *The Suicide Squad* in 2018, he had a pretty good idea of the kind of film he wanted to make—a Super-Villain version of Robert Aldrich's 1967 convicts-at-war movie *The Dirty Dozen*. But where David Ayer had similar ambitions when formulating his 2016 *Suicide Squad* film, Gunn had a different tone in mind—a freewheeling war caper movie along the lines of Brian G. Hutton's 1970 World War II

"They're dying to save the world."

Marketing tagline

comedy-drama heist flick *Kelly's Heroes* (which starred Clint Eastwood, Telly Savalas, and Donald Sutherland as a group of rogues on the make). Moreover, Gunn wanted to make a film free from restrictions, with no set-in-stone first act/second act/third act structure, and no PG-13 rating—in short, a film with no rules.

By the time he came to *The Suicide Squad*, James Gunn already had a proven track record in ensemble comic book movies, having written and helmed both *Guardians of the Galaxy* (2014) and

Originally, James Gunn tested a hammerhead design for King Shark, before deciding that the character's eyes being so far apart made it awkward for him to interact with other performers.

The Suicide Squad—Joel Kinnaman's Rick Flag, John Cena's Peacemaker, Margot Robbie's Harley Quinn, and Idris Elba's Bloodsport—stride into action, with Peter Capaldi's reluctant Thinker in tow.

On the streets of Corto Maltese, Ratcatcher (Daniela Melchior) and Bloodsport are faced with an army of citizens enslaved by the giant alien Starro.

During the Suicide Squad's assault on what they believe is an enemy base, King Shark makes a meal of an unfortunate guard.

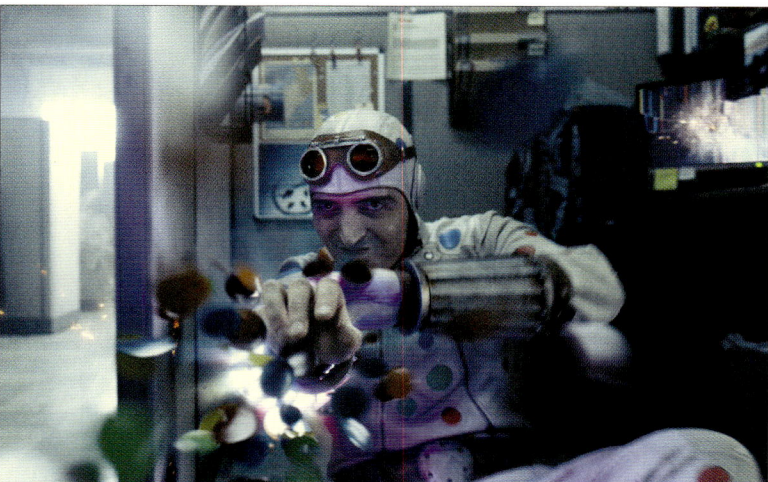

David Dastmalchian saw his character, Polka-Dot Man, as someone who has experienced a lot of pain, shame, and solitude in his life.

After shooting the dictator of Corto Maltese, Harley Quinn is imprisoned and tortured—until she makes her escape and slaughters the palace guard.

Guardians of the Galaxy Vol. 2 (2017). Gunn had loved John Ostrander and Luke McDonnell's original 1987 Super-Villain-starring *Suicide Squad* comics series, as well as Adam Glass and Federico Dallocchio's 2011 New 52 volume, and had always thought the concept would make for a great movie. He felt a little envy when David Ayer had gotten to make his *Suicide Squad*. But in tandem with the comics concept, what excited Gunn was the idea of bringing back the genre of war caper movies he had loved as a kid, epitomized by *The Great Escape* (1963), *Where Eagles Dare* (1968), and—of course—*Kelly's Heroes* (1970).

Knowing the sort of story he wanted to tell, Gunn's first step in formulating *The Suicide Squad* was to pick characters. For days, the director pored over DC's enormous library of characters, pinning pictures on the wall as he tried to figure out which would work with which. Gunn wanted each member of his Suicide Squad to hail from a different movie or TV genre, whether that be Idris Elba's Bloodsport, who Gunn pictured as coming from a modern, grim and dark movie; John Cena's Peacemaker, who in Gunn's mind hailed from a 1970s TV show; David Dastmalchian's Polka-Dot Man, who Gunn envisioned as having originated in a sad version of the 1966 *Batman* TV show; Daniela Melchior's

Far left: While much of *The Suicide Squad* was shot at Trilith Studios in Atlanta, the final battle with Starro was filmed in Colón, a seaport city in Panama.

Left: Bloodsport and the Suicide Squad don civilian guises to go undercover in a Corto Maltese nightclub in order to grab Project Starfish lead scientist the Thinker.

Ratcatcher, who to Gunn was a character from a horror movie; or Margot Robbie's returning Harley Quinn, who couldn't have originated from anywhere but the DC universe.

OUTFITTING THE SQUAD

The disparate nature of the characters flowed through to their costumes, Gunn noting to costume designer Judianna Makovsky that they didn't need to look as though they originated from the same film. Makovsky worked in close collaboration with production designer Beth Mickle and the movie's concept artists to conceive the squad's outfits, among them Harley's practical battle outfit, which Gunn wanted to be closer to the character's red-and-black comics costume. One surprise was Peacemaker's helmet, a shiny chrome take on the character's comic book helmet that went through multiple iterations before the final design was settled on. Originally envisioned as being used only for the occasional hero shot, the helmet was such a hit with Gunn and director of photography Henry Braham that it was used throughout the film.

While many of the characters were clothed in practical costumes, some needed to be realized with the help of CGI. Voiced by Sylvester Stallone, King Shark was performed on set by Steve Agee, who also appears in the film as John Economos, an aide to A.R.G.U.S. director and Suicide Squad commander Amanda Waller (Viola Davis, returning from 2016's *Suicide Squad*), a role he would reprise in the 2022 *Peacemaker* TV show. The 6-foot 7-inch (2 m) actor and comedian wore an outside torso rig and wire-frame shark head, which were then used as reference by the visual effects team to help create the final King Shark.

An even more spectacular CGI creation came in the form of Starro the Conqueror, the gigantic starfishlike alien the squad have been sent to Corto Maltese to destroy. Originally created in 1960 as the first villain to be faced by the newly formed Justice League of America, Starro had terrified James Gunn as a kid, hence why the director chose the alien—that, and Gunn believed the ridiculous nature of Starro would fit with the tone of his film. Certainly Starro, after escaping confinement—in the process killing his tormentor, Project Starfish lead scientist the Thinker, played by Peter Capaldi of Doctor Who fame—provides a suitably over-the-top spectacle for the film's finale, as the Suicide Squad battles the cerulean blue starfish and its army of enslaved Corto Maltese soldiers and citizens.

Peacemaker star-maker

In summer 2020, as he was finishing editing *The Suicide Squad* during a coronavirus lockdown, James Gunn started writing a TV series. Gunn wrote a season's worth of stories in eight weeks, mostly for his own amusement, as he didn't believe it would actually happen. When DC then asked him which character from *The Suicide Squad* he would choose to make a TV show about, Gunn had a ready answer—Peacemaker. Debuting in 1966 as a peace-loving diplomat-turned-adventurer, Christopher Smith, alias Peacemaker, had been reinvented 20 years later as an excessively violent vigilante and occasional government operative. It was this version that James Gunn selected to feature in *The Suicide Squad*, played by former WWE star John Cena, whose performance convinced the director that there was a lot more potential in both actor and character.

The first season of *Peacemaker* debuted on HBO Max at the start of 2022, with Cena's character recruited into an assassination squad dubbed Project Butterfly alongside Chukwudi Iwuji's Clemson Munn, Jennifer Holland's Emilia Harcourt; Steve Agee's John Economos; and Danielle Brooks's Leota Adebayo, daughter of Suicide Squad head Amanda Waller. Freddie Stroma's Vigilante, a sociopathic reworking of *New Teen Titans* spin-off character Adrian Chase, also appeared. A hit with both audiences and critics, a second season was immediately put into the works.

THE BATMAN

Release date: March 2022
Starring roles: Robert Pattinson, Zoë Kravitz, Paul Dano, Jeffrey Wright, John Turturro, Peter Sarsgaard, Andy Serkis, Colin Farrell
Director: Matt Reeves

Screenplay: Matt Reeves and Peter Craig
Cinematography: Greig Fraser
Music: Michael Giacchino
Running time: 176 minutes
Box office: $772,245,583

Matt Reeves's first exposure to Batman came in early childhood, courtesy of the 1966–1968 *Batman* TV show, which the director (born in 1966) would have watched in repeat. In a similar manner to so many other kids who grew up in that era, including Dark Knight Trilogy director Christopher Nolan, it wasn't the irony or comedy of the show that the young Reeves responded to, but the theatricality—the Batsuit, the Batmobile, the gadgets.

"Unmask the Truth"

Marketing tagline

Five decades later, Reeves would use those elements in service of a deeply personal psychological story set during Batman's second year of operation, rooted in a heightened reality and utilizing some of the same British studios as Nolan (notably Bedfordshire's Cardington Sheds). But in contrast to the British-born director, Reeves would employ a range of cutting-edge digital methods—from virtual reality previsualization to digital cameras, to shooting in the volume—as he worked to craft a motion picture with emotional heft, even as he and his crew faced unprecedented challenges in the shape of a global pandemic.

A DIFFERENT VISION

When Matt Reeves was first approached by Warner Bros. about directing *The Batman*, he was deep in postproduction on *War for the Planet of the Apes* (2017). Unable to turn his thoughts to what he would do with a Batman movie, the *Cloverfield* (2008) and *Let Me In* (2010) director was given the space he needed to finish his second Apes film (following 2014's *Dawn of the Planet of the Apes*) before starting to write *The Batman* early in 2017. Had Ben Affleck remained in the role he had inhabited from *Batman v Superman: Dawn of Justice* (2016) through to *Justice League* (2017), Reeves's film would have been about a Batman struggling with disillusion; but when it became clear that Affleck would no longer be involved, Reeves was free to pursue a different vision, separate from the continuity of prior DC films.

The elements of the Batman mythos that had enthralled Reeves as a child—the Batsuit, the equipment—would be key to his conveying the kind of character he envisioned: a younger Batman

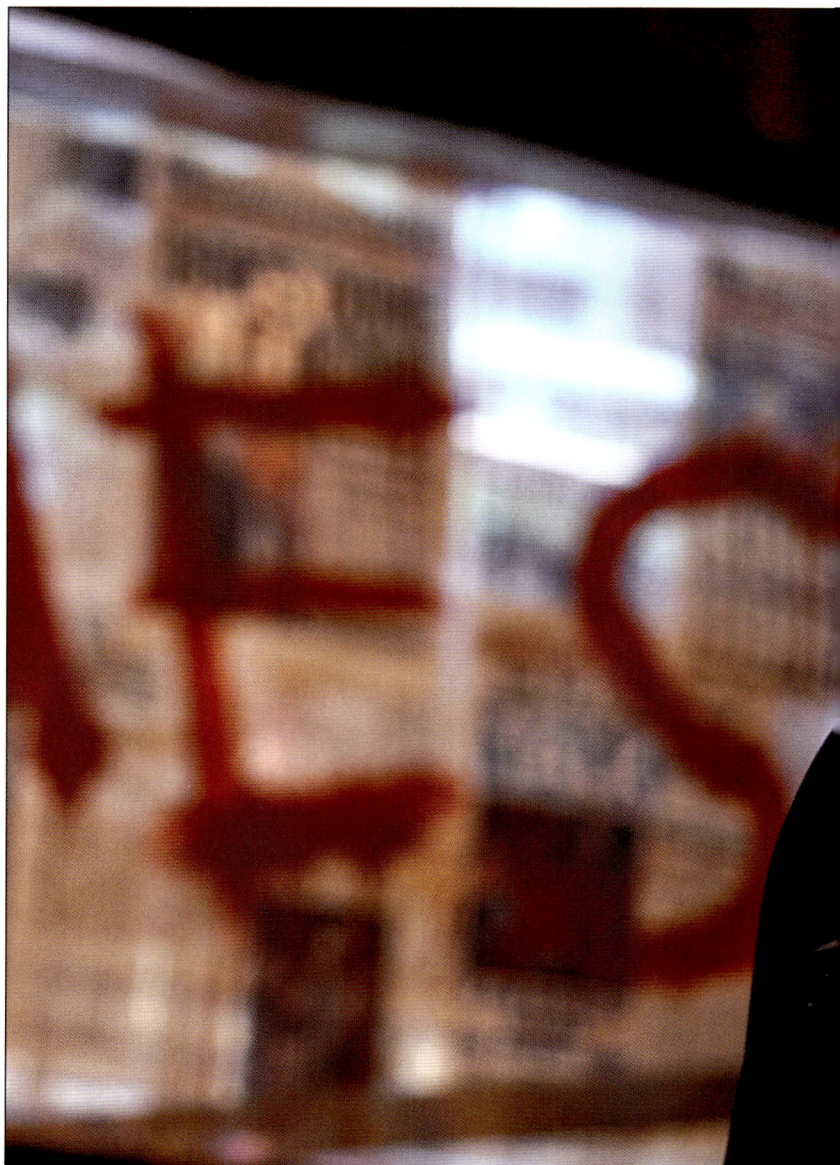

Robert Pattinson as the Batman surveys The Riddler's gruesome work at Mayor Mitchell's mansion, the "lies" daubed on newspaper cuttings of the late mayor's achievements indicating the dark secrets about to be uncovered.

Far left: Built into a train terminal underneath Wayne Tower—the gothic building in the heart of the city where Bruce Wayne lives—the Batcave of *The Batman* is a work in progress, much like Batman himself.

Left: Jeffrey Wright saw his character, Lieutenant Gordon, as an overwhelmed everyman, struggling to keep his head above the mire of crime and corruption in Gotham City.

To build a Batsuit

Director Matt Reeves's desire to ground his tale of a formative Batman in a believable verisimilitude flowed through to the Batsuit. One of Reeves's inspirations while writing the movie was writer Brian Azzarello and artist Lee Bermejo's 2019 graphic novel *Batman: Damned*, in which Batman wears a militaristic tactical suit replete with pockets and gadgets, not a million miles from riot control gear. Reeves wanted the Batsuit of *The Batman* to adhere to a similar utilitarian logic and aesthetic—to be an intimidating yet practical, protective suit that appeared as if it had been pieced together by a young Bruce Wayne, something that could evolve over time.

Translating Reeves's ideas into reality were Batsuit costume designers Glyn Dillon and David Crossman, who formulated a suit that was divided into panels to allow Robert Pattinson a full range of movement, with a skull-like cowl where the stitching was visible. Everything on the suit had a function, whether it be the tasers in the gloves; the ballistic protection on the body; the chest Bat-logo, which could be detached and used as a knife; the wrist grapple guns, which were inspired by Travis Bickle's homemade wrist-ejecting gun in *Taxi Driver* (1976); or the inflatable wingsuit (*pictured*), which a somewhat nervous Batman uses for the first time to escape the GCPD, with near-fatal results.

LED volume screens were employed for numerous scenes in *The Batman*, affording digital views of Gotham City that could be adjusted as needed.

At the behest of Matt Reeves and Paul Dano, costume designer Jaqueline Durran researched the kinds of surplus store clothing The Riddler might have used to create his outfit.

in the formative stages of his crime-fighting career, building the tools and arsenal he needed for his mission, but unsure even who Batman is and whether he can accomplish his goals. In common with Affleck's Batman, this younger version would struggle with despair at the seeming futility of his mission, almost succumbing to darkness in the form of vengeance, only to fight his way through and find hope toward the end of the film—an emotional arc that was of paramount importance to the director.

Just as important was the question of who would play Bruce Wayne/Batman. As he was writing his film, Reeves was captivated by former *Twilight* star Robert Pattinson's powerful performance as a desperate, destructive bank robber in Josh and Benny Safdie's crime thriller *Good Time* (2017). Reeves had been playing a track by Nirvana, "Something in the Way"—eventually used near the start and at the end of *The Batman*—while picturing Bruce Wayne, Gotham City's tragic orphaned prince as a tortured rock star recluse akin to Kurt Cobain. Pattinson's nihilistic turn in *Good Time* convinced Reeves that the actor could play such a role.

DETECTIVE COMICS

Accompanying Reeves's conception of Batman in the second year of his career was the notion of the character being the World's Greatest Detective, an aspect dating back to his earliest Bob Kane/Bill Finger comic book appearances, but one that hadn't really been explored in film. In Reeves's movie, the series of crimes Batman has to solve, in conjunction with Lieutenant Jim Gordon (Jeffrey Wright) and a Gotham City Police Department uneasy

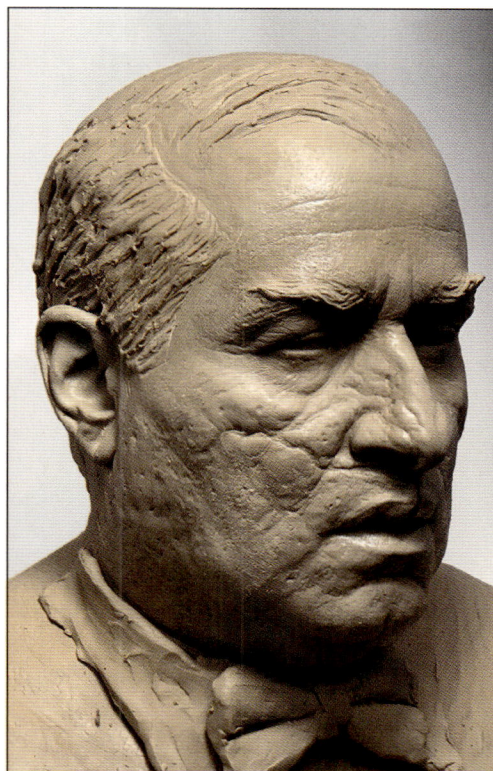

Far left: For production designer James Chinlund, the look of the Batmobile was rooted in Bruce Wayne's appreciation of American muscle cars, and Batman's functional need for the vehicle to be powerful and impenetrable.

Left: As seen on this maquette for The Penguin, prosthetic makeup designer Mike Marino and prosthetic artist Mike Fontaine shaped penguinlike eyebrows and the suggestion of a bird beak in the nose.

about working with, as Officer Martinez (Gil Perez-Abraham) puts it, a "goddamn freak," take the form of gruesome murders of Gotham City's political elite by The Riddler, played by Paul Dano (*Little Miss Sunshine*). Reeves read John Douglas and Mark Olshaker's *Mindhunter* as he was writing, bringing to mind the Zodiac killer and his primitive costume. The director channeled that image into his version of The Riddler, who in the narrative leaves cryptic clues and cyphers at his crime scenes, exposing the corruption in Gotham City and pointing to the involvement of Bruce Wayne's late father, adding a personal, emotional dimension that challenges Bruce to be a better Batman.

The aftermath of The Riddler's first murder, of Gotham City Mayor Don Mitchell Jr. (Rupert Penry-Jones) at his mansion, was the first scene to be shot when principal photography commenced in January 2020. For cast and crew, those early days were about working out how to make a masked, caped vigilante walking into a crime scene feel real: how Robert Pattinson's Batman sounded and moved; how the cops and other characters reacted to him.

Also of importance early on in presenting a believable Batman was striking the right balance between light and shadow when lighting the Batsuit. Director of photography Greig Fraser (*Zero Dark Thirty*, *Rogue One*) researched thousands of images in order to put together a reference document for Matt Reeves titled "Light for Dark," cinematographer and director using Frank Miller and David Mazzucchelli's 1987 graphic novel *Batman: Year One* as inspiration to compose film frames that straddled the line between unreadability and overly bright. Production designer James Chinlund (*War for the Planet of the Apes*), meanwhile, took inspiration from the films of Wong Kar-Wai in the textures and patterns of street scenes, such as the neon-lit red-light district where Selina Kyle lives.

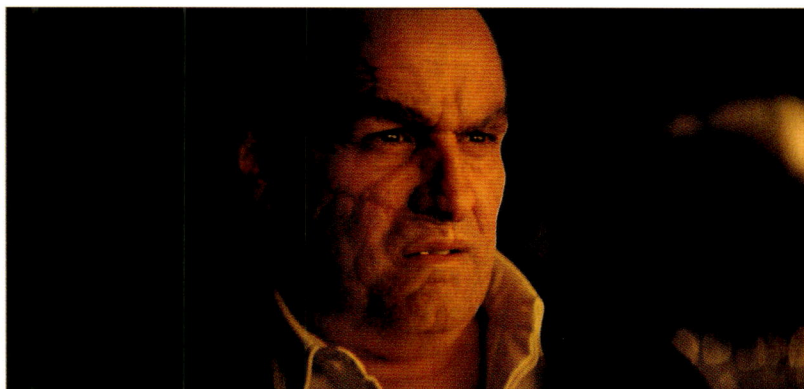

Playing Oswald Cobblepot, alias The Penguin, Colin Farrell wove a personal history for his character from the scarred prosthetics that adorned his face.

After bludgeoning Gotham City Mayor Mitchell (Rupert Penry-Jones), The Riddler wraps the politician's head in duct tape, scrawling "No more lies" on it.

For Andy Serkis, the survivor's guilt that Alfred feels was key to the tension between the bodyguard-turned-surrogate father and his ward, Bruce Wayne.

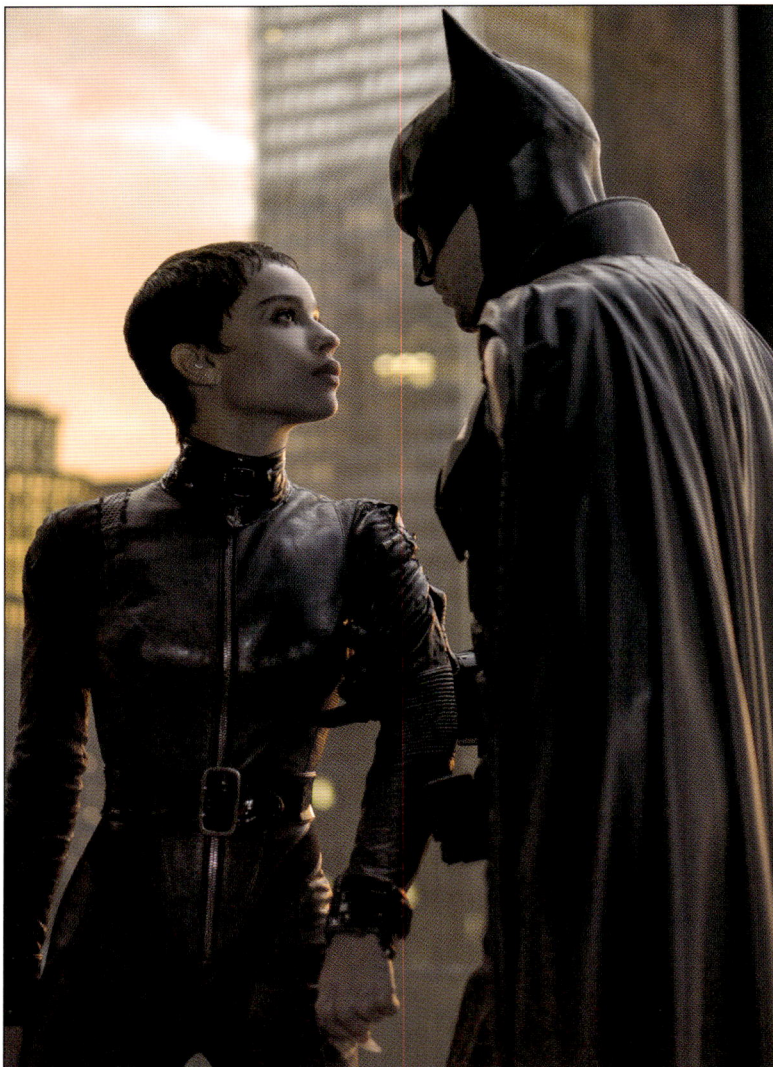

In the abandoned building housing the Bat-Signal, Selina reveals that her father is Carmine Falcone, leading to a deeper understanding between herself and Bruce/Batman.

THE BAT AND THE CAT

Playing Selina would be Zoë Kravitz, who had recently turned heads with her performance as Bonnie Carlson in HBO's *Big Little Lies*. The actress had secured the part of Selina following an electrifying chemistry read with Robert Pattinson in October 2019, with Pattinson, whom Kravitz had known for years, wearing the still-in-development Batsuit. Taking a lead from *Batman: Year One*, the Selina of *The Batman* has yet to fully assume the persona of Catwoman. Costume designer Jacqueline Durran conceived a jumpsuit that had a practical basis behind it—Selina rides a motorcycle—yet gave the impression of the beginnings of a catsuit.

The criminal underworld that Selina moves in in the movie necessitated a number of looks involving different colors, textures, and wigs, not least for the scenes in the Iceberg Lounge, the club where she works. The site of a bruising battle between Batman and a succession of hired thugs, the Iceberg Lounge and its nefarious inner sanctum 44 Below are owned by Oswald "Oz" Cobblepot, alias The Penguin, played by Colin Farrell (*Phonebox*, *The Banshees of Inisherin*), almost unrecognizable under layers of prosthetic makeup. As directed by Matt Reeves, prosthetic makeup designer Mike Marino and prosthetic artist Mike Fontaine referenced the late actors Bob Hoskins and John Cazale, especially the latter's performance as Fredo in *The Godfather* (1972), in formulating a scarred, grizzled countenance; this fed into Farrell's performance, the actor inventing backstories for every facial scar.

BATMAN YEAR TWO

In the narrative, Oswald Cobblepot's boss is mafia don Carmine Falcone, a character who had debuted in *Batman: Year One* and had previously been played by Tom Wilkinson in *Batman Begins* (2005). Asked by one of the production's casting crew, Cindy Tolan, what type of actor Matt Reeves saw as Falcone, Reeves said his ideal would be someone like John Turturro. Tolan suggested simply asking Turturro, who responded positively to Reeves's complex characterization. Falcone's backstory is intertwined with both Selina Kyle's and that of Bruce Wayne's late father, Thomas, further enhancing the personal nature of Batman's mission.

Simultaneously assisting Bruce in that mission and worrying about his mental well-being is Alfred, played by Andy Serkis, who had previously played the evolved chimpanzee Caesar in Reeves's two Apes movies. This version of Alfred has a military background, which in his guilt at allowing Bruce Wayne's parents to be killed he has channeled into training Bruce. But despite Alfred's assistance—particularly in cracking The Riddler's cyphers—this Bruce is very much a self-made Batman, exemplified by his Batmobile.

For Matt Reeves, the Batmobile needed to be a vehicle that Bruce could conceivably build: welded together from other cars, displaying the methodology of function over form, yet with the power to intimidate. Recalling the possessed car of Stephen King's *Christine* and John Carpenter's movie adaptation (both 1983), Reeves pictured the vehicle emerging from the darkness like a terrifying monster, a vision that with the help of production designer James Chinlund, special effects supervisor Dominic Tuohy, and cinematographer Greig Fraser he was able to realize when the Batmobile roars to thunderous life in pursuit of The Penguin.

Far left: Trying to unravel The Riddler's clues about Gotham City's corruption, Bruce Wayne lays out all the related evidence—with himself and his family at the center.

Left: Visiting a captured Riddler in Arkham Asylum, Batman finds there is more to the criminal's plans than he suspected, prompting him to fly into a rage demanding to know what the villain has done.

IN MEMORIAM

On March 14, 2020, filming for *The Batman* was suspended as the COVID-19 pandemic gathered pace. Two weeks later, one of the production's dialect coaches, Andrew Jack, died from coronavirus complications. As the pandemic intensified, Matt Reeves and his film crew had no idea when or even if they would be able to resume production. When they at last did that September, it was with the most stringent safety precautions in place. By the time the film wrapped in March 2021, the production had been running for a year and a half; Reeves and his team—indeed the whole world—experienced something that no one had ever been through before. Through all of that, Reeves and crew had made a movie that heralded a bold new start for the Dark Knight. A remarkable film made in extraordinary circumstances, it was dedicated in the end credits to the memory of Andrew Jack.

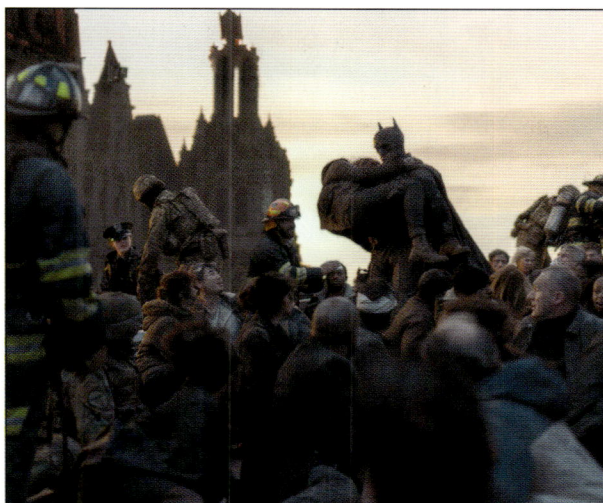

Assisting with rescue efforts in the wake of The Riddler's plan to drown Gotham City by blowing up the sea wall, Batman realizes there is hope for the city.

Visions of Gotham City

There have been numerous screen versions of Gotham City, from the stylized city of Tim Burton's *Batman* (1989) and *Batman Returns* (1992), to the increasingly realistic conurbation of Christopher Nolan's Dark Knight Trilogy (2005–2012), to the prequel town of TV show *Gotham* (2014–2019) and its successor *Pennyworth* (2019–2022). For *The Batman*, Matt Reeves wanted to realize a Gotham City that built on the gothic architecture of an actual city with sets and visual effects to create an original vision: a believable American metropolis that felt familiar but was still unique to the film.

An example was Gotham City Hall *(pictured)*, where the The Riddler gatecrashes Mayor Mitchell's funeral with a car containing District Attorney Gil Colson (Peter Sarsgaard) wired to a bomb. Exteriors were shot at St. George's Hall in Liverpool, with interiors constructed at Cardington Studios (the design and tone of the set taking visual inspiration from Liverpool) and then extended digitally. Other sets, such as the half-constructed building where the Bat-Signal is situated and where Batman meets both Jim Gordon and Selina Kyle, made use of the volume, LED walls displaying sprawling, moving cityscapes that reflected onto the actors, and which they in turn could react to. Moreover, courtesy of production designer James Chinlund's innovation of designing sets in virtual reality, in previsualization Matt Reeves was able to don a headset and walk around VR sets, even using them to plan shots once the physical sets had been built.

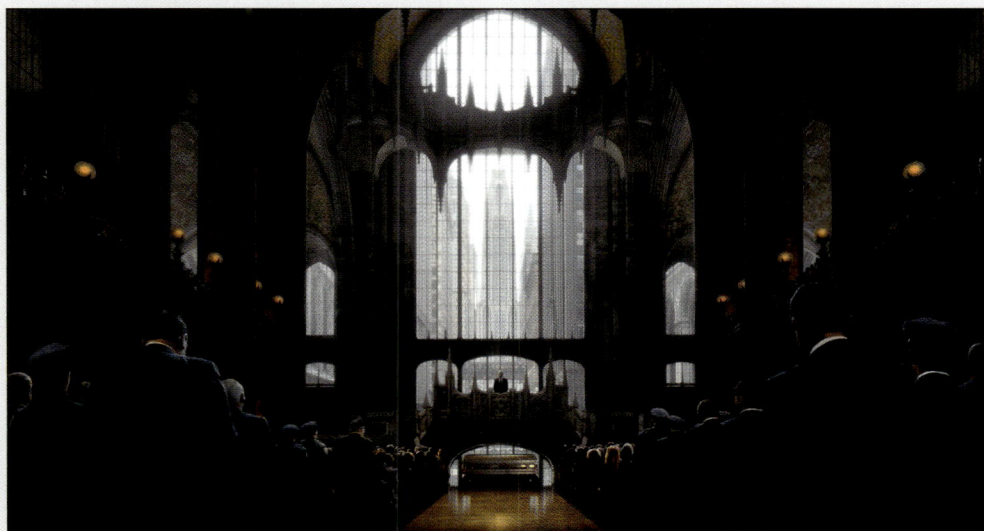

BLACK ADAM

Release date: October 21, 2022 (US), October 3, 2022 (Mexico)
Starring roles: Dwayne Johnson, Sarah Shahi, Aldis Hodge, Pierce Brosnan, Quintessa Swindell, Noah Centineo, Marwan Kenzari, Bohdi Sabongui, Jalon Christian

Director: Jaume Collet Serra
Screenplay: Adam Sztkiel, Rory Haines, Sohrab Noshirvan
Cinematography: Lawrence Sher
Music: Lorne Balfe
Running time: 125 minutes
Box office: $393.3 million

Everyone knows a great superhero story is impossible without a great villain. And sometimes their path to glory evokes enough empathy for them to be the hero of their own story. In an era where modern sensibilities welcome complex renegades and mavericks, it was a given that audiences were ready for heroes to step over ethical lines. DC had been publishing one for decades.

"Violence is always necessary."
Black Adam

Growing out of preproduction work on *Shazam!* (2019), *Black Adam* was the eleventh chapter of the DC Extended Universe. Producer and star Dwayne Johnson had been interested in the role since 2007, and in 2014 was officially attached to the character wherever he ultimately materialized. After many permutations, Johnson's Seven Bucks Productions, New Line Cinema (and its owners Warner Bros.) released a dark saga of vengeance and redemption that also introduced DC's oldest, most revered super-team—the Justice Society of America—to the big screen.

A TOUCH OF EVIL

A throwaway villain created by Otto Binder and C. C. Beck for team title *The Marvel Family* (issue #1, December 1945), Black Adam was the mysterious Wizard's original champion, corrupted by his own power and exiled by magic "to the farthest star." Flying through space for five millennia, the villain's rampaging vendetta resulted in his death at the end of the story.

Predating Greco-Roman gods and the heroes empowering the 20th-century Marvel (now Shazam) Family, the ancient Egyptian miscreant called upon Shu's stamina, Heru's swiftness, Amon's strength, Zehuti's wisdom, Aten's power and Mehen's courage. When DC revived Captain Marvel in 1972, his ages-old antithesis was also eventually resurrected in *Shazam!* #28 (April 1977).

Following repeated clashes against the child-heroes in adult form, Black Adam survived *Crisis on Infinite Earths* and subsequent reboots to become a menace to many Super Heroes in the unified post-Crisis continuity. Dark, brooding, visually striking and extremely charismatic, Adam spearheaded a growing trend for conflicted antagonists and was a frequent foe for the Marvel Family, Superman, Hawkman and the

Justice Society of America. *Black Adam*'s first movie trailer launched on June 8, 2022—the anniversary of C. C. Beck's birth.

Over its convoluted cinematic journey, *Black Adam* engaged the talents of numerous concept artists, with the ideas of Kode Abdo, Robert Baricevic, David Levy, Victor Martinez, Andrea Onorato, Paul Ozzimo, and Christian Scheurer eventually informing the final film. Narrative thrust and numerous uncompromising action scenes were storyboarded by Jeffrey Henderson, Josh Shepperd, and Aaron Sowd. Costumes were designed by the team "Kurt and Bart" (*Deadpool 2*, *Ghost in the Shell*), covering everything from iron-age warriors and slaves to ultramodern uniforms for Intergang and a squad of new/old superheroes.

EVIL UNDER THE SON

Originally intended as the Super-Villain in the child-centered fantasy *Shazam!*, Black Adam was now able to tell his own story thanks to Catalan director Jaume Collett-Serra (*The Shallows*, *Unknown*), who came up as a possibility after being invited to helm *The Suicide Squad* (2021). At that time, however, he instead opted to direct Johnson in *Jungle Cruise*.

The story is as much about Kahndaqi archaeology professor, single mom, and freedom-fighter Adrianna Tomaz (Sarah Shahi)

A tailor-made role, years in the planning, Dwayne Johnson's first major superhero outing was as the nuanced, amoral messiah Black Adam.

Dr. Fate is one of DC's oldest heroes. As Lord of Order Nabu, his in-world backstory reveals him to be active in ancient Kahndaq beside Hawkman and Teth-Adam.

Cursed to reincarnate and battle forever, Hawkman uses weapons and wings made of alien "Ninth" metal—later "Nth Metal"—on crooks, Super-Villains, and devils out of hell.

Pierce Brosnan's first brush with the DC cinematic universe was auditioning for the part of Bruce Wayne/Batman in Tim Burton's *Batman* (1989), a role that eventually went to Michael Keaton.

Overtones of wry political satire abound as well-meaning, idealistic, impetuous young American, Atom Smasher, continually blunders, wrecking a city that has survived threats for 3,000 years.

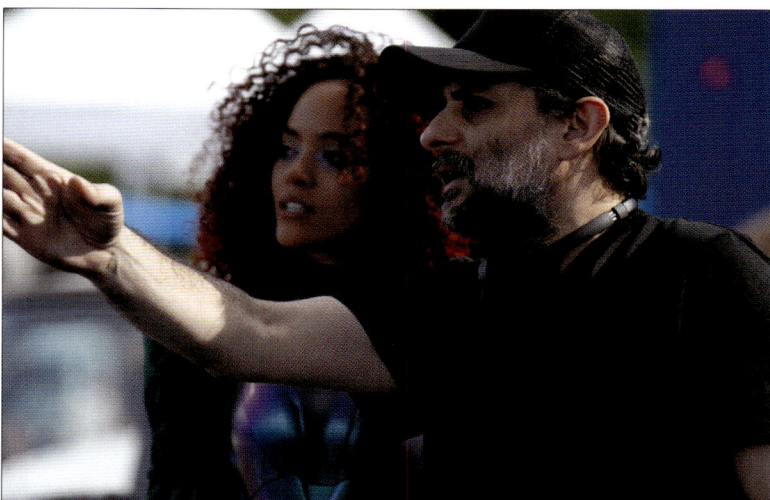

Director Jaume Collet-Serra steers Quintessa Swindell—who incorporated modern dance techniques into her portrayal of the Super Hero Cyclone—on the most visually expressive way to fight oppression.

as it is a classic antihero's return. Living under oppression in a fictional modern-day Middle Eastern nation, Tomaz draws inspiration to resist from her country's foundation myth, unaware it has become corrupted over five millennia.

The oldest democratic nation on Earth has been conquered by crime cartel Intergang, ruthlessly plundering its resources for nearly three decades while searching for every instance of the wonder-mineral Eternium. Tomaz's quest to keep mystic relic The Crown of Sabbac from them inadvertently leads to the advent of a very bloody messiah in the form of Black Adam.

Adrianna's son Amon (Bodhi Sabongui) adores Western culture and is obsessed with American ideals of freedom—as learned from imported movies and comic books—and inspires the awakened Adam to nobler aspirations. Technically, Sabongui reprised his part, having been Behrad Tarazi (an alternate-Earth analog of Amon Tomaz) in 2018's *Legends of Tomorrow* episode "Necromancing the Stone."

Adrianna herself was based on a comics character who debuted in weekly maxi-series *52* (issue #16, July 2006). She married Black Adam and was transformed into nature goddess Isis, with her brother Amon becoming the godling Osiris. When both were murdered, a bereaved Adam declared war on the world. Prior to DC acquiring the character, Isis originated on television as half of the *Shazam/Isis Hour*, and gained her own DC comics tie-in title, *The Mighty Isis*, which ran from October 1976 to January 1978.

LIBERATION, TRICKS, AND VISIONS

Scriptwriter Adam Sztykiel (*Made of Honor*, *Scoob!*) drafted a screenplay that underwent many changes as the film nudged forward. Rory Haines and Sohrab Noshirvan (co-writers of *Informer* and *The Mauritanian*) delivered a final screenplay that also underwent further revisions from David Leslie Johnson-McGoldrick (*Aquaman*), before the primordial Man in Black was ready to take on the modern world.

After completing work on Todd Phillips's *Joker* (2019), cinematographer Lawrence Sher (*Garden State*) shot principal photography at Trilith Studios, Atlanta in Georgia, with extensive set-building beginning in mid-March. Once again pandemic-generated delays deferred the formal start date of July 2020 to April 10, 2021, when filming finally commenced. Johnson completed his on-set scenes on July 15, before shooting of his remaining scenes was extended. Filming only completed on August 15, after the shoot relocated to Los Angeles.

BAFTA and Academy Award–winning Rhythm & Hues alumni Bill Westenhofer (*The Golden Compass*, *Wonder Woman*) was visual

Far left: *Black Adam* conjures up a true hell on Earth with the visceral horrors of criminal enslavers, catalysmic collateral damage from Super Hero clashes, and even a zombie apocalypse.

Left: Powered by nether demons Satan, Aym, Belial, Beelzebub, Asmodeus, and Crateis, Sabbac was created by Otto Binder and Al Carreno (*Captain Marvel Jr.* #4, February 1943). His righteous destruction at the hands of Black Adam is brutal and explicit.

effects supervisor, coordinating and overseeing a roster of third-party vendors, including Scanline VFX, Digital Domain, Rodeo VFX, Lola VFX, Cantina Creative, Tippett Studio, and Wētā FX, whose work on the final battle against villain-turned-demon, Sabbac, required many purely digital sequences.

In one technological triumph, body double Benjamin Patterson supplied a regulation-sized frame for enslaved Kahndaqi Teth-Adam in his mortal form, before digital mapping superimposed Johnson's face, while Miles Humphus (*Jungle Cruise, Jumanji: Welcome to the Jungle*) was Johnson's fully ripped stand-in on other scenes. Carrying tone and mood to the action-packed extreme, composer Lorne Balfe (*The Dark Knight Trilogy, The Lego Batman Movie*) wrote the music.

Initially rated "R," the original film required cutting and carefully edited fights and inventive death scenes, before *Black Adam* could qualify for a lower—and more commercially rewarding—PG-13 classification.

ENTER THE JSA

Adhering to DCEU continuity, Teth-Adam's revival alarmed Task Force X chief Amanda Waller (Viola Davis), who rejected her usual Suicide Squad solution in favor of delivering a clear message. She instead dispatched America's greatest heroes—The Justice Society—to end the escalating violence in Kahndaq. Her decision introduced audiences to veteran heroes Hawkman (Aldis Hodge) and Doctor Fate (Pierce Brosnan), as well as novices Cyclone (Quintessa Swindell) and Atom Smasher (Noah Centineo).

Between July 5 and October 4, the JSA's film debut was augmented and anticipated by DC, who published tie-in comic books with both illustrated and photographic covers for each team member, collected as a graphic novel, *Black Adam: The Justice Society Files.*

In September 2022, one month before the premiere, Dwayne Johnson was recalled for an end-credit sequence, accomplished remotely using body doubles and with Superman (Henry Cavill) literally phoning in his part from London. The revenge-and-redemption epic ends with newly redesignated Black Adam a global pariah confined by his own promise to stay in Kahndaq as its protector, while Superman and the superhuman community prepare for an inevitable future clash.

JSA screen shots

In 1940, the publishers of Superman and Batman revolutionized comics books for a third time. With publishing partner All American Comics—and at the suggestion of AA editor Sheldon Mayer and writer Gardner Fox—a joint venture united their less popular costumed characters to fight evil together. Dubbed the Justice Society of America in their premiere appearance (*All-Star Comics* #3 "Winter Issue," November 22, 1940) they were the first Super Hero team in history.

On screen, the JSA's appearances were confined to television, initially appearing on the animated adventure shows *Justice League, Batman: The Brave and the Bold,* and *Young Justice.* Their live-action debut was in 2010 on *Smallville* in two-part storyline "Absolute Justice." This was a hardline team from an earlier, less forgiving era and primarily featured Hawkman, Dr. Fate, and Stargirl, with flashback cameos of the full membership. This was followed by "The Justice Society of America" (October 20, 2016) on The CW's DC's *Legends of Tomorrow.* Here, Hourman, Commander Steel, Obsidian, Stargirl, Vixen, and Dr. Mid-Nite are in their element, bravely battling Nazis in WWII.

In *Stargirl* (2020–2022, pictured above), the eponymous hero bridges two generations of JSA: the (murdered) original team and a new modern-day squad including S.T.R.I.P.E., Dr. Mid-Nite/Beth Chapel, Hourman/Rick Tyler, and Wildcat/Yolanda Montez. *Black Adam* was the JSA's movie debut, and they were namechecked in 2023's *Shazam: Fury of the Gods*, with the promise of bigger and better to come in the form of their own feature film.

SHAZAM! FURY OF THE GODS

Release date: March 14, 2023 premiere (Fox Village Theater, LA), March 17, 2023 (US general release)
Starring roles: Zachary Levi, Asher Angel, Jack Dylan Grazer, Grace Caroline Currey, Ross Butler, Rachel Zegler, D.J. Cotrona, Meagan Good, Djimon Hounsou, Helen Mirren, Lucy Liu

Director: David F. Sandberg
Screenplay: Henry Gayden, Chris Morgan
Cinematography: Gyula Pados
Music: Christophe Beck
Running time: 130 minutes
Box office: $133.8 million

The huge success of *Shazam!* in 2019 made a sequel starring the teen hero and his foster siblings a certainty. However, with the global COVID-19 pandemic closing theaters and decimating the uniquely skilled workforce of technical staff required to complete such effects-heavy projects, delays and compromises were unavoidable. So, in 2023—after many shifts and reshuffles of story, staff, and schedules—the Shazam Family finally took to the skies again.

"Unleash the Chaos."
Kalypso

The first indication of New Line Cinema's intentions came as early as April 8, 2019 (11 days after *Shazam!*'s US release), when *The Wrap* reported a sequel was already in development. With director David F. Sandberg, producer Peter Safran, and writer Henry Gayden reunited to continue the saga, the studio announced in December 2019 a scheduled released for April 1, 2022, but it wasn't until March 17, 2023, when the magic words rang out again.

LUCK OF THE GODS
The pandemic endangered the entire film industry and changed how movies were accessed. Denied venues to show their movies, studios turned to streaming services or delayed major releases. Warner Bros. was no exception and initially moved *Shazam!: Fury of the Gods* from April to November 4, 2022—the date previously earmarked for *Aquaman and the Lost Kingdom*—before shifting it again to June 2, 2023, and then back to December 16, 2022. This was after Sandberg delivered his film ahead of other DC features fighting deadlines and staff shortages. Further changes ultimately deferred it to the spring of 2023.

Compared to getting the film to fans, producing it was relatively straightforward, but by then it had become a far different beast

Above: In a moment of comic book razzle-dazzle and disaster-movie action, the assembled "Shazamily" prepare to save imperiled commuters on the iconic Benjamin Franklin Bridge connecting Philadelphia, Pennsylvania to Camden, New Jersey.

Far left: Anthea (Rachel Zegler) and Freddy (Jack Dylan Grazer) provide a tortured but triumphal romantic dimension to the sequel after losing their godlike powers and being targeted by Kalypso's dragon Ladon.

Left: In mythology, Kalypso, Hespera (pictured) and Anthea are Hesperides—the spirits of the sunset. Anthea was patron deity of gardens, swamps, and human love and Kalypso (a.k.a. Calypso) was a witch.

than originally envisioned. Comic fans' hopes were high, anticipating an epic clash between the Shazam! Family and Black Adam (Dwayne Johnson) and the returning Sivana (Mark Strong) with evil worm Mister Mind (voiced by director Sandberg) in tow.

Instead, Greek gods Hespera (Dame Helen Mirren), Kalypso (Lucy Liu), and Anthea (Rachel Zegler) imprison the wizard (Djimon Hounsou) in the Gods' Realm, intent on restoring their vanished kin and kind with a magic apple hidden in the Rock of Eternity. When dissent divides the sisters, chaos-bringer Kalypso punishes humanity with a terrifying dragon, using the apple to recreate her lost world in Fawcett City as it lies trapped under a magical dome. Shazam's childish champions are her only obstacle. Now the heroic team confront the loss of their powers as the angry goddesses attack, bringing a war of monsters to the streets. In the end, Billy is the last hero standing and must sacrifice himself.

EASTER EGG HUNT

Early in development, the worm Mister Mind was included, but his subplot would have impacted both run time by overburdening the plot and draining precious, scarce digital resources. His moment was held over for another time in favor of a storyline exploring the Shazam! Family growing apart while menaced by their own foundational mythology. That same thinking saw Superman and Batman's prospective appearances—failing to break the dome over Fawcett City—cut. However, a hilarious running gag and third act cameo for Wonder Woman (Gal Gadot) is included as Billy is stricken by an embarrassing boyhood crush.

The in-joke, Easter-egg-packed script was co-written by Chris Morgan, the scribe of many *The Fast and the Furious* films, leading to wry digs from Billy proclaiming, "I've seen all of *The Fast and the*

Mythologically, the dragon Ladon guards the Golden Apples of the Hesperides—a child of sea gods Phorcys and Ceto. Its animated tree makeover was conceived by digital games artist Scott Gessler.

Gods and monsters

As well as supplying super-strength to the Shazam! Family, demigod Hercules also contributed to the storyline. When Kalypso vengefully implants a Golden Apple from the Rock of Eternity in Pittsburgh's soil, it unleashes a Hellenic host of mythical monsters that run rampant through the city. which is now encased in glass.

Concept artists Rodion Vlasov of Parallax Studios and Kelton Cram rendered 3D models of the cyclopes, minotaurs, manticores, harpies, unicorns, and other fabled creatures based on the classical Eleventh Labor of Hercules. It was then down to the digital effects teams to bring them to cinematic life for the thrilling hunt scenes in the movie.

Furious movies" to elemental villain Hespera, played by Helen Mirren, who has starred in three movies from the franchise. When the foster siblings flee for their lives from the rampaging mythical monsters, one bystander—a cameo from Michael Gray wearing a red-and-yellow T-shirt just like the one he wore as Billy Batson in 1970s TV series *Shazam!*—calls the lightning-wielding hero "Captain Marvel."

The first *Shazam!* film also included many sly treats for diligent moviegoers among the artifacts seen in "Shazamily's" Rock of Eternity lair. These included the burning violin of 1940s villain Oggar; the Ibistick wand of Shazam!'s ally, Ibis the Invincible; and a mirror with a face in it from Shazam!'s New 52 comic era. In the sequel, they are topped by the affably sentient self-writing pen "Steve"—a hilarious advance on the Golden Age heroes' all-knowing eldritch database "the Histo-rama," plus other arcane references that only dedicated fans might recognize.

After decades of comic book reboots—the most successful being Jerry Ordway's mid-1990s run based on the Republic movie serials—Shazam!'s New 52 incarnation by scriptwriter Geoff Johns and artist Gray Frank was closely followed for the films. It led to Johns's appointment as an executive producer on the sequel, which eventually adopted all-original antagonists.

In *Shazam!* Billy shared his Super Hero powers with his foster siblings before destroying the wizard's staff that facilitated the process. The fallout from that rash act now allows Hespera, Kalypso, and Anthea to attack humanity, painfully aware that the stamina of their dead father Atlas empowers their enemies.

Acting couplets Faithe Herman and Meagan Good (Darla), Ian Chen and Ross Butler (Eugene), and Jovan Armand and D. J. Cotrona (Pedro) return, but Grace Caroline Currey (née Fulton) plays Mary in both roles, thanks to some careful cosmetic

The COVID pandemic even affected fantasy romance. Rachel Zegler's standard on-screen "chemistry test" with Jack Dylan Grazer was conducted long-distance, with director Sandberg assessing their compatibility via three-way Zoom call.

Despite having the NCam system, which provided real-time "in-camera" shots of anticipated CGI effects while filming, Sandberg soon discarded the technology, as it slowed down the shoot.

touches to her hair and makeup. Jack Dylan Grazer and Adam Brody again comprise both Freddy Freemans, who supplies poignant romantic interest by his connection to—and ultimate redemption of—Anthea. Asher Angel reprises Billy, with Zachary Levi and stunt doubles David Castillo and Eddie Davenport parlaying Shazam!.

STAIRWAYS TO HEAVENS

Shot by Hungarian cinematographer Gyula Pados (*Kontroll*, *Jumanji: Welcome to the Jungle*), principal photography took place in Atlanta, Georgia from mid-May to August 31, 2021, with location shooting in Greece—at the Acropolis Museum in Athens—Toronto, Canada; and Philadelphia. When the cameras stopped rolling, third-party visual-effects companies Weta FX, DNEG, Pixomondo, Territory Studios, Static Chair Productions, Scanline VFX, Method Studios, RISE VFX, and Stereo D parceled out and enhanced the scenes at a frantic pace.

Storyboard artists David E. Duncan, Vincent Lucido, Jim Magdaleno, Thomas A. Nelson, and Bridget Shaw choreographed the saga while concept artists including Danar Worya (who visualized the Rock of Eternity chamber and the Hellenic funeral gardens), Scott Gessler, Kelton Cram, Matt Codd, and Daniel Garelik of Pixomondo communally conceived the look of three worlds and the creatures who dwelled in them.

Online media was used to promote the film and update potential viewers, and the film featured heavily during virtual event DC Fandome, but the attention proved a double-edged sword when news of Gal Godot's guest appearance was revealed months before the film's release. Not spoiled was a cheeky midcredits moment as Billy/Shazam is disappointingly headhunted for the Justice Society by Task Force X agents Emilia Harcourt (Jennifer Holland) and John Economos (Steve Agee). This scene was also bumped from an earlier script, originally intended for the midcredits of *Black Adam*.

Embracing yet challenging superhero tropes, Billy and Hespera have a snack and a talk about trading hostages before resorting to another spectacular battle.

THE FLASH

Release date: June 2023
Starring roles: Ezra Miller, Sasha Calle, Michael Shannon, Ron Livingston, Maribel Verdú, Kiersey Clemons, Antje Traue, Michael Keaton
Director: Andy Muschietti
Story: John Francis Daley, Jonathan Goldstein, Joby Harold

Screenplay: Christina Hodson
Cinematography: Henry Braham
Music: Benjamin Wallfisch
Running time: 144 minutes
Box office: $270,633,313

For over 60 years, the Multiverse had been an intrinsic part of DC comics lore, reaching its ultimate expression in the 1985–1986 maxi-series *Crisis on Infinite Earths*, in which multiple versions of Earth—and multiple versions of Earth's heroes and villains—were wiped from existence (at least for a time; most later returned in one form or another). The notion of the Multiverse was baked into DC's comics history—yet to date, DC's movies had barely touched on the idea, with only *Batman v Superman: Dawn of Justice* (2016) and *Justice League* (2021) suggesting the possibility of an alternate timeline in their dystopian Knightmare sequences. With *The Flash*, however, the Multiverse would take center stage—entirely appropriately, as it was The Flash who had instigated the concept all those decades ago.

TWO WORLDS COLLIDE

In 1961, writer Gardner Fox and artist Carmine Infantino formulated a landmark story in the pages of *The Flash* #123. In "Flash of Two Worlds!," The Flash, alias police scientist Barry Allen—the character who with his 1956 debut had kickstarted

"Worlds Collide."

Marketing tagline

Promotional poster for *The Flash*, showing newcomer Sasha Calle as Kal-El's cousin Kara Zor-El—better known to comic book fans as Supergirl.

After infiltrating the Batcave by vibrating his molecules, an awestruck Barry Allen of 2013 pulls back a dustsheet to behold the Batmobile.

Having unwittingly wound up in 2013, Barry Allen encounters an alternate version of his younger self—who, suitably freaked out at meeting himself, promptly passes out.

The Flash gets ready to run from Central City to Gotham City—only to be interrupted by bystanders excited to see their hometown hero in action.

Flashpoint and the New 52

In summer 2011, DC published *Flashpoint*, a five-issue comic book miniseries plus associated tie-ins that precipitated arguably the biggest revamp in the company's history—though *Flashpoint* wasn't originally intended as the launchpad for that revamp ...

Conceived and written by DC's then-CCO Geoff Johns, with art by Andy Kubert, *Flashpoint* sees Barry Allen waking up in a twisted alternate reality where Batman is a murderous Thomas Wayne rather than Bruce Wayne, the Amazons have conquered Britain, and Aquaman has sunk western Europe. As the story unfolds, Barry learns that he himself created this dystopia by stopping his time-traveling nemesis the Reverse-Flash from killing Barry's mother.

The original plan after Barry set things right at the end of *Flashpoint* was for the DC universe to be restored and a number of new titles launched, including one starring Wally West, the former Kid Flash who had taken on the mantle of The Flash for two decades after Barry's apparent death in 1985–1986's *Crisis on Infinite Earths*. Instead, something much more radical happened. In May 2011, not long after the first issue of *Flashpoint* hit the stands, DC announced the New 52, a relaunch of every DC series with a new number-one issue. Four months later, at the end of *Flashpoint*, DC's decades-long continuity was reset, its heroes and villains revamped as younger versions—for a while, anyway: five years after the launch of the New 52, the Rebirth initiative reintroduced much of the pre-New 52 DC universe, merging the two continuities together.

Originally designed for Tim Burton's *Batman* in 1989, the Batwing was given an upgrade for *The Flash* to make the plane appear more modern.

This concept art delineates the scene where The Flash uses his super-speed to save numerous falling babies from a collapsing Gotham City building.

As well as featuring three seats rather than the original's one, the new Batwing boasted a gyroscopic cockpit, so Batman remained upright when the plane rolled.

the Silver Age of Comics—unexpectedly finds himself on an alternate Earth after using his super-speed to vibrate his molecules. It transpires that the world he has wound up on is the home of the original Flash, alias Jay Garrick, the Golden Age version of the character who was published from 1940 to 1951. With that one story, the idea of multiple Earths existing parallel to one another—a Multiverse—was born, and from the very beginning, The Flash was at the heart of it.

MULTIVERSAL MASTERS

Fifty years later, it was another Flash-centered Multiversal story, the 2011 crossover event *Flashpoint*, that would lay the foundations for *The Flash*. The concept of a solo movie of The Flash had been in various stages of development for decades, but with the advent of *Man of Steel* in 2013 and the notion of a shared continuity between DC's movies, more concrete moves toward a Flash film were made. In 2014, actor Ezra Miller (*The Perks of Being a Wallflower*) was cast as Barry Allen/The Flash, ostensibly to appear in the in-production *Batman v Superman: Dawn of Justice* and subsequent *Justice League* (2017), but with the idea that a Flash solo project would follow. Even so, it would be another five years before director Andy Muschietti (*It, Mama*) came on board, and another year and a half before principal photography could begin in April 2021, with preproduction complicated by the COVID-19 pandemic.

The story that Muschietti and the film's writers alighted on would see Barry Allen travel back in time to prevent the murder of his mother, Nora (Maribel Verdú), and the consequent incarceration of his father, Henry, for a crime he didn't commit. Ron Livingston (*Band of Brothers*, *Office Space*), played Henry, replacing the unavailable Billy Crudup who had filled the role in *Justice League*. However, on his way back to the future, Barry lands in 2013 on the eve of General Zod, Faora-Ul (Michael Shannon and

Supervising art director Jason Knox-Johnston collaborated with a forensic technician to give the crime lab where Barry works a functional, state-of-the-art appearance.

Antje Traue, returning from *Man of Steel*), and the Kryptonian insurgents' attack—but a 2013 where there is no Superman. With the help of his 2013 younger self—performed in person by Ezra Miller's acting double Ed Wade wearing a volumetric capture camera, with Miller subsequently reenacting the 2013 Barry part— Barry enlists the aid of a bitter, retired Batman, played by Michael Keaton, and Kal-El's cousin, Kara Zor-El/Supergirl, played by feature-film newcomer Sasha Calle.

KEATON'S BATMAN

With Keaton making a return to the role he portrayed in iconic fashion in Tim Burton's *Batman* (1989) and *Batman Returns* (1992), *The Flash* also marked a return in the movie's opening sequence for Ben Affleck as Batman; Gal Gadot as Wonder Woman; and Jeremy Irons as Alfred, who requests Barry's assistance with a robbery gone wrong in Gotham City. Irons' part was the first moment of the film to be shot, his Batcave scene filmed against green screen during preshoots. The scene sees the debut of The Flash's new suit, which Andy Muschietti felt would have been refined by Barry and Bruce Wayne in the five years since *Justice League*. Costume designer Alexandra Byrne (Marvel's *Avengers*) and costume effects supervisor Dan Grace (*Wonder Woman 1984*) devised a Flash suit that was closer in appearance to the comics incarnations, yet incorporated The Flash symbol and lines of circuitry that lit up and could be enhanced in postproduction with a flowing golden glow effect.

Those visual effects come into play when The Flash runs from his home of Central City to Gotham City, Ezra Miller suspended from a wire on a treadmill and filmed at 48 frames per second rather than the usual 24. An even more ambitious sequence comes once The Flash arrives in Batman's hometown and must deal with a collapsing hospital with nearly a dozen babies, a nurse, and a

Costume effects supervising modeler Pierre Bohanna wanted The Flash suit worn by the Barry of 2013 to appear as if it were hastily made.

Freed from captivity by Barry, Barry, and Batman, Kara Zor-El dons her Supergirl suit at Wayne Manor and restores her power with the Sun's rays.

Racing to a fateful encounter with General Zod, the Barry of 2013 sneaks a quick pic of Supergirl as she flies alongside the Batwing.

In the alternate reality of 2013, a somewhat different Justice League forms in the Batcave, one dubbed by Batman as an "interesting group."

Even the combined might of two Flashes and Supergirl isn't enough to defeat Zod and the Kryptonian insurgents on the battlefield.

therapy dog all plummeting to earth—and having to recharge his metabolism midair with snacks from a falling dispenser. Achieved via a combination of practical filming and visual effects, the scene involved the construction of a nursery capable of tilting 20 degrees, a mixture of live and dummy babies, and Ezra Miller suspended on wires to achieve The Flash's gravity-defying rescue.

The dramatic Gotham City scene also sees the debut of an updated, partially armored Batsuit for Affleck's Batman and a new Batcycle. Responding to Andy Muschietti's direction that the Batcycle should be built like a tank, production designer Paul Austerberry and special effects supervisor Dominic Tuohoy used an electric motorcycle as the basis for a practical vehicle that was almost 10 feet (3 m) long and could be ridden at speeds of over 80 miles per hour (128 kph).

BACK TO THE BATCAVE

While the Batcycle ridden by Ben Affleck's Batman was all-new, the Batmobile used by Michael Keaton's Batman was an original working prop from the 1989 movie, carefully transported from a secret location to Leavesden in Watford, Hertfordshire, where Keaton's Batcave was built. In overseeing the design and construction of the huge set, which incorporated an LED volume wall digitally displaying a waterfall, Paul Austerberry's two main inspirations were the 1989 Batcave with certain aspects of the version from Christopher Nolan's Dark Knight Trilogy, not least the scale. The set included a rostrum for the Batmobile, requiring the vehicle to be hydraulically elevated on the back of a truck, then slowly driven onto the rostrum and into position.

When Michael Keaton saw the Batcave for the first time, he was so stunned that he filmed the set to send to Tim Burton. Once he

Far Left: An early development image of Supergirl released after decades of imprisonment.

Left: In the basement of the stricken Gotham City hospital, The Flash ties together power cables to prevent a fire—not realizing that the entire building is about to collapse.

had donned the Batsuit, the actor asked Andy Muschietti to take pictures to preserve the moment for Keaton's grandson. The Batsuit was a newly created version of the costume originally worn by Keaton, this time boasting a full range of movement, meaning that Keaton could turn his neck and head. Once of the scenes filmed in the Batcave set was the moment where Keaton in his Batsuit strides to a balcony and declares, in an echo of the 1989 movie, "Yeah, I'm Batman."

INFINITE EARTHS

Also shot at Leavesden was the carousel-like "Chronobowl," the temporal plane accessed through the Speed Force, from which The Flash can view and access the past. Unlike the Batcave, the Chronobowl was created in postproduction using a photorealistic volumetric capture technique, but Ezra Miller and their double were present on the green-screen set in costume, along with a third Flash, an older version of 2013 Barry who has become corrupted over the course of his multitudinous attempts to travel back through time to defeat Zod and save the Earth. It's during the maelstrom of Barry's struggle with his future self that the full scope of the film's Multiversal ambition comes into play, as the fabric of reality begins to fracture, affording glimpses of everything from the 1940s Jay Garrick Flash, to the 1960s TV Batman, to Nicolas Cage as Tim Burton's unrealized vision of Superman.

While the film's final battle takes place in the Chronobowl, the real climax comes with a much quieter moment in a supermarket, where Barry replaces a can of tomatoes on a shelf, thus correcting the tiny alteration to the past he made to save his mom's life. For Andy Muschietti, for all *The Flash*'s time-traveling, Multiversal shenanigans, the emotional foundation of the film was the relationship between Barry and his mom, encapsulated by the moment where a tearful Barry bids farewell to Nora for the final time.

The Flash on TV

In October 2014, the same month that Ezra Miller was cast as Barry Allen, The Flash began what would turn out to be a nine-season, nine-year run on television. Developed by Greg Berlanti (*Dawson's Creek*), Andrew Kreisberg, and Geoff Johns as a spin-off from Berlanti and Kreisberg's Green Arrow-starring CW show *Arrow*, which had launched in 2012, *The Flash* featured Grant Gustin (*Glee*) as forensic crime-scene investigator Barry Allen, who gains the power of super-speed after being struck by lightning caused by a particle accelerator explosion. As The Flash, Barry battled a succession of criminals who had gained powers in the same accident that had given him his abilities, but as the series continued into season 2 and beyond, the show became more Multiversal in nature, introducing comics concepts like Earth-2, the Speed Force, and Flashpoint. Grant Gustin's The Flash even got to meet Ezra Miller's The Flash in the 2019–2020 CW Arrowverse crossover "Crisis on Infinite Earths."

Miller's The Flash wasn't the only Flash encountered by Gustin's The Flash in that crossover, however. At one point, Barry meets a Flash from another reality who sacrifices himself so that Barry can live. This alternate Flash was played by John Wesley Shipp, who two decades before had starred as Barry in *The Flash*, a TV series which aired on CBS. A fairly faithful take on the Flash comics, the show lasted just one season from 1990 to 1991, but is fondly remembered by fans, not least the makers of *Crisis on Infinite Earths*.

BLUE BEETLE

Release date: August 2023
Starring roles: Xolo Maridueña, Bruna Marquezine, Damián Alcázar, George Lopez, Adriana Barraza, Belissa Escobedo, Elpidia Carrillo, Susan Sarandon, Raoul Max Trujillo
Director: Ángel Manuel Soto

Screenplay: Garth Dunnet-Alcocer
Cinematography: Pawal Pogorzelski
Music: Bobby Krlic
Running time: 127 minutes
Box office: $129,288,072

Ángel Manuel Soto never expected to make a superhero movie. Growing up in the 1980s and 1990s on the streets of Santurce, one of the most populated areas of Puerto Rico, Soto didn't think he would get such an opportunity, instead later channeling his experiences into a series of gritty short films and features, including crime drama *La Granja* (2015) and coming-of-age movie *Charm City Kings* (2020). But when the filmmaker was presented the chance to direct the first live-action superhero movie centered on a Latino character, starring an actor of Mexican, Cuban, and Ecuadorian descent surrounded by a similarly Latin American cast and penned by a Mexican writer, Soto saw an opportunity to make not just a superhero movie, but one of the most personal films of his career.

INTO THE BLUE

The fourth character to bear the name Blue Beetle—counting the 1939 Dan Garret original, the 1964 Dan Garrett revamp, and the 1966 Ted Kord version—Jaime Reyes debuted in 2006 during that year's *Infinite Crisis* crossover event, his powers derived from a mystical alien scarab once owned by his Blue Beetle predecessors. It was this incarnation of the character that DC began to develop as a movie in 2018, bringing writer Gareth Dunnet-Alcocer (*Miss Bala*) on board to pen the screenplay.

"He's the first Super Hero in his family."
Marketing tagline

When Ángel Manuel Soto was subsequently contacted about potentially directing a DC movie, the director prepared himself to pitch ideas, including one centered on an origin story for Batman villain Bane (previously played by Tom Hardy in 2012's *The Dark Knight Rises*). Instead, when he was asked if he would like to take on the Jaime Reyes incarnation of Blue Beetle, Soto saw a way of combining his own background with the kind of action-adventure movies he had always loved, from *Raiders of the Lost Ark* (1981) to *Mission: Impossible* (1996).

For the part of Jaime Reyes, Soto had one name in mind—Xolo Maridueña. The director had encountered Maridueña at the 2017

The Blue Beetle scarab and exoskeleton grant Jaime Reyes a range of powers, including the ability to create energy constructs.

Far left: The Reyes family urge Jaime to open the box containing the scarab entrusted to him by Victoria Kord's niece Jenny.

Left: Removed from its box by Jaime, the scarab begins to crackle with energy—a foretaste of the body horror to come!

Filming the emotional scene where Blue Beetle defends his family from the forces of Victoria Kord, only to see his father suffer a heart attack.

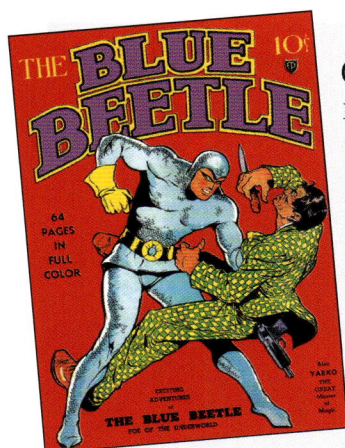

Comic book Beetle

Decades before Jaime Reyes assumed the mantle of Blue Beetle in 2006, the character had a long and twisting comics career. Originally published by Fox Comics, Blue Beetle debuted in 1939 as rookie policeman Dan Garret, who donned a bulletproof costume and fought crime with the aid of a strength-enhancing formula, Vitamin 2X. In 1964, Blue Beetle was revived by Charlton Comics, who had bought the rights from the defunct Fox. Now named Dan Garrett, two "Ts," this Blue Beetle was an archaeologist who discovered a blue-hued ancient Egyptian scarab that granted him great power when he uttered the words "Kaji Dha." Two years later, Blue Beetle was reinvented again, this time by Spider-Man co-creator Steve Ditko, who introduced Ted Kord, an inventor who used his technical know-how to fight crime, with the assistance of an airship, the Bug.

When DC acquired the Charlton library of characters in the mid-1980s, Blue Beetle and his Charlton Action Hero cohorts, as they were called, almost ended up as the protagonists of Alan Moore and Dave Gibbons's *Watchmen*, until it was decided to use analogs in that soon-to-be-classic 1986–1987 maxi-series (Blue Beetle was reworked as Nite Owl). Instead, Ted Kord was incorporated into the DC universe, joining the Justice League as part of Keith Giffen, J. M. DeMatteis, and Kevin Maguire's wildly successful 1987 relaunch and forming an enduring partnership with time-displaced adventurer Booster Gold. Ted was killed off for a time, murdered by former Justice League financier Max Lord just before 2006's *Infinite Crisis* event and replaced by Jaime Reyes, but he has since been resurrected, his ongoing story becoming intertwined with Jaime's.

Sundance Film Festival before the young actor found fame as the lead in *Karate Kid* sequel *Cobra Kai*. Even then Maridueña had struck Soto as a young man with strong family values. Later, after Soto had witnessed the actor's charm and authenticity in *Cobra Kai*, he knew Maridueña was right for the role of Jaime Reyes.

FAMILY TIES

Aptly, the story that Soto and Dunnet-Alcocer put together would focus on the Reyes family almost as much as Jaime himself. Set in the working-class neighborhood of Edge Keys in the fictional Palmera City—a conglomeration of Puerto Rico, where much of the movie was shot, with elements of El Paso, Miami, and Barcelona—the film follows Jaime as he is bonded with the alien scarab, gaining a carapace exoskeleton and incredible abilities. This pulls him and his family into a deadly struggle for the scarab with Kord Industries CEO Victoria Kord, played by Susan Sarandon (*Thelma and Louise*), and her bodyguard, the armored Ignacio Carapax (Raoul Max Trujillo).

For Soto, the film offered the chance to tell the story of someone searching for their purpose in life, with Jaime's resilience and determination in the face of adversity reflecting Soto's own struggles to become a filmmaker. But it was also an opportunity to show three Latin American generations under one roof, from Jaime's hardworking, caring father Alberto (Damián Alcázar) to his conspiracy-theorist uncle Rudy (George Lopez) to his Nana (Adriana Barraza), a character with a revolutionary history that would come in very handy toward the end of the movie.

ACTION HERO

For all of the film's by-turns comedic and touching family dynamics, *Blue Beetle* still needed to deliver on the costumed action front. Taking inspiration from the Jaime Reyes Blue Beetle's first appearance in *Infinite Crisis* #3 (February 2006), and the character's appearances in the *Young Justice* and *Batman: The Brave and the Bold* animated shows and *Injustice 2* video game, Soto and costume

Left: After bonding with the alien scarab, alias Khaji Da, and manifesting the Blue Beetle exoskeleton for the first time, an astonished Jaime is propelled into space, before rocketing back down to Earth.

designer Mayes C. Rubeo (*Apocalypto*) designed a suit that merged insectoid elements with alien technology. To build the costume, the filmmakers worked with Jose Fernandez's Ironhead Studios to come up with an outfit that was flexible enough for Xolo Maridueña to perform in, comprising a fabric undersuit and urethane-cast plates.

In conceiving the energy constructs that the scarab—which in the movie calls itself Khaji Da, after the Dan Garrett Blue Beetle's "Kaji Dha" incantation—gives Jaime the power to create, especially the huge sword he conjures, Soto cast his mind back to the anime he watched growing up and the kinds of outsize swords he always wished he could wield. For the film's fight sequences, Maridueña could call on the karate and stamina training he underwent while making *Cobra Kai*, but in addition the actor was required to increase his strength and gain weight so that his body could handle being in the costume.

ALL IN THE FAMILY

As extraordinary as Blue Beetle's powers are, for Ángel Manuel Soto and Gareth Dunnet-Alcocer, one of Jaime Reyes's greatest superpowers is his family, reflecting the director and writer's own lived experiences. It's telling that when the scarab first affixes itself to Jaime and he is transformed into Blue Beetle—a scene that Soto wanted to recall the body horror of David Cronenberg ... but for kids—the scene takes place in Jaime's home with his suitably horrified family around him. As Soto and Dunnet-Alcocer reasoned, there was little point in Jaime having a secret identity when his close-knit family would have found out about his secret anyway. After all, Soto figured, whenever someone in a Latino family is in trouble, the first thing they do is call their parents.

Ultimately, Soto wanted to make a family movie that his family—his nephews, his nieces, his community—could be entertained by and recognize aspects of themselves in. In *Blue Beetle*, he had made a Super Hero movie, but one that, growing up, he wished had been made for him.

Xolo Maridueña found the Blue Beetle costume incredible, and even more so once it had been enhanced with visual effects in postproduction.

AQUAMAN AND THE LOST KINGDOM

Release date: December 2023
Starring roles: Jason Momoa, Patrick Wilson, Yahya Abdul-Mateen II, Amber Heard, Nicole Kidman, Randall Park, Temuera Morrison, Dolph Lundgren, Martin Short
Director: James Wan
Story: James Wan and David

Leslie Johnson-McGoldrick and Jason Momoa & Thomas Pa'a Sibbett
Screenplay: David Leslie Johnson-McGoldrick
Cinematography: Don Burgess
Music: Rupert Gregson-Williams
Running time: 124 minutes
Box office: $423.5 million

If *Aquaman* (2018) was James Wan's aquatic take on *Romancing the Stone* (1984)—an action-adventure romantic comedy—then *Aquaman and the Lost Kingdom* would be the director's homage to the Sylvester Stallone and Kurt Russell–starring *Tango & Cash* (1989): an action-adventure buddy comedy. Stepping up to star opposite returning headliner Jason Momoa would be long-time James Wan collaborator Patrick Wilson (*The Conjuring*, *Watchmen*), whose role of Orm, alias Ocean Master, Arthur Curry/Aquaman's half-brother, would be significantly expanded for the new film.

More significantly in the broader scheme of DC filmmaking, *Aquaman and the Lost Kingdom* would represent the final installment in the sequence of interconnected DC movies that had begun back in 2013 with *Man of Steel*, in effect bringing an era of DC cinema to a close.

SEVEN KINGDOMS

The seeds of the story for *Aquaman and the Lost Kingdom* were sown during production of *Aquaman*. For James Wan, the notion of the seven kingdoms of Atlantis outlined in the first movie presented a suite of tantalizing storytelling possibilities for the sophomore film. For his part, Jason Momoa also had a strong sense of where any potential sequel should go. When *Aquaman* wound up earning over a billion dollars at the worldwide box office, that sequel became much more of a certainty.

"One king will lead us all."

Marketing tagline

The key to the direction the film would take lay in its eventual title (revealed by James Wan in June 2021 as the movie entered preproduction). *Aquaman* had alluded to a seventh kingdom, lost when Atlantis had sunk beneath the waves; *Aquaman and the Lost*

A flashback details the ancient battle between King Atlan and his brother, Kordax, that resulted in Atlan defeating the ruler of Necrus by splintering the Black Trident.

Found by Black Manta broken in two pieces, when reassembled the Black Trident shimmers with an occult energy that channels the dark power of Kordax.

David Kane becomes possessed by the undead spirit of Kordax—signified by the green glow in his eyes—who fuels Black Manta's quest for vengeance.

Promotional poster art for *Aquaman and the Lost Kingdom* showing Jason Momoa's Aquaman astride a new addition to the array of cinematic Atlantean creatures—his steed, the seahorse Storm.

Tom Curry (Temuera Morrison) and Arthur perform a ceremonial Haka to a delighted Mera (Amber Heard), Atlanna (Nicole Kidman), and Arthur Jr. at Amnesty Bay.

The beloved scion of Aquaman and Mera, Arthur Jr. is placed in mortal danger when Black Manta kidnaps the infant child to use his blood in a ritual to release Kordax.

Concept art delineating one of Atlantis's new locales unveiled in *Aquaman and the Lost Kingdom*—the dazzling and bustling Night Market—lit by bioluminescent jellyfish.

Kingdom would zero in on that mysterious realm. However, the sequel would also elevate David Kane, alias Black Manta, into an even more formidable threat not just to Aquaman but the entire world, affording Yahya Abdul-Mateen II (*Candyman, Watchmen*) the opportunity to flesh out the antagonist he had played in the first film. In the narrative, Kane's storyline intertwines with that of the eponymous kingdom, as Black Manta's quest for vengeance against Aquaman—whom he blames for the death of his father—leads him to the Black Trident. This powerful ancient weapon was once wielded by Korda, brother of King Atlan and ruler of the Lost Kingdom of Necrus. Both possessing and possessed by the Trident, Kane and his crew set about liberating deposits of the volatile fuel Orichalcum from Atlantean storage depots, in the process plunging the world into crisis by elevating global temperatures and causing outbreaks of plague in Atlantis.

Besides Jason Momoa, Patrick Wilson, and Yahya Abdul-Mateen II, also returning for the sequel were Nicole Kidman (*The Others*) and Temuera Morrison (*The Book of Boba Fett*) as Arthur Curry's parents, Atlanna and Tom—now also grandparents to the infant son of Arthur and Mera (Amber Heard), Arthur Jr.—and Dolph Lundgren (*Rocky IV*) as King Nereus. New additions to the cast included Indya Moore as Karshon, in comics lore a mutated radioactive shark, but here a much more humanoid member of the Atlantean High Council and a political opponent for Arthur, and Martin Short as the voice of Kingfish, ruler of the underwater pirate realm the Sunken Citadel.

SEALIFE CENTERS

While James Wan would have loved to build practical underwater cities and dominions, as in the first film the realization of Atlantis and other aquatic realms again required extensive visual effects. There was room to significantly expand those underwater worlds, however, introducing new domains and spotlighting aspects of Atlantis not seen before, such as the Night Market, a jellyfish-lit

Left: Concept art for the Whale Harbor, Atlantis's transport hub, featuring a pair of Octobots making off with a store of Orichalcum during Black Manta's raid on the city.

Below: In this concept art of Aquaman riding his steed, Storm, the original Silver Age comics incarnation of the gigantic seahorse is given a modern sheen, not least with the addition of armor.

milieu based by production designer Bill Brzeski and his team on Bangkok's floating markets. The Night Market was one of the settings for a chase sequence between Aquaman and Black Manta showcasing a succession of Atlantean locales, a scene for which Brzeski and co. looked to classic car chases from the likes of *Bullitt* (1968) and *The French Connection* (1971).

As with its predecessor, visual effects were also employed to envision many of the ocean's denizens, not least Aquaman's steed, a giant seahorse named Storm. Originally hailing from the Silver Age Aquaman comic books, here it was brought to vivid life by visual effects supervisor Nick Davis and his team. Presenting in an albino form above the waves, this 25-long (7.5-m)-long CGI creation turned a bioluminescent blue underwater. This required a delicate balancing act on the part of Davis and his colleagues to achieve a natural match to the way Aquaman perched on the creature.

While Storm was a new addition to Aquaman's cinematic world, another undersea creature was returning from the first film, albeit in a more prominent role. Glimpsed in *Aquaman* playing the bongos, the octopus Topo was granted the opportunity to spread his tentacles in *Aquaman and the Lost Kingdom*, which reflected the character's comics incarnation by becoming something of a sidekick for Aquaman. In the film, the cephalopod was granted greater status as an Atlantean secret agent, his name revealed as an acronym: Tactical Observation and Pursuit Operative.

HORROR OF THE DEEP

Storm and Topo's roles in *Aquaman and the Lost Kingdom* encapsulated the sense of adventurous fun James Wan wanted to infuse the film with, much as he had with *Aquaman*. But Wan also wanted to lean into his heritage as a horror filmmaker, one who could not only boast a back catalog which included *Saw* (2004) and the "Insidious" and "Conjuring" franchises, but in the interim between the two Aquaman movies had reaffirmed his horror roots with *Malignant* (2021). Accordingly, Wan and his co-writer, David Leslie Johnson-McGoldrick, looked to Italian director Mario Bava's sci-fi horror flick *Planet of the Vampires* (1965) and the work of stop-motion animator Ray Harryhausen in the likes of *The Voyage of*

Left: Not only did *Aquaman and the Lost Kingdom* bring Storm to the big screen, but another of Aquaman's comic book sidekicks, Topo, was given a much bigger role than before.

As Black Manta makes his escape from Atlantis with his haul of Orichalcum, Aquaman gives chase, only to be repelled by a sonic blast from Manta's submarine.

With the power granted him by the Black Trident, Black Manta becomes an even more dangerous opponent for Aquaman, as their fight in Manta's lair, Devil's Deep, amply demonstrates.

The final battle takes place in Necrus, where Aquaman, Orm, and their allies face legions of undead warriors, animated by the dark magic of King Kordax's Black Trident.

Sinbad (1958) and *Jason and the Argonauts* (1963) to formulate the retro feel of the film and the dark nature of Necrus and the Black Trident.

That sensibility manifested in many locations throughout the movie. This included Black Manta's refinery-based lair inside Devil's Deep, a dormant volcano in the South Pacific where a pitched battle between Arthur, Orm, and Manta unfolds, and the undead legions of Necrus at the film's climax in the Sunken Citadel. Black Manta's undersea hideaway was one of numerous sets built at Warner Bros. Studios, Leavesden, UK, which also served as the production's primary base. However, these horror touches were lightened by a spirit of adventure and comedic banter between Arthur and Orm, especially on Devil's Deep island, a lush paradise corrupted by Orichalcum, resulting in the perilous presence of giant rapacious mutated plants and insects.

Also sporting the influence of Ray Harryhausen, not to mention H. P. Lovecraft and Jules Verne, were the Octobots—squidlike mechanical submersibles displaying a distinct steampunk design aesthetic. Hailing from Necrus and utilized by Black Manta's crew, these one-man machines could operate underwater, on land, and even use their whirling limbs to propel themselves through the air.

The Octobots were among the more visible examples of the advances in visual effects between the making of *Aquaman* and its sequel, but there were less immediately apparent technological leaps, too, especially in how the filmmakers captured the performers underwater. While on *Aquaman* the "tuning fork" harnesses employed to suspend the actors had been effective in conveying the weightlessness of being underwater, the apparatus had proved uncomfortable for the cast and restricted camera positioning. For *Aquaman and the Lost Kingdom*, Wan and his team employed volumetric capture to create a 360-degree aquatic environment, with the actors performing inside a circular booth of plasma walls, their performances captured by 136 cameras in fixed positions. The arrangement allowed the actors a greater freedom of movement, with room even for a mechanical horse for the performers to mount to simulate riding sea creatures. Additionally, other cast members could perform before cameras outside the booth, with their facial performances superimposed on CGI avatars on the plasma screens inside the booth.

BROTHERS IN ARMS

Visual effects may have been vital to the realization of *Aquaman and the Lost Kingdom*'s underwater worlds, but the emotional core of the film remained its themes of redemption and reconciliation, encapsulated by the odd-couple pairing of Arthur and Orm. Incarcerated in the arid Deserter Prison since the events of *Aquaman*, his body emaciated through lack of access to water, Orm is sprung by Arthur—in a scene featuring footage shot on location at Saunton Sands beach in Devon, UK—in order to help face the global threat of Black Manta and the Black Trident. Unsurprisingly, however, given their former enmity, the half-brothers' reunion is anything but friendly.

While the aforementioned *Tango & Cash* was a touchstone for James Wan in formulating the siblings' relationship, another

Far left: As they traverse the jungle surrounding the Devil's Deep volcano, the contrast between the outgoing, fun-loving Aquaman and his overly serious, buttoned-down brother becomes more pronounced.

Left: As well as being Aquaman and Orm's mother, Atlanna became a trusted royal advisor, using the benefit of her wisdom and insights into Atlantean politics to assist a king who is still new to his role.

comparison to the pair's dynamic, as noted by producer Peter Safran in *Entertainment Weekly* (September 13, 2023), would be Nick Nolte and Eddie Murphy's bickering partnership in Walter Hill's *48 Hrs* (1982), or Will Smith and Tommy Lee Jones in Barry Sonnenfeld's *Men in Black* (1997). In *Aquaman and the Lost Kingdom*, Jason Momoa brings a larger-than-life quality to Arthur while Patrick Wilson plays Orm as the straight man. Momoa and Wilson relished the opportunity to transform the half-brothers' tumultuous bond into an unlikely bromance. Momoa in particular was gratified to further develop a character he had been portraying for the best part of a decade, ever since Zack Snyder had cast him in the role for *Batman v Superman: Dawn of Justice* (2016). It was only after the film wrapped that it became evident it might be his final time playing Aquaman.

In January 2023, Peter Safran and *The Suicide Squad* (2021) director James Gunn announced a new beginning for DC's cinematic endeavors. If the film was the last hurrah for both Jason Momoa's Aquaman and the cinematic universe he inhabited, the actor was sad but philosophical, proud of his time in the role and of the films. Safran, who had worked with the actor since *Aquaman*, pointed out that not only was Momoa the definitive Aquaman, but that he would always have a home at DC.

Patrick Wilson, alias Orm Marius, on the Devil's Deep set with director James Wan, who has directed the actor in half a dozen films.

Animated Aquaman

Not only has James Wan helmed two Aquaman movies, but the director was instrumental in granting the character his own animated show, more than 50 years on from Aquaman's inaugural animated series. In 2021, Wan executive-produced the HBO Max animated show *Aquaman: King of Atlantis*, which ran for three weekly installments that year before airing as a feature-length film on Cartoon Network the following year. Developed and written by Victor Courtright and Marly Halpern-Graser, and directed by Keith Pakiz, all of whom had worked together on *ThunderCats Roar* (2020), the series was a decidedly quirky and comedic take on the character and his world, with an animated style evidently inspired by *ThunderCats Roar* and *Adventure Time*.

It was certainly a departure from the approach to Aquaman's prior animated exploits, which largely adopted a more straight-faced tone. Introduced as the "bold and daring King of the Seven Seas," Aquaman made his TV debut in Filmation's *The Superman/Aquaman Hour of Adventure* on CBS in 1967 (pictured), with his segments subsequently repackaged simply as *Aquaman* and running until 1970. But though it would be half a century before Aquaman headlined in his own animation series, in the interim he made numerous appearances in DC animated shows, from *Super Friends* (1973–1985) to Bruce Timm and co.'s *Justice League* (2001–2004) and *Justice League Unlimited* (2004–2006), where his bearded countenance (which reflected the sea king's 1990s comics look) was not a million miles from Jason Momoa's later incarnation.

251

INDEX

INDEX

ACKNOWLEDGEMENTS

Neal Adams, Ryan Benjamin, Steve Bissette, Brian Bolland, Wayne Boring, Brett Breeding, Nick Cardy, Darwyn Cooke, Tony DeZuniga, Dale Eaglesham, Lou Fine, Dave Gibbons, Joe Giella, Dick Giordana, Gurihiru, Everett E. Hibbard, John Higgins, Dan Jurgens, Bob Kane, Stan Kaye, Jack Kirby, Scot Kolins, Alex Kotzky, Mort Meskin, Sheldon Moldoff, Win Mortimer, Steve Oliff, Jerry Ordway, Harry G. Peter, Eric Powell, Joe Quinones, Paul Reinman, George Roussos, Marco Santucci, Ira Schnapp, Dick Sprang, Curt Swan, John Totleben, Rick Veitch, Tatjana Wood.

PICTURE CREDITS

The publisher would like to thank the following for their kind permission to reproduce their photographs:

(Key: a-above; b-below/bottom; c-centre; f-far; l-left; r-right; t-top)

1 Alamy Stock Photo: Everett Collection Inc (clb). **10-11 Alamy Stock Photo:** Everett Collection Inc. **12 Alamy Stock Photo:** Everett Collection Inc (tr); Everett Collection, Inc. (cl). **13 Alamy Stock Photo:** Everett Collection Inc (tl, tc, c); Pictorial Press Ltd (bl). **14 Alamy Stock Photo:** Album / Columbia Pictures (cla, tr). **15 Alamy Stock Photo:** Everett Collection Inc (cl, tc); Moviestore Collection Ltd (tl). **16 Alamy Stock Photo:** SilverScreen (cla). **17 Getty Images:** CBS Photo Archive (cb). **18 Alamy Stock Photo:** Cinematic Collection / ABC (tr); Everett Collection Inc (cl). **19 Alamy Stock Photo:** Everett Collection Inc (tl, tc, c, cb, bl). **20 Alamy Stock Photo:** Everett Collection, Inc. (cla). **21 Alamy Stock Photo:** Everett Collection Inc (tl, tc). **22 Alamy Stock Photo:** Everett Collection Inc (bl, br). **23 Alamy Stock Photo:** Moviestore Collection Ltd. **24 Alamy Stock Photo:** Everett Collection Inc (cl). **25 Alamy Stock Photo:** Everett Collection Inc (tc). **26 Alamy Stock Photo:** Everett Collection Inc (cl, tr); Everett Collection, Inc. (bl). **27 Alamy Stock Photo:** Everett Collection Inc (t); Everett Collection, Inc. (bl). **28 Alamy Stock Photo:** Everett Collection Inc (t, clb). **29 Alamy Stock Photo:** Everett Collection Inc (tl, tr). **30 Alamy Stock Photo:** Associated Press / Anonymous (br); Sam Kovak (tr). **31 Alamy Stock Photo:** Allstar Picture Library Ltd / AA Film Archive. **32 Alamy Stock Photo:** Allstar Picture Library Limited (tl); Photo 12 / Fox Television (bl); Everett Collection Inc / © 20thCentFox (tr). **33 Alamy Stock Photo:** Allstar Picture Library Ltd / AA Film Archive / ABC (tc); Everett Collection Inc / © 20thCentFox (tl, c); Moviestore Collection Ltd (bc). **34 Alamy Stock Photo:** Everett Collection Inc / © 20thCentFox (tl, cl, bl). **34-35 Alamy Stock Photo:** Everett Collection Inc / © 20thCentFox (tc). **35 Alamy Stock Photo:** Everett Collection Inc / © 20thCentFox (tc). **42 Alamy Stock Photo:** Everett Collection Inc (tl). **44-45 BFI National Archive.** 'Flying Ballet production design by Ivor Beddoes for SUPERMAN (1978) by Ivor Beddoes © 1978 Estate of Ivor Beddoes, courtesy of The British Film Institute: (tr). **46 Alamy Stock Photo:** Everett Collection Inc / © Warner Bros (crb). **47 Alamy Stock Photo:** Allstar Picture Library Ltd / AA Film Archive / WARNER BROS.. **48 Alamy Stock Photo:** Everett Collection Inc (tl). **49 Alamy Stock Photo:** Album / Warner Brothers (tc). **50 Alamy Stock Photo:** Allstar Picture Library Limited (tl). **51 Alamy Stock Photo:** Everett Collection Inc / © Warner Bros (tl). **52 Alamy Stock Photo:** United Archives GmbH / IFTN (bl); United Archives GmbH / IFA Film (br). **53 Alamy Stock Photo:** United Archives GmbH / IFA Film. **54 Alamy Stock Photo:** Everett Collection Inc / Ron Harvey (tl); Everett Collection Inc / © Embassy Pictures (bl). **55 Alamy Stock Photo:** Album / Swampfilms (tc); United Archives GmbH / IFA Film (tl); Everett Collection Inc / © Embassy Pictures (c). **56 Alamy Stock Photo:** United Archives GmbH / Impress (br). **59 Alamy Stock Photo:** Everett Collection Inc (c). **68 Alamy Stock Photo:** Everett Collection Inc / © Warner Bros (br). **70-71 Alamy Stock Photo:** Everett Collection Inc / © Warner Bros (tc). **73 Alamy Stock Photo:** Photo 12. **74 Alamy Stock Photo:** Everett Collection Inc / © Lightyear Ent (bl); Photo 12 (tl). **74-75 Getty Images:** Moviepix / Michael Ochs Archives (tc). **75 Getty Images:** Moviepix / Michael Ochs Archives (tc). **78-79 Alamy Stock Photo:** Entertainment Pictures / SNAP (tc). **81 Alamy Stock Photo:** Album / Warner Bros / DC Comics (tl). **83 Alamy Stock Photo:** Entertainment Pictures / SNAP (cl); ScreenProd / Photononstop (tc). **84 Alamy Stock Photo:** United Archives GmbH / kpa Publicity Stills (tc). **85 Alamy Stock Photo:** Entertainment Pictures / SNAP (tc). **98 Alamy Stock Photo:** Album / Greenlawn Productions (clb). **107 Alamy Stock Photo:** Pictorial Press Ltd (cb). **124 Alamy Stock Photo:** UPI / Bill Greenblatt (tl). **131 Alamy Stock Photo:** Everett Collection Inc / © 20thCentFox (bc). **134 Alamy Stock Photo:** Entertainment Pictures (tr). **137 Alamy Stock Photo:** Album / Warner Bros. Pictures (tc); Landmark Media (crb). **145 Alamy Stock Photo:** Cinematic / Warner Bros. (cr). **148 Alamy Stock Photo:** Album (bl). **150-151 Alamy Stock Photo:** Everett Collection Inc / © Warner Bros (tc). **159 Alamy Stock Photo:** Everett Collection Inc (bc). **187 Alamy Stock Photo:** Everett Collection Inc / Ron Harvey (tr). **196 Alamy Stock Photo:** Everett Collection Inc (tl). **199 Alamy Stock Photo:** Landmark Media (tl, crb). **214 Alamy Stock Photo:** Cinematic / ABC (cb). **217 Alamy Stock Photo:** Moviestore Collection Ltd (bl). **231 Alamy Stock Photo:** Everett Collection Inc / © Warner Bros (cr). **246 Alamy Stock Photo:** Landmark Media (tr, cr). **247 Alamy Stock Photo:** Landmark Media. **248 Alamy Stock Photo:** Landmark Media (bl, tl). **250 Alamy Stock Photo:** Landmark Media (tl, bl). **251 Alamy Stock Photo:** Landmark Media (tc).

All other images © Dorling Kindersley Limited